ALBYN

MacDiarmid 2000
the Collected Works
from Carcanet

Selected Poetry
edited by Michael Grieve
and Alan Riach

Selected Prose
edited by Alan Riach

Complete Poems I and II
edited by Michael Grieve
and W.R. Aitken

Scottish Eccentrics
with a note on the author
by Norman MacCaig

Lucky Poet
edited by Alan Riach

Contemporary Scottish Studies
edited by Alan Riach

The Raucle Tongue: Hitherto Uncollected Prose I
edited by Angus Calder, Glen Murray & Alan Riach

Hugh MacDiarmid

ALBYN

Shorter Books and Monographs

Edited by Alan Riach

CARCANET

This edition first published in
Great Britain in 1996 by
Carcanet Press Limited
402-406 Corn Exchange Buildings
Manchester M4 3BY

A CIP catalogue record for this book
is available from the British Library.
ISBN 1 85754 233 9

The publisher acknowledges financial assistance
from the Arts Council of England.

Set in 10pt Sabon by Bryan Williamson, Frome
Printed and bound in England by SRP Ltd, Exeter

Contents

Acknowledgements

Acknowledgements are due to the Institute for Advanced Studies in the Humanities at the University of Edinburgh where I held a Fellowship from February to April, 1995; and to the University of Waikato Research Committee, who have generously supported my work on the 'MacDiarmid 2000' project and whose Academic Visitors Award allowed Angus Calder to visit the University of Waikato in December 1995 to work on the project.

Most grateful thanks are tendered to the staff of the National Library of Scotland, Edinburgh University Library, the Mitchell Library, Glasgow (particularly to Hamish Whyte), the British Library, London (particularly to Richard Price) and the University of Waikato Library, particularly the reference and interloans section. My warm thanks are due also to Robert Creeley and Robert J. Bertholf of the State University of New York at Buffalo, U.S.A. Their part in the production of this book is more fully explained in the introductory note to the appendix.

Thanks for personal kindness, support and generosity towards the project are due to W.R. Aitken, Kenneth Buthlay, David Daiches, George Davie, Duncan Glen and Edwin Morgan; G. Ross Roy and Patrick Scott of the University of South Carolina; my parents Captain J.A. Riach and Mrs J.G. Riach; my wife Rae; and my colleagues at the University of Waikato, Marshall Walker and Jan Pilditch. I would also like to make grateful acknowledgement of the trust of the MacDiarmid Estate and Deirdre Grieve, and of the professionalism, commitment and patience of Carcanet Press, especially Michael Schmidt and Robyn Marsack.

Portals of Discovery
An Introduction to *Albyn: Shorter Books and Monographs* by Alan Riach

This volume brings together all Hugh MacDiarmid's shorter books and monographs with the exception of those published in the *Selected Prose* (Carcanet, 1992). These works span his entire career, from 1927 to 1972, and might be read as portals to the larger concerns of the periods in which they were written and as complementary to the poetry of his developing *oeuvre*. The shape of MacDiarmid's poetic career is well known; the shape of his career as a journalist, polemicist, political and aesthetic commentator and *provocateur*, while notorious, is only now becoming clearly visible. With the publication of *Contemporary Scottish Studies* in 1995 and of *The Raucle Tongue: Hitherto Uncollected Prose* in 1996 and 1997, Carcanet will have made available a massive selection of MacDiarmid's prose writings which demonstrate the enormous range of his work in these capacities.

While *The Raucle Tongue* gathers mainly journalism, *Albyn* collects items MacDiarmid saw fit to publish as small books or pamphlets, or to distribute and list as off-prints from journals, individual in themselves. There are overlaps, of course. MacDiarmid is rightly famous for the degree to which he appropriated and re-used his own writing, as well as that of others, and the further one reads into his prose, the more the broader arguments become clear as the single articles lead to the grand construction of a life's work.

Some portions of the writing in *Albyn: or Scotland and the Future* reappear in journalism of the period. *The Present Condition of Scottish Music* appeared as a series of articles in a newspaper, *The Border Standard*, before appearing as a pamphlet. *The Present Condition* (sometimes the title is given as *Position*) *of Scottish Arts and Affairs* was printed at the office of *The Stewartry Observer*, one of the many newspapers throughout Scotland to which C.M. Grieve contributed syndicated articles. This essay had first appeared in *The Stewartry Observer* as an anonymous article on 24 November 1927 as by a 'Special Correspondent'. Such articles appeared with ferocious frequency in the press; readers must have followed them on their first printing with keen pleasure. Here was passionate concern and revolutionary fervour beating the drum in local Scottish newspaper columns alongside items on village sport competitions, Burns supper jamborees, adverts for cures for back ailments, corsets and chicken feed.

The Scottish National Association of April Fools appeared as an article in a short-lived but fascinating journal which announced its commitment to Scotland's *ur-motives* in its very title: *The Pictish Review*. Here Grieve adopted the cod-Gaelic pseudonym 'Gillechriosd Mac a'Ghreidhir' and joined forces with the Honourable Ruaraidh Erskine of Marr, founder of the Scots National League and one of the co-founders of the National Party of Scotland, whom MacDiarmid described as 'one of the most remarkable personalities of modern Scottish history, the very core and crux of the *Gaeltacht*.' With Erskine of Marr, he set out to co-edit *The Scottish Review* in 1926, and they were invited by the Tailltean Games Committee and the Irish nation to attend the festivities in Dublin in 1928 as 'distinguished guests' along with Compton Mackenzie. MacDiarmid had a wonderful fortnight in Dublin, meeting De Valera ('and his chief henchmen') taking tea with the Minister of Defence, having a 6.30 to 1.00 a.m. discussion with Yeats, A.E., F.R. Higgins and others, being flown ('in an Arvo-Anson 5-cylinder plane') and driven by car about 1000 miles by Oliver St. John Gogarty (the 'Buck Mulligan' of Joyce's *Ulysses*). The visit was important to him, and the 'April Fools' article, though written earlier, clearly springs from the same dynamic as that which would lead a passionately nationalistic, intellectually and aesthetically committed Scot to look to developments in the new Republic for models or precedents for a Renaissant Scotland.

That forward-looking republicanism was deep in MacDiarmid's hopes. A year later, in *The Scots Independent*, he entitled an article 'Fifty Years Hence' and sketched his provocative vision of a Scotland which had taken charge of its own affairs, paying due attention to the Gaelic component and the cultural resources of Gaeldom, and following the political examples of Italy and Ireland. Published as a pamphlet, *Scotland in 1980* is a concise summary of MacDiarmid's political and cultural ideals in the late 1920s. Ireland had been crucially important to him throughout his life. His recollection of the Easter Rising in a 1977 radio interview, a year before his death, was an evocation of divided commitments: 'I was in barracks, in Sheffield of all places, in 1915, and I was there when the Easter Rising took place in 1916. If it had been at all possible I would have deserted at that time from the British Army and joined the Irish.'

In a later unpublished interview for Radio Telefis Eirann with Michael na hUanachain, recorded in the year of his death, MacDiarmid said that his greatest disappointment was that the republican idea did not develop in Scotland into a fully empowered political movement. The condition of Ireland's independence may have been intolerable to James Joyce and may have remained intolerable to Sinn Fein and the IRA, but the strength of the Republican movement in Ireland has been a far more serious political force than the bourgeois nationalism and devolutionist tokenism which has been repeating on Scotland throughout the twentieth century.

The present volume also collects MacDiarmid's extended essay *Aesthetics in Scotland*, an unusually considered and calm appraisal. Essays on the lives and works of the writer R.B. Cunninghame Graham and the composer F.G. Scott follow, and the book-length essay *Burns Today and Tomorrow* is a comprehensive statement of MacDiarmid's judgement on Burns, his achievement and his legacy. Two items on David Hume offer MacDiarmid's opinion of a different facet of eighteenth-century Scottish writing and the essays on Ian Hamilton Finlay, John Gawsworth and Sydney Goodsir Smith bring us closer to the contemporary scene.

The range of tone in these items is extremely varied. MacDiarmid's vituperation is notorious, but the qualities of loyalty, warm affection, deep friendship and trust are evident in his writing about Goodsir Smith and Gawsworth, for example, and there is a zestful humour in his toast to Goodsir Smith which is inimitably quick.

The final item, *A Political Speech*, returns us to the concerns of the earlier pieces. It is an eloquent, vibrant assertion of MacDiarmid's undaunted conviction that the status of an independent republic is the only desirable destiny for Scotland because only in such a state might the people of the country find fulfilment. He rests his case on the virtue of his personality and the strength of his determination; if only that were all it might take.

Note

Footnotes in the text are MacDiarmid's, except where noted.

Albyn:
or Scotland and the Future

To what genius are addressed the disquietudes stirred in our conscience by a setting so poor and so strong?

MAURICE BARRÈS

All despair in politics is an absolute stupidity.

CHARLES MAURRAS

I

The forces that are moving towards a Scottish Renaissance are complex and at first sight incompatible. The movement began as a purely literary movement some seven or eight years ago, but of necessity speedily acquired political and then religious bearings. It is now manifesting itself in every sphere of national arts and affairs, and is at once radical and conservative, revolutionary and reactionary. Engaged in traversing the accepted conceptions of all things Scottish, it is in keeping that it should not have set the heather on fire. But it has made far greater headway than what has appeared about it in the English or Anglo-Scottish Press would indicate. For obvious reasons these are concerned to minimize or ignore its manifestations. The movement has had various more or less short-lived organs of its own; it will undoubtedly acquire others. But in the meantime it lacks any and its progress is correspondingly obscure but none the less real. Its inception synchronized with the end of the War, and in retrospect it will be seen to have had a genesis in kin with other post-war phenomena of recrudescent nationalism all over Europe, and to have shared to the full in the wave of Catholic revivalism which accompanied them. It took the full force of the War to jolt an adequate majority of the Scottish people out of their old mental, moral and material ruts; and the full force of post-war reaction is gradually bringing them to an effective realization of their changed conditions.

At first blush there may seem little enough connection between such phenomena as the Clyde Rebels, the Scottish Home Rule

Movement, the Irish Invasion of Scotland, and the campaign to resuscitate Braid Scots and Gaelic. But, adopting the Spenglerian philosophy, the Renaissance movement regards itself as an effort in every aspect of the national life to supplant the elements at present predominant by the other elements they have suppressed, and thus reverse the existing order. Or, in terms of psychology, the effort is to relieve the inhibitions imposed by English and Anglo-Scottish influences and to inhibit in turn those factors of Scottish psychology which have rendered it amenable to the post-Union state of affairs. In closer consideration, then, it will be seen that the four phenomena mentioned correspond to pre-Union conditions in Scotland. The first takes us back beyond the demoralizing concept of the Canny Scot, which has conduced so largely to Scottish denationalization, and re-establishes a psychology in keeping with the independent traditions of the country. The majority of the Scottish Labour members returned to the House of Commons went there as 'internationalists'. They were very lukewarm Home Rulers. A short experience of Westminster transformed them completely. They found the vote of the majority of the Scottish electorate systematically vetoed by an English majority, and saw how Scottish affairs were treated in the House of Commons. This saltatory emergence of a Socialist preponderance in the Scottish representation is a post-war product, and is interpreted from the Renaissance point of view as a significant reassertion of the old Scottish radicalism and republicanism. Prior to the Union Scotland was always 'a nest of rebels' and 'never noted for loyalty to Monarchy', and the old Scots' Parliament, though far from being a democratic body, placed on its statute book measures of social reform in many directions in advance of any yet enacted by the Mother of Parliaments. An analysis of the difference in psychology and 'direction' between the English and the Scottish Labour and Socialist movements shows that this interpretation is by no means far-fetched. The English movement is constitutional and monarchical; the Scottish revolutionary and republican.

The Scottish Home Rule movement is re-orienting itself along realist lines, and has ceased to be mainly sentimental. For the first time it is looking before as well as after. It is concerning itself less with the past and more and more with the present and the future, and its membership is growing in direct ratio to its increased practicality. Most significant of all is the fact that these developments are marked by an ascending claim. It is now generally realized that no form of devolution without fiscal autonomy will meet the case, and that merely constitutional means may not suffice. Bill after Bill, backed by four out of five of the Scottish representatives of all parties, has been thrown out by the overwhelming majority of English members. This is a state of affairs which will not be tolerated indefinitely. A premium is being put upon militant effort; and the fact that the Scots National League which is out for complete independence is now growing very much more rapidly than the moderate Scottish Home Rule Association is significant in this direction. At present the nationalist Press consists of two small monthly organs; and all the daily, and practically all the weekly, papers are anti-Home Rule, just as they are all anti-Socialist, although the Scottish Socialist vote represents a third of the electorate. Scottish journalism is, therefore, almost wholly untrustworthy in relation to Scottish opinion. Realistic nationalism and the majority elements of the Labour movement solely, or at all events, predominantly concerned with bread-and-butter politics, have naturally a great deal in common in the existing state of affairs, and it is not surprising that Scottish nationalism and Scottish Socialism should be making joint cause. Nor is the attitude of those Liberal and Conservative politicians who are opposing Scottish Home Rule, or modifying their interest in the subject, because it would probably mean a Scottish Socialist Government, failing to produce its own effects. Constitutionalism that fears and evades the will of the people signs its own death-warrant.

Lord Haldane recently commented on the stimulating and beneficial effects of such an admixture of races as is at present taking place in Scotland, and especially on Clydeside. There has been a tremendous 'pother' about the 'Irish Invasion' in certain quarters. We are told by some Protestant leaders that Scottish nationalism is in danger. This is a new-found zeal for nationalism, however, obviously dictated by emptying churches. These gentlemen represent the very factors which have been mainly responsible for the desuetude of Scottish nationalism. Their anti-Irish propaganda has been of the most unscrupulous character and depends for its principal effects on the use of the terms 'Irish' and 'Catholic' as synonymous. But, large as the Irish influx has been, the recent rapid development of which throws an adequate light on the real motives of the protesters, representing as they do churches which are about to achieve Union, really a prelude to the inevitable re-union of the Protestant Churches and Rome, through the indifference instead of the enthusiasm of their remaining members and without consultation of the Scottish people, *via* a Parliament systematically anti-Scottish in its policies. From the Renaissance point of view the growth of Catholicism, and the influx of the Irish, are alike welcome, as undoing those accompaniments of the Reformation which have lain like a blight on Scottish arts and affairs. In this connection it is useful to remember that the Shorter Catechism, like the concept of the Canny Scot, the myth which has facilitated the anglicization of Scotland, was an English invention. The revival of Catholicism means the restoration of the atmosphere in which Scottish arts and letters flourished in a fashion they have far from paralleled at any time since the Reformation. I am not contending that Protestantism is essentially antagonistic to arts and letters. That would be absurd. But Scottish Calvinism has been: and just as many of the great figures in the Irish literary movement have been Protestants, so, on the other hand, if there is to be cultural progress in Scotland, must many of the emerging artists be Catholics.

As to Scots, here, again, its desuetude was largely due to the Reformation and to the Union with England. Its 'direction' is completely at variance with the 'direction' of English; and the present state of English literature on the one hand, and the newer tendencies in Europe to which London is most antipathetic on the other, considered in conjunction with the special virtues of Scots, suggests that the psychological moment for its revival has arrived and that through it lies a way for the successful re-entry of distinctively Scottish culture into the European stream. The Burns influence has been wholly bad, producing little save puerile and platitudinous doggerel. It is necessary to go back behind Burns to Dunbar and the Old Makars — great Catholic poets using the Vernacular, not for the pedestrian things to which it has latterly been confined, but for all 'the brave translunary things of great art'. The younger Scottish poets are repossessing themselves of noble media and high traditions; and a splendid mystical and imaginative spirit is reuniting them over a period of five centuries with their mighty predecessors. Even the Burns cult itself, which long confined itself to an 'annual guzzle' on the poet's birthday, is now proclaiming itself a Scottish literary and patriotic organization, and advocating the teaching of Scots in the schools. And the Scottish Education Department is reported to be favourably disposed. Can the headway that has been made during the past few years be more impressively illustrated?

The Scottish Renaissance Movement is even more concerned with the revival of Gaelic than of Scots. It regards Scotland as a diversity-in-unity to be stimulated at every point, and, theoretically at any rate, it is prepared to develop along trilingual lines. Actually the revival of the Gaelic — and the output of Gaelic letters of quality, despite the efforts of the Hon Ruaraidh Erskine of Marr, is lagging behind in comparison with Braid Scots, and it is questionable whether Gaelic has any similar alignment with the 'becoming tendencies' in *Weltliteratur*. Or it may be that the present position calls in the first place for recognition, and modern applications, of the Pictish rather than the Gaelic elements in Scottish culture. On the other hand, proposals for the establishment of a great Gaelic College have been taken up enthusiastically by the Clans Association in America, and are already well advanced. Far-reaching developments are imminent in this direction. Here again, materialism is giving way to new spiritual ideals, and in Gaelic we return closer than ever to the old Scotland.

All these movements then represent so many antitheses of the tendencies which have dominated Scotland since the Union and have conjointly driven it so far along the road to Anglicization. They are asserting themselves and have arrested the tendency to assimilate Scotland to English standards just when it seemed on the point of complete success. Lost ground is being rapidly recovered; efforts are being made once more to create distinctively Scottish literature comparable in artistic quality and tendencious force to the contemporary output of other European countries, and to regain the independent cultural position of Scotland in Europe; efforts are being made to create a Scottish national drama and Scottish national music — both of which Scotland alone of European countries entirely lacks, mainly because of Calvinistic repression — and all these efforts are achieving a measure of success. Scottish genius is being liberated from its Genevan prison-house. But the centralization of British arts and affairs in London is still restricting it in ways that can only be redressed by that re-orientation of facilities which would follow the re-establishment of an independent Scottish Parliament, or, in the event of a return to the system of Provinces, a federation of assemblies. The movement cannot manifest its full stature and move freely, save within that framework of a Scotland become once again a nation in every sense of the term for which it has been designed.

II

In the foregoing chapter I have given an account of the movement upon which it seems to me the future of Scotland depends — or, rather, a Scottish future of Scotland. Scotland, of course, may have another future. It may become a Roman-Catholic country with a predominantly Irish population. Or its progressive anglicization and provincialization may continue until it becomes to all intents and purposes a part of its English neighbour. The latter is still the likeliest; the former has only within the past few years emerged as a serious competitor. But the main point to seize upon in the meantime is that, apart from the 'Scottish Renaissance Group', the rest of the Scottish people in Scotland today are not Scottish in any real sense of the term. They have no consciousness of difference except in detail; 'distinctions without difference'. They are all the less Scottish in proportion to their ardour as Burns enthusiasts, members of St Andrew's and Caledonian Societies and the like. Just as the majority of Socialists become conscious of the economic causes of their plight but retain (often in an exacerbated form) the types of ideas on other matters which spring from the same source, so the vast majority of Scots today — even Scottish Home Rulers — regard as typically Scottish the very sentiments and attitudes which are the products of their progressive anglicization. Scotland is suffering from a very widespread inferiority complex — the result of the psychological violence suffered as a consequence of John Knox's anti-national policy in imposing an English Bible (and, as a consequence, English as the basis of education) upon it, and of the means by which the Union of the Parliaments was encompassed and by which its inherent intention of completely assimilating Scotland to England has since been pursued. Weaker minds find compensation in a 'romantic nationalism' — sedulously dissociated from politics and practical realities of every kind. The others accept the situation and transcend it; that accounts for such phenomena as Scottish Prime Ministers, Archibishops of Canterbury and York, 'heids of departments' of all kinds, the ubiquitous Scotsman generally, most of the Scottish aristocracy, and such writers of English as R.L. Stevenson, R.B. Cunninghame Graham and Norman Douglas. But these — or some of them — are only exceptions that prove the rule that the Anglo-Scottish symbiosis leads to nullity. There is a third class who are 'more English than the English' — who become panicky immediately any question arises as to the benefit to Scotland of its present relationship to England, who regard everything 'Scottish' as beneath contempt, and, in short, manifest all the symptoms of a 'specific aboulia' in the presence of any challenge to their submerged nationalism. They have been un-Scotched and made 'damned mischievous Englishmen'. The 'nationalism' of the first of these three classes is such that it has been unable to create any literature, music or drama of more than a local value. It is hopelessly provincialized. The history of Scottish Vernacular poetry, for example, since the days of the Auld Makars, is a history of the progressive relinquishment of magnificent potentialities for the creation of a literature which might well have rivalled the English. The only challenge to the decline was that of Allan Ramsay and Ferguson [*sic*] — which Burns, in the last analysis, betrayed. The influence of Burns has reduced the whole field of Scots letters to a 'kailyard'. So with music. Scottish mediæval music was ahead of English. Today, Scotland is the only country in Western Europe which has failed to develop an art-music, though it has as available basis perhaps the finest inheritance of folk-song in the world. Scarcely any effort is being made even yet to create a national school of composers in Scotland, although the creation of such national schools in every other country in Europe — at their third and fourth stage of development now in most of them — has constituted during the past half century or so one of the greatest revolutions in music. So far as Scottish music is concerned it remains at best practically where it was in the sixteenth century. Music in Scotland is another matter. An effort is presently being made to found a Scottish Academy of Music in conjunction with a Chair of Music in Glasgow University. But the title is a misnomer. It will be merely an Academy of Music in Scotland — probably under a Welshman. In his new book, *Music: Classical, Romantic, and Modern*, Dr Eaglefield Hull deals very succinctly with the position of Scottish music today. 'Scotland,' he says,

> the country with the loveliest scenery, the most thrilling history, a rich inheritance of literature, and hundreds of the finest love songs in the world, has no national school of musical composition. Mac after Mac goes down into England and loses his musical soul for a mess of pottage! It is useless to ask whether Scotland stands where she did in music, for apart from folk-music she has no standing at all. It is indeed high time that she set to work to put her house in order. In Donald Tovey, David Stephen, Francis George Scott, Erik Chisholm, and others, there is fine material which must be utilized. But the cultivation of a School of Scottish composers can only be carried on within its own borders.

But he goes on to throw out a suggestion of no little significance. 'Perhaps,' he says,

> Scotland is waiting for some awakener from outside to make her thrill to a sense of her great mission, such as John Field in Russia, Glinka in Spain, and Jean Aubry in England. The spark is undoubtedly there, and only needs fanning.

Association of ideas leads me to think how the distinctively Scottish genius has manifested itself in alien fields, however inhibited it may have been at home. My main purpose here is not to discuss the lets and hindrances which have prevented the development of modern arts in Scotland, nor will my space permit me to analyse the complexities of Scottish character and circumstances responsible for our comparative failure to find expression on the higher levels of culture. But it is curious to find that in relation to the cultures of other countries, or in association with foreign elements in the constitution of the individuals concerned, Scotsmen, or half-Scotsmen have, with a surprising consistency, continued to manifest elements distinctively Scottish which clearly relate them to the Auld Makars, to the ballad makers, to our mediæval Scots musicians, and to that elusive but unmistakable thread of continuity which attaches the work of Norman Douglas, for example, to that of Sir Thomas Urquhart, the translator of Rabelais. Wergeland, the Norwegian poet, was conscious of the idiosyncratic power of the Scottish blood in his veins. So was a greater poet — the Russian Lermontov. So was Hermann [*sic*] Melville; so — to take a living example — is Walter de la Mare, whose *diablerie*, the finest element in his work, is probably attributable to his Scottish blood, as, in his case, were some of Browning's amusing tortuosities and prepossession with dialectical excesses. This Scottish strain is tremendously idiosyncratic, full of a wild humour which blends the actual and the apocalyptic in an incalculable fashion. In his able analysis of the complexities of the Scottish genius Professor Gregory Smith has called it 'the Caledonian antisyzygy' — a baffling zig-zag of contradictions — and he traces it down the centuries in a most interesting fashion, remarking that

> There is more in this Scottish antithesis of the real and fantastic than is to be explained by the familiar rules of rhetoric. This mingling, even of the most eccentric kind, is an indication to us that the Scot, in that mediæval fashion which takes all things as granted, is at his ease in both 'rooms of life', and turns to fun, and even profanity, with no misgivings. For Scottish literature is more mediæval in habit than criticism has suspected, and owes some part of its picturesque strength to this freedom in passing from one mood to another. It takes some people more time than they can spare to see the absolute propriety of a gargoyle's grinning at the elbow of a kneeling saint.

And Professor Gregory Smith goes on to express the opinion that this incalculable Scottish spirit will continue to survive in English arts and letters pretty much as a dancing mouse may manifest itself in a family of orthodox rodents — as something disparate, an ornament, or an excrescence, but irreconcilable to any major tradition and incapable of affording a basis for any higher synthesis of the Scottish genius.

That may be; on the other hand, its expansion may await a conjunction of conditions which have not yet arisen. It has affiliations to the baroque and the rococo, and evidences are not lacking of a widespread renewal of interest in these modes. But a more important fact is that this complicated wildness of imagination is, in Scots literature, associated with a peerless directness of utterance

Nae bombast swell,
Nae snap conceits.

The language of the Greeks is simple and concrete, without *clichés* or rhetoric. English is, by contrast, loose and vague. But what Greek epigram has a more magical simplicity than Burns's

Ye are na Mary Morison,

or where shall a parallel be found for the terrific concision, the vertiginous speed, of *Tam o' Shanter*? The future of the Scots spirit may depend upon the issue of the great struggle going on in all the arts between the dying spirit of the Renaissance and the rediscovered spirit of nationality. Today there is a general reaction against the Renaissance. Observe the huge extent to which dialect is entering into the stuff of modern literature in every country. Dialect is the language of the common people; in literature it denotes an almost overweening attempt to express the here-and-now. That, in its principle, is anti-Renaissance. Basil de Selincourt[1] and many others observe that modern English shows signs of fatigue in comparison with Chaucer's. Chaucer was a poet with this power of plain speech. He never flinched from the life that was being lived at the moment before his eyes. A farmyard, with its straw, its dung, its cocks and hens is not, some people have thought, a poetic subject; Chaucer knew better. Dunbar with the aid of Scots achieved effects beyond Chaucer's compass with an utterance even more simple and straightforward. It has been said that Dunbar had for his highest quality a certain unique intensity of feeling, the power of expressing that passionate and

---

1 See his *Pomona: or the Future of English*, in this series.

peculiar force which distinguishes and differentiates us people of the North from our Southern neighbours. What is this unique intensity of feeling, this power of direct utterance, but the pre-Renaissance qualities of which I am writing? Braid Scots is a great untapped repository of the pre-Renaissance or anti-Renaissance potentialities which English has progressively forgone.

> In days when mankind were but callans
> At grammar, logic and sic talents,
> They took nae pains their speech to balance
> Or rules to gie,
> But spak' their thoughts in plain braid lallans
> Like you or me.

But it goes far deeper than language, this 'Caledonian antisyzygy', and music in the long run may utilize it more fully and finely than literature. It is here that I join issue again with my essential theme — to find what I have said concerning the persistence of this queer Scots strain extraordinarily exemplified in modern music in the work of Erik Satie. Satie's middle name was Leslie; his mother was a Scotswoman. Satie was a 'musical joker'. His distinctive and important work was a species of fantastic experimental clowning, hardening later into satire. His work and his methods should have the special consideration of every Scottish artist — every musician in particular — who is puzzled as to how he may profitably exploit the peculiarities of Scottish psychology of which he is conscious. Paul Landormy calls him 'a freakish musician, more inventor than creator, the composer of "Pieces in the form of a Pear", of the "Bureaucratic Sonata", and other fantastic products of a whimsical yet quite elegantly witty imagination', but — and this is the vital thing — he admits that 'he furnished certain elements of that new language which the composer of *Pelleas* used for loftier ends'. This is no little understatement of Satie's significance. Dr Eaglefield Hull says:

> This kind of musical irony is the most individual and personal of all types of art. The composer writes for a few detached individual people, who would scoff at the rest of humanity. Only very 'superior' people can appreciate such irony, which passes from an elegant wit to a brutal sarcasm.

But he goes on to say:

> Historically Satie was of immense importance. The music on Satie's twelve pages (of his first work, *Sarabandes*, 1887) is even

> a greater landmark than either Debussy's or Chabrier's work. The 'diaphony' of his sevenths and ninths was to become part and parcel of the harmonic decoration of Debussy and the Impressionists.... He was the father of atonality in music. Side by side with all his strangeness and boldness are passages of the most amazing commonplaces, which are difficult to explain except as satirical allusions.

Exactly! What is this but the 'Caledonian Antisyzygy' precisely as Professor Gregory Smith describes it, but manifesting itself in modern music to ultimately triumphant effect. There is no need, then, for Dr Hull to say 'His father was French and his mother Scottish. We wonder to which source his outstanding characteristic of humour is due.' Surely it is along similar lines in Scotland itself that our difficult national characteristics may yet be turned to musical account and make the basis of a new technique, at once completely modern yet intimately related to the whole history of Scots psychology and conjoining in the closest fashion the artists we are about to become, if the Scottish Renaissance realizes its objectives, with the Auld Makars and the ballad-makers whose achievements we have yet to parallel and continue.

As with literature and music so with drama and dancing this tale might be continued. The explanations of Scotland's leeway lie in the Reformation, the Union with England and the Industrial Revolution. If I isolate the second of these as the main cause, it is because it was indispensable to the consummation and continuance of the first and largely determined the effect upon Scotland of the third. There are people who imagine that but for the Union with England Scotland would still be destitute of all the blessings of modern civilization. They find no difficulty in associating this belief with the idea that Scotsmen are thrifty, hardworking, exceptionally well-educated, law-abiding and home-loving. I am not one of them. I believe that the Industrial Revolution would have spread to Scotland much less injuriously if England had suddenly disappeared about 1700. I believe that the concept of the 'canny Scot' is the myth (as M. Delaisi puts it) which has made Scotland governable by England and has prevented the development since the Union of any realistic nationalism worth speaking about. True, it has been so insidiously and incessantly imposed that the great majority of Scots have long been unable for all practical purposes to do other than believe it themselves. Yet there are notable exceptions; the traditions of Highland soldiering, for example — the 'ladies from Hell'. Even the 'canniest' Scot does not repudiate these as un-Scottish. At all events the effect of all these three causes was overwhelmingly repressive and anti-Scottish. The Reformation, which strangled Scottish arts and letters, subverted the whole national psychology and made the dominant characteristics of the nation those which had previously been churl elements. The comparative cultural sterility of the latter is undeniable. A premium was put upon Philistinism. There has been no religious poetry — no expression of 'divine philosophy' — in Scotland since the Reformation. As a consequence Scotland today is singularly destitute of æsthetic consciousness. The line of hope lies partially in re-Catholicization, partially in the exhaustion of Protestantism. The Union with England confirmed and secured the effects of the Reformation. It intensified the anglicization that the introduction of an English Bible and the *Shorter Catechism* (with which England itself so promptly dispensed) had initiated. It progressively severed the Scottish people from their past. The extent to which this has gone is almost incredible — especially if taken in conjunction with the general attribution of an uncommon love-of-country to the Scots. English has practically vanquished Scots (which is not a dialect but a sister language to English, with different but not inferior, and, in some ways, complementary, potentialities) and Gaelic. There is very little Scottish Education in Scotland today. The type of international education which is everywhere gaining ground today is that which seeks to perfect, and even to intensify, different cultures already existent among different peoples, and sets for its ideal that each people has, first, the right to its own interpretation of life; and, second, the duty of understanding, and sympathizing with, the different interpretations given by its neighbours as fully as possible. Back of this type of international education lies the belief that differentiation in matters of culture is more valuable to life than a stereotyped homogeneity. This, so far as Scotland is concerned, is the aim and object of the Scottish Renaissance movement; and it is high time that the Scottish Educational System was attempting to change-over to this type of education rather than adhering partly to the imperialistic and partly to the eclectic types, both of which, as Professor Zimmern says, 'belong rather to the past than to the present', except, alas, in Scotland, which once prided itself on leading the world in matters of education. A recent Committee of Enquiry, set up by the Glasgow branch of the Educational Institute of Scotland, reports that no school-book dealing with Scottish history is of a satisfactory character. This, although a remarkable advance in professional admission, is a sheer understatement. Scottish history is only now in the process of being rediscovered and, once the labours of the new school of Scottish historical researchers come to be synthetized, it will be found that even such comparatively 'Scottish' Scottish Histories as Hume Brown's have to be thrown overboard, as little more than a mass of English propaganda. It is only within recent years that any attempt has been made to teach even such 'Scottish history' in Scottish schools, and then subsidiarily to English, and, as it were, as a make-weight or after-thought — to the older children. Scots literature is in even worse case, although here, too, there has been a slight improvement during the past decade. The increasing — if still insignificant — Scoticization of Scottish Education during recent years is, of course, not a product of the propaganda of the Scottish Renaissance Group. To what is it attributable? How can it be accounted for if the policy of England and, even more determinedly, of Anglo-Scotland, let alone the over-riding tendency of modern industrialism, is towards the complete assimilation of Scotland to England? In my opinion it is a product partly of the latent criticism of the industrial order and partly of a realization of the cultural exhaustion of English (*vide 'Pomona'*) — an instinctive protective re-assembling of the forces suppressed by the existing order of things which has made for the predominancy of English. This explanation accords with the doctrine Spengler expounds in his *Downfall of the Western World.* 'The Caledonian Antisyzygy', instead of being a disparate thing destined to play a baroque, ornamental, or disfiguring rôle — *chacun à son goût* — in English literature may be awaiting the exhaustion of the whole civilization of which the latter is a typical product in order to achieve its effective synthesis in a succeeding and very different civilization. In the history of civilization therefore the sudden suppression of Scots, with all its unique expressive qualities may prove to have been a providential postponement; it may have been driven underground to emerge more triumphantly later. Its coming musicians and writers must address themselves to it, as Mussorgsky, following Dargomisky's dictum that 'the sound must express the word', addressed himself to Russian — with Mallarmé's 'adoration for the property of words'; just as they must recollect that the 'pure poetry' of some of the contemporary Continental expressionists was anticipated and carried far further long ago in their *Canntaireachd*, or mnemonic notation of the MacCrimmons — a basis upon which they may profitably build. To detail the arguments in support of this 'theory of Scots letters' would take up more space than I can afford; but I must interpolate a brief outline of them here, for they bear in one way and another on all the issues with which I am concerned.

III

Not Burns — Dunbar! That is the phrase which sums up the significant tendency which is belatedly manifesting itself in Scots poetry today. At first it may seem absurd to try to recover at this time of day the literary potentialities of a language which has long ago disintegrated into dialects. These dialects even at their richest afford only a very restricted literary medium, capable of little more than kailyard usages, but quite incapable of addressing the full range of literary purpose. They are the *disjecta membra* of a language; the question is, whether they can be re-integrated and re-vitalized. Can these dry bones live? Like feats have at all events been accomplished elsewhere — in regard to Provençal in France, Catalan in Spain, the Landsmaal in Norway, and so on. Those who would try it in Scots must first of all recover for themselves the full canon of Scots used by the Auld Makars and readapt it to the full requirements of modern self-expression. This is no easy task. Why should it be attempted? One answer is because English is incapable of affording means of expression for certain of the chief elements of Scottish psychology — just as English has no equivalents for many of the most distinctive words in the Scots vocabulary. Another answer is that there is a tendency in world-literature today which is driving writers of all countries back to obsolete vocabularies and local variants and specialized usages of language of all kinds. This is not the place to more than indicate considerations such as these. Suffice it to say that a little group of Scottish writers today are alive to them and conscious of an overwhelming impulse to return more deeply 'into the pit whence we were digged' than any Scot has felt impelled to go for several centuries. Burns, although he used a certain amount of synthetic Scots of his own, not sticking to any one dialect and recovering words that had ceased to be used, did not know the works of his great fifteenth-century predecessors well enough to make anything like full use of the linguistic material available. This is what makes Carlyle say that if Burns had been 'a first-class intellectual workman he might have changed the whole course of literature'. That opportunity still remains open, however, for anyone who can revive the potentialities of the Scots language manifested in Dunbar and since then almost wholly forgone in favour of the very different potentialities of English.

The effect of Burns' work on Scots poetry is well-known. It has reduced it to a level that is beneath contempt. Little or no poetry that has been produced in Scots since Burns' day has been of a quality to support comparison for a moment with the average of contemporary poetry in any other European country. It is all of the kailyard kind; sentimental, moralizing, flatfooted, and with little or no relation to reality. I have suggested in the preface to my selection of Burns' work in Benn's *Augustan Poets* that critical revaluation of Burns is overdue — or has, perhaps, been tacitly accomplished — except by Burnsians and anthologists. Perhaps poetry-lovers have carried the winnowing process too far. Reacting from hackneyed favourites, and immune from the Burns cult, they have not troubled to go over his work again — still less considered it from the standpoint of what is best by Scottish, if not by English, standards. Much of the best, and least known, of Burns depends for appreciation on a thorough knowledge of Scots. This is its 'growing end'. His poetry in English is wholly negligible, and of his work as a whole it may be said that it rises in poetic value the further away from English it is, and the stronger the infusion of Scots he employs.

But it is not a question of language only but of content. A great deal of Burns' work is eighteenth-century conventionalism of a deplorable kind. Most of his love-songs have a deadly sameness. The task of Scottish poetry today is to rise out of the rut in which it has so long been confined. It is here that the return to Dunbar is of the utmost value. It means that Scots poetry may be rescued at last from the atmosphere of hopeless anachronism which has long kept it so 'fushionless'. It has been said that if Burns is the heart, Dunbar is the head, of Scottish poetry: and certainly at any time during the past century Scots literature has had desperate need to pray Meredith's prayer for 'More brains, O Lord, more brains'. Dunbar is in many ways the most modern, as he is the most varied, of Scottish poets, whereas all but a fraction of Burns' work (and that fraction by no means confined to the most generally known portion of it) is irrevocably dated and almost indistinguishable from the ruck of imitations of it to which Scots poets have so largely confined themselves during the subsequent century and a half. Even Professor Gregory Smith admits that

> there cannot be any quarrel about the richness of the Scottish vocabulary, its frequent superiority to English in both the spiritual and technical matters of poetic diction, its musical movement and suggestion, and, generally, what have been called the 'grand accommodations' in the craft of writing as well.

Intelligent young Scots a few years ago might very well have been excused for failing to detect any of these great qualities in the very inferior types of Scots literature they came into contact with. Scottish children are only taught a little Burns and a few of the ballads. They are not taught anything of the Auld Makars. For the most part their attention is confined to English literature. It is not surprising, therefore, that they should regard Scottish literature as a mere sideline, and that, in consequence, Scottish literature should lose the greater part of those who should be contributing to it rather than to a foreign literature, which, in any case, prefers its own sons and daughters. But with the rediscovery of Dunbar in particular by young Scottish poets during the past few years new possibilities have opened up. They realize now upon what grounds testimony is borne to the richness and resource of the Scots language. In Dunbar they see them displayed in a way far beyond anything accomplished since. They see Scots allied to noble ideas, high imaginings, 'divine philosophy', and no longer confined to the foothills of Parnassus, and when they re-survey the problem of the revival of Scots from that angle, many of the difficulties of readjusting and utilizing it to serious literary purpose which have hitherto proved baffling are dispelled. Most of the people who are trying to revive the Doric are, at the same time, trying to maintain its 'pawkiness', its 'canniness', its kailyardism and so forth — in a word they are trying to revive Scots and yet remain within the stream of tendency responsible for its progressive decay. It would be truer to say that it is Braid Scots — not Scots — with which they are concerned. Their method is that of exact dialectical demarcation — they do not believe in mixing dialects — they contemplate no synthesis. What alienates the young creative writers, conscious of the inadequacy of their purpose alike of English and of what has still any currency as Scots, from the Vernacular Circle people is precisely that the latter have anything but a literary purpose. Not one of them is capable or desirous of envisaging the creative potentialities of Scots or sufficiently involved in questions of literary technique and tendency to appreciate that so far as the literary outcome of what they are professing to attempt goes it must depend, not only on intuitions in profound harmony with the phonetic and expressive genius of Scots, but also in effective relation with some major tendency in European literary evolution. If there is to be further writing in Scots these people want it to be as like what has gone before it from Burns' time as possible: otherwise they will be the first to condemn it as un-Scottish. But they are not caring much about further writing in Scots at all; they want to maintain the Burns cult and the cult of such lesser lights as Tannahill and *Johnny Gibb o' Gushetneuk*. Any Scottish aspirant worth a bawbee is bound to recognize that this is hopeless. The Vernacular Circle is a 'vicious circle'. No revival of Scots can be of consequence to a literary aspirant worthy of his salt unless it is so aligned with contemporary tendencies in European thought and expression that it has with it the possibility of eventually carrying Scots work once more into the mainstream of European literature. The rediscovery of Dunbar can solve the difficulty for every would-be Scots writer who stands divided between his reluctance to go over bag and baggage to English literature and his inability to rise above the Kailyard level through the medium of Kailyaird Scots. Dunbar stands at the opposite pole of the Scottish genius from Burns. The latter has ruled the roost far longer than it is healthy for any literature to be dominated by a single influence. It is time, and more than time, for a swing of the pendulum which, if it carries us back over the centuries to Dunbar, may also regain for Scots literature some measure, at all events, of the future that was foregone at Flodden.

It is the possibility and increasing probability of such a swing of the pendulum that Mr G.M. Thomson seems to me to have disregarded in his cogent, but far too pessimistic, essay on *Caledonia: or the Future of the Scots* in this series. But I am at one with him in regard to the desperate state of Scottish arts and affairs today and in the absence of such developments as I indicate and their timely expression in an effective form, my anticipations could not materially differ from his. His melancholy outlook is due to his failure to recognize that the Scottish Home Rule Association, the Scots National League, the Scottish National Movement, the Scottish National Convention, the Scotland's Day Committee, the Scottish Renaissance Group and other bodies fully realize the position he describes, and have been making marked headway during the past two or three years. Mr Thomson's reference to the Porpoise Press (which has done excellent work) does not excuse his failure to give credit to *The Scottish Chapbook, The Scottish Nation, The Northern Review, The Scots Independent, Scottish Home Rule, Guth na Bliadna*, and other organs which, severally and jointly, have been of far greater consequence in this redevelopment of cultural and political nationalism. Nor — otherwise accurate as is his account of Scotland's industrial plight — can he be excused for failing to realize the significance of the electrification policy. Scotland would never have been selected for this purpose if it had been so destitute of an industrial future as surface appearances suggest. The North of England is suffering in many respects just as Scotland is doing, but Mr Thomson should have realized the import of the map on the cover of *The Northern Review*, which showed not only Scotland but England as far down as Hull and Liverpool. The country between the Humber-Mersey line and the Forth and Clyde line corresponds to the old Brythonic kingdom. This is our real centre of gravity. Most of our heavy industries are centred there — most of our mineral wealth — and statistics show that an overwhelming percentage of Scottish and English genius alike of all kinds has come from that area. Politics have led to an extraordinary distortion; but there can be little doubt that economic realities will yet redress the balance as between London, on the one hand, and that area on the other, and in effect endorse the Southward policy of the old Scots Kings. In any case there is still an ample Scottish population in Scotland to redevelop the essential nationalism — if they can be aroused to a recognition of the necessity of it and, with the support of the international tendencies to which I have referred (which in turn they would strengthen) avert the calamity he indicates. The calamity, however, is imminent; and all but a moiety of the people are unconscious of its imminence or indifferent. The conscious minority has, perhaps still a decade in which to develop a 'Scottish Idea' complementary to Dostoevsky's 'Russian Idea' (Dostoevsky's mistake was to imagine that Russia alone could prevent the robotization of Europe) and in so doing to demonstrate that Professor Denis Saurat divined aright the larger hope of the Scottish Renaissance Movement when he wrote that in achieving its immediate objectives it might do more — it might save Europe. It is significant that Spengler and Laurie Magnus in his *Dictionary of European Literature*, both look to 'one of the smaller countries' with a similar hope. But, as Saurat says, to 'burn what we have hitherto adored' is the prerequisite of such a Scottish Renaissance.

IV

With increasing frequency there is a paragraph in the Scottish papers — more particularly the local papers, not the 'national' organs — telling how a debate on the question of Home Rule for Scotland has been held here or there, and, almost invariably, the paragraph ends with the statement that, on a vote being taken, there was a large majority in favour of it. That is to say a majority of that small minority who attend meetings. No one who is in the habit of going up and down the country and coming into varied contact with the public can fail to observe that more and more are inclined to the movement with a sympathy which has greatly intensified within the past few years. These are they, in my opinion, who 'feel in their bones' the larger issues of which I have been speaking, but have not yet developed more than a political reaction to them. Observers of very different shades of political opinion agree that the time is ripening for a new political nationalism, as part and parcel of a general national awakening. There is little agreement, however, as to how this widespread latent feeling may be crystallized, in the best interests of Scotland and the wider interests inevitably involved. Partial views, and partial solutions, abound; but none of these proffered precipitants are powerful enough to act on more than a small proportion of the flux of opinion that is obviously awaiting effective redirection. What is it that intervenes in ninety-nine cases out of a hundred, to prevent the sympathetic Scotsman from giving any practical effect to his feelings on such a matter?

Scotland is unique among European nations in its failure to develop a nationalist sentiment strong enough to be a vital factor in its affairs — a failure inconsistent alike with our traditional love of country and reputation for practicality. The reason probably lies in the fact that no comprehensive-enough agency has emerged; and the commonsense of our people has rejected one-sided expedients incapable of addressing the organic complexity of our national life. For it must be recognized that the absence of Scottish nationalism is, paradoxically enough, a form of Scottish self-determination. If that self-determination, which, in the opinion of many of us, has reduced Scottish arts and affairs to a lamentable pass, is to be induced to take a different form and express itself in a diametrically opposite direction to that which it has taken for the past two hundred and twenty years, the persuading programme must embody considerations of superior power to those which have so long ensured the opposite process. Scottish opinion is anachronism-proof in matters of this kind. The tendency inherent in the Union, to assimilate Scotland to England, and ultimately to provincialize the former — the stage which has been so unexpectedly but unmistakably arrested at the eleventh hour — has, as a matter of fact, not yet been effectively countered by the emergence of any principle demanding a reversed tendency. That is why, despite the persistence in Scotland of an entirely different psychology, the desire to retain and develop distinctive traditions in arts and affairs, and the fairly general recognition that the political, economic and social consequences of the Union have never been by any means wholly favourable to Scottish interests and have latterly, in many ways, become decreasingly so to a very alarming degree, there has nevertheless been at most little more than a passive resistance to complete assimilation masked by an external acquiescence. This is because Home Rule has been conceived for the most part, even by its advocates, merely as a measure of devolution — a continuance of substantially the same thing as prevails at Westminster; not something fundamentally different and answering to the unexpressed needs of the Scottish spirit. It is this passive resistance which accounts, for example, for the comparative paucity and poverty of distinctively Scottish literature since the Union. Only that fringe of the Scottish genius amenable to Anglicization has continued to find expression; the rest has, practically, 'held its tongue', and, to a large extent, its powers of expression have atrophied. A similar phenomenon manifests itself in our schools. Many teachers tell me that the children's abilities to express themselves, and, behind that, to think, are largely suppressed by official insistence upon the use of 'correct English'. They actually think, and could express themselves a great deal more readily and effectively, in dialect. This tenacity of Scots in the life of our people is extraordinary. Observe the way even 'educated people' lapse into it on convenient occasions, or when they are genuinely moved. To ban it from our schools is, therefore, a psychological outrage. A distinctive speech cannot be so retained in the intimate social life, in the thinking of a people without an accompanying subterranean continuance of all manner of distinctive mental states and potentialities. The inhibition of these is all the worse when, as in Scotland today, they are denied their natural pabulum — when, for example, as so often happens, an appeal to Scottish sentiment is applauded by those who, owing to the way in which our educational system has been organized, have little or no knowledge of our separate history and culture, and have been taught to take it for granted that Scotland's future is wholly identified with England's, and that economic and social expediency are best served by discarding the shibboleths of 'a distinction without a difference'. It is upon these camouflaged or hidden forces, however — many of them unconscious — that the ultimate direction, if it has any, of 'Scotland — a Nation', must depend. Only so can Scotland, as such, re-enter the mainstream of European arts and affairs. This reservoir of 'difference' has not yet been tapped by any of our Scottish nationalist movements; few, indeed, have realized its existence or made it their objective. That is why they have been so ineffective. But latterly there has been a significant change. Its promise lies in the fact that it is not limited to Scotland, but, as Dr J.M. Bulloch has said, is a world-movement, naturally becoming specially well-defined in Scotland, to 'set up a resistance to the efforts, many of them due to mechanisms and not a few to political theories, to make us all of one mind'. It is manifesting itself in many diverse ways — not yet co-ordinated into a comprehensive reversal of the general tendency it is arresting.

The recent Scottish breaks-away from English domination in regard to such widely-separated interests as the lifeboat service and the protection of birds are straws which show the way the wind is blowing. Cultural forces have manifested themselves and demonstrated the timeliness, if not the necessity, of specifically Scottish developments in relation to the European situation as a whole. Religious forces are now manifesting themselves. The 'Irish invasion' may be the 'point of departure'. Happily it is already clear that we have here far more, and far other, than (as Dr G.F. Barbour puts it) 'the ominous beginnings of a form of controversy from which Scotland has long been free — that regarding religious education'. Art and religion — if these two are being nationalistically stirred, we have the conditions we have hitherto lacked for the re-creation of a dynamic Scottish nationalism. These are factors of incalculably greater power than those which have already produced the meagre and ineffective phenomena of Scottish nationalism since the Union — and factors leading right back into that 'reservoir of indifference' of which I have spoken. It is not surprising to find, with the emergence of significant developments in these two great fields of consciousness, a simultaneous leap in the membership of the political nationalist societies. That membership has more than trebled itself within two years. And the measure of autonomy which is being contended for has increased proportionately. So long as Scottish Home Rule was regarded as, more or less, an end in itself, it was incapable of attracting a sufficient measure of active support to demonstrate the falsity of calling it — as most of the papers persist in calling it — 'the absurd demand of a handful of fanatics'.

There is a time-factor in all these things. The discoveries which have recently revolutionized physical science are due to a strain of 'heresy' in mathematics, long ridiculed and sterile, but now come to its own as the medium of stupendous discoveries the heretics themselves never anticipated in their wildest dreams. The position in regard to Scottish Nationalism today is not dissimilar. A form of Scottish Home Rule would probably ultimately have been granted, if for no other reason than the congestion of business at Westminster — a matter of mere administrative convenience; and the present attempt to destroy the last vestiges of Scottish control of Scottish affairs by the wholesale transference of Departments to London is probably due to the realization that this goal, which was almost within grasp, is unaccountably receding. It would have made for greater efficiency, and, temporarily, for economy — but it would not have been utilizable for the deeper purposes I have indicated. On the contrary it would have represented the last step in the assimilation of Scotland to England. Scottish Home Rule Societies in the past have sought little more; and have encountered, in Scotland, the overwhelming objection to a 'glorified County Council'. The deep intuitions of the people were right. The time had not come. All the bills hitherto promoted to give Scotland this or that measure of self-government have been inadequate means to the ends in reserve. Has the time come now? Unlike any of its predecessors the latest Draft Bill is 'nation-size' and in significant alignment, if only in the steepening of its demands, with those profounder stirrings of the national consciousness to which 'mere politics' are comparatively irrelevant, although in the last analysis they may be dependent upon them, as the big things in life often are upon the little.

The Bill as an end in itself would still be of little consequence perhaps; but as a means to steadily emerging ends which cannot yet be clearly defined, but which it is obviously anticipating and likely to facilitate, it is on a different plane. And its promoters cannot realize too clearly that, as Charles Maurras has said,

> The man of action is but a workman whose art consists in taking advantage of the lucky chances. All politics come back to this art of lying in wait for the *combinazione*, the happy chance. A moment always comes when the problem of success is a question of insight, and reduces itself to a search for what our Ancients called *junctura rerum*, the place where the bony structure bends, though it is rigid elsewhere, the place where the spring of the action will play.

Success may be unexpectedly near, and stupendous in its sequelae.

V

In the meantime the extirpation of 'a Scottish accent' in the Scottish schools continues almost unabated, although, as Lady Margaret Sackville says, and as the cultural poverty of post-Union Scotland amply attests,

> language imposed mechanically upon a people without understanding of their peculiar ways of thought can only be stultifying; and it is an impertinence to substitute a pert, half-baked, and complacent education for the very ancient culture which the Vernacular represents. Let education rather work hand in hand with this culture and humbly learn from it to its own great gain.

But the general attitude to England, and Scotland's relation to it, is far deeper, and for the most part other than mere 'protective mimicry'. Apart from the claim to which I have referred there is a widespread reluctance to think about the matter — to discuss it in any way. No probable, perhaps no possible, development of Scots Nationalism could lead to a complete disjunction of the two countries; or preclude their remaining parts of the British Empire. Opponents of Scottish Home Rule, of course, generally argue that such a measure would be a piece of retrogressive parochialism at variance with the part we are called upon to play as citizens of a great Empire. Especially is this argument being used against the newer forms which that demand is taking. The reason for this is that they represent that growth or rebirth of national sentiment in Scotland in recent years, which has brought with it the increasing realization that any measure of devolution which does not carry with it full financial autonomy is not worth having. Besides, the powers granted to the Irish Free State render it impossible, as derogatory to its historical status as a nation, that Scotland should accept any less. The latest Draft Bill meets these considerations, and is thus a far more advanced measure than any of its eleven predecessors. A typical comment runs as follows:

> The Old 'Home Rulers', while they aimed at autonomy for the management of the strictly domestic business of Scotland, jealously safeguarded Scotland's position in the United Kingdom and the Empire. Nothing was more repugnant to them than the idea that the country should cease to have its full representation in the Imperial Parliament. In the new Bill that ceases, and Scotland in nearly everything but a joint interest in the armed forces becomes detached and isolated; and provision appears to be made for the severance at some future time of even this link.... It is a reversal of the whole process of constitutional progress which governs British history.

This is the generally accepted view. But — apart from the fact that Great Britain occupies an altogether disproportionately important place in the Empire which the growth of the other elements must drastically correct in time — it is, nevertheless, completely at variance with the history and present prospects of our constitutional evolution. So far from being a reversal of the process of constitutional progress which governs British history, it is a fresh and salutary manifestation of it, and constitutional experts are increasingly realizing and proclaiming that it is only by a general extension and speeding-up of this process that the Empire can be maintained and prevented from sharing the fate of all the other great centralized Empires of the past. 'Empire', as a matter of fact, is now a misnomer; the term ought to be the 'British Association of Free Peoples'. Upon the development of the utmost freedom of each and the inter-relations with each other of the various elements in this great diversity-in-unity the future of the 'Empire' depends.

This point of view is admirably expressed by Viscount Dunedin, who says:

> The secret of the tie that unites the Empire — the rock on which it is built — is the autonomy of local law. And not merely local law, but autonomy of local law making — in other words — legislation.

And he pointed out that the Privy Council had been more solicitous of the principle of legislative autonomy than the Dominions themselves. The Scottish Home Rule demand is, therefore, strictly in accord with the very life-spirit of the Empire, and it is the attempt to assimilate Scottish law and legislation to English and to secure uniformity, instead of permitting the free development of inherent diversity in accordance with distinctive national genius that is anti-Imperial.

The opponents of the new Draft Bill cannot have it both ways. The same type of people have objected to all the previous bills on the ground that these would only result in transforming Scotland into a 'glorified County Council'. It is the realization of the truth of this that has prompted the greater demand embodied in the present Bill. Without the power of the purse a Scottish Parliament would, indeed, have been a mere glorified County Council, and such a measure would have completed, instead of reversing, the shameful provincialization of our country.

The Empire not only stands in no danger from Scotland coming into line with the other component parts of it, but it will give Scotland for the first time an effective say and share in Imperial affairs. Scotland has contributed far too much to the upbuilding of the Empire to want to withdraw from it. It is, indeed, the very opposite motive that is at work. It is the recognition of how grossly anomalous it is that Scotland, which has contributed so preponderantly to Imperial development, should be relegated to so inferior and ineffective a place in it, and have no voice in determining and disposing its future. Scotland has been placed at an intolerable disadvantage in this connection compared with almost every other part of the Empire, and the newer developments of autonomy in the Dominions are relegating Scotland to a more and more subordinate rôle, entirely out of keeping with its due as one of the great founder nations of the Empire. The new Bill is designed to rectify matters and accord to Scotland its due place in the economy of the Empire. Under it, Scotland will re-acquire a real part in relation to Imperial and world affairs. At present it has no effective part in either. The constitution of the House of Commons is such that the Scottish vote is subject to the perpetual veto of the English majority, although English political psychology is profoundly different from Scottish and the economic conditions and requirements of Scotland profoundly different from those of England. Scotland, today, has no effective representation anywhere — on the Imperial Conference, on the League of Nations, on Inter-Parliamentary Delegations and on any of the other great international bodies which are playing rôles of cumulative importance in world-affairs: but, given a distinctive place again, there is every reason to hope that this old historical nation, which once occupied so notable a place in Europe, and which has been one of the main sources of our Imperial power, may again play a part proportionate to its past and in keeping with its particular genius.

What is commonly forgotten, too, in matters of this kind, is that Scotland itself is part of the Empire. A concern with Scottish domestic welfare is just as much an Imperial consideration as preoccupation with the affairs of any other part of the Empire. The welfare of the Empire depends upon the welfare of each of its component parts. Scotsmen may help the Empire best by keeping the heart of it — the source of much that is best in it — sound at home. Surely it cannot be contended that Imperial policy demands the dereliction of Scotland? Will it not serve the Empire best in the future, as it has done in the past, if Scotland can once again become the home of a vigorous and multiplying people from which the Colonies can continue to draw robust settlers? The idea that Scottish Home Rule is at variance with Imperial tendencies and requirements is, in fact, an erroneous and short-sighted one, while the contrary opinion is supported by the recollection of the great part Scotland has played in Imperial affairs in the past — and cannot, assuredly, continue to play if its population is to be decimated, its industries ruined, and its countryside depopulated and thrown out of cultivation. Yet the latter is the effect of the neglect of Scottish affairs which is the settled — and natural — policy of the overwhelmingly English House of Commons. It represents a greater menace to the Empire than any Separatist movement can ever become because it strikes at the very heart of Imperial strength. The present policy of encouraging emigration in regard to Scotland is nothing more or less than a killing by our overseas dominions of the goose which has hitherto laid many of the best clutches of their golden eggs.

Let me add here that Scotland is not only the most neglected country in Europe today, but the most highly taxed. A vehicular and passenger bridge across the Forth is refused to Scotland by Englishmen, but Scots must contribute towards the £7,000,000 or £8,000,000 granted for a bridge across the Thames. Scotland's housing is a disgrace to Western civilization, although Scots builders are such efficient workmen that they are welcomed in England and overseas. Scotland has the highest death-rate, the highest sickness-rate, and the highest infant mortality rate in the British Isles, although naturally it is no less healthy than England, Ireland or Wales. Scotland contains 2,000,000 acres of land which are certified as suitable for cultivation and small holdings, although during the last ten years her agricultural population decreased by 15,000. There are fewer small holdings in Scotland now than in 1911, when the Small Landholders Act was passed by the London Parliament. Like facts can be adduced in regard to every other aspect of Scottish affairs. They are the inevitable counterparts of her cultural declinature. Verily 'Without the Vision the people perish'.

VI

Several reviewers of the Rt Hon H.A.L. Fisher's biography of the late Viscount Bryce have expressed their surprise that Bryce had not at least some measure of practical success with his first legislative love, the Bill to give free access to Scottish mountains and moors. As one of them well remarked,

> Forty years ago there was no more popular measure. The mention of it on a public platform never failed to jog a lackadaisical audience into enthusiasm. How thankful many a Liberal orator felt that he could wind up by declaring his 'whole-hearted concurrence

> in principle and in part with that measure sponsored by the Member for South Aberdeen, which would give the people of Scotland freedom to enjoy their health-giving heritage'. It was a measure easy to advocate and difficult to oppose, even in the days before the motor car had driven the pedestrian from the by-ways as well as the highways. But to this day not one practical step in its realization has been taken; there is still no legal access to Scottish mountains and moors.

It is, indeed, one of the most curious of all puzzles in political psychology. Of the reality of the need for it, and of the abundance of public support, there is no question. Why, then, is nothing done? Whoever can answer that question can explain the whole position of Scotland today. It is not enough that a measure should be clamantly called for by the needs of the Scottish situation; it is not enough that the mere mention of it should be sufficient to jog the most apathetic body of Scottish electors into enthusiasm; it is not enough that it should have the support of the overwhelming majority of the Scottish MPs of all parties. All these three considerations can be fulfilled, and have been fulfilled, in respect to Scottish Home Rule and other questions, and yet not only is nothing at all done, but the proposed solution never even emerges into what is known as 'the sphere of practical politics'. Why is this?

But, whatever the reason, it is obviously not to the credit of the Scots MPs and their constituents that such measures should have to be supinely forgone; the realities of the Scottish national position treated as unrealities while the catch-vote tactics of professional politics are permitted to monopolize public and Parliamentary attention; and the whole principle of democracy in regard to Scottish affairs stultified in this obscure but overwhelming fashion. Somehow or other the situation must be changed, so that measures corresponding to the actual requirements of our nation can be carried into the field of practical politics — and not allowed to 'fail to carry' in this way. The whole impression of Scottish politics is like that of a man dominated by a sort of nightmare he cannot shake off. He would fain get back to his true self — but he cannot move. Just as reading certain papers one gets a wholly disproportionate and unfortunate conception of the world as a place where murders, divorces and all sorts of sensations and scandals are dominant — so the present political system entirely distorts and misrepresents the real condition of Scottish affairs and bogs the attention of the electors in all manner of 'professional political' issues which have little or no bearing on their interests, while the latter are excluded from the 'sphere of practical politics'. What is wanted is a movement to shake off all the old shibboleths, the tyranny of the catch-phrases; and to found a new conception of politics on the basis of a practical concentration upon the actualities of our national situation.

The Scottish Protestant Churches have manifested increasing alarm for several years over what has become known as the 'Irish Invasion' of Scotland. There is no dispute as to the facts. The Irish population is rapidly increasing; the native Scottish population is rapidly declining. The former is mainly confined to the big industrial centres; the latter is leaving the cities, but to a still greater extent is leaving the countryside. The position is that, owing to Irish, and other alien immigration, our urban congestion is not being relieved by the continual drain of emigration. All that is happening is that a certain proportion of Scottish people is being replaced there annually by an equivalent of un-Scottish people. While this is happening in the towns, which, despite all the emigration, continue to show 50 per cent more unemployment than in England, our rural areas are being steadily depopulated of their irreplaceable native peasantry — and nobody is taking their place. The seriousness of the matter on either count cannot be exaggerated. But the vital thing is not the influx of Irish and other aliens, but the exodus of Scots. It is due to our present economic system — to the condition of Scottish industries on the one hand which renders them incapable of paying adequate wages to Scottish employees and ready, therefore, to supplant them with cheaper Irish labour, and, on the other hand, to the lack of a progressive and native agricultural policy. The causes are political and economic, and if the consequences have religious and social bearings, these should not lead to any misconception as to the causes and any confusion as to how these can, and should be, dealt with. Sectarian trouble, for example, over a purely economic question, is not likely to help matters. This is the danger some of the Scottish Protestant Ministers are running. Their failure to penetrate to the real causes is blinding them to the only solution. That solution is a reorientation of Scottish affairs on such a basis that Scottish industries and interests would not be systematically sacrificed to English, but developed in accordance with the particular requirements of Scotland, as they could be developed if Scotland were not compelled to pay, as it is under the present system, upwards of £120,000,000 per annum to the Imperial Exchequer, out of which it receives back only some £30,000,000. If the Scottish contribution were equitably applied, many millions a year would become available for Scottish commercial and industrial developments, and not only could the flow of Scottish emigration overseas be arrested, but a stream back to Scotland would speedily set in if Scotland could offer its exiled people anything like the conditions they are obtaining in the colonies. They did not want to emigrate. Economic conditions forced them. Only economic conditions can bring them back. This will never happen so long as a system is applied which is willing to spend £2,000 in settling a Scot overseas, but unwilling to spend £1,000 to settle him at home — although the percentage of such home settlements as have been effected (a miserably small percentage of the applications) which has been successful has been much greater than amongst overseas settlements, relatively expensive as the latter are. Most important of all is the necessity for devising and financing a thorough-going agricultural policy for Scotland, designed to do for it, in accordance with its specific requirements, something like what Denmark and other small nations have achieved for themselves by co-operative methods. But what hope is there for the initiation of any such policy under the present system? Scottish Independence is an indispensable preliminary to any attempt to solve Scottish problems in such a fashion as may arrest the deplorable efflux of Scottish people and the progressive dereliction of the Scottish soil.

Dealing with the question of Irish Immigration, the Committee on Church and Nation of the Established Church of Scotland says:

> There are only two explanations of the great racial problem that has arisen in Scotland — the emigration of the Scots and the immigration of the Irish people. There does not seem to be any hope of alleviation of this problem in the future. All available evidence points to its intensification. The outlook for the Scottish race is exceedingly grave. If ever there was a call to the Church of Scotland to stand fast for what men rightly contend dearest — their nationality and their traditions — that call is surely sounding now, when our race and our culture are faced with a peril which, though silent and unostentatious, is the gravest with which the Scottish people has ever been confronted.

This is true — but not exactly in the sense the Committee intends. It will not do to identify Scottish nationality and traditions wholly with Protestantism. There has always been a considerable native Catholic population, and most of the finest elements in our traditions, in our literature, in our national history, come down from the days when Scotland was wholly Catholic. Neither, in speaking of a 'silent and unostentatious peril' will it do to overlook the fact that

Scotland has been steadily subject to Anglicization ever since the Union. This, since it does not raise the 'religious bogey' in the way the Irish immigration does, is apt to be overlooked, but it should have at least as much attention as the other from the 'Scottish' Churches, if at last they are seriously concerned with Scottish nationalism, and not merely with a sectarian issue. Until they face the whole issue of Scottish Nationalism and define what they mean by it and by a national culture, they will be suspected of merely using the term to cover an interest in special issues by no means synonymous with it, however importantly they may be related to it. But the part is not greater than the whole, and an all-round statesman-like attitude is what is necessary, and should be forthcoming from a Church that is truly Scottish and has the deepest interests of Scotland at heart. Nor will these ministerial protagonists gain anything by suggesting that 'Scottish employers of labour ought to do their utmost to retain their fellow-countrymen at home'. The suggestion takes no cognizance of economic realities. Nor is the suggested restriction of immigration any more feasible under the existing system. It is impossible to discriminate against the Irish in that way as long as we are co-members of the British Empire. If anything is to be done it must be along the lines of re-acquiring Scottish control of Scottish affairs, and more particularly such a measure of financial autonomy as would enable projects like the mid-Scotland ship canal, land settlement on a far greater scale, the creation of co-operative agencies in our agriculture, afforestation and so forth, to be developed in a way the House of Commons has not allowed — in short, to undo the present neglect of, and contempt for, Scottish affairs, and their treatment, where they have had any, within the limits of alien and inappropriate conceptions, which are largely responsible for the pass to which we have been brought, and which cannot be undone until we have once again a Parliament of our own and are free to move on the axis of our own mentality.

VII

'We should be the last to assert that there are no aspects of the smaller nationalism worth conserving,' says another opponent;

> there are many, but the best of them are alive and effective in Scotland today, and they have no necessary connection with the structure of Government. But Scotland, without losing her sense of

> herself as a Scottish nationality, has attained to a full and complete sense of a larger nationality, and she is not going to throw off that sense of partnership in larger nationality under the leadership of archaic and thrown-back minds, all of them belonging to the largely denationalized region of Clydeside.

Now the fact of the matter is that no valuable aspect of 'the smaller nationalism' is permitted to function, except under extraordinary handicaps, by the conditions of progressive Anglicization (in violation of even such safeguarding clauses as the Treaty of Union contained), which have increasingly dominated Scotland during the past hundred years. Scotland has ceased to hold any distinctive place in the political or cultural map of Europe. The centralization of book-publishing and journalism in London — the London monopoly of the means of publicity — has reduced Scottish arts and letters to shadows of their former or potential selves, qualitatively beneath contempt in comparison with the distinctive arts and letters of any other country in Europe. There is no Scottish writer today of the slightest international standing. Scotland connotes to the world 'religious' bigotry, a genius for materialism, 'thrift', and, on the social and cultural side, Harry Lauderism and an exaggerated sentimental nationalism, which is obviously a form of compensation for the lack of a realistic nationalism. No race of men protest their love of country so perfervidly as the Scots — no country in its actual conditions justifies any such protestations less. Every recent reference book in any department of human activity shows the position to which Scotland has degenerated. *Europa 1926* (although it is presumably designed for British readers) lists contemporary Czech and Bulgarian poets, litterateurs, musicians, etc. (the bare names — which convey nothing!) but it excludes Scotland completely. Ireland, on the contrary, has a section to itself, and a special article on the boundary question. Professor Pittard's *Race and History*, doing justice to every other people under the sun, deals only very slightly and imperfectly with Scotland, and fails to take account of any of the newer material, *e.g.*, the works of Tocher. Like examples can be multiplied in every direction.

Again, letters from Paris, or 'Our Irish Letter', etc., are familiar features of English newspapers. Whoever saw a 'Scottish Letter'? Concern with Scottish interests of any kind has been so completely excluded from publicity, has been made so completely a case of 'beating the air', that the usual headlines following a 'Scottish Night' at Westminster are 'Absent Members — Empty Benches — During

Discussion on Scottish Estimates', while from the report it appears that the debate resolves itself into a potpourri of stale jokes. Scotland alone of all European countries that have ever been in anything like its position relatively to any other country, has failed to develop a Nationalist Movement capable of affecting the practical political situation in some measure or other. Why have the Scottish members of all parties who have supported the numerous successive Scottish Home Rule measures acquiesced so tamely in their defeat at the hands of the English majority? There must be more in this acquiescence than meets the eye. It represents an abrogation of themselves, for all effective purposes, as the political leaders of Scotland of which it is inconceivable that they should be guilty, unless — behind the ostensible position — they were cognizant of a power against which they were incapable of contending, a power so possessed of the monopoly of mass publicity that it could completely stultify them by its all-pervasive *suppressio veri, suggestio falsi* the instant they went beyond a given line.

Contrasting the pre-Union achievements and promise of Scottish arts and letters with the beggarly results since, it is not too much to assert that Scottish Nationality was sold for 'a mess of pottage', and that Scotland has since been paying the price by submitting to the diversion of her entire energies into purely materialistic channels — not, however, as the present condition of Scotland and Scottish industries shows, for its own benefit. For whose, then? That I shall attempt to indicate. But, first of all, it cannot be too strongly stressed that its social, commercial, and industrial conditions today afford strong *prima facie* evidence that if, as is commonly contended, Scotland has owed a great deal materialistically (whatever it may have lost in other directions) to its Union with England, it has now wholly ceased to derive any such advantages; the boot, indeed, is on the other foot; and on that, as on other grounds, it is high time to reconsider the relationships between the two countries.

What prevents the development of well-informed and positive policies in regard to such problems as that of the Scottish Highlands? Col. John Buchan, MP, expressed the opinion in a letter to the present writer that 'it is impossible to make up one's mind on the Scottish Home Rule question — the necessary facts, and figures are not available'. Why are they not available? In certain directions these have been systematically refused by Government Departments — or purposely embodied along with the English in such a way that comparisons between the two countries cannot be instituted. In other directions the refusal of financial facilitation, as Mr William Graham,

MP, has pointed out, has resulted in the creation of a tremendous leeway in the economic and social documentation of Scotland, so that in practically every direction laborious independent research is necessary to get at the facts and figures. They are nowhere readily available.

The vested interests of the Scottish daily papers are all part and parcel of the sequelæ of the Union. They all 'make a show' of Scottishness by dealing in windy and suitably contradictory generalizations with Scottish topics — but they all toe the secret line. Letters sent in by readers are carefully censored. Opinions may be expressed (preferably anti-nationalist, or, better still, merely sentimentally nationalist), but facts and figures are not permitted — or, at all events, only isolated ones. Nothing can get published that attempts to relate facts and figures in regard to Scottish subjects to each other, and thus, to a national policy of any kind. There is not a single paper that dare publish a series of articles dealing thoroughly and systematically either with the case for Scottish Home Rule or with any of the major social or economic problems of Scotland. Nor dare they relax their vigilance in respect of the utterance of Scottish MPs in Parliament. Only so much is allowed 'through'; the rest must be kept back in the sieve. What does appear must appear so fragmentarily and disjointedly — and be so offset by the facetiousness and belittlement of leaders and tittle-tattle paragraphs — that it cannot conduce to the creation of any 'well-informed and positive policy'. What hidden interests behind the newspapers dictate this corruption of their natural functions and insist upon a journalism to bamboozle rather than educate the public — a journalism to make 'confusion worse confounded' rather than to clarify national issues in a systematic and rational fashion? What is the meaning of the whole position and policy that is, superficially, so determinedly unintelligble?

It is utterly irrational to find all the real practical issues of a nation 'outwith the sphere of practical politics' and that sphere monopolized by professional-politician issues, few of which have the most indirect bearing upon national realities. It is utterly irrational to find a whole electorate bemused and misled (for all practical purposes) by such an abracadabra. That is the position of Scotland today. All the Scottish papers aver that the demand for Scottish nationalism is made by 'a handful of fanatics', and has no real weight of 'public opinion' behind it — but what is 'public opinion', and how far is it reflected by a Press which, in a country which has always been overwhelmingly radical and republican, and where today a third of the entire electorate vote Socialist, is solidly sycophantic and anti-socialist?

The Glasgow Herald, in a recent leader, observed that there was no need for street-corner oratory in these days of a great free Press whose columns are open for the expression of all manner of opinion, and its editor, Sir Robert Bruce, is frequently to be heard dilating on the high status and professional integrity of the journalist today. Yet it is a simple fact that there is no free Press and that journalists hold their jobs by opportunism and cannot afford to 'own their own souls'. A man with 'ideas of his own' is of no use in a modern newspaper office. The vigilance of the Press censorship — the ubiquitous range and insidiousness of the policy behind it — is such that even *The Glasgow Herald* does not, and cannot, permit signed correspondence on such subjects as Scottish music or drama, for example (let alone politics), if these go against the ideas of the vested interests concerned with these departments, not to speak of the veiled interests behind these vested interests which 'hold all the strings in their hands'. Interplay of opinion is confined to opposing views within a certain range; but the essence of the matter all the time, so far as the ultimate interests are concerned, is 'Heads I win, tails you lose'. It is this that makes a goblin of the vaunted Scottish hard-headedness and practicality — induces the amazing supineness of the successful protagonists of Scottish Devolution Measures when these are rejected by the English majority at Westminster — prevents any real Scottish issue emerging into the realm of 'practical politics' — makes the systematic neglect of Scottish interests of all kinds a subject for stereotyped jokes in the Scottish Press (professedly favourable to 'legitimate' nationalist aspirations — in China) — prevents different sections of the Scottish public realizing that their diverse grievances and difficulties spring from a common centre and denies them those publicist services which would effectively relate consequence to cause — and foists, not least upon Scotsmen themselves, that stock conception of the 'canny Scot', which is so belied by the actualities of our national position that it can only be accounted for by saying that if, as M. Delaisi argues, government is impossible unless a myth of some kind is foisted upon the 'people', then, so far as Scotland is concerned, its present disastrous condition is due to the fact that the existing myth is out of touch with realities to a degree so abnormal that history presents no parallel to it.

Discussing the possibilities of a Scottish Renaissance I have written elsewhere that the Credit Reform proposals of Major C.H. Douglas will be 'discerned in retrospect as having been one of the great contributions of re-oriented Scottish genius to world-affairs', and that I wished to record my unqualified pride and joy in the fact that of all people in the world a Scotsman — one of the race that has been (and remains) most hag-ridden by commercial Calvinism, with its hideous doctrine of 'the need to work', 'the necessity of drudgery', and its devices of 'thrift', and the whole tortuous paraphernalia of modern capitalism — should have absolutely 'got to the bottom of economics', and shown the way to the Workless State.

It is significant that practically the only, and certainly the only real (if, unfortunately, only very partial and temporary) political triumph Scotland has scored over England since the Union of the Parliaments took place just over 100 years ago: and was associated with the name of a great Scotsman and with precisely the type of business which it has since become almost physically impossible to think — let alone speak — about. The Banking System! I refer to Sir Walter Scott's *Letters of Malachi Malagrowther*. Just how much Scott (albeit a Tory of Tories, and a national liability rather than an asset in most respects), was roused by the Government's proposal that Scottish Banks should cease to issue notes 'in order to unify paper currency throughout the United Kingdom', can be gauged from his veiled threat that 'claymores have edges'. Scott's agitation was so far successful that the Government dropped their proposals inasmuch as they related to the Scotch pound notes — for the time being. 'Very probably,' says a recent writer, 'they realized that there was real determination behind Scott's reference to claymores — even if it did not actually mean the wielding of these lethal weapons to enforce the protest.' All who are in earnest about Scottish Home Rule should take a note of that. Evidences of 'real determination' must be forthcoming if anything is to be achieved. The Parliamentary record of the Scottish Home Rule question would long ago have driven protagonists of any mental and moral calibre to the realization that an irresistible premium had been put upon the recourse to militant methods, and that anything else is a waste of time — 'an expenditure of spirit in a waste of shame'.

But a great deal has happened since 1826. The existence of a Scotsman of Sir Walter's calibre was a nasty snag for the Government of the day — but the policy behind them could afford to wait, to pretend to yield; it is not every generation, happily, that throws up such a figure to thwart its purposes, although Lord Rosebery *did* concede that Scotland is 'the milch cow of the Empire'. There has appeared no Scotsman since of equal size to do anything analogous and to expose the tremendous losses to Scotland through the financial unification of Scotland with England that has since been consummated. The dangers that Scott apprehended and warded off a hundred years ago are fully battening on Scottish interests today, and they are powerless to defend themselves. How powerless is indicated by the fact that the Scottish Press (whose columns are shut to all discussion of national realities) gives prominence to such ridiculous statements as that of Mr Ridge Beedle, prospective Unionist candidate for the Camlachie Division of Glasgow, who says that 'it is owing to the Scottish Home Rule Movement that new industries are not settling in Scotland; industrialists are preferring locations in England where continuity and settled conditions are assured'. Thousands upon thousands of Scottish electors are so hopelessly bemused that they swallow an absurdity like that as if it were a self-evident truth. If it were, the difficulties of Scottish Nationalism would be over. Our English competitors would be falling over each other to subsidize it and ensure its success.

VIII

Here the connection between the diverse movements in Scotland I indicated as so superficially incompatible becomes clear. The Credit Reform Movement is essentially one for the removal of all the false restraints under which humanity is labouring. It is not without significance that its leader, Major Douglas, should belong to the race which has suffered most abominably from the forms under which it has been subjected to two of the greatest agencies — the Reformation and the Industrial Revolution — which the impelling force, which has multiplied these restraints until 'civilization' is tending to reduce the majority of mankind to the condition of robots, has utilized in securing that stranglehold on life which it is now visibly exercising. Will Scotland yet produce

> Eighth marvel of seven on earth,
> A Douglas at peace?

Do not the intolerable conditions to which it has been reduced, the unparalleled anomalies in its 'national' finance, suggest that a flanking movement against the Powers of Finance may be best achieved through it. This is 'the place where the spring of action will play' — where alone a counterforce to that which is not only making for centralization in all directions and superannuating such agencies of differentiation as Scots and Gaelic, but would eliminate religion by completely mechanizing the masses of mankind and make Socialism the last and worst stage in capitalism — the Servile State — rather than the first in a new and nobler order, can be generated. Here is the 'comprehensive-enough agency' — 'the nation-size principle' — the meeting ground of Scottish Nationalists, Catholics and Socialists, those diverse elements upon whose recognition of their interdependence, their need to complement and moderate each other, depends not only the realizable proportion of the ideals of each but a Scottish Renaissance of international consequence. Let us not fight with enemies — England, commercial Calvinism, 'Progress', thought-hating democracy — which are merely the agents of the foe that is really worthy of our steel, the cause that lies behind them all; but, in concentrating on the latter, remember that every other nation has suffered in like fashion to some degree from its operations, and make common cause with the elements in all these other countries which are seeking to overcome it.

It is noteworthy that banking and national interests in Scotland are far more conspicuously divorced from each other than in most countries. There is less 'cover' here than at the centre. Leading Scottish bankers do not discourse, like their English brethren, on current topics; they confine themselves to the business in hand. Mr McKenna and the like may create a diversion by pretending to let, not the cat, but one or two of its meows out of the bag occasionally, but in Scotland the public is too docile even to need 'circuses'.

The amalgamation of the Scottish banks with the English, along with such subsidiary developments or sequelæ of the same policy, as the amalgamation of the railways, and the English control of Scottish newspapers, represents one side of that picture of which the inevitable obverse is the fact that the collective area of deer forests (1,709,892 acres in 1883) is now 3,599,744 acres; seventeen Scottish counties today have a population less than it was fifty years ago, eleven have less than in 1821, and five less than in 1801; and of the remaining population of the country more than 45 per cent (over two million people) live more than two in a room!

These tendencies are continuing at an accelerating rate. This is the price Scotland is paying for its 'sense of participation in a larger nationality' — a sense that even then must be qualified by recognition of the fact that the 'larger nationality' will in turn be subjected to the same 'policy' as the 'smaller' (although both, no doubt, may continue a while longer to have a sense of 'Empire') — unless Scotland comes to the rescue of England in the manner suggested.

The Scottish Convention of Burghs (of which I have been a member) is the oldest municipal institution in Europe — it is also the most effete and powerless. Otherwise its continued existence would not be tolerated for a moment. Let it discuss with any 'real determination' the effect of the amalgamation of the Scottish banks, railways, etc., with the English — or the relation of the banking system to the policy of neglect and deliberate 'misunderstanding' which is eviscerating Scotland — and it will speedily see the end of its long history.

Scotland's, and more than Scotland's, only hope — albeit yet a slender one — is through the Scottish Socialist movement, and, it may be, one of its Irish Catholic leaders. The closer inter-relationship of the Scottish Socialist and Nationalist Movements, their increasing identity of personnel, and happily, their tardy concentration on the financial aspect, is the one promising feature in the situation, unparalleled in history, in which a whole nation, reputedly hard-headed and patriotic, have been almost ineradicably persuaded by (mainly alien — or alienated) financial interests that black is white and white black until they wax only the more perfervid in their patriotic protestations, and the more diligent in their Sisyphus task of futile 'thrift', the more their country is denuded of population, status, and prosperity, and themselves of all that makes life worth living. It is significant that *The Scotsman* and other Anglo-Scottish papers dealing with the new Draft Bill, are increasingly conceding the 'advantages' of sentimental nationalism, but simultaneously warning their readers that 'realistic nationalism' will be reactionary and profitless — 'what Scotland wants is not a Parliament of its own, but more employment, new industries', etc, as if the present system were supplying these, and nationalism threatened the supply. Happily, as I have said, the Scottish Home Rule Movement is rapidly re-orienting itself along realist lines, but the degree of realism achieved has not yet reached through to the financial backwork of our affairs, the real manipulation area, without control of which 'self-determination' is only a delusion and a snare. This is not surprising — when that stage has not even been reached in the Irish Free State despite the long history of intense nationalistic activity there and the relatively great measure of 'political success' achieved. But the Scottish psychology differs from the Irish, and, nationalistically laggard as Scotland has been in comparison with other countries, there are grounds for anticipating that, once it does waken up, it will redeem the leeway at a single stride and be the first to penetrate into that arcanum which still foils even Mr de Valera with its intangible and ubiquitous barriers.

Whether 'dreamers of dreams' can still prove themselves 'movers and shakers of the world' or not, the protagonists of a Scottish

Renaissance are dreaming the dream outlined in these pages, and have already earned at least the right to say to their countrymen in the words of Jaurès: 'It is we who are the true heirs of the ancestral hearth: we have taken its flame while you have kept but the cinders'.

The Present Position of Scottish Music

I

What is the present position of Scottish music? The question is a deceptively simple one, susceptible of a great variety of partial answers. Within brief compass it is impossible to deal with the manifold issues it raises. As a rule when the question is put in the form in which I have given it the answers show that the word 'music' is apprehended as synonymous with 'musicality', and that 'Scottish music' is taken to mean 'the cultivation and appreciation of music in general in Scotland'. That the question should be habitually so taken is an illuminating fact. The contrary would hold good in France or Italy, for example. The question would be taken in a different sense: and answered as if it meant either 'How do French or Italian composers today compare with, say, contemporary Russian or Spanish or German composers?' or, 'How do French or Italian composers today compare with their predecessors; what is the relative value of our new developments in music?' Each of these countries has made great contributions to the art of music and is vitally involved in its further evolution. A cultured European of any country, in replying to a question equivalent to mine, would naturally think first of all of composers. Anything else would be a very secondary consideration at best. In Scotland we think first of all of audiences, or choirmasters, or gramophone records, or wireless programmes — of anything and everything but composers. A cultured European would be puzzled to know what kind of creature his interrogator was if he went on to say — 'I am not asking about the new tendencies in music. What I am wondering is whether the masses of your people are musically inclined or not? Is there a constant multiplication of musical activities in their midst; is every village organist vying with every other village organist; have you organized competitions amongst your workpeople?' I should dearly love to hear such an interrogation. But I cannot imagine the most egregious Scotsman with heather in his hair asking any such questions — on the Continent. They are for home use only. The dumbfounded Frenchman would raise protesting hands to Heaven. 'Ah, I beg your pardon. I haf mistook your question. You are a sociologist then — not a musician.' It would be a great joke; but, as I say, I cannot imagine it happening. That is the attitude we adopt to music in Scotland; but we know that it is otherwise in France and Italy. We summon up our knowledge of French and Italian music. We remember that these are countries with great musical traditions — with peoples whose psychology (we are content to assume) is very different from ours. They produce music: we apply a certain amount of musicality to a certain amount of it — for our own local purposes. Again, almost wholly, for home consumption only. They not only produce the music; they supply most of the musicality too. Their artistes monopolize our high-class concerts; their conductors conduct our Scottish Orchestra. In a word, the countries that produce the creators produce the executants. To all intents and purposes Scotland produces neither. That is one — and the main — answer to our question (or, as another writer puts it, 'we have cultivated and worshipped foreign art classics so long that to produce native art up to the level of Continental art seems an impossibility, and among those educated in music the mention of Scottish music arouses feelings of contempt and disgust'); but, before going on to consider the whys, and wherefores of it, the position may be illuminated from another angle.

II

The leading Scottish daily newspaper the other week published a big advertisement appealing, over several well-known names, for substantial funds to make up the balance necessary, along with very large sums already provisionally given by several business magnates, to establish what it called 'A Scottish National Academy of Music' in Glasgow, and to set up at the same time, and in connection therewith, a Chair of Music in Glasgow University. A leading article supported the appeal. It is fairly well-known that I am not a millionaire. But it is equally well-known that I have taken a very active part in regard to Scottish arts and letters during recent years. The newspaper in question has frequently referred in flattering terms to my services in that connection. One understands, of course, that the pressure on space in regard to the correspondence columns of a great daily paper is at least equally great, but the best traditions of British journalism in this respect were that the available space for letters to the editor should as far as possible be allocated amongst competing correspondents on the basis of merit, with due regard to giving the different sides of the question fair proportion. In other words, the editor did not take it upon himself to support one point of view by denying expression to others. It will be agreed that such a practice is indefensible and may amount to an unscrupulous manipulation of public opinion. What happened in this particular case — not by any means for the first time in connection with this paper, which is not only no worse in this respect but a great deal better than all the other daily papers in Scotland today — was that I sent a very short letter to the editor asking for information as to the proposed scheme. I asked whether 'Scottish National Academy of Music' was not a misnomer and whether it was not the case that in so far from doing anything to promote distinctively Scottish music the proposed institution would 'thirl' us more completely to England. I asked whether, indeed, that might not be the unavowed intention — not of the donors of the money — but perhaps those who hoped that the subsequent control would be left to them. I pointed out that the dominant feature of modern music in every other country in Europe had been the evolution of national schools of composers — most of these now in their third or fourth stage of development — but that there was as yet little or no sign of any equivalent tendency in Scotland. I suggested that to make up that leeway was our main business in music as a nation, and that unless the proposed Academy was to be organized to that end — or to that end primarily — it was not only a misnomer but would prove a further stumbling block. The money might be much better applied in other directions. I said that the scheme as formulated might deceive the Philistines, but that, if it went through, those (no doubt comparatively few) who knew the true inwardness of Scotland's position in music today would, according to temperament, either regard it as a more hopeless proposition or a greater stumbling block than ever. With regard to the proposed Chair in Glasgow University, I asked what Scotsman we had to occupy it who was a representative national musician or whether here again we were to be in the absurd position of falling back on an Englishman — and in parenthesis I added — (or Welshman). I believe that parenthesis sealed the fate of my letter — for, of course, it did not appear. It was really a very short letter — not more than a 'stickful'. It has taken me several times the space it would have occupied to describe it here. I submit that all these questions were very proper and relevant questions in the circumstances. I submit that things have come to a pretty pass when a comparatively well-known writer is debarred from raising such an obviously important issue in connection with a public project. I submit that the editorial attitude is peculiarly and significantly petty — and not to be submitted to. What, in the nature of the scheme, required this extraordinary editorial vigilance? What made it so necessary that there should be no discussion of the questions I raised? I cannot imagine that my letter would have jeopardized the raising of the balance required. I am not so puffed up with hope as to imagine for a moment that it would have had the slightest effect on those who had already provisionally intimated munificent donations (in the way of making them withdraw their offers, that is — though it might have led them to reconsider whether they could not improve their scheme and have their money more profitably administered) — certainly not those in the background. Nor do I imagine that the editorial decision not to publish my letter was dictated by any fear that it might have any such effect. What, then, was the reason for it? I feel sure it was that wretched parenthesis. I am not a prophet nor the son of a prophet, but I shall be agreeably surprised if a Welshman is not the first occupant of the forthcoming Chair of Music in Glasgow University.

What really impressed me with the strength of the determination behind the scenes that the particular aspects of the matter I was raising must not penetrate through in public if that could possibly be prevented was the fact that on the offchance, as an added inducement, I had taken care to append to my signature the mystic initials 'J.P.' A poet is, of course, neither here nor there.

> Rattle his bones over the stones,
> Only a poor critic whom nobody owns.

But a J.P.! What is Scotland coming to?

III

I fancy that once it is put to him in this way, however, any intelligent Scot will see the point and recognize its paramount importance. His natural desire will be to know exactly how Scotland stands to other nations in respect of its contribution to the art of music — and why. It will be apparent to him that the relative quality of the likes and dislikes of the relatively uninstructed masses will not compensate for the absence of Scottish composers comparable in significance to those of other countries. It may even be obvious to him that if other countries produce the music and support scores of important composers they must also have a public responding to music to a far greater extent, and in a far more important way, than ours. The facts can be stated quite bluntly. Scotland in this respect (whatever it may be in others) is like the snake; it has not a leg to stand upon. Compare Babtie's *Musical Scotland: a Dictionary of Scottish Musicians from 1400 Onwards*, with Landormy's *History of Music* for example, or Eaglefield Hull's *Dictionary of Modern Music* — the one an enumeration of stocking-makers, precentors and gangrel scrape-guts; the others with thousands of names each one of which represents a positive giant in comparison with anything Scotland has ever produced. As the writer I have already quoted says:

> In Scotland we have to bewail the fact that there is no art-music literature; if there happens to be any it is never heard, and there seems to be little desire for the creation, stimulation or development of it. Obviously for a nation this is a calamitous condition of affairs, and we cannot claim to be on an equality with intellectually and artistically alive countries. This unproductiveness spells stagnation equally in music as in commercial concerns.... It is said that art is international. Surely this means that art is intercommunicable and for mutual interest and example, and thus it is clear that as we have nothing to communicate we continue to be parasitic, and in the mind of the foreigner, this country as regards art-music does not exist.

And the reason, paradoxically enough, is largely because of what Scotland is — or is not — in other respects. We have ceased to exist on the map of European arts precisely for the same reason (or from the same causes) that have rendered it possible for foreigners to address letters to 'Edinburgh, England'. The Scot is apt to have a good conceit of himself. In almost every respect — and certainly in respect of all the arts (all the things, in other words to which everything else should be the means) — his conceit has scant justification, and when the position of Scotland is compared with that of other countries, none. Even the smaller countries — Norway and Sweden and Denmark — are far ahead of us in regard to all; Ireland is ahead of us in regard to all save music; Wales is at least slightly ahead of us in regard to music if in regard to nothing else — if only in respect to Cyril Jenkins! This finds its reflection in the world-judgement of us summed up in the term 'the canny Scot'. For

> ...prudence is the deadly sin
> And one that groweth deep into a life,
> With hardening roots that clutch about the breast.
> For this refuses faith in the unknown powers
> Within men's nature; shrewdly bringeth all
> Their inspiration of strange eagerness
> To a judgement bought by safe experience;
> Narrows desire into the scope of thought.
> But it is written in the heart of man,
> Thou shalt no larger be than thy desire...

But it ought to be remembered that this conception of the Scot is wholly a post-Union thing. Prior to the Union Scotland was notoriously 'a nest of rebels': literature should have flourished in it, for, as Thomas Hardy has said, 'literature is the written expression of revolt against accepted things', and the like is true of all the arts. The arts did flourish in Scotland prior to the Union and the Reformation in a way they have never come within a million miles of flourishing since. What is today almost universally regarded, and most dogmatically by the vast majority of Scots themselves, as typically Scottish, is either quite un-Scottish — in fact, anti-Scottish — or represents the least worthy traits of the lower orders of Scottish life thrown into demoralizing prominence by the suppression of the better and more distinctive elements. These plebeian elements were happily inarticulate in the heyday (such as it was) of the Scottish arts: thanks to continual war and internecine strife and the general poverty of the country and the smallness of the population a 'shilpit' enough affair! With the single exception of Burns, all Scotland's great poets have been aristocrats — highbrows and necessarily so. It is only today that the petty demagogues of the arts are so organized that they can prejudice the public against work that is outwith their range, or defies their professional control, as if there were peculiar virtues in limited accomplishments and popular ignorance. The Reformation threw a blight over the arts in Scotland from which they have never recovered. It fell with especial severity on music and the drama. Scotland is the only country in Europe which has no native drama. Scotland is almost the only country in Europe which has failed to develop a distinctive national art-music on the basis of its native folk-song. Can we name a single Scottish poet or prose-writer today of the slightest significance as compared with dozens we can enumerate for every other European country. We cannot. I do not believe that the Scottish people are inferior in their natural endowments to every other

European race, or so markedly different that they are destitute of abilities akin to those which have built up great music and drama and living literature elsewhere. Despite the unique severity of the Calvinistic period in Scotland, I believe that our creative instincts would have reasserted themselves long ere this — if there had been any national centre to which they could rally; and that they still will do so, as soon as there is any such centre. I attribute our deplorable national backwardness in these respects, not so much to Calvinism, as to the diverse agencies responsible for our steady denationalization. Scotland has been almost completely provincialized. In every direction the contemporary culture of Scotland is overwhelmingly a thing superimposed from without, instead of evolving from within, and is therefore comparatively ineffective — excluding and atrophying the distinctive elements of the Scottish character so that the entire population (in addition to the handicap that attaches to provincialism) is, in respect of all cultural and æsthetic issues, in the position we describe when we say that a writer 'had not found himself'. We mean that what he writes is in a given convention — it might as easily be the work of any other undistinguished writer. His development as a creative artist has been arrested; he has not pierced through to personal expression. Scotland has not pierced through to distinctive national expression. It has not found itself. There is no country in Europe perhaps whose people are more perfervid in their lip-service to it. There is certainly none where there is a greater discrepancy between the professed pride — and the actual facts. Scotland sold its heritage for a mess of pottage, and it is a striking commentary on our suppositious hard-headedness that we have been diddled out of that too. Our businessmen, our engineers, are not better than the equivalent products of other countries; our present commercial and industrial position shows that. But other countries do not confine themselves to the production of businessmen and engineers, or pride themselves upon the production of them in the way they pride themselves upon their artists and composers and poets. We do. We forget entirely the tremendous element of truth that lay in the response of the young artist during the late war 'to save civilization' when a lady asked him why he was not in khaki. 'Madame,' he replied, 'I am the civilization they are fighting to save.'

It is very questionable whether Scotland has derived any material advantages out of the Union with England that the industrial revolution would not have brought to it almost synchronously in any case, and perhaps — if it had remained independent — without some of the evil accompaniments with which we are now contending; it is certain that it has ceased to derive any — that English interests (as in the case of Rosyth) are increasingly being favoured at the expense of the Scottish; that Scotland is so disproportionately taxed (by far the most heavily taxed country in the world) that the Government have refused to make any separate returns which would afford an includable basis of comparison — that our economic conditions are such that we are being increasingly depleted of our best manhood and womanhood; that the shameful depopulation of our countryside is counterbalanced by some of the worst slums in the world, peopled largely by aliens attracted hither by the fact that our industries cannot pay a better type of citizen a living wage; and that, to compensate ourselves for this shameful state of affairs, we cultivate a sentimental nationalism at complete variance with reality and seek to camouflage our position by defending as Scottish the very products of our national decadence — Harry Lauderism, the egregious Burns cult, the peculiar thing that is generally meant when we speak of a 'Scotch Concert'. Such matters as these should surely be the principal preoccupation of papers calling themselves Scottish papers. Instead of that all manner of unreal 'professional political' questions are canvassed to the exclusion of any discussion of Scotland's vital issues. It is easy to understand that papers subservient to the forces which have brought about the state of affairs in Scotland that I have just described will not give space to anything calculated to reawaken a realistic Scottish nationalism. And a realistic Scottish nationalism is a prerequisite of a Scottish Artistic and Literary Renaissance on any considerable scale — or any scale that would ever materially reduce the leeway. In other words, our backwardness in music and the other arts is a natural and inevitable concomitant of our political, economic, and social position. That we are so backward artistically brooks of no denial — and if we are not in a false and singularly calamitous position politically, economically, and socially, then the only other explanation is that in comparison with every other race in Europe we are spiritually deficient to an appalling degree.

I do not envy Scotsmen who are prepared to agree to that latter alternative, although I quite understand how, by the processes which have produced them, thousands of Scots can regard the absence of any Scots music or drama as matters of indifference. But Scotsmen who profess to be musicians, for example, are in a different category, and when they begin to talk about a Scottish National Academy of Music it is high time they were brought to book. For the fact of the matter is that it is the professional musician in Scotland today who (when he is not simply a 'blind leader of the blind' and 'there are none so blind as those who will not see') is perpetuating the dual standard of judgement — applying one standard to foreign art and condoning what passes for Scottish music by another, as if the two things had anything in common. He knows that national awakenings have been the vital feature of modern music in every other country: he knows, or should know — precisely how these developments were encompassed: he cannot deny that such developments are of infinitely more consequence to each country concerned and to the world at large and to the art of music than anything that is happening in Scotland. Why, then, is he not bent before all things on stimulating a like development in Scotland? Why, instead of being so bent, is he so implacably determined that nothing of the kind will transpire if he can possibly prevent it? He is not only doing this, but he is interposing between music and the masses and delimiting their capacities for appreciation in accordance with his professional interests — systematically pandering to them instead of educating them — and, above all, boycotting every tendency to creative development that manifests itself. Let me describe exactly how it is done — and why — and by whom.

IV

But stay a minute! What about our famous Scottish Educational System? Well, what about it? It must be judged by its fruits. If what I have said about Scotland's position relatively to other countries in regard to the Arts is true, that surely throws a peculiar light upon it. It has produced an abundance of lawyers and doctors and ministers and business and professional men of all kinds: but, judging by the present material condition of Scotland as compared with other European countries of comparable size — Denmark for example — Scotland has derived remarkably little profit from its investments in these directions; and I have still to find even a Scotsman who will place his hand upon his heart and aver that, if he had to choose for his country, he would speak in reverse terms to Fletcher of Saltoun and say 'Let who will make Scotland's songs: I am more concerned about its laws'. Is it not in the very nature of the Scottish Educational system to produce anything and everything but artists; and to turn out that anything and everything, however diverse in vocational accomplishment, so much of a pattern mentally and spiritually that the term 'Scottish' calls up a panorama of undifferentiated Philistines incapable of any cultural life? The first thing to do, then, is to alter the educational system. It is rooted in Calvinistic repressions. The last thing that would occur to the vast majority of Scottish parents is to train up any child to be an artist. The typical Scottish father or mother would be horrified at the mere idea of any child of theirs wanting to be anything so eccentric as a composer. There is no doubt that this attitude to the arts — a legacy of the Reformation — is largely responsible for Scotland's deplorable position and the miserable tone of contemporary Scottish life. 'Where there is no vision the people perish.'

I remember how perturbed my own parents were over my early poetical proclivities. There is no money in poetry. The Civil Service is the thing. A Scottish musician was telling me the other day, too, of how Roger Ducasse, the French composer, received the information that he (the Scot) was not a professional composer — he had not been trained as a composer — but as a teacher. M. Ducasse could not imagine a country where anything so uncivilized could happen. The last thing the average Scottish schoolmaster concerns himself about is what violence the application of a uniform system may do to the emotional nature of an individual child — particularly the more sensitive (and probably secretive) child — in a word, the potential creator. He 'larns them'. They are ruthlessly compelled to conform, and their own home atmosphere is even worse. 'Stop that reading, Johnny, and get on with your sums.' The first thing is to alter the educational system — to shift its barbarous emphasis — but the first thing according to the self-constituted leaders of Scottish musical life is to have more teaching. When we call a man a musician in Scotland 999 times out of 1000 he isn't — he is a teacher — and not merely in the sense that appalled M. Roger Ducasse, but on an infinitely lower plane than he could have conceived the existence of. I do not intend to labour this point here. I have dealt with it more fully elsewhere.[1]

But apropos of musical education and such additional facilities as the proposed Scottish Academy is designed to give, I may quote what Arnold Schönberg says:

---

[1] See *Educational Journal*: 'Creative Art and Scottish Education', issues of Nov. 5 and 19, 1926.

> He has not technique who can just skilfully imitate something given: rather he is the slave of technique — the technique of another. Whoever is capable of perceiving aright must realize that such technique is fraudulent. Nothing really fits in properly — it is merely put together with some skill. In such a case nothing is exact, nor develops out of itself, nor holds together; viewed from a distance, however, it seems genuine enough; but invention must create its own technique.[2]

The utilization of acquired foreign technique by Scots — the superimposition of it on Scottish themes even — does not produce Scottish music. It does not make Scottish composers. Substantially the same results could have been obtained by composers of any nationality applying the same technique to the same subjects. That is not how musical work of any consequence is done. And all that the proposed Scottish Academy of Music seems at all likely to do is to enslave Scottish pupils of music more thoroughly than ever to other people's technique — all that constitutes the alleged musicality of almost all teachers of music in Scotland is prostituted to this form of fraud. The files of our Scottish papers may be scanned and all the references to music matters read — nowhere will there be found any appreciation — at all events in relation to Scotland — of the fact that 'invention must create its own technique'. It must come from within; it cannot be superimposed from without. Nor will any reference be found to any attempt to devise any such technique in Scotland — to create a distinctive national idiom — to do what Scotland alone of European countries has failed — create an art-music of our own on the basis of our native folk-song, take our native rhythms and idioms and raise them to classical rank, or, if the time for that is past, as is probable, elide that stage and apply the full range of modern technique in a distinctively Scottish fashion. An ounce of creative impulse is worth tons of polite accomplishments. Scottish musicality is organized to promote the latter and to preclude the former. Let us revert to the questions which I propounded before I deviated to the subject of Scottish Education.

---

2 See his *Problemen des Kunstunterrichtes.*

V

What is the reason of 'this thusness'? The attitude of the professional musician — of the newspaper critic — ultimately of the general public (which is at their mercy) — is all dictated by the same thing — vested interests. It is the aspect so far as music is concerned of the commercialism of our age, accentuated in Scotland by our denationalization and provincialization. Sir Thomas Beecham has recently been inveighing against the present condition of affairs musically in England — against the way in which wireless and other mechanical agencies which 'make all good music sound bad and bad music sound good' and confound all values in the interests of mediocrity are rendering the position of the creative artist or genuine interpreter hopeless. He points out that it is not due to 'financial stringency'. Despite our economic position as much money is turned over nightly in many a degenerate nightclub as would subsidize a genuine artistic development. It is not the effect of the war years. Germany and France suffered even more than we did, but their artistic vitality so far from having been impaired is — comparatively — as high as ever. All sorts of little journalistic nonentities, pandering to the public who are not prepared to believe any ill of themselves or of their likes and dislikes (unconscious of how these are created for them for somebody else's profit), in their usual way, have had the impertinence to set up their petty sycophantic views against Sir Thomas's, and to question if he is not over-pessimistic. A few of the 'yellower' ones have even attributed his outburst to personal disappointment. It was due to personal disappointment — but the disappointment of the artist — not of the profiteer or careerist. The mere existence of these gadflies is another proof of the pass to which we have fallen — largely due to the hatred of real distinction by the plethora of nonentities in an age of democratic decadence when 'Jack is as good as his master — if not better'. The arts are not democratic. There is no equality in them. If democracy and creative art are incompatible, democracy will go — for 'without the vision mankind must inevitably perish'. The trouble is that the swing back to sanity may not come in time to save European civilization.

The organization of modern business is ousting the small firm and building up monopolistic combinations which depend upon mass production. This affects music as it affects everything else. Music in Scotland is in the hands of two or three firms. Their interest is to make it pay as much as possible. They involve the public taste in a vicious circle. This is the explanation of the increasing diffusion of a uniform standard of appreciation — its limits are determined by the publishing and other interests of the firms in question. They want to create a condition of public taste which will enable them to circulate a given sort of thing as widely as possible. Like the newspapers, also dependent on big national circulations, they are careful not to pitch their standard too high. They make more off the thing (however inferior in quality it is) a hundred thousand people want than of the thing, say, a hundred people want. In their own measure the great majority of music teachers are in like case — they want an adequate number of pupils, not one incipient genius who would probably prove intractable. They do not want the fatigue of trying to keep abreast of contemporary musical tendencies — they do not want to be constantly varying their repertoire and learning new works, especially some of these modern compositions which are so difficult to play. So they create an atmosphere of prejudice against everything that is beyond their range or outwith their control as 'highbrow stuff' or 'foreign'. Professional singers 'play safe'. They 'play to the gallery' — singing and re-singing the same old hackneyed 'favourites' ad nauseam — rather than venture any experiment with new work. And 'public opinion' is manipulated to respond to the professional interest.

It is a sentimental delusion in the public, sedulously and incessantly cultivated, that they like these so-called 'favourites' instead of being sick to death of them. The Man in the Street is 'disinterested'. He has 'no axe to grind'. He would respond to the new work if he was given the chance of hearing it — before the middlemen, the parasites, had imbued him with the prejudices necessary to their business. Musical progress depends upon going on from one stage of appreciation to another — not going round and round in a circle like a squirrel in a cage. When they are so organized that they are engaged in promoting this progressive appreciation, our music teachers and firms will be performing the function they would have in a civilized society — and Scotland would be beginning to have a position in music. New music is created by action and reaction upon a given position at a given moment. It stands to reason that it must be opposed to the big trade interests — to the prejudices of the ruck of mediocre teachers — to the likes of the general public. It is an acquired taste — not for everybody — at first. But it is the most important thing, nevertheless, and everything else should be related to it. We want a new synthesis — not with the oldest elements but the newest. It is the newest tendencies with which people should be familiarized first. Then they can turn to the past stages with an appreciation of their historical position. That would prevent the accumulation of prejudices which prevents most people ever reaching an appreciation of the contemporary music to which, if it could be got across to their unprejudiced minds, they would respond most readily, seeing that it is an expression of contemporary psychology of which in some direction or another they are already cognisant. But they fail to realize these two things. That is because the professional educators interpose and clutter up their mind with hoary conceptions — useful enough in proper historical perspective but stultifying otherwise. The Musical Festival Movement is, of course, dominated by trade interests. That is why it has such a 'good press'. Newspapers nowadays are not controlled by their editors but by their advertising managers; and the bulk of 'musical criticism', 'book reviews', and the like is camouflaged publicity matter.

VI

All this may seem only remotely, if at all, related to the present proposals to establish a Chair of Music in Glasgow University and to set up a 'Scottish National' Academy of Music. And these are designed to crown and complete the edifice I have been describing — to provide culminating facilities for the attitude to music developed in Scotland from the infant school upward — to fit into the 'cultural' landscape that has just been depicted. Let us consider them separately for a moment. If the donors of the money have the interests of music in general, and Scottish music in particular, at heart — or if those in the background upon whom they may be relying for advice or in whose hands they are prepared to allow the project to take practical shape, are so inspired — it is to be presumed that they have thought out the whole position and can present a reasoned and purposive attitude towards it. In that case they would naturally welcome any discussion of the vital issues involved as a means of clarifying the position, creating further public interest, and, above all, enlisting the energies of all who are keenly concerned in Scotland in such matters. There is no need for a 'dog-in-the-manger' policy. There is still less need to follow the example of the ostrich. A good case does not fear thorough investigation; a public-spirited project invites the consideration of the public. I should like to be told in a convincing fashion just what good those who are promoting it think is likely to accrue to Scottish music from the establishment of ANOTHER Chair of Music in Scotland.

It may put Glasgow University upsides with Edinburgh University, and please those who care about petty matters of that sort; but, from the purely musical point of view, have we not in Professor Donald Tovey one of the ablest of living critics, imbued with the true juice of classical tradition? And yet what has his chair done in the direction of stimulating and developing the creation of an art music in Scotland and enabling us to entertain comparison for a movement with even the most backward of other European countries in this respect? The answer is — Nothing; and, that being so, the establishment of another such Chair in Glasgow seems utterly superfluous from any point of view concerned with significant development. Indeed, it may make matters worse instead of better. Even if the Glasgow occupant is of equal calibre to Professor Tovey, his effect can only be to increase the production of Mus. Bacs. and Mus. Docs., until, perchance, we have the whole country overrun with them, all scrambling for posts under Education Authorities, reproducing their own kind in every possible direction and degree, and accelerating for all they are worth the infernal mill of Education, Education — Light and yet more Light! — for a nation dead to any intuition of the functions of art or response to it. Is this really what the donors of the money intend? Is this all that their advisers can suggest? If there is more to it than this — and other — surely some statement could be issued to the public indicating how such a result is to be provided against — what safeguards have been taken — upon what grounds the promoters are confident that the establishment of this Chair will lead to more profitable results than Professor Tovey has been able to inspire. The promoters must have some intentions in regard to who — or what type of man — is to fill the Chair. A great deal may depend upon that. It would illuminate the whole matter from the most essential angle if any statement could be issued showing just what is intended, or hoped for, in relation to the issues I am raising. The public are being asked to subscribe for a practically-undefined object. If the promoters have any real grounds for supposing that the scheme as they intend to give effect to it will do anything at all to remove the existing reproach from Scotland in regard to music — will do more than Professor Tovey's Chair has done (and if so they must have a very different type of man in view, and the tenure of the Chair must carry with it an obligation upon the holder to construe his primary function in a very different fashion) — let them frankly say what they are. As matters stand it seems exceedingly improbable that anything but a White Elephant can ensue. Then as to the proposed Academy, it seems to me, as presently informed, that all that is to happen is that the local (Glasgow) Athenæum of Music is to become an annexe of the Royal Academy of Music, and no doubt the staff will be largely recruited from the headquarters in London. The idea apparently is to have the University as the academical training ground for Mus. Bacs. and similar degrees, and the Athenæum as the practical school. It will be obvious that if this is the intention it will worsen rather than improve the national position. Any creative talent that ever does emerge in Scotland will be up against a more hopeless position than ever. The so-called 'National Academy' will be his main opponent. These are the vital issues — who is to fill this Chair, and who is to man the practical school, and what will be the nature of the training given under the conditions likely to obtain? That the public have not been taken into the confidence of the promoters on these issues is a significant and suspicious circumstance. Everything hinges upon them. To contribute to the scheme in the absence of precise information on this point is to assist in buying a pig in a poke. To call it a 'Scottish National' Academy does not help matters. If it is a National movement, who are really behind it? In whose hands, once the money is subscribed, is the thing to lie? Are there any signatories to the appeal who have shown any such appreciation of, or concern over, the national position in regard to music as to engender confidence that if the necessary funds are placed at their disposal they will do anything to improve it? Has really representative, and musically competent, national opinion been sought before launching the appeal or deciding upon the policy to be pursued? It would appear, unless the issues that I have been raising, are yet taken into consideration and whatever provisional scheme may have been drafted re-modelled in accordance with the obvious requirements of the situation if the use of the terms 'Scottish National' is to be in any way justified, that all that it will amount to will be — London at second-hand, at the very best, instead of a living and creative contact with Continental movements. If that is so, it would be infinitely better to have it manned with Talichs from Czechoslovakia and be done with it — and call it, not a Scottish National Academy, but the Central European Conservatorium, and let Glasgow 'fidge fu' fair'.

I remember what the late Gerald Cumberland once said about Wales (and the same thing applies to Scotland) in reply to someone who said: 'Wales is too small a country to absorb the culture of the entire world: you might as well ask a squirrel to assimilate a granary'. 'Wales cannot absorb the culture of the whole world?' said Cumberland.

> Well, so much the worse for Wales. I believe she can: and she will begin to do so the moment she recognizes that music is not solely an emotional art, but an art demanding rigorous intellectual application. But it is not so much a question of Wales's power to assimilate foreign culture; rather is it a matter of the ability of a Welsh man of genius to do so. Music, of course, is a living growth: year by year it expands and discovers a greater diversity of means of expression. An English writer of today does not use the vocabulary of Chaucer, but the typical Welsh composer employs only the technique of a century ago, when modern music was in its childhood. No; Wales, being isolated, is content to crawl while the rest of the world is marching forward. Her music — the music she herself creates — is beneath contempt, and it will remain so as long as men she respects continue to assure her that all is for the best in her best possible musical world.

The same thing applies to Scotland: and it is precisely that assurance — to a greater extent than ever — that the promoters of this appeal are giving to Scotland. The complement of the full national position, in addition to Cumberland's remarks, lies in the old text: 'What shall it profit a man, though he gain the whole world, if he lose his own soul?'

VII

In his brilliant book, *Science and the Modern World* (Cambridge University Press), Professor A.N. Whitehead points out that one of the great facts confronting the modern world is the discovery of the method of training professionals (i.e. the top-notchers amongst our so-called musicians in Scotland) — and that, while that has accelerated human development in many ways, it has its dangers, dangers which, if uncorrected, may soon completely outweigh and stultify its values. 'It produces minds in a groove.' And he goes on to say:

> In every country the problem of the balance of the general and specialist education is under consideration.... I do not think that the secret of the solution lies in terms of the antithesis between thoroughness in special knowledge and general knowledge of a slighter character. The makeweight which balances the thoroughness of the specialist intellectual training should be of a radically different kind from intellectual analytical knowledge.... The

> general training should aim at eliciting our concrete apprehensions, and should satisfy the itch of youth to be doing something. There should be some analysis even here, but only just enough to illustrate the ways of thinking in different spheres.... The type of generality, which above all is wanted, is the appreciation of variety of value. I mean an æsthetic growth. There is something between the gross specialized values of the mere practical men, and the thin specialized values of the mere scholar. Both types have missed something, and if you add together the two sets of values you do not obtain the missing elements.... What I mean is art and æsthetic education.

And he goes on to show that what he means by art and æsthetic education are precisely what the Glasgow School of Art, for example, does not mean and can never give, any more than the proposed Scottish Academy of Music will. He means, on the contrary, precisely what Dr Pittendrigh Macgillivray meant when he declared recently that 'Art schools are not, and seem unlikely ever to be, in effect, what was expected. The education busines — School Board and University — all round is little better than a beautifully painted balloon, the pricking of which is about due.' And what Mr A.S. Neill meant when he said 'Any village cobbler will tell you that MAs in Scotland are as common as "dugs gaen barefut"'. Surely we are an instructed nation. But the disturbing question arises — 'Is an MA educated?' In exactly the same way, with reference to music, the question arises — 'Is an LRAM musical?' What Will-to-Significance is being inculcated? What recognition is there among Scottish music-teachers that, as Egon Wellesz puts it, 'the right relation between pupil and teacher lies, not in the pupil's learning to become like his teacher, but in his being led by him to the development of his own innate powers'? On the answer to that question hangs the answer to the question with which this paper begins. And Professor Whitehead puts the reason for Scotland's backwardness in regard to the creative arts in a nutshell, and shows that the only way to a better condition is along the lines I have indicated, when he says:

> The analysis of reality indicates the two factors — activity emerging into individualized æsthetic value. Also the emergent value is the measure of the individualization of the activity. We must foster the creative initiative towards the maintenance of objective values. You will not obtain the apprehension without the initiative or the initiative without the apprehension.... Sensitiveness without impulse spells decadence.

That is certainly what would be in the mind of the cultured European I postulated if he heard of this remarkable country where the general appreciation of music is alleged to be so widespread and yet (for the two things are incompatible) where there is no creativity worth mentioning.

> *The fertilization of the soul is the reason for the necessity of art. A static value, however serious and important, becomes unendurable by its appalling monotony of endurance. The soul calls aloud for release into change. The importance of a living art, which moves on and yet leaves its permanent mark, can hardly be exaggerated.*

That should be of all intelligent activities in relation to Scotland in particular — for it needs it more than any other country in Europe — as the quotation is of this paper.

The Present Position of Scottish Arts and Affairs

Scottish literature is generally regarded as a subordinate element of English literature. It is known, of course, that there is an ancient Gaelic literature, and that, prior to the Battle of Flodden, foundations were laid for a literature in the Scots Vernacular potentially no less great than that which has subsequently evolved in English. But there is only a very small body of readers today for that old Gaelic or old Vernacular literature, and it is generally assumed that the effects of the Reformation, the Industrial Revolution, and the Union with England in putting an end to the development of separate literatures in these ancient tongues are irreversible. The Gaelic speaking and Gaelic reading public has steadily diminished. The Scots Vernacular long ago disintegrated into dialects incapable of being made the media of high literature. A little stream of work has been maintained in each; but for the most part this has either been mere pastiche of the old models, or 'popular' work with little or no claim to be regarded as literature. For several centuries the great majority of Scottish writers have written in English — yet with a difference. This Scottish contribution remains a thing apart from the mainstream of English literature. It is very questionable whether any Scottish writers can be regarded as integral and indispensable to the evolution of English letters, and be accorded a place in the great succession, beginning with Chaucer, Shakespeare, Milton, Pope, Dryden, and so on, down to Wordsworth, Shelley, Keats and Tennyson, among the poets, or, in prose, can claim to rank in the sequence of Fielding, Sterne, Thackeray, Dickens, down to Hardy and Wells. The withdrawal of the Scottish contributions would scarcely affect the main body of English letters. No Scots writer except Sir Walter Scott has assimilated himself so well to the English tradition or won so high a place in it as, for example, the Pole, Joseph Conrad. The greater Scottish writers in English have either been disparate, 'kenspeckle' figures like Carlyle, or, too sedulously aping English models, have, like Stevenson, (in so far as the bulk of his work is concerned — he had, of course, another side to him which is purely Scottish) become more 'English than the English', and failed as a consequence to reach the front rank. A few, following the example of Burns and Fergusson, have turned their backs on English, and written their best work in Scots, where, however, they have had to be content with a restricted public and a degree of recognition qualified by the contempt in which dialect work is commonly held.

It is only within the past few years — as part and parcel no doubt of the widespread post-war intensification of nationalist sentiment all over Europe — that there has been a tendency to reverse the process that was threatening to assimilate Scotland wholly to England, and to ask whether the facts that no Scots writer using English has reached the front rank, that the Scottish contribution has proved practically irrelevant to the development of English literature, and that quantitatively as well as qualitatively the Scottish literary output has been markedly inferior to that of the English, do not imply that the whole process has been a misdirection from a Scottish standpoint. It is claimed that to regard work in Scots as merely 'dialect' work is wrong; and that it is fairer, even to those Scottish writers who have used English, to reassess their value as contributors to an independent Scottish literature rather than, treating them as contributors to English literature, misprise them on account of Scottish national qualities admittedly incompatible with English traditions. The result has been the beginning of a Scottish literary revival. The latest and most promising literary products of Scotland cannot be regarded as contributions to English literature at all; they are as far removed from it — and from the practice of the majority of Scottish writers since the death of Burns — as are the old Gaelic literature on the one hand, or, on the other, the products of the fifteenth-century Makars in the Vernacular, while their relation to these is clearly established. Apart from form and content, there has been a revival and definite accentuation of linguistic difference — in the revived use and creative development of Scots and, to a lesser extent, of Gaelic, and even in the devisal of a strongly-differentiated Scottish use of English. Scottish literature today is therefore once more claiming separate recognition, as something not only not contributing to English literature, but in many respects opposed to English literature, and certainly with separate functions and a different destiny of its own. It claims recognition as a national movement, in unbroken descent from our racial beginnings — the inheritor of the traditions of Gaeldom on the one hand and the Old Makars on the other.

The term 'unbroken descent' can be used because, despite the overwhelming Anglicization of the past two and a quarter centuries, the separate streams of Gaelic and Vernacular literature have continued to flow, albeit in a subterranean fashion. They are now winning to the daylight again with every manifestation of undiminished potentiality and force.

The writers who have rendered this revival possible, by continuing these separate traditions despite the overwhelming tendencies which are only now being successfully challenged, are in the nature of things practically unknown outside Scotland itself; but the older group of Scottish writers — living in Scotland and dealing mainly with Scottish subjects — deserve mention here. The centralization of British literature in London has deprived them of due recognition. They occupy a very subordinate place in contemporary English literature; but they should be recognized as nationally representative of Scotland at a time when distinctive Scottish letters were handicapped by progressive Anglicization. Novelists and poets, such as John Buchan and Neil Munro; short story writers like R.B. Cunninghame Graham and the Misses Findlater, have honourably maintained the Scottish note in English literature in direct descent from Scott and Stevenson. The two Vernacular poets, Charles Murray and Mrs Violet Jacob — like their forerunners J. Logie Robertson ('Hugh Haliburton') and 'J.B. Selkirk' — may rather be regarded as the heralds of the new vernacular revival. A less popular but far more important poet is Dr Pittendrigh Macgillivray, the King's Sculptor for Scotland, who, as the Scottish Renaissance makes headway, will undoubtedly assume increased stature as one of the most significant figures in the continuance of distinctive Scottish standards, through Burns, from Dunbar. Mention should also be made of the poems of Sir Ronald Ross, Douglas Ainslie (the translator of Croce), General Sir Ian Hamilton, and Mrs Rachel Annand Taylor, and of the fiction of such writers as J.J. Bell, Frederick Niven, and the late J. M'Dougall Hay. There are other writers — poets, novelists, and critics — who have perhaps scarcely received their due because they have been regarded as English rather than discerned as Scots. Professor H.J.C. Grierson, for example, is likely to be esteemed in retrospect as having had bearings which can be much better appreciated in relation to Scottish literature than in relation to English.

The new tendencies which are now manifesting themselves have so far been most prominently displayed in poetry. Writers such as Edwin Muir, perhaps the finest critic Scotland has yet produced, Frederick Branford, John Ferguson, William Jeffrey, and George Reston Malloch have produced in English a body of poetry which is yet on analysis distinctively Scottish and on a higher level than all but a very small proportion of the poetry Scottish writers have contributed to poetry in English. The Vernacular Revival is represented by a very virile group who are re-establishing a full canon of 'literary Scots', and applying to it the whole range of modern technique, while linguistic experiments towards a synthesis of dialects (resembling the Norwegian Landsmaal) and toward usages akin to the 'skaz' and 'zaumny' of contemporary Russian writers, have been initiated and have also produced a crop of very distinctive and dynamically racial work. The principal poets in this group are Lewis Spence, Lewis Coutts, Marion Angus, Helen Cruickshank, Alexander Gray (who has translated the Songs and Ballads of Heine into Scots with fine effect), William Ogilvie, Margaret W. Simpson, and 'Hugh M'Diarmid'.

A new school of critics has come into being as an accompaniment to these developments. They display a new consciousness of Scotland as a separate cultural entity, and manifest a full sense of relationship with our pre-Union writers and with the Gaelic background. They seek new affiliations with European literature too, along lines consonant with the differences, rather than, as hitherto, with the resemblances of Scottish psychology and English. Their propaganda is developing a marked political aspect, and most of the prominent young Scottish writers are active protagonists of Scottish Home Rule. These publicists and critics include William Power, Lewis Spence, the Hon Ruaraidh Erskine of Marr, William Gillies, Donald Carswell, G.M. Thompson, R.T. Clark, and C.M. Grieve, and a recent welcome addition to their number has been Compton Mackenzie the novelist.

There is also a new school of Scottish historians and researchers who are rapidly setting aside a considerable portion of Scottish History as little more than English propaganda. Outstanding amongst these are Alan Orr Anderson, Professor J.T. Baxter, Dr Geo. P. Insh, M.V. Hay, and Evan Barron.

The literary revival of the Scots Vernacular has been accompanied by a big popular movement inaugurated by the Vernacular Circle of the London Burns Club, and since taken up and extended by the World Federation of Burns Clubs. Vernacular Circles have been established in Edinburgh and Glasgow. More 'fundamental' than these is the Scots Language Section of the Scottish National Movement, the Secretary of which is Miss H.H. Guthrie. The Scottish Education Department have intimated their approval of the teaching of a certain amount of Scots Language and Literature in the schools, and in other directions there has been a slight re-Scoticization of our educational system, while the British Broadcasting Corporation have manifested a willingness to help in the redevelopment of 'literary Scots' rather than mere dialect by favouring the broadcasting of suitable work on the higher level.

Just as the Scottish Nationalist Movement has developed a strong Vernacular Section, so another of the political-nationalist organizations — the Scots National League — manifests a keen interest in the maintenance and revival of the Gaelic Language and Culture, while a society — An Comunn Litreachais — has been formed to secure the publication of literary work of high quality in Gaelic which cannot secure publication through ordinary commercial channels — centralized as most of the media of publishing and journalism are in London. The biggest body in this connection is An Comunn Gaidhealach, which has also recently shown progressive tendencies in a fashion not dissimilar to those manifested by the Burns Federation with regard to Scots. Donald Sinclair is perhaps our most important Gaelic poet and dramatist.

The latest development of this many-sided and widespread national movement is an effort at synthesis and the establishment of a common front amongst the various political and cultural organizations, so that these may be brought into a definite and progressive relation to each other and effectively related to the Gaelic background into which, it is felt, a return must be made before a foundation can be secured for the creation of major forms either in arts or affairs.

This movement is also manifesting itself in efforts to establish a Scottish National Drama and a Scottish school of composers. In Drama the older and less aggressively national tendencies are represented in the work of the Scottish National Players and the plays of such writers as John Brandane, J.A. Ferguson, Naomi Jacob, and Joe Corrie; and the newer and more 'integral' tendency in the propaganda of R.F. Pollock and his 'Little Theatre' productions of plays by Alexander M'Gill, George Reston Malloch, Lady Margaret Sackville and others.

In music the older tradition is represented by the Hebridean songs of Mrs Kennedy Fraser, and the newer tendency in the song-settings of Dunbar, M'Diarmid, and other poets by Francis George Scott, by far the greatest composer Scotland has yet produced.

The development of aggressive nationalist tendencies has been reflected in fiction in a new attention to Scottish actualities, and a young Glasgow school of novelists has come into being, the principal figures in which are George Blake, John Carruthers, and John Cockburn, while Neil M. Gunn deals in a similarly realistic fashion with the Highlands, and James Bryce with the Central Scottish countryside. Excellent historical novels have been written by Winifred Duke, Violet Jacob, Edward Albert, and J.M. Reid, and the Scottish short story has become more vital and tendencious in the work of 'Dot Allan', Joe Corrie, Edward Scouller, and 'Hugh M'Diarmid'.

Little is heard in the English literary press of most of these writers, and the tendencies they embody; but foreigners who wish to know what Scotland is thinking and doing today, and what kind of future it is preparing for itself, can confidently be recommended to the writers who have been named, who represent, in their varying degrees, as interesting and promising a national rebirth as is to be found anywhere in Europe today.

The Scottish National Association of April Fools

Those of us who have been opposing the project to transfigure the Glasgow Athenæum into a so-called Scottish National Academy of Music are highly amused, and not surprised, to find that the First of April has been selected as the date upon which the change of name is to take effect. What could be more appropriate? It is the very date we would have selected if we had been approached in the matter. It has not been chosen by chance. Truth *will* out. An engaging picture of the promoters at work presents itself. Immersed in the details of their great undertaking, they were naturally oblivious to the implications of a mere date. But occultists, alive to the baffling properties of number, will, even in the absence of Cratylus, have some appreciation of what has actually happened — though only musicians will savour the true inwardness of it!

This latest evidence of the bias towards absurdity inherent in their plans should give the promoters pause. The enterprise is discovering a disconcerting, and cumulative, capacity for self-criticism of this singular kind at every stage of its development. Its sponsors are in the position of worthy but utterly humourless parents whose darling child is discerned by everyone else as a veritable *enfant terrible*. One trembles in anticipatory laughter at what may happen next. But, after all, Sir Daniel Stevenson has himself to blame if, in an allegedly musical matter, he brushes aside competent technical criticism as 'highbrow' stuff, and appeals (as he did, and as this Academy certainly only can) 'to more prosaic minds'.

Look at what has happened already. There was first of all the delightful *non sequitur* responsible for the proposal. It was evolved as follows: 'Scotland's position in regard to music is hopelessly inferior to that of any other country in Europe. *Therefore* let us establish a Scottish National Academy of Music.'

That 'therefore' is the crux of the whole thing. It is like saying: 'The creature has no intelligence. Let us make him Minister of Education.'

A normal intelligence would have said:

> What — no national music? This won't do. Let us find out why — and do all that money and concentrated effort can to make good this appalling deficiency. First things first. An Academy will doubtless follow in due course when we have something to academize upon. In the meantime, it will cost infinitely less, and be a great deal more to the point, to subsidize two or three composers to apply themselves systematically to the problem of creating a Scottish national music idiom. Once they initiate the process, however faultily, others of a more fundamental cast will follow, and we may ultimately discover the goods.

But no! The promoters of the scheme are not concerned with the realities of the Scottish musical position. It is difficult (for any intelligent person) to know what they *are* concerned about. They are exceedingly reticent on the subject. Apparently all that is in their minds is to continue what has been happening (namely, nothing) on a greater scale than ever and under a more grandiloquent title, with — this seems the main point — themselves posing as the Leaders of Music in Scotland. Their attitude is simply an inversion of the old proverb, 'Give a dog a bad name'. Call it, they say, a Scottish Musical Movement — and it will be so. All that they have condescended to make clear is that they want the public to pay — without knowing what for, except the name. They are equally determined to call it a Scottish National Academy, and to keep it a private affair. The next thing is to register Scotland itself as a limited — very limited — company, with Roslyn Mitchell, Hugh Robertson, F.H. Bissett, and Joseph Laing Waugh as directors, with a subsidiary company (under the same directorate) for each of the arts.

Scotland, however, definitely refused to buy this 'pig in a poke', and the refusal has had some astonishing sequelæ. An embassy was sent to the United States, for example, another country with no music of its own worth talking about. The ambassadress bore the fine old Scottish name of Jacobsen. She is no doubt a very estimable lady; she may even be a Scotswoman. I am merely recording the fact. From my point of view, it would not have made the slightest difference if her name had been Annie Laurie. But it isn't. And I venture to think that if there had been a National Guessing Competition (which, incidentally, might have solved the financial problem — the whole thing has been deplorably mismanaged from a publicity point of view) as to the name of any lady likely to be chosen to canvass America on behalf of a Scottish national project, exceedingly few of the competitors would have suggested 'Jacobsen'. We live in complex days, however, and this is just another illustration of the incredible hazards which have attended this apparently simple project all the way through.

It reads like a romance. Miss Jacobsen went to America and pleaded her cause so successfully that she actually gained the benediction of the gentleman whom the profane H.L. Mencken terms 'the incomparable Cal'. In other words, President Coolidge received the lady and blessed her mission. It moves me unspeakably to think of all the myriad momentous matters with which the Chief Executive of 'God's Own Country' is incessantly engaged being temporarily dismissed from his mind while he gave his undivided attention to the naive Caledonian appeal. That's your Olympians for you! Only the truly great can condescend to the infinitely little in this way.

So far, so good! But the cash value of Cal's benediction proved disconcertingly small. Negligble, in fact! I understood — on the very worst of authority — that the aid of Mussolini was next to have been invoked. If this had proved correct it would have shown that the promoters had at last adopted one of my suggestions. For this (subject to a trifling difference in spelling) was what I had urged all along. To the Duce with it!

But that has been rendered unnecessary. Some other Good Samaritan has come to the rescue. It was announced at a meeting of the Carnegie Trustees the other day that the necessary sum had been secured. The Earl of Elgin, who presided, mentioned at the same time that the Trustees' Publication of Music Scheme had now been done away with. Conditions had changed since it was inaugurated — and there was now no difficulty for composers with the ability to compose anything of consequence to secure publishers. Ye gods and little fishes! The fact of the matter is that in music as in literature ease in obtaining publication is in inverse ratio to the excellence of the work. All sort of worthless stuff finds the readiest of markets, but it is easier for a camel to go through the eye of a needle than for any musical score of consequence to secure a publisher. The very people who are associated with this Scottish National Academy of Music know that — and are taking every possible precaution to prevent it becoming less difficult. That is one of the reasons why I dislike them: but there are others.

The major reason for my dislike is simply that — *ex nihil, nihil fit*. The personalities and records of these people are a sufficient condemnation of any movement with which they are connected. All they want in connection with anything Scottish is the name. All they want in regard to any of the arts is 'the more prosaic people' who will take them at their own valuation. They have not an idea worth a boodle amongst them, and are organizing themselves as strongly as they possibly can between the Scottish public — and anyone who has. Their pseudo-nationalism represents the greatest possible menace to the new spirit of Scottish nationalism, just as their artfulness represents the greatest possible menace to any new spirit in the Scottish arts.

Happily, it is at last becoming widely recognized among the intelligent minority in Scotland — the class from which any Scottish cultural or political development must come — that the inter-relation of the so-called Scottish Musical Festival Movement, Country Dance Society, National Theatre Society, Verse-Speaking Movement, and proposed Academy of Music, represents a positive conspiracy to subvert Scottish arts and affairs in the interests of a group of mediocrities behind whom monopolistic trade interests appear to be at work. The personnel of these various organizations is practically identical. The use of the term 'Scottish', in connection with their activities, is seen in its true light if their programmes and the lack of any progression towards the creation of new Scottish art-products of the slightest consequence are studied. The promoters of these movements want no such development; there is nothing they dread more. They will go to any length in boycotting anything that threatens to introduce a new creative principle. They only want to exploit the creators in other countries and keep Scotland itself safe for artistic parasites. The calibre of these societies is best appreciated when the fact is noted that they are wholly run by persons utterly destitute of accomplishment themselves. Not one of those concerned has the slightest standing in relation to any of the arts involved. Their presumption, however, is unbounded. It is not generally known, perhaps, that the close co-operation of adjudicators who have established themselves by means of these movements can command as much as £25 per day in fees. Yet these are the gentry who go about denouncing the 'pot-hunting' spirit, and demanding competition for art's sake alone and free of any mercenary taint. The hypocrisy of the whole thing is astounding, and it is no wonder that trained musicians of high ability — such as Mr A.M. Henderson and Mr Herbert Fellowes — are at last coming into the open in their denunciations of it. It is bad enough that men with no professional training or standing whatever should take it upon themselves to act as adjudicators — and, mark you, not in one department only. All's grist that comes to their mill; they are authorities alike on music, dancing, elocution, and theatricals! It is still worse when the programmes disproportionately reflect the music published by a certain firm to the exclusion of better music; when such good work as is being done towards the creation of a Scottish art-music is being rigidly excluded; and when silly little 'arrangements' by some of the *dilletanti* prominently associated with these movements are, on the contrary, being boosted 'all over the shop'.

The criticism that has been directed against these movements, by myself and others, on Scottish nationalist grounds, is being met in a characteristic way. Some time ago I had an urgent message from a friend that Mr Rosslyn Mitchell, MP, would take it as a very great favour if I would let him have a brief note of my objections to the proposed Scottish National Academy of Music. I did so; I also sent him a pamphlet I had published on the subject, and referred him to other relevant writings. That was several weeks ago. He has not yet had the courtesy to send even a bare acknowledgement. But he has not been idle in the interval — nor, it would seem, uninfluenced by my contentions (one of which was that if there was to be a Scottish Academy of Music, it should be under a Scotsman — not an alien). Dr Arthur Somerville (an Englishman) is retiring shortly from the post of Inspector of Music to the Scottish Board of Education, and a deputation consisting of Messrs Hugh Robertson, Rosslyn Mitchell, and F.H. Bissett have, I understand, interviewed the department and successfully represented that Dr Somerville ought to be succeeded by a Scotsman. Unfortunately, quality has been left out of consideration — and it is stated that the appointment is likely to be given to Mr Herbert Wiseman. Why didn't they make it Sir Harry Lauder or Mr Will Fyfe when they were at it? Or Mr Robertson himself? That is the worst of being a highbrow; one is so apt to be misunderstood by groping intelligences. No doubt they were really endeavouring to give effect to my wishes; but my point was that *competent* Scotsmen, where available, should be preferred for such posts, and definitely nationalistic Scots at that, i.e. Scots who would not pursue alien and irrelevant artistic traditions instead of devoting themselves to those national creative developments which Scotland pre-eminently requires — and to which any Scotsman with a brain worth talking about will naturally address himself today, since there lies not only his duty as a Scotsman, but his greatest opportunity as an artist. But the last thing in the world I should have been taken as implying is that any Scotsman is preferable to any foreigner. The very reverse holds true so far as most of the gentlemen I have named are concerned.

I expressed fears in the pamphlet in question lest the Principalship of the proposed Scottish National Academy of Music — and, with it, the new Chair of Music in Glasgow University — should go to Dr Walford Davies (although who gets either of them is relatively a secondary matter, and only comes within my purview as a kind of 'making the best of a bad job!'). That would have been bad enough; but the pseudo-nationalism of the junta of nonentities who are now dominating these movements may do even worse than that by appointing such a Scotsman as, for example, Mr F.H. Bissett.

That will be the last straw; but happily there are already signs that that will suffice to precipitate the long-overdue reaction against all these associated futilities on the part of professional musicians and others who appreciate what is happening. Decent standards may be re-erected, and, of course, if any real genius wins through, the gaff will be blown on the whole caboodle.

In the meantime they are having things all their own way. Even Dr George Dyson, the Cramb lecturer on music at Glasgow University, has been inveighing against the intolerable intellectualism of ultra-modern music and advising his hearers to have no hesitation 'in refusing to listen to it, but simply to get up and walk out of the hall'. Where would the art of music have been if this course had been generally followed? Most great composers were little esteemed in their own day except by small coteries, and it is upon small coteries — and not great mobs — that the progress of all the arts depends. But there is no such coterie in Glasgow. To advise Glasgow people to entertain nothing but contempt for composers they had never heard was carrying coals to Newcastle with a vengeance. Why — the place hasn't even a contemporary Music Circle!

But it's going to have a Scottish National Academy of Music whose emblem should be a Gowk rampant!

Scotland in 1980

Wad that I held Staoiligary
  And the four pennies o' Drimisdale,
And had never seen a news-sheet,
  No' even *The Daily Mail*.
The fifteen generations afore me
  Could lippen me no' to fail
Into the darkness o' alien time,
  To carry my sang and sgeul
As the duck when she hears the thunder
  Dances to her ain Port a' Beul!

So a Scots poet sang in 1929; and already in these lines we see a complete reversal of the tendency and temper that had dominated Scotland for several centuries — still albeit with a doubt of success. The scornful reference to journalism — 'back-stairs gossip writ large', as a publicist of the period described it — is extraordinarily accentuated by the inverted reference to *The Daily Mail*. A year or two earlier the line would have been written 'let alane' instead of 'no' even'. A profound difference! Scottish verse was beginning to get its head well above 'the kailyaird tradition', as it was called. This new finesse was partly due to the consciousness of the pioneers of the Scottish Renaissance Movement of their need to return to the background of Gaelic culture before they could secure a basis for the creation of major poetry. It is, indeed, this re-fertilization by Gaelic influences which gives quality to the lines. Staoiligary and the four pennies of Drimisdale were probably unintelligible references to the great majority of even so-called cultivated Scots at that time. Since then they — and a whole beautiful geography which had become grossly overlaid with mere feudal and subsequent place-names, destitute of spiritual significance and associative interest — have been brought back into the vital consciousness of the whole nation.

Goal of the Renaissance

Writing in Scots (with a greater and greater infusion of Gaelic and the substitution in imagery and general background and atmosphere of terms and figures drawn from Celtic culture and consonant with Gaelic psychology and modes of living for the chaotic medley of Judaic, Greek, Roman, Anglo-Saxon, and cosmopolitan influences which characterized English and Anglo-Scottish literature and finally so de-classicized, confused and muddled them) has, of course, become quite a minor element in the literary output of Scotland — 80 per cent of all the creative literature of any value published in Scotland last year was in the new standard Gaelic, approved by the Scottish Academy of Letters in 1969 — but, nevertheless, in its refined form it has distinctive qualities, values and functions of its own, and Scots literature would be the poorer if this subsidiary element were to disappear altogether, just as the beauty of the sickle moon is enhanced by a star at its nether horn.

It should never be forgotten, however, that it was creative writers in Scots who really forwarded the Renaissance at a time when one of the great spirits of Gaeldom, the Hon R. Erskine of Marr, writing of the Movement, said:

> There is a Renaissance — a turning round of the eye of the nation's soul towards original cultural values in general, to employ a platonic figure — going on in Scotland; and there are high hopes, and some good grounds to believe that, in course of time, the movement I speak of may yet embrace the Gaelic poets, jolting them out of their present semi-moribund state into some more lively, if not more tradition, consciousness of art than they have so far shown, into some due understanding of the magnitude of their errors and wanderings from the professional paths chalked out to them by the great poets of Gaelic times. So far, however, there are few signs that the Highland poets of the day have been much impressed by the intellectual phenomena about them, or that, in obedience to the demands of the Renaissance, they are prepared to mend their poetic ways. They continue to turn out poetry on the old familiar lines, some of it meritorious enough, no doubt, a part tolerable, and the rest — wholly negligible; but, on the whole, no matter what the merits of particular parts may be, condemned beforehand by reason of a certain uniformity of rustic mode and theme and form in which this modern 'bardachd' is invariably cast. To throw Gaelic poetry out of this lowly rut, to

draw it back to its first cultural principles — this is one of several necessary things that the Renaissance must do, if it is to justify the high hopes that its prophets and leaders entertain of it.

The Gaelic Revival

It is indeed amazing to reflect that these sentences were penned only a little over half-a-century ago. One feels as a reader might have felt about that time on discovering that Russian literature, then so tremendous a phenomenon in *welt-literatur*, was only about a century old; a mere child in comparison with many European literatures, but one which had suddenly sprung to titanic maturity. Modern Scottish Gaelic literature in the past quarter of a century has developed to a like degree. How astounded Dr Nigel MacNeill would be if he could be made aware of it! But more of him in a moment!

The lines quoted at the beginning show a deliberate effort to resume the ancient historical continuity — a new creative pride in the old traditions — a growing hatred of the dingy promiscuity of industrial civilization, with a sense of its mortal dangers and a keen desire to break away from it — and, in general, the beginning of that new, aristocratic, 'integral' spirit which so speedily revolutionized the national psychology and inaugurated the new era of Scottish Independence. So far as the application of the new spirit in practical political directions and its diffusion in every department of national activity was concerned, that began with the saltatory development in Glasgow University in 1928. The conditions under which this surprising *kulturkampf* began are well depicted in the following poem of the time:

A Visit to the Four Universities in Scotland

Oor four Universities
  Are Scots but in name;
They wadna be here
  If ither folk did the same
— Paid heed tae a' lear
  Exceptin' their ain,
For they'd cancel oot syne
  And leave us wi' nane.

I summoned the students
   And spiered them to tell
Where Trenmor triumphed
   Or Oscar fell.
'Dammit,' I cried,
   'But here is a mystery —
That nane o' ye ken
   The first word in history!'

I tested them neist
   In geography and there
Their ignorance was such
   As gar'd me despair.
Innis Fada and Rosnat
   Made them look green as
I'd spoken o' places
   On the faur side o' Venus!

But, och, when I cam'
   To Arts and Letters,
The gomerils gapit
   And shamed their begetters!
— Even Muireadach Albannach,
   Lachlan Mor of his stem,
And Finlay Macnab
   Meant naething to them!

The professors were waur
   Than the students were even,
And yattered in Sanscrit
   Or Czech — wi' a leaven
O' some kind o' English,
   A leid o' their ain;
God grant I may never
   Hear the like o't again!

'I'm beggin' your pardon,
   A mistake has been made.
It was *Scots* Universities
   I was seekin',' I said.
'To condemn your ignorance
   'Ud indeed be to wrang you
When in Hell here there isna
   A Scotsman amang you!'

These verses show how furiously the new National consciousness was beginning to rise. But already An Comunn Gaidhealach had embarked on a progressive policy; the schools in the Highland areas were being rapidly re-Gaelicized; and Clann an Fhraoich — vowed to speak and write Gaelic on every possible occasion — had been brought into being — largely through the instrumentality of Captain Moffat Pender, who, however, stood at the General Election in 1929, not on behalf of the National Party of Scotland, but, curiously enough, as a candidate of the Conservative Party, one of the English-controlled organizations; a fact which illustrates the extraordinary confusion which still prevailed, but was so soon to disappear.

The trend of the time was seen in the scornful protests which greeted the appearance of a new edition of Dr Nigel MacNeill's *The Literature of the Highlanders* in May, 1929. It was edited by Sheriff J. Macmaster Campbell, who, unfortunately, in no way attempted to bring it up to date, although a great deal had happened in Gaelic scholarship since its original publication in 1892. He did not seem at all aware of its appalling defects — not only in scope and detail, but in method and spirit. He ought to have compared it with Dr Douglas Hyde's *Literary History of Ireland*, or that wonderful study of the Munster poets, Daniel Corkery's *Hidden Ireland*, and he would have seen that it was a national ignominy to republish so lopsided and defective a volume, destitute of literary acumen and spiritual understanding, and lick-spittle to the Sasunnach prejudice prevalent forty years before, but at that time quickly disappearing. True, Sheriff Macmaster admitted that 'the author's Church history, and his allusions to matters ecclesiastic are occasionally tinged with the "odium theologicum"' (but this was putting it very mildly!), and Dr MacNeill himself acknowledged that Scottish Gaelic literature had been very inadequately explored. The book amply necessitated both apologies; it was little more than a 'catalogue raisonnée' of petty clerical bards and minor versifiers, rank with sectarian bias, and in general tone and substance similar to Baptie's *Musical Scotland* with its list of negligible scrape-guts and village organists (and not a sizeable composer amongst them) or the interminable series of Edward's *Minor Scottish Poets*, all of whom are now happily forgotten as if they had never been. *Hidden Scotland* remained hidden; its rediscovery has been the triumph of the last half-century.

But the reissue of this precious volume evoked sharp protests, mainly on account of the author's scurvy, Anglophil treatment of William Livingston, which left no doubt as to the way in which the wind was blowing in younger Scotland. Livingston was, of course, the greatest Gaelic poet of the nineteenth century, although the best of his work was 'difficult' and caviare to the general. He had suffered unmerited neglect and contumely in his life-time and since; but the tide had at last turned in his favour. He has now come fully 'into his kingdom'. Dr MacNeill wrote of him in such amazing and shameful terms as these:

> The duties which he assigned to himself were the lashing, in Wallace and Bruce fashion, of the Teutonic invader from the south of the Tweed and the special vindication of the Celtic character from the continual aspersions of the uncircumscribed Saxon. He did his work with a will, but there was no need for it. It was as uncalled for as Thomson's work on 'Liberty', which, undertaken in an unwise moment, the public, not without reason, condemned to 'gather spiders and to harbour dust'. When highly needed work goes without its reward it cannot be a matter of surprise that unnecessary ebullitions of patriotism do not always pay; so poor Livingston, like not a few of the order of Bards, died somewhat neglected in an obscure street of the philanthropic city of Glasgow.

These sentiments may have been generally endorsed in the 'nineties of last century; but happily they met with a very different reception in 1929; and today they read as curiously as the old Anglo-Scottish idea that the Gaels were a cultureless pack of blue-painted slavering savages.

The controversy that arose over this book — and the growing realization of the chaotic conditions of Scottish studies in general — led to an intensified demand for the re-Scoticization of Scottish education. Already some headway had been made with this in the schools and colleges. Further concessions were demanded — and, perforce, conceded — all along the line. These were supplemented by the development of a Scots Colleges Movement, somewhat on the lines of the Workers' Educational Association but devoted to Scottish subjects — Gaelic, Scots, Scottish history, literature, music, etc — instead of, like the W.E.A., Economics and Sociology. It was an instant success, meeting a felt want, for, apart from 'politics' altogether, the new Movement in Scottish arts and letters had brought home to the great bulk of Scottish people the ignominy of their ignorance of national subjects of all kinds, thanks to the progressive Anglicization of their education and journalistic and literary environment. They hastened to take advantage of it. All the ablest of the younger Scottish school of writers, artists, musicians, and historians were on the Headquarters' panel of lecturers. Study circles were formed in every town and village in Scotland. Auxiliaries were developed in all the Scottish colonies abroad. A change of psychology soon manifested itself as a result of this change of cultural interests and influences, which inevitably soon set up corresponding phenomena in the spheres of politics, commerce, and industry.

Clann Albann's Victory

In a way this was part and parcel of a wider movement, shifting the emphasis of interest in the civilized world from economics and sociology, which had too long monopolized attention, to spiritual values. The younger people who had never been subjected to the demoralizing influence of the old Anglo-Scottish party political system, speedily repudiated the methods and ideology of organized — and English-controlled — democracy then in vogue; and, no longer confining themselves to English precedents, availed themselves readily of the examples of Italy and Ireland, and, powerfully re-enforcing the transitional organization of the Scottish Nationalist Party (up till then still deplorably liberal and Anglophile) with their militaristic neo-Fascist auxiliary, 'Clann Albann', carried the Movement to the successful conclusion we know of by 1965, and re-established the ancient Gaelic Commonwealth in Scotland on a modern basis.

In the early days of the National Party superficial critics, who forgot that the destinies of peoples always lie with a handful of determined souls, jeered at its predominantly literary leadership; but they failed to realize that, while party-political hacks merely scratch the surface of things, literary men work directly on the national psychology and penetrate to the springs of action. R.B. Cunninghame-Graham, Compton Mackenzie, Lewis Spence, and their coadjutors knew what they were about. Their names are secure in Scottish history. But who today could name half-a-dozen of the Scottish MEPs during the whole long period of the Parliamentary subordination of Scotland? — who today could name even three of the so-called 'Secretaries of State'? — servile English agents who did their utmost to prevent that great belated movement of the Scottish spirit which threw off the Sasunnach yoke and restored Scotland to its rightful place in the comity of nations.

Aesthetics in Scotland

In a recent article Mr John Tonge said:

> That factory of the arts, the modern art school, could help by teaching the young artist not only his craft, but by clarifying the role of the twentieth-century Scottish artist in Scotland and in society. The national tradition is some kind of a handrail in this 'museum without walls'.

The reference in the last sentence is to M. André Malraux's book, *Psychologie de l'Art*, published by Roto-Sadag in Geneva last year. Further reference will be made to it later. But the increasing sense and use of our national tradition in the way suggested by Mr Tonge has been an outstanding feature of the past ten or twelve years and has borne good fruit.

Mr Tonge himself was a pioneer in this connection with his admirable little book, *The Arts of Scotland*, published in 1938 at the time of the Burlington House Exhibition of Scottish Art. It will be remembered that Sir William Llewellyn, the then President of the Royal Academy, confessed that he had had no idea before he saw that Exhibition that Scotland had such a rich and distinctive tradition of its own in the art of painting, and a tradition so dissimilar to the English tradition. The Exhibition was, he declared, an eye-opener. Most of the art critics in our leading British newspapers and cultural periodicals wrote in the same strain. It did not occur to any of them, however, to examine more deeply this extraordinary situation in which of two countries linked together under a common Crown and Parliament for two and a half centuries one of them remained utterly ignorant of, and indifferent to, so important a part of the other's life as its paintings, nor did it stimulate them to enquire whether or not the English, while seeing to it that their language, history, literature and other arts, had a virtual monopoly in our Scottish schools and colleges (without any reciprocal attention to their Scottish counterparts in the English educational system) were equally ignorant of Scottish literature, Scottish music, and, for the matter of that, the whole range of Scottish national affairs. It will be clear that the exclamations of astonished — and, in some quarters, incredulous —

discovery evoked in England and elsewhere by the Burlington House Exhibition disclosed a very serious state of affairs and threw a thoroughly disconcerting light on the general assumption that the Scots-English relationship was a satisfactory one. It is obviously inevitable that a Union under which the arts of one country are almost entirely unknown to the other, while the arts of the latter, entirely different in character and tendency to its own, are given an overinfluence in the former through the educational system and through the press, platform, and other media of publicity, to the virtual exclusion of any attention whatever to its native products must be equally unsatisfactory in political, commercial, social and all other connections. These implications — which are responsible for the increasing nationalist ferment in Scotland during the past quarter of a century — have proved highly unpalatable to most of the English writers and speakers who have got so far as to realize them at all. Most of them have reacted by a 'conspiracy of silence'. Others have gone out of their way to belittle Scottish culture in one way or another. The bad feeling that exists in many quarters cannot always be hidden or camouflaged, however. It manifests itself occasionally as in the review of Mr Stanley Cursiter's book, *Scottish Art*, in *The Listener* of 7th April 1949, which said:

> Scotland is a long way off, even by train; but distance is not the factor which produces a national school of painting, and demonstrations of such a school in the smaller dependent countries [note that phrase!] are tatty, and, to the outsider, unconvincing to the edge of pathos. Out comes the brush. A great many names and a great many inferior pictures are dusted out of the corners and tidied together with a few good pictures into a school which no one else in the world acknowledges. It is a compulsion, and Mr Cursiter, having directed the National Gallery at Edinburgh, could not escape. Yet how much stronger our impression of Scottish painting, or painting by Scotsmen, would be if Mr Cursiter could blow off all the dust! We ourselves have to blow it off. We have to clean off Allan Ramsay, and Geddes and Raeburn and Wilkie, as well as a few altogether unfamiliar artists, who need pushing into our more sceptical sight. Mr Cursiter quotes Northcote on a likeness of Queen Charlotte which Ramsay painted 'a profile, and slightly done, but it was a paragon of excellence. She had a fan in her hand; Lord how she held that fan!' Excellent; but the scope of Ramsay's power is not always acknowledged. It hardly *excites* Mr Cursiter. Yet Allan Ramsay may seem to an

> Englishman, remembering the portrait of his wife and some others which Mr Cursiter reproduces, more deliciously appetizing than any painter who ever came down from the north. But is he Scottish, or is he European? Or even English? Mr Cursiter might have told us more, for example, of Ramsay's assistant David Martin, and more of Thomas Graham (1840-1906), in deference to two of the pictures reproduced; he might have told us less of the many Victorian academicians and the late Victorian namby-pambyists of one type and another. But he is kindly. He is mild rather than critical or selective and he has to keep the Scottish flag well aloft. To those who might be Englishmen or Frenchmen or Americans matters up north seem to go like this: 'There were painters called Impressionists in France, whom the world thinks of very highly. You know in Scotland we had a painter called McTaggart who painted a little impressionistically. *We* had our Impressionist. What a great painter our Impressionist was!'...Whereas he was not. He painted pictures (out with the red jacket before the Lowland bull) which are frail, flat, and provincial. There it is...there indeed is the trouble of the dust-panning of a pseudo-national school: it must capture the eyes of the Scottish young and the Scottish innocent. Provinciality must be posed as the real thing in the guise of patriotism. It would be better patriotism to act less patriotically.

The Listener is one of the official organs of a public Corporation. The vicious anti-Scottish attitude of that anonymous spokesman of the English *herren-volk* must therefore be taken as a reflection of Government policy, and as an accurate index of the general attitude of the English *cognoscenti* to Scottish cultural issues. Nor is it an isolated phenomenon. *The Listener* is closed to Scottish talks — only the talks from the English programmes are reproduced in it. That is characteristic. It is not a matter only of today, however. Fears are expressed in many quarters lest the Scottish discontent with Londonization should lead to anti-English feeling in Scotland. Right down our history, however, anti-Scottish feeling has been strong in England. Scotland has produced no anti-English writers to compare with the whole sequence of anti-Scottish writers from Charles Churchill and Dr Johnson to our own day who have been so marked an element in English literary history.

That this deplorable state of affairs does not apply to painting only, but to the whole range of Scottish arts and affairs, is clear from any consideration of the history of the independent Scottish literary tradition. I can only give one illustration here. In his splendid study of the fifteenth-century Scottish poet, Robert Henryson, Professor Marshall W. Stearns of Cornell University says:

> The reputation of Robert Henryson is still in the process of being established. Even his own countrymen found little merit in him until comparatively recently. The first adequate estimate of the poet was made by William Ernest Henley in 1880.... Recognition of Henryson in the United States was even more delayed. In 1888 James Russell Lowell condemned fifteenth-century Scottish poetry in general and the Middle Scots dialect in particular, while four years later Professor T.R. Lounsbury observed [in the very tone of *The Listener* review I have just quoted] that Henryson 'is one of those early writers whom Scottish patriotism struggles energetically to consider a poet'.

The tide began to turn in England after that, however. W.W. Skeat in 1897 singled out Henryson's *Testament of Cresseid* as the best Chaucerian poem, and in the following year Professor George Saintsbury said of Henryson's poems:

> The total bulk is not large, but the merit is, for the fifteenth century more particularly, very high, and the variety of directions in which it is shown is extremely remarkable,

and he ranked the *Testament of Cresseid* with, if not above, the best work of the century. If space permitted, I could show that in many other directions Scottish work is still grossly underprized or completely neglected, and the extremely belated rehabilitation of Henryson in his proper place as a great poet after the lapse of several centuries is only a pointer to the sort of revaluation or rescue work which must yet be effected in many fields of Scottish Arts and Letters.

Far more serious, however, is the indisputable fact that the Scottish people themselves were — and the vast majority of them still are — as ignorant as the English with regard to the Scottish tradition in literature and the arts, and, indeed, with regard to Scottish interests in the whole range of affairs. It is that ignorance and indifference that has at long last begun to be rectified in some measure. But only the fringe of it has been touched so far. Far too many Scots are still utterly insensitive to the arts — a higher proportion, I think, than can be found in any other Western European country. One of Scotland's greatest men, David Hume, the philosopher, blandly admitted that he was constitutionally incapable of taking any interest in any of the arts. The Scottish novelist, Tobias Smollett, was equally uninterested.

I am afraid that what Mr William Power says in his book, *Literature And Oatmeal*, is still only too true of a very large section of our people.

'In a compartment of the Flying Scotsman, roaring north along the central rock-ridge of the Merse,' says Mr Power,

> I began to dilate to a companion on the part that the canyon of Pease Dean, near Cockburnspath, had played in Scots history. I spoke of Cromwell and the Battle of Dunbar, Scott, and *The Bride of Lammermoor*. A man in a landward corner of the compartment broke in: 'Ugh! That's history. An' literature, I suppose'. He was burly and fiftyish, with a bristly moustache. He wore a good suit of rough brown tweed, and there was a horseshoe pin in his ugly tie. His boots had cost a good deal more than sixty shillings. I guessed him to be a prosperous contractor and general merchant in a country town, grazing beasts on a couple of 'led' farms.
>
> 'Don't the history and literature of your own country mean anything to you?' I asked.
>
> 'Not a bit. Just nonsense. The stuff we used to get in school. Ugh!...' His contempt was beyond articulate expression. In the attitude of this man, I reflected, there was more than mere indifference. There was a positive element. History and literature, particularly those of Scotland, were somehow inimical to his way of life. He had a bad conscience concerning them. The outlook in such matters that usually confronts one in Scotland is curiously different. It is one of amiable nescience. Anyone who begins to talk of history or literature in a chance company is listened to with polite inattention, as if he were a foreigner who was inadvertently speaking his own language. But nobody is ever rude about it.

To blame all this on Calvinism in Scotland is stupid. It not only ignores the facts which are admirably set out in Dr Mary Ramsay's *Calvin And Art*. It ignores also the fact that it is quite unjust to attribute to Calvinism a crude Philistinism which was, in fact, bred by the Industrial Revolution and aggravated by the loss of our own national roots. It ignores also the fact that on the admission of the Church of Scotland a third of our entire population today have no church connection of any kind, while another large section are Roman Catholics and have no more aesthetic interest or sensitivity than either the heirs of the Calvinists or the neo-Pagans. Then, again, what are we to make of the fact that Calvinism in other countries — Holland, for example — did not prevent great schools of painting? While efforts have been made in the last quarter of a century to correct this deplorable anti-aestheticism of the Scottish people, these efforts have so far been of a very sporadic and superficial kind, and have not yet succeeded in ramming home even to the most alert of our countrymen the great fact stated by the German poet, Hölderlin, that 'Nothing is so difficult to learn as the mastery over our natural national gifts'.

Hölderlin put the matter very clearly — and what he says in the following passage must be applied to our own case and thoroughly learned and digested before there can be a real national awakening in regard to the arts in Scotland — when he wrote:

> It sounds paradoxical, but I repeat and leave it to you to test in theory and practice, natural qualities always become in the process of learning the lesser merit. On that account the Greeks are less masters of sacred passion because it was innate in them; on the other hand they are excellent at representing from Homer onwards, because this extraordinary man was large-minded enough to appropriate and make use of Western Junonian clear-headedness for his Apolline sphere, and thus truly to assimilate elements foreign to him. With the Germans the opposite was the case, and it was for that very reason necessary for them to study the Greeks, both their nature and their art, in order to gain knowledge of themselves and what should be the aim of their art. But we have to win knowledge of our own faculties just as much as of those of others. That is why the Greeks are indispensable to us. Only we shall not be able to cqual them in the qualities natural to us, because, as was said already, mastery over one's own nature is the most difficult of all.

One of the most characteristic American cartoons I have seen depicted a prosperous citizen being sucked down a manhole in Fifth Avenue by an octopus. A listless crowd stands round and watches his agonized face on the point of disappearing. A prosperous citizen in a top-hat remarks to his friend: 'Anything will collect a crowd in New York.'

Thanks to the activities of Dr Honeyman and the Saltire Society, the Arts Council, and other bodies, art is beginning to attract increasing crowds in Scotland today. Before going on to ask what art, and to what effect, I must make it clear that I do not think art in Scotland is in the grip of an octopus and being sucked down a drain. On the contrary I do not think the public response to art in Scotland was ever greater in quantity or better in quality than it is today or the prospects better not only for art in Scotland and a genuine appreciation of it among our people, but also — a far harder thing — for the consolidation and development of our distinctive Scottish tradition, and for constructive criticism (that is to say, criticism helpful to the artists) and the elucidation and elaboration of a complementary aesthetics and the building-up of an adequately impressive organization to secure for Scottish art a fair share of recognition and attention throughout the world. In short, we are, in my opinion, getting past the stage now in which there seemed a real danger of our becoming bogged not long ago — the stage of having 'all the culture of the world on tap and none of our own'. It has been said, 'If we want an art that will express the values of our democratic society, we must provide the artist with a growing audience whose judgement he does not despise'. I think we are building up in Scotland today an adequate public of that sort, despite the fact that art education in the ordinary schools is poor, because most teachers are not expected to have any standards of appreciation or knowledge beyond those of the general public, and specialized art teaching is bad, because it has to turn out designers who are neither required nor encouraged to do good work — although there has perhaps been a little improvement in that connection in the past year or two. But so far as the public at large is concerned, any art teaching they may have had is vastly supplemented by the tremendous number of excellent art-books of all kinds available to them at little cost or through the public library system; and by admirable radio talks; and by the fact that art treasures of all kinds are open to their inspection to an infinitely greater extent than has been the case at any previous period in human history.

Mr Tonge's book to which I have referred is not only an admirable introduction to the subject, giving all the most essentual factual information in a lucid and highly readable form, but it was the first book on its subject which was highly intelligent, widely informed, thoroughly up-to-date, and, in short, deserving of shelf-room alongside the average of the books of real value produced in the past half-century or so on the arts of other small European countries. Most of these countries, however, have scores of such books to their credit. This was literally Scotland's first. There had been other books on the subject, but they were all hopelessly out-of-date and in any case were little more than unintelligent catalogues of names, diversified with insignificant personalia, chit-chat, comments of the most hackneyed kind, stock platitudes, banal bromides and clap-trap generally.

As Mr Tonge himself said in his preface: 'There is no book giving the kind of all-round view of art and *Kunstgewerbe* popularized on the Continent in such works as Hamann's *Geschichte der Kunst* or Burckhardt's *Renaissance*'; and he goes on to say that while the two volumes published by Messrs Maclehose after the 1888 and 1901 Exhibitions respectively — namely *Scottish National Memorials* and *Scottish History and Life* — bring together a good deal of expert information, the pages he had devoted to the crafts of Scotland had had to be supplemented by reference to Mr J. Arnold Fleming's writings on pottery and glass, the literature on Communion Plate, and other specialized works.

The rapidly developing momentum of our contemporary Scottish Movement is shown by the fact that the few years which have elapsed since the publication of Mr Tonge's book have been signalized by a whole succession of books and pamphlets far superior in every way to anything previously available. We are entitled to assume that that indicates a corresponding growth of a well-informed and intensely interested public in our midst. The publications I have in mind include Mr Ian Finlay's *Scotland*, his *Art in Scotland* and his *Scottish Crafts*, Mr Stanley Cursiter's *Scottish Art*, Dr Honeyman's monograph on Leslie Hunter, and the two volumes now published in Messrs Wm. MacLellan's Modern Scottish Painters series, namely *The New Scottish Group* and *Scottish Painters: Donald Bain*. To these must be added the excellent 'Scottish Tradition' pamphlets published by the Saltire Society, and including *Pottery* by Iain Paul, *Burgh Architecture* by Iain Lindsay, *Silver* by Ian Finlay, *Printed Books* by W.R. Beattie, and *Photography* by R.O. Dougan. Mention must also be made of *The Scottish Art Review*, the quarterly magazine of the Glasgow Art Gallery and Museums Association, which has now developed into more than a Glasgow publication of restricted interest, and is reaching out into the wider field of art appreciation in general. All these together with the lectures given under the auspices of the Saltire Society, some of the talks on the Scottish BBC, and various other activities in Scotland today, amount to nothing less than a revolution compared with the position twenty-five years ago.

This development has been given the general name of the Scottish Renaissance Movement — a name which does not imply that that has been achieved, but simply that it is what is being aimed at. It has been remarked that interest in the corresponding arts of other countries is never keener than where a revival movement is afoot in a nation's own arts. Scotland has an unparalleled record of international interest and interaction, and it is good to see this feature so prominent again in the art products, writings and speeches of those who are most active in the Scottish Movement today. Not only has the level of debate risen immensely — not only is a far higher degree of intelligence and wealth of information and the power to assimilate and apply it being manifested, but in books like Mr Tonge's and Mr Finlay's at any rate real and very able attempts are made to grapple with the basic psychological and philosophical problems and to deduce the significance of these in relation to the ecology and ethos of our people. We find Mr Tonge, for example, dealing with M. Henri Focillon's terms, *espace-milieu* as opposed to *espace limite* — that is to say, constructed with reference to space and not framed off from it like the Pyramids or the Parthenon, and going on to say: 'The filigree technique so common in Celtic art presents a very obvious example of an art in which it is difficult to say whether the tangible forms or the immaterial intervals are the more important.'

Again he says:

> The New Town that Edinburgh built when, after centuries of turmoil, she turned her back on Prince Charles and Celtic Scotland, is so different from that of the Old Town of Edinburgh as to raise the question of whether such a classicism is in Scotland part of the artistic cycle into which Adama van Scheltema resolves all artistic movements, or a departure from a racial norm, or both. For Celtic Art comes within Worringer's category of Nordic Arts, and from his viewpoint Scotland, in the neo-Greek movement, could be regarded as indulging in something like the German *Sachlichkeit*, a merely temporary reaction from the characteristic Nordic *Expressionismus*.

Mr Tonge sums up his whole position in the following passage, I think.

> Scottish art as a whole — one must not forget the smooth façades and ordered simplicity of the New Town of Edinburgh — is much more involved and restless and dynamic than English art, and these characteristics we find in the asymmetrical intricate organic Celtic art. Scottish architecture — and architecture is the mother of the arts in Scotland no less than elsewhere — at its most characteristic evolves like a cellular structure, not from the tectonic piecing together of elements in classical fashion. It should not be forgotten, too, when the filigree technique of Celtic brooches, or the patterning of the Crosses is under consideration, that precisely the same technique characterizes the consummate and intricate atonal art-music of the composers of piobroch, some of the greatest of whose works date from as recently as the seventeenth century.

Writing of Rosslyn Chapel, Mr Tonge says that its

> rich ornament people who think of Scotland only as chaste and severe have been tempted to attribute to Burgos or Oviedo — to anyone except the Gael. Foreign workmen helped to build the chapel, as they did Holyrood, and there was foreign influence too; but when was there not foreign influence in the Middle Ages? There is nothing exotic in the plan, and the ornament is Celtic — not archaistic, but adapting intertwining coils and the rest to mediaeval ends. Its ornate qualities derive not from contemporary Renaissance work, which was relatively simple, but from the Celtic love of elaboration. The makers of Rosslyn did with English Gothic what the Makars did with the English tongue. Precisely the same juxtaposition of incongruous motives, the same crowded and firmly controlled ornament, is found in William Dunbar's aureate diction. And like Dunbar — Rosslyn is either warmly admired or as heartily hated.

Mr Ian Finlay is in general agreement with Mr Tonge in his insistence on the supreme importance of our Gaelic background. That point of view is so generally accepted by the leading controversialists on the subject of the arts in Scotland today (I share it fully myself) that it is desirable perhaps to quote a critic who is not a Scotsman on the subject. This is what Dr Herbert Read says in his book, *The Meaning of Art*, and, before quoting it, I may refer gratefully to the period in the 1920s during which Dr Read occupied the Chair of Fine Arts in Edinburgh University and stirred up the dovecots there with his lively modernistic doctrines and impatience with pompous humbugs.

'The ornament of the early Celtic period,' says Dr Read,

> is linear, geometric and abstract; the type most familiar is the interlaced ribbon or plaited ornament vulgarised in present-day 'Celtic' tombstones. It is seen in all its purity in the Book of Kells, the eighth-century manuscript belonging to Trinity College, Dublin. The real nature of this ornament has been well described by a German historian of art, Lamprecht, in the following words: 'There are certain simple motives whose interweaving and commingling determine the character of this ornament. At first there is only the dot, the line, the ribbon; later the curve, the circle, the spiral, the zig-zag, and an S-shaped decoration are employed. Truly no great wealth of motives! But what variety is attained by the manner of their employment! Here they run parallel, then entwined, now latticed, now knotted, now plaited, then again brought through one another in a symmetrical checker of knotting

and plaiting. Fantastically confused patterns are thus evolved, whose puzzle asks to be unravelled, whose convolutions seem alternately to seek and avoid each other, whose component parts, endowed as it were with sensibility, captivate sight and sense in passionately vital movement.'

Dr Read goes on to say that this non-organic, super-organic type of art is

> a mode of expression in direct contrast to the classical mode, which is organic, naturalistic, serene and satisfying. The significance of the Northern mode lies precisely in its life-denying qualities, its completely abstract character; and in this character, in these qualities, one must see a reflection of the spiritual life of these Northern people — 'the heavily oppressed inner life of Northern humanity', as Worringer has called it. Into this gloomy and abstract field of art, the symbols of Christianity come like visitants from an exotic land. In a prickly nest of geometrical lines, two birds of paradise will settle, carrying in their beaks a bunch of Eastern grapes. David comes with his harp and the three children in the furnace; Adam and Eve, and the sacrifice of Isaac, are represented in panels reserved among the bands of abstract ornament; and finally the stone is dominated by Christ in Glory and the company of angels. Such stones will stand where they were erected centuries ago in Ireland and Scotland; and no monuments in the world are so moving in their implications; they symbolize ten thousand years of human history, and represent that history at its spiritual extremes, nearest and farthest from the mercy of God.

From some of the phrases in that paragraph I think Dr Read has mistaken the matter. Worringer was referring to the Scandinavian peoples who are extremely neurotic and heavily-oppressed in their inner life. Such terms are quite inapplicable to the Gael. The Gaelic people were gay and fantastic. Classical Gaelic literature is merry and quite unburdened by the spiritual excesses subsequently wished on the Gaelic genius during the so-called 'Celtic Twilight' period. Not twilight but the clear sun was the symbol of the classical Gaelic spirit. But Gaeldom stands outside Europe altogether. Its affiliations are with the East. And it is not to Worringer's Nordic Arts but to the arts of the East we must look when we seek to understand Gaelic Art.

In one of my own books, I have said with reference to this matter,

> The ideas of the East-West synthesis and the Caledonian antisyzygy merge into one and lie at the root of any understanding of,

for example, that great Scottish musical achievement, the *piobaireachd* or great pipe music, and it is impossible to communicate any idea of pibroch to people who are not effectively seized of this joint-idea. Mr Harold Picton's *Early German Art and Its Origins, from the beginning to about 1050* (published in 1939) emerges from a grasp of related factors in the same field. This important book is the first in English — and probably in any language — to give a general account of what may be termed the non-classical standpoint of the origins of German art and thus of Northern European art generally. In an appreciative foreword Professor Josef Strzygowski, the leading authority on early European art, confirms the validity of the orientation adopted by Mr Picton in this work. Tracing the characteristics of Germanic art from the earliest beginnings, the author makes clear the large part played by Syria, Armenia, and the East in general in the development of the arts of Building, Ornament Painting, Carving, Goldsmith's Work, Enamel and Sculpture. He shows how the influence of the South often perverted into naturalism the talent of the Germans for pattern, fantasy, and abstraction, while the effect of the East often confirmed and stimulated that talent. One of the most important features of the book is the wealth of well-reproduced illustrations with which the wave of Eastern influence, and the backwash of this influence from Ireland, is brought out.[1]

I have quoted Mr Tonge's references to pibroch music and to Dunbar's poetry in connection with the arts of painting and sculpture — and I might have culled similar analogies drawn from a wide intimacy with science, literature and history from the pages of Mr Ian Finlay and others — for the special reason that they illustrate a pronounced and I think very valuable tendency which has developed to an enormous extent in certain countries and has only shown the most tentative beginnings so far in Scotland where it can certainly be pursued immensely further with vast profit. It has been remarked that, like all other sciences, that of aesthetics has undergone decisive changes during the past three-quarters of a century, both in method and in scope. 'It is,' says one writer,

> difficult even to compare the present with the early stage in which it is still to be found in some countries, where the science has

---

[1] Hugh MacDiarmid, *Lucky Poet* (1943; Carcanet, 1994, pp.375-6) — Ed.

remained under the spell of narrow preoccupations with theories of beauty and with those based on idealistic metaphysics. The term aesthetics as it has been used during the last century is derived from Baumgarten's work, *Aestetica* (published in 1750), but a strictly scientific view of aesthetics was first developed by Kant in his *Kritik der Urteilskraft*, published in 1790. Recent decades have shown an intensification of aesthetic activities such as has never been known before. Art history has been developed from a descriptive and classifying doctrine to a science which takes into account not only the stylistic aspects but also deeper connections with the general ideas of mankind. The Swiss, Heinrich Wölfflin, is the chief exponent of the first line of thought (*Die Grundbegriffe der Kunstgeschichte*), and the Viennese, Max Dvorak, who saw the history of art as a history of the human spirit, expounds it in his *Kunstgeschichte als Geistgeschichte.* Dvorak liberated art history from the methods applied by the natural sciences. Modern psychology has had a tremendous impact on art history and art theory; a new term had to be invented to cover the entire field of knowledge. This German term, *Kunstwissenschaft*, the science of art, includes not only the history of art but also art theory and art criticism, the development and periodicity of styles and techniques, the relation of spiritual culture and material civilization (as in Jacob Burckhardt and certain Marxist thinkers), and the analysis of the creative processes themselves (as in Freud, Jung, Lévy-Brühl, Worringer), from which point of view the life of the artist, his journals, his manifestoes and theories became of greater importance. The interrelations of the arts — as the different forms of expression of the human psyche and probably the purest sources of human experience, and the crisis of art as a symptom of the spiritual crisis of our highly-mechanized life — are the latest fields of research. With this widening of interest in the arts, the literature of the subject has become more diverse. The mass of popular books on art is overwhelming. Their characteristic is a kind of general or panoramic approach to the problems and 'isms' of art and its personalities, based mainly upon illustrations, often uncritical and subjective. General histories of art and critical biographies, when written by experts, represent the next step. A wide range of psychological, philosophical, and sociological works are also devoted today to problems of aesthetics; they are written by scientists who, like the late Dr A.N. Whitehead, are convinced that 'the most fruitful, because the most neglected, starting-point of philosophic thought is that section of value theory which we term aesthetic'.

A model book in this connection is Professor Charles Gauss's *The Aesthetic Theories of French Artists*, published early this year. In it, Professor Gauss takes the writings of modern artists as the basis of research. Beginning with Courbet and his manifestoes on realism, the books goes on to the theories of impressionism of the two great independents, Cézanne and Renoir, of Symbolism (Synthetism) and Fauvism (Gauguin, Denis, Matisse), of early Cubism (Gleizes, Metzinger), and finally of Surrealism (Breton, Ernst, Dali). Professor Gauss challenges the views of such theorists as Curt Ducasse who insisted that it was wrong to see in the artist an expert, because the production of works of art was something very different from dealing with theoretical questions. Professor Gauss shows clearly how these manifestoes can be critically used to elucidate the new methods and the revolutionary character of contemporary art. The book has a second outstanding merit — and this seems to have been the author's main concern — and that is to show that each aesthetic theory reflects a philosophical background and that therefore the problems of the artist are the problems of the philosopher, namely the enigmas of the external world. It is revealing to see how realism and Comte's positivism as well as Saint Simon's social ideas are related; how impressionist theories of light coincide with the research work of Augustin Fresnel, Helmholz, and M. Chevreul; how the philosophical parallel of Renoir's repudiation of any connection between science and art is the Bergsonian metaphysic; and how there is an analogy between Cézanne's idea that artistic creation depends upon the acceptance of an ordering principle of sensation, and Poincaré's demonstration of the reason for hypotheses in scientific method. The inner connection of Symbolism and Fauvism with Schelling's romantic philosophy and with the anti-intellectualism in contemporary French thinking, is shown to be as convincing as the identity of the cubist theories, and the critique of scientific methodology made by Meyerson. The theoretical background of Surrealism, besides the Freudian and Jungian psychology, is also Hegel's principle of dialectic and Lobatschewsky's discovery of a non-Euclidean geometry. Such books as Professor Gauss's are important because they break down the barriers which specialization has built up between the sciences. Specialization prevents us achieving a unified picture of the world as reflected in all intellectual activities.

> It is the unification, the wholeness of an outlook on life, that is the sign of the maturity of a genuine culture.

We are a long way from anything of that sort in Scotland yet. Nevertheless progress is being made. As with Mr Tonge's, the great virtue of Mr Finlay's work is that it is the record of a mind earnestly striving to get away from vague abstractions, meaningless catch-words, and facile clichés. Both write with that vividness and conviction which come from living contact with the subject under discussion. This is something quite new in Scottish art-writing. And with that remark I come to the heart of my subject — 'Aesthetics in Scotland'. One of the few books of any consequence published in recent years dealing with the aesthetic doctrines of Scottish philosophers is a two-volume study in Italian by an Italian scholar, well-known to many of us in Scotland today, Signor Mario Rossi. His book is entitled *L'Estetica dell' Empirismo Inglese*, that is to say, *The Aesthetics of the English Empiricists*, and appeared in 1946 in a series published by the firm of Sansoni under the general title 'Scrittori d'Estetica'. I will not pause at the moment to object to the adjective English in the title, when half the Empiricist philosophers dealt with are in fact Scotsmen, including David Hume, Lord Kames, Dugald Stewart and others. Signor Rossi has no difficulty in showing, in his introduction, that the aesthetic theory of the Empiricists, so far as it could be called a theory, failed to establish 'The true character of the universality of the beautiful', and that their illegitimate progress from the perceptions of the senses to the apprehension of universals vitiated the whole of their arguments, even those of Lord Shaftesbury which were directed to establishing the universality of the beautiful. Seen in the light of the progress in transcendental philosophy since Kant and of the more modern discoveries in the field of psychology, the common-sense aesthetics of the seventeenth and eighteenth centuries appear rather faded and only distinguished by the grace and urbanity of their presentation. They were not concerned with art in the sense in which we conceive the subject today at all. What they were concerned with was moral philosophy. None of them seem to have had any actual acquaintance with the arts or with artists and where they deal with the subject of beauty they do so in forms of more or less thinly disguised theology. None of them condescend to show any knowledge of or interest in objects of art. Blake stressed the importance of minute particulars and stigmatized those who traffic only in generalities as knaves and fools. And certainly the Scottish philosophers I have in mind avoided particulars like the plague. They wrote in fact *in vacuo* and that — and the nature of the presuppositions with which they came to their task — vitiated their work and makes it today, if not altogether unreadable, extremely transpontine and practically valueless. They knew and cared little or nothing about the arts — only about Art with a capital A, which means nothing at all.

The trouble with all these philosophers — Sir William Ferguson, Dr Blair, Lord Kames, Adam Ferguson, Francis Hutcheson, and so on — and the trouble indeed with most of the Scots who have written on art until quite recently is, in fact, the trouble that afflicted the greatest writer on art Scotland has yet produced. I refer to John Ruskin. We are still apt to forget that Ruskin was a Scotsman. The trouble with Ruskin is described by R.H. Wilenski as follows:

> He was addicted from childhood onwards to a drug which he was forced to take in daily doses in the nursery until he acquired the taste for it. In youth and maturity he fought against the abuse of the drug; but he fought in vain; when at last he was immuned by satiety his power of action was all spent. The drug, of course, was the emotive language of the Bible. Ruskin, as everyone knows, was made to read the Bible *aloud* every day in childhood and early youth. He was started at the beginning, taken through to the end, and then back to begin again. He was also made to memorise long sections of the text. This continued until he went to Oxford. He then knew by heart Exodus, Chapters XV and XX; Deuteronomy, Chapter XXXII; 2 Samuel, Chapter I from 17th verse to the end; 1st Kings, Chapter VIII; Psalms XXIII, XXXII, XC, XCI, CIII, CXIX, CXXXIX; Isaiah, Chapter LCIII; Matthew, Chapters V, VI, VII; Acts, Chapter XXVI; 1st Corinthians, Chapters XIII, XV: James, Chapter IV, and he had thousands of other phrases in his head. He continued to read the Bible as long as he read anything. He was always obsessed with the emotive rhythm, the sonority, the obscurity, the archaism, and awful associations of this living text within his brain. We shall never know to what extent the obsession impeded his power of thinking, but no one who has really studied his writing will, I am convinced, deny that this obsession fatally impeded the precise externalization of his thought. The remembered language continually intervened between the thought and its expression, and often sidetracked the thought itself. Ruskin, it is quite clear, struggled to use language as a means of precise communication. He fussed about the derivations of words to persuade himself that he was learning to use

> words with scientific care. But in fact he continually failed to achieve sustained control of his vocabulary. Again and again he began by making sentences in which the words exactly represent the thought; and then some remembered emotive words and phrases would rise to his mind's surface, and he would take first one sip of the fatal drug, and then another, till, finally, he would abandon the hard task of precise externalization of thought, and yield to the pleasure of making 'some sort of melodious noise about it'. Again and again a paragraph begins as precise writing, and ends as emotive rhetoric recalling the Bible. In book after book the words on the first few pages have no power themselves, but submissively obey the thought; then gradually the words become more Biblical, and so emotive, till, in the end, the thought is dancing to their tune.

There is a great deal more to be said about Ruskin than that, however. He was a man of indubitable genius. After a long period of obloquy and belittlement, he is now happily being restored in critical esteem. There have been many good books about him recently. But all that Mr Wilenski says in the passage I have quoted is true enough; and the same thing is true of most of our Scottish philosophers. The same thing is still true of almost all of us, although few of us nowadays perhaps are over-dosed with the Bible. Yet thinking as distinct from rationalization is extremely rare among us in every connection. There is even a widespread prejudice against the use of exact terminology. The general preference is for the time-honoured commonplaces, windy abstractions, and bromides. Careful study, thorough knowledge, and precise expression are generally at a discount. With all the facilities at their disposal nowadays most people steer clear of equipping themselves with information about the things they go to see. They do not — or will not — understand that they can only receive from works of art in proportion to what they bring to them. They continue to refuse to prepare themselves in any way, and, confronted with works of art, give vent to expressions of opinion of the most irresponsible and imbecilic kind — at the same time not hesitating to insist that every man is entitled to his own opinion and that their opinions are just as much entitled to consideration as anybody else's. It never occurs to them that they lack even the minimum basis for the formation of any opinion, and when they say, 'Of course, I am not an expert', or 'There's nothing highbrow about me', what they are really doing in regard to Art is what most of them also do in regard to Philosophy, or, as Thomas Davidson put it,

> What shall we say of people who devote their time to reading novels written by miserable ignorant scribblers — many of them young, uneducated, and inexperienced — and who have hardly read a line of Homer or Sophocles or Dante or Shakespeare or Goethe, or even of Wordsworth or Tennyson, who would laugh at the notion of reading and studying Plato or Aristotle or Thomas Aquinas or Bruno or Kant or Rosmini? Are they not worse than the merest idiots, feeding prodigally upon swinish garbage, when they might be in their father's house, enjoying their portion of humanity's spiritual birthright? I know of few things more utterly sickening and contemptible than the self-satisfied smile of Philistine superiority with which many persons tell me, 'I am not a philosopher'. It simply means this, 'I am a stupid, low, grovelling fool, and I am proud of it'.

The type of all these Scottish philosophers — and indeed of the whole tribe of the pompous platitudinarians still so rife in Scottish public life — was Professor John Wilson, better known as 'Christopher North', who occupied the chair of Moral Philosophy in Edinburgh University and knew so little about his subject that he was only able to keep going year after year in hand-and-mouth fashion, dependent on receiving in time for his next lecture a few notes and suggestions from a humble and little-known friend who supplied him in this way during the whole tenure of his Chair. 'Wilson,' says Miss Swann, his biographer,

> never fully formulated his moral philosophy, for the Professor's ideas were always a little vague, and somewhat cloudy through lack of disciplined thought. His own doctrines were never quite fixed, and he stated publicly to the class at the close of his last session that he had all along been conscious there was some gap in it. He read widely, but in a haphazard and desultory way that never digested the reading so that it became an organic whole in his being; consequently he could not only contribute nothing new to philosophy but because he would not make the intellectual effort of absorbing his material had much ado to keep going as a lecturer. He shuffled along in a hand-to-mouth existence, fed with assiduous small scraps from Blair [the correspondent I referred to], in letters that arrived frequently. With a few crude notes of his own on the backs of envelopes, and chiefly with his gift of impassioned rhetoric, Wilson contrived to fill out the daily lecture and enflesh the few philosophical bones at his disposal with the juicy meat of his eloquence. The hungry sheep looked up and they were

duly fed; but the more intelligent discovered later that there was surprisingly little sustenance in the fare provided by the persuasive shepherd. He was a hollow man, and he knew it better than anyone else. The knowledge made him awkward and *gauche* with Thomas Carlyle, because he sensed that Carlyle had looked within and seen his hollowness, as, of course, Carlyle had, with a most rare perception. Wilson, however, felt safe before the rest of the world, who accepted him at his face-value — provided that Blair stood behind him, and plied him with the means to keep up appearances.

While few of our people today have any exact knowledge of Scottish Philosophy — or the Common Sense Philosophy as it was called — and the names of Thomas Reid, Dugald Stewart, Sir William Hamilton, Francis Hutcheson and the others are hardly known at all save to students of the subject — a hangover from it conditions the general mentality of our people to an enormous extent. Speaking in Edinburgh University recently the Earl of Lindsay (Crawford) renounced Picasso's work and influence as destructive of all sound and normal values, all the decencies so laboriously built up in the course of civilization. This sense of what is 'sound and normal' is simply a hangover from Reid and the others. Is there any good basis for it? A great American scientist, Dr Trigant Burrow, has recently written about it in the following terms:

> Let us look into this attitude of normality, so called, upon which individuals and communities commonly pride themselves. Let us examine this social state of mind with its underlying trend toward conflict and antagonism. We might consider the generally accepted covenants upon which this social fabric rests. For the prevailing pattern of 'normality' is as yet an unexplored field. It embodies habits of behaviour that we hold sacrosanct. Indeed, nothing so commands the fealty of human communities as the socially established average of conduct known by universal assent as normality. Nothing exerts a more irresistible influence over the processes of men than this criterion of behaviour embodied in the currently accepted social reaction-average, and this criterion of conduct dominates man's thinking and feeling today no less than in the earliest period of human history. The traditions of normality are preserved in literature, art, religion and philosophy.
>
> Its tenets are securely embalmed within the structure of the law. It is the warp and woof of politics, the raison d'être of psychiatry, the foundation of our educational systems. It enjoys the solemn

endorsement of Church and State. Among all individuals, professional as well as lay, among all groups and all communities, it is 'normality' that regulates and determines the behaviour of family, home and country. It is the standard by which we measure all behaviour and indict as subversive or pathological whatever conduct deviates from this popularly cherished 'norm'. Very early in our analysis of groups we found that this social confederacy, this mentally conditioned state we credit as 'normality' possesses certain special and distinctive marks — marks that cannot be too strongly emphasized. In the first place, the standards of normality are completely arbitrary and mutable; they are alterable in accordance with personal volition. Though socially ubiquitous, this mental habitude rests upon no determinate premise; its dicta are wholly esoteric; it possesses no objectively stable constant. Besides, the motivation underlying this esoteric normality was found to activate equally the behaviour of the isolated neurotic and that of the socially adapted individual. It activates the teacher as well as the pupil, the governing alike with the governed, the parent no less than the child, the presumably strong and upstanding personality along with those presumed to be weak and ineffectual. As a gauge of interindividual conduct, 'normality' bears no dependable relation to reality, but is supported only by capricious community preconceptions. It is supported by one-sided ideologies, or, if I may recall the term I first used years ago, by arbitrary *social images*. What is more, normality as now constituted is sustained by a secret and unconscious prerogative that jealously preserves its partisan viewpoint against all inquiry. The shrine of normality at which all of us devoutly worship must on no account be examined into. The old-time religion is good enough for normality, and any investigation into its sacred rites and ordinances is taboo. For in its widebound conditioning, normality is always 'right' and the least infringement upon this interrelational mode of feeling and thinking calls forth a reflex defence reaction in individual and community.

To question the prerogatives of this social consensus of behaviour is the unpardonable sin, the irreconcilable affront. By the universal manifestoes of unwritten law this criticism of human adaptation we call 'normality' is the great Sir Oracle. As the sworn custodian of the bidden ulterior aim, normality promptly frowns upon any suggestion that presumes to question its established dogmas. According to the adherents of normality, its subjective conviction of rightness and security leaves nothing to be desired.

Enjoying supreme authority over man, this fanciful pattern of human conduct possesses the credibility of a superstition and is by common consent immune to the scientific tests of objective actuality.

As to the variability and inconsistency of the standards of normality, examples are legion. We are supposedly a democratic country, but we are largely ruled by professional lobbyists. Overtly we support a war for world unification, but our ulterior intention leans strongly to the side of nationalism. In our commercial relations secret cartels often take precedence over our boasted policy of free enterprise. Everywhere codes of morality are juggled beyond recognition. Only a few years ago children stood in awe of their parents, now it is parents who stand in awe of their children. Divorce was formerly anathema, but today no stigma whatever attaches to it. One advocates democratic policies in his public life, but not infrequently adopts an attitude of imperialism in his home. Such will-o'-the-wisp principles of human behaviour and a thousand other catch-as-catch-can precepts are shared in varying forms by all peoples and bespeak once more the perennial imbalance and conflict, the vacillating factionalism and partitiveness that mark the habitual mode of adaptation we cherish as 'normality'.

Happily for the credit of Scottish intelligence today, the Earl of Lindsay is counterbalanced by the great Scottish dramatist, James Bridie, who boldly declares that Picasso is one of the outstanding geniuses in the world today and that if Picasso is not normal he would rather stand with Picasso than with all the hordes of the normal.

The stupidity of these diehard reactionary attacks on an artist like Picasso, an author like James Joyce, and other leaders of modernist developments in the arts can best be appreciated when we reflect that Joyce's unrewarded attempt to establish the first motion-picture theatre in Ireland is only another chapter in the history of his misunderstandings with his country, but he fully understood the technical possibilities of the new medium. He keenly perceived — in spite of his defective vision — that the cinema is both a science and an art, and therefore the most characteristic expression of our time. Joyce's own technique shows the confluence of many modern developments in the arts and sciences. The impressionistic painters, by defining their object through the eyes of the beholder, gave Joyce an example which his physical handicap may have encouraged him to follow.

The 'ineluctable modality of the whole' was narrowed down for him, so that blurred sight looked for compensation in augmented sound. The Wagnerian school, with its thematic blend of music and ideas, had its obvious lesson for a novelist who had wanted to be a lyric poet or a professional singer. The international psychoanalytic movement, under the direction of Jung, had its headquarters in Zurich during the war years while Joyce was writing *Ulysses*, and he could scarcely have resisted its influence. And, although philosophy could not have offered him much in the way of immediate data, it is suggestive to note that Bergson, Whitehead, and others — by reducing things-in-themselves to a series of organic relations — were thinking in the same direction. Thus the very form of Joyce's book is an elusive and eclectic *Summa* of its age: the montage of the cinema, impressionism in painting, *leit-motif* in music, the free association of psychoanalysis, and vitalism in philosophy. Take of these elements all that is fusible, and perhaps more, and you have the style of *Ulysses*. To characterize this style, we must borrow a term from either German metaphysics or French rhetoric; we may conceive it as *Strom des Bewusstseins* or again as *monologue intérieur*. Of its prototype, Edward Dujardin's *Les lauriers sont coupés* it has been well observed that

> it seems to bear the same relation to ordinary fiction that the film does to the stage. For, to find ample literary precedent for the internal monologue, we need only turn to the theatre. The conventions of Elizabethan drama permitted Shakespeare to marshal the arguments for and against suicide in Hamlet's soliloquy or to mingle desperation with prose and song in the distractions of Ophelia's madness. Recent playwrights, like Eugene O'Neill, have renewed their license to soliloquize. Poets like Browning and T.S. Eliot have never abandoned this prerogative.

Something very similar can be said of Picasso. But when Lord Lindsay attacks him in the name of normality, Lord Lindsay needs to be reminded of the queues at every picture-house and of the fact that the man-in-the-street and his wife — although they may jeer at and condemn a modernist picture or poem are at the very same time assimilating its techniques every time they go to the 'movies' and are also taking it into their homes in the patterns of their new carpets and in the design of all sorts of other domestic gadgets.

The prejudice against modern innovations is that of Lord Lindsay and other reactionaries; the general public have none of it. As Justice Brandeis said, 'ordinary men and women can grasp the essentials of any situation, no matter how involved its details, if the facts are adequately presented to them'. When the people of Mexico after the Revolution were given their first opportunity to hear the classics of European music at concerts in the public parks, it was not Bach and Mozart and Beethoven that evoked their enthusiasm but the most difficult atonal music of Schoenberg and his followers. It was with the dance as with music. Emmanuel Eisenberg reports that Anna Sokolow in introducing modern methods of choreography and novel dance technique for the first time into Mexico found that working-class pupils in that stronghold of folk-lore and ritual took to them readily and without any difficulty of adjustment.

It is exactly what the group of intellectual girls defying tradition and founding an association called Anggana Raras in Java with R.M. Kordat as leader have (again in dancing) done in another part of the world, influenced, as their spokesman R. Abdul Latief says, by what he calls 'the new and young idea; back to your own culture, developing it in modern direction'. That is the best possible advice for Scotland too, and is, in fact, exactly what the Scottish Renaissance Movement set out to do. The mass of the people will react all right if they get a chance. It is the stupid conservatism of their self-styled 'betters' that is the danger. One sees easily enough why a great modernist poet and poetic dramatist like T.S. Eliot says that as far as his work is concerned he would prefer an audience of illiterates to an audience of half-educated conventionalists.

Another hang-over from the worst elements of the Common Sense Philosophy was represented by the plea put forward for amateurism by Sir Alexander Gray the other day. Sir Alexander denounced the radio, and the other modern facilities which have concentrated the arts more and more in the hands of professional artistes, and done away with the happy old times when far more people played an instrument in their own homes and associated with neighbours and friends in all kinds of humble social music-making. Whatever may be said of that from a merely human point of view, there can be no question that this development has been immensely to our artistic betterment. Vast numbers of people now hear first-class executants playing important music who would in former times — even as recently as fifty years ago — never have had any such opportunity. A vast amount of excellent instruction in appreciation of music and art and literature is constantly on the air. Amateurism has always been the curse of the arts in modern Scotland — amateurism, and, along with it, the inveterate predilection to 'domesticate the issue'. What Sir Alexander Gray recommends may suit the book of local exhibitionists, anxious to impress the neighbours, but the progress of the Arts in Scotland is dependent upon precisely the opposite course — upon, that is to say, the wider appreciation and striving after the highest possible standards.

Now in view of all I have said so far, it must surely come as a surprise when I have to go on to point out that in the article on Aesthetics in the 11th Edition of the *Encyclopaedia Brittanica* — after listing and discussing the great Greeks and the great Germans and French and others who have contributed importantly to this branch of philosophy and devised the various systems of aesthetics — we come to what are called the 'English writers' on the subject — and find that thirteen of them are allotted separate paragraphs in which their contributions are described and assessed, and that of these thirteen no fewer than eight are Scots — namely, Francis Hutcheson, Thomas Reid, Sir William Hamilton, Lord Kames, Archibald Alison, Dugald Stewart, Alexander Bain, and John Ruskin. Not only so, but the text contains references to two other Scots, James Mill and Francis Jeffrey. Numerically at least that is an extraordinarily good proportion for Scotland compared with England in relation to a subject on which, I think, it would have been generally expected that Scotland would make a comparatively very meagre and miserable showing indeed. And on the strength of it I think I am justified in once again registering an emphatic protest at England's appropriation of Scottish writers in this way to hide or camouflage her own lamentable deficiencies. Not only are the Scots in the list more numerous; they are also more important — one of them, indeed, Ruskin, is as important as all the rest of the thirteen put together. Moreover the list is incomplete and excludes one important and far too little known Scottish writer, Aeneas Sweetland Dallas (1828-1879) of whose significance I must have a good deal to say before I finish. I am one of that very few and far between sort of Scotsman sufficiently interested in theories of art to look for and read all I can lay my hands on in this connection, and I may be allowed to reinforce what I have just said about the monstrous trick of describing Scottish writers as English by pointing out that in a recently-published massive volume in German, *Kunst und Literatur*, the writings of Engels and Marx dealing with the arts, I find that while Burns is properly described as a 'schottischer Volksdichter' no less a person than Thomas Carlyle is listed as 'englischer Schriftsteller', Sir William Hamilton as 'englischer Philosoph der schottischen Schule', and John Stuart Mill as 'englischer Philosoph und Okonom'. The lines of Scottish thought and of the arts in Scotland have developed so differently from their English counterparts and point in such entirely different

— and, indeed, opposed — directions that it is important to clear up this kind of confusion and put these men all in their proper places in the traditions to which they really belong — and apart from which they cannot in fact be properly appraised at all.

I have pointed out elsewhere that any attempt to carry forward the Scottish philosophy — somewhat inaccurately called the Common Sense Philosophy — is discouraged by the Philosophy Professors of our universities and consequently little or nothing has been done about it in modern times. On the Continent, however — and in the United States of America — it has attracted some very able students and several important books on it have appeared there in recent years. For general reading, Dr Henry Laurie's book, *Scottish Philosophy In Its National Development*, published in Glasgow in 1902, remains the best available. He devotes a chapter each to all the principal men — from Francis Hutcheson, Andrew Baxter, and David Hume, through Kames, Adam Smith, Thomas Reid, Dugald Stewart, and several others, down to Sir William Hamilton and James Frederick Ferrier. His phrase about 'thoughtful minds occupied with philosophical questions in theological disguise' accurately describes most of the work of all these men. And, conveniently for our purpose, he has a separate chapter on 'Aesthetic Theories'. As he says,

> the aesthetic theories favoured by writers of the Scottish school, from Hutcheson downward, are marked by a strong family likeness. They are almost unanimous in adopting a psychological method of inquiry, discussing the characteristics of our feeling of the beautiful and asking by what quality or qualities it is excited.

He proceeds to discuss Hutcheson's essay 'Of The Standard Of Taste', Adam Smith's *Theory of Moral Sentiments*, Alexander Gerard's 'Essay on Taste', Dr Hugh Blair's essay and Thomas Reid's and Lord Monboddo's and Dr Archibald Alison's contributions to the subject, finishing up by considering Francis Jeffrey's 'Essay on Beauty', Dugald Stewart's *Philosophical Essays*, Thomas Brown's treatment of the Beautiful, and Sir William Hamilton's *Lectures*, remarking that for his theory of the sublime and beautiful Hamilton was indebted to Kant far more than to any of his Scottish predecessors (though he might have added that Kant himself was of Scottish descent). He sums up by remarking that

> on the whole Scottish philosophy has been psychological in its treatment of these questions, its starting-point being the recognition of the emotion of the beautiful as a part of conscious experience, and its next step an enquiry into the source or sources of this

peculiar emotion. This is still represented [he was writing in 1902] in some quarters as the only scientific method of inquiry. In the hands of the Scottish thinkers, at least, it did not lead to any triumphant success. From a psychological point of view, we are struck by the vagueness of the characterization of the feeling of the beautiful. They were right no doubt in describing it as a pleasurable and disinterested emotion of a peculiar kind. But this did not carry them far into inquiring into its causes. It did not even relieve them from the ambiguity of the word beautiful, sometimes restricted in its application to nature and art, and sometimes extended to the world of mind. They were fortunate in lighting on the old conception of unity in multiplicity as a condition of beauty. But it was not till the influence of German philosophy began to be felt that an attempt was made to exhibit any rational connection between this condition and its effect. In the absence of such an explanation, they were naturally led to ask if the emotion of beauty might not be excited by a variety of external causes, or accounted for by a connected flow of ideas. Recent theories of Aesthetics have sought to surmount these difficulties by a more exact delimitation of the region of inquiry, concentrating attention more particularly on the Fine Arts. This, however, would have been impossible to Scottish writers in the eighteenth century. The tardy development of art in Scotland sufficiently explains the scantiness of their references to the nature, the history, and the masterpieces of music and the plastic arts, and even in literature the superficial judgement which preferred Corneille and Racine to Shakespeare [Dr Laurie is referring here to certain notorious expressions of opinion made by David Hume] prevented their recognition of the catholic aims of art as the interpreter of nature and of human life in their fullest details and deepest meaning.

How far we have travelled since these vague explorations of 'the feeling of the Beautiful', may be illustrated by quoting Dr Herbert Read. 'The concept of beauty,' he says,

> is, indeed, of limited historical significance. It arose in ancient Greece, and was the offspring of a particular philosophy of life. That philosophy was anthropomorphic in kind; it exalted all human values and saw in the gods nothing but man writ large. Art, as well as religion, was an idealization of nature, and especially of man as the culminating point of the process of nature. The type of classical art is the Apollo Belvedere or the Aphrodite of Melos — perfect or ideal types of humanity, perfectly formed,

> perfectly proportioned, noble and serene; in one word, beautiful. This type of beauty was inherited by Rome, and revived at the Renaissance. We still live in the tradition of the Renaissance, and for us beauty is inevitably associated with the idealization of a type of humanity evolved by an ancient people in a far land, remote from the actual conditions of our daily life. Perhaps as an ideal it is as good as any other; but we ought to realize that it is only one of several possible ideals. It differs from the Byzantine ideal, which was divine rather than human, intellectual and anti-vital, abstract. It differs from the Primitive ideal, which was perhaps no ideal at all, but rather a propitiation, an expression of fear in the face of a mysterious and implacable world. It differs also from the Oriental ideal, which is abstract too, non-human, metaphysical, yet instinctive rather than intellectual. But our habits of thought are so dependent on our outfit of words, that we try, often enough in vain, to force this one word 'beauty' into the service of all these ideals as expressed in art. If we are honest with ourselves, we are bound to feel guilty sooner or later of verbal distortion. A Greek Aphrodite, a Byzantine Madonna and a savage idol from New Guinea or the Ivory Coast cannot one and all belong to this classical concept of beauty. The latter, at least, if words are to have any precise meaning, we must confess to be unbeautiful or ugly. And yet, whether beautiful or ugly, all these objects may be legitimately described as works of art.

Mr Eric Newton in his book on *The Meaning of Beauty* published the other day, stresses that the love of pictures has to be acquired with great patience. The only way of learning to enjoy pictures is to spend a lot of time looking at them and for most people this is impossible. Literature has been made easily available by printing, music by the gramophone and the radio; but painting remains difficult of access, for even the best coloured reproductions of a Titian or a Velasquez are no more faithful than old phonograph cylinders. 'Art,' says Mr Newton,

> is no more than the expression of human experience, and the understanding and enjoyment of art is no more than the capacity of the spectator to relate the work of art to his accumulated store of experience. It follows that the spectator's reaction to the work of art is limited by the scope of his experience.... Yet Human beings continue to quarrel among themselves about what is, or is not, beautiful, rather than about who is and who is not capable of recognizing beauty.

'Such a distinction,' Mr Raymond Mortimer said in a review,

> it will be said, is shockingly undemocratic: paintings ought to please the average man. But will even the most bigoted Marxist impose the same obligation upon chess-problems? By 'experience' Mr Newton means not only study in museums but habitual responsiveness of eye in daily life. Most people use their sight very negligently except for an ulterior purpose such as to hit a ball, to avoid a fishbone, to appraise the expression, or the hat worn by a friend. The painter is continuously fascinated by appearances as such, by the mere look of everything — of slugs, of barbed wire, of old sardine-tins. So also is the lover of painting. This disinterested delight in shapes and colours can become one of the major rewards of living, but it is commonly sought only in things well-known to be beautiful — sunsets, for instance, and flowers and porcelain ornaments.

The reader who does not wish to read a book like Dr Laurie's systematic philosophical exposition may find all he wants or needs about the earlier Scottish writers on aesthetics in J.H. Millar's *Literary History of Scotland* published a year later than Laurie's book, that is to say, in 1903. The book created a furore, evoking no little of that defence-reaction Dr Trigant Burrow describes in the passage I quoted dealing with normality. Dr Millar was a wit and he exposed in a devastating way the absurdities and windy pretentiousness of much in the writings of the Scottish philosophers. He may be claimed by and large to have been the initiator of many of the leading ideas of the Scottish Renaissance Movement today and his most amusing attacks on the writers of the then popular Kailyaird School — Ian Maclaren, S.R. Crockett, J.M. Barrie and others — struck pain and alarm into all the mindless sentimentalists round the parish pumps and bonnie briar bushes. Of Thomas Reid, he said:

> Reid's philosophy has suffered to some extent from his employment of so ambiguous an expression as 'common-sense'. Passages like the following 'brust' of eloquence are not likely to restore confidence in that touchstone, or its champion: 'Admired Philosophy! daughter of light! parent of wisdom and knowledge! if thou art she, surely thou has not yet arisen upon the human mind, nor blessed us with more of thy rays than are sufficient to shed a darkness visible upon the human faculties, and to disturb that repose and security which happier mortals enjoy, who never approached thine altar nor felt thine influence! But if, indeed thou hast not

> power to dispel those clouds and phantoms which thou hast discovered or created, withdraw this penurious and malignant ray; I despise Philosophy and renounce its guidance — let my soul dwell with Common Sense.'

Despite this ridiculous and all too typical flight of rhetoric, Dr Millar recognized that there was a real core of substance in Reid all the same, and went on to say:

> But, in making his appeal to Common Sense, Reid did not desire to take the judgement of the man in the street. He meant to appeal to those principles which are common to the understanding of all men, and which are the indispensable conditions precedent to an act of judgement on the part of any one.

More recent writers have tended to re-establish Reid as no unworthy antagonist of Hume himself — Hume of whom Sir Leslie Stephen said that the failure of English thinkers to face up to some of the problems posed by Hume, and by Hume alone, accounted for the pusillanimity and ineffectiveness of all subsequent English philosophy.

Of Sir William Hamilton's work, Dr Millar says that many are now disposed to think his abilities were sadly wasted in wedding the philosophy of the unconditioned to the philosophy of 'common-sense'. Elsewhere Dr Millar had said of Hamilton,

> as a Professor he was a great success, commanding in all cases the attention and respect, and in not a few the enthusiastic devotion of his pupils. His favourite doctrines were championed by one of the ablest metaphysicians who adorned Oxford during the century, and denounced by one of the feeblest logicians that ever attempted to reason accurately. Yet now, there is scarce a Hamiltonian in the land. He is repudiated with zeal alike by empiricits and neo-Hegelians. His influence is imperceptible in modern thought; and there is no sign that the wheel of fashion will bring even a modified form of his system into vogue again. Wherein, then, lies the secret of the eclipse of this once brilliant luminary?

But I am not so sure that a measure of rehabilitation will not come to him even yet. I know that the late Lord Tweedsmuir (John Buchan) was keen to attempt it. He told me that he had always cherished the hope of writing a study of Hamilton. His tremendous activities in other fields of literature and public life prevented him doing so. But the task may be discharged by some one else.

Of the other Scottish Philosophers Dr Millar says enough to show that they owed most of what repute they had in their day to their fine presence and imposing personalities and gifts of eloquence, but that they added precious little of any value to the subjects on which they expatiated and have certainly little to yield to students of aesthetics today. Mr A.D. Woozley's edition of Reid's *Essays on the Intellectual Powers of Man*, published in 1941, makes out a good case for Reid *vis-a-vis* Hume. And Dr Norman Kemp Smith's book, *The Philosophy of David Hume*, a critical study of its origins and central doctrines, published in 1941, is a brilliant reassessment which does ample reparation to an ambiguous shade and marks the highest point of that apotheosis of Hume which had been proceeding throughout the previous decade. These studies, however, have little to do with our specific concern — that department of philosophy which is called aesthetics. Nor is there much to our purpose in Mr Jerome Hamilton Buckley's book, *The Victorian Temper* (1952), although it does introduce the reader to the now forgotten but once influential critical pronouncements of the Rev George Gilfillan, and the much sounder achievement of David Ramsay Hay, who carried on the tradition of Kames and Alison by founding at Edinburgh in 1851 the Aesthetic Society, with the avowed object of discovering the objective principles which governed the creation of beauty.[1]

It is very otherwise with A.S. Dallas, whose most important work, published in two volumes in 1866, bears the reassuring title of *The Gay Science*. Dallas was born in Jamaica in 1828. As a young man he studied Philosophy at Edinburgh, under Sir William Hamilton, from whom he learned to apply psychology to the study of aesthetics. His first book, *Poetics, an essay in poetry* (1852) was a first draft for ideas which he developed fully in *The Gay Science*, but it has been remarked that it shows an acute and appreciative mind, scholarship, and a lively prose style, and is diversified with a wealth of anecdote, illustration, apt metaphor and shrewd incidental judgement. An article on criticism which he published in *The Times* revealed the same qualities, and Dallas became, and remained for many years, a member of *The Times* staff. He wrote fluently and accurately on politics, biography, criticism and other subjects. At the time of his death, in January 1879, he was preparing a new edition of the Maxims of La Rochefoucauld and his long essay on that subject is still unprinted. In addition to the two volumes of *The Gay Science* two others, dealing

---

[1] The last sentence of this paragraph (from 'Nor is there much…') seems to have been added in 1952. — Ed.

with the practical application of critical principles, were promised, but the first two were so poorly supported that the others were never written.

True criticism, Dallas contended, is threefold. It involves, first, the comparison of all the arts with one another, and a discussion of the common element which they are generally admitted to possess. Second, it involves a study of psychology, a comparison of all the arts with the nature of the mind, its intellectual structure, and its ethical needs. Third, it involves a comparison between the results thus obtained, and the facts of history, the influence of race, religion, and climate. 'The great fault of criticism is its ignorance — at least its disregard — of psychology.' Even Aristotle, for all his shrewd observation, provides no basis for a systematic criticism.

> His leading principle, which makes all poetry, all art, an imitation, is demonstrably false, has rendered his Poetics one-sided (a treatise not so much on poetry as on dramatic poetry) and has transmitted to all after criticism a sort of hereditary squint.

All ages have agreed that the aim of art is pleasure: the pleasure of imitation, said the Greeks. But the inadequacy of the Aristotelian conception was shown by the elder Scaliger: if all poetry is imitation, then prose is also imitation. The object of art is the pleasure of the beautiful, said the Germans; losing themselves in a cloud of transcendental tautologies. 'The beautiful,' says Hegel, 'is the perfect expression of the perfect idea — my grand idea of the absolute, in which contraries are at one, and the all is nothing.' The object of poetry is a pleasure of the Imagination, say English critics from Webbe to Johnson, using the word 'imagination' vaguely and ambiguously. History, science and poetry, says Bacon, are the products of memory, reason and imagination respectively. But in the account of our faculties given by Locke, and almost every other English psychologist down to Herbert Spencer, the imagination is disregarded. 'Imagination is the Proteus of the mind, and the despair of metaphysics.' Addison uses the term merely to describe the power of visualizing. The Germans pile confusion on confusion: Die Phantasie ist die Weltseele der Seele, und die Elementargeist der übrigen Kräfte. Coleridge is at his most portentous:

> The imagination I consider either as primary or secondary. The primary imagination I hold to be the living power and prime agent of all human perception, and as a repetition in the finite mind of the eternal act of creation in the infinite I AM. The secondary I consider as an echo of the former.

'Oh gentle shepherds,' cries Dallas, 'What does this mean? It reminds me of a splendid definition of art which I once heard: when the infinite I AM beheld His work of creation, he said Thou Art, and Art was.'

Dallas himself says that imagination or phantasy is a special function, not a special faculty, of the unconscious mind: 'It is a name given to the automatic action of the mind or any of its faculties — to what may not unfitly be called the Hidden Soul'. His object, he says, is not so much

> to identify imagination with what may be called the hidden soul, as to show that there is a mental existence within us which may be so called — a secret flow of thought which is not less energetic than the conscious flow, an absent mind which haunts us like a ghost or a dream and is an essential part of our lives. Incidentally there will be no escaping the observation that this unconscious life of the mind — this hidden soul — bears a wonderful resemblance to the supposed features of imagination.... To lay bare the automatic or unconscious action of the mind is indeed to unfold a tale which outvies the romances of giants and ginns, wizards in their palaces and captives in the Domdaniel roots of the sea.... The hidden efficacy of our thoughts, their prodigious power of working underhand, can be compared only to the stories of our folk-lore, and chiefly to that of the lubber-friend who toils for us when we are asleep or when we are not looking.

The concept of the 'unconscious mind' was not new; it had been recognized by Leibnitz, and in Germany the notion had already taken root and run to seed in the 'absurdities and extravagances' of the transcendental philosophy. More recently it had been resuscitated in more measured terms by Sir William Hamilton, John Stuart Mill, and Herbert Spencer. Dallas, however, was making a definite contribution to the theory. He summarizes the evidence for unconscious memory, and unconscious reasoning, but then adds: 'There is in the mind, as I shall afterwards have to show, a genuine creative process, over and above the seeming creativeness of unconscious memory'. Further he traces the relation of dreams and the unconscious: 'The realities of our hidden life are best seen in the darkness of slumber'. Indeed a *lack* of conscious effort seems to be necessary for the production of some works. 'If you think how you are to write,' said Mozart, 'you will never write anything worth hearing.'

Dallas did not, of course, completely forestall the psychoanalytic method: he did not explicitly enunciate the doctrines of transference and substitution; but he did see that the ways of the conscious mind can only be explained by assuming that it is sometimes fulfilling desires of which it is not aware, or is providing a substitute for those desires, and that the instincts often offer the plainest example of unconscious motives. He identifies the life of the unconscious mind with the inner life of the mystic as well as the inspiration of the poet.

> The great fact out of which it springs is the felt existence within us of an abounding inner life which transcends consciousness. We feel certain powers moving within us, we know not what; we know not why — instincts of our lower nature, intuitions of the higher, dreams and suggestions, dim guesses, and faint, far cries of the whole mind. There is a vast and manifold energy, spontaneously working in a manner which at once reminds us of Cuvier's definition of instinct as akin to somnambulism.

'All good poetry,' says Dallas, 'has a latency of meaning beyond the simple statement of facts,' and the similarity of the arts lies in the fact that they act directly on the unconscious to produce an effect not wholly described or accounted for by the conscious thought which they arouse: the scientific 'meaning' of Beethoven cannot be 'compared' with that of Shakespeare. If we attempt to interpret music we are trying to produce through another medium effects in the hidden mind similar to those which were produced by the original. The pleasure which the artist aims at giving arises from 'the quiet of the mind' but that quiet is not the quiet of inaction, but of harmony. Harmony itself may be indefinable, but we may nevertheless distinguish dynamic harmony and static. The former follows the contemplation of specifically dramatic effects, and corresponds to a mixed pleasure and a balance of conflicting emotions. As Dallas points out, we have no form of words which will rid us of this contradiction — that the contemplation and experience of pain may itself give rise to pleasure. Static harmony springs from the contemplation of things which are eternally and intrinsically beautiful: pure colours, straight and curved lines and the solids they generate, pure concords, and elegant theorems in mathematics, and all those objects whose absence is unfelt and painless but whose presence produces pleasure.

The effects of tragedy and comedy on the one hand, and 'pure beauty' on the other, are both legitimate objects of the artist. But there is a third, which is concerned not with the harmony of the will or of the conscious mind, but with the hidden soul. This third type Dallas calls 'the weird'; and the pleasure which it gives is neither the 'mixed pleasure' of comedy or tragedy, nor the 'pure pleasure' of impersonal beauty, but a specific excitement which is related directly to the hidden working of the mind, and is the essential mark of poetry and art. 'You can,' says Dallas, 'have great art which is dramatic, you can have great art which is not beautiful, but you cannot have great art which is not weird.'

This concern of art with the unconscious explains the relation of art and morality. Art, in so far as it is 'weird', is not consciously concerned with morality. In art, as in religious ceremony, the symbolism and the effect upon the unconscious mind are the most important elements. Some critics have rated the activity of the conscious mind above all human values, and there are moralists who value a circumspect and conscious rectitude more highly than a natural and instinctive virtue. 'The essence of life lies in thinking, and being conscious of one's soul,' says Matthew Arnold, translating the French writer, Joubert. 'In point of fact,' Dallas replies, 'it is out of a flourishing self-consciousness that suicide springs.' It has been observed that there are moments, indeed, when Dallas seems an earlier and less harassed D.H. Lawrence, as when he speaks contemptuously of 'the modern disease — excessive civilization and overstrained consciousness'. 'Intense consciousness,' he says, 'is the all-in-all of philosophy; therefore philosophers think it must be the all-in-all of life.' The method of Christianity, on the other hand, has often been to cherish impulse and to control the instinctive actions by the manipulations of the hidden soul; and, says Dallas, 'Art is so far like the religion of the Gospel, that it is not satisfied with that righteousness which is of the law, and which is called virtue. It would fain put love instead of law, and the sense of delight for that of duty.'

Poetry is thus the ethics of the unconscious. It operates through fictions, ideas which would be false, or meaningless, or inaccurate for any purpose other than that for which they were put forward. Similarly, the lines and points of the mathematicians, and the legal fictions of the constitution, are inapplicable except within the framework for which they were devised. Poetry is essentially religious in temper, even when it shows some doubt of current dogma. 'The poets whom we condemn for their scepticism,' says Dallas,

> saw before them but two types of theology — theology in the cold-blooded school of Paley, reduced to a system of clever contrivances, with springs and pulleys and most ingenious machinery; or theology in the more ardent school of the Wesleys and Whitefields, reduced to a system in which there was less of love and

> mercy than of hell and damnation. If thus in the earlier half of the century there flourished among us a misshapen theology, a clock-making theory of the universe which represented the Almighty as a sempiternal Sam Slick, hard of heart, but of infinite acuteness and softness of sawder, those are not wholly to be blamed who revolted against the creed because in their zeal they carried the revolt too far.

Dallas's significance can be best appreciated when his whole line of argument is set against Stanley Cursiter's bald statement (in his *Scottish Art*) that 'Imagination has played only a small part in the art of Scotland. Portrait painters, landscape painters, painters of *genre* and of history, we have had in plenty, but works of real imagination have been few.'

New life, Dallas contends, may have visited the Church, but the progress of the Church has been as nothing in comparison with the progress of the people. In the race between the press and pulpit, the pulpit has lost so much ground that it may even be said that the authors and journalists are now the true working clergy of the British Isles. Furthermore,

> the development of literature in our day — the new power which we possess of acting on the masses and of being acted on — has led and is leading to many changes, but none more important than the withering of the individual as hero, the elevation and reinforcement of the individual as private man.

In art, it marks the culmination of a change which has been in progress from the time of Greece. 'There was a time,' says Dallas,

> when we could draw a pretty clear line of demarcation between the private life and the public life — between private virtues and public virtues. Now the private virtues are becoming public, and the private life is rising into public importance. Publicity is the order of the day.

All this is influencing the intention and the method of the artist. 'It is curious,' says Dallas,

> that at the very moment when we are proclaiming that party is dead, and that henceforth we must no more consider men, but measures, the biographical element predominates in our literature, and in public life the personal overrides almost every other consideration. We are not only deluged with biographies of all sorts and conditions of men, women, and children, from the pet

> parson to the pet pugilist, and from Mr Bowen's three wives to the sweet infant who was perfect in lollypops and Dr Watts; we have biographies of horses, biographies of dogs, and everything is more or less regarded from the personal point of view.

To condemn these tendencies and struggle against them without tracing their causes is useless; but Dallas sees in them the symptoms of a widespread disease in the body politic. 'There is,' he says,

> a pregnant saying of Goethe's...that thought widens but lames; that action narrows but quickens. The individual feels how thought cripples him; the nation feels how discussion cripples it; and we are keenly sensitive to the lameness thus produced.

In the reaction against excessive intellectualism there is a demand for violent sensation. Literature becomes the study of the abnormal. In reaction against the brutality of the new commercial system there is an idealization of the weak and the incompetent; 'in modern literature,' as Dallas says, 'we have the same phenomenon — the weak and the foolish made much of, and treated as of equal accounts with demigods...And so thoughout the art of the day.'

I agree with an anonymous essayist who says:

> Against such disorder the work of Dallas stands as a dignified but ineffectual protest. He was concerned no less than modern writers with the relation of the individual and the mass, the life of the instincts and of the intellect, but he recognized that such critical work can take effect only when social conditions are in its favour and when it serves to crystallize opinions already widely but inarticulately held.

The two volumes of *The Gay Science* produced little effect in their own time, but they are still worth reading. In some of his opinions Dallas had been forestalled — his theory of poetry is essentially that of Shelley, for whom poetry was 'not subject to the control of the active powers of the mind' — but Dallas was remarkable not only for his outline of a psycho-analytic theory of art, but also for the acumen with which he observed and analysed the prevailing tendences of his age. Finally, the anonymous essayist says:

> It is not easy to judge the strongest undercurrents of our day, but in his obituary notices in *The Times* of Lord Minto, Metternich, Macaulay, Thackeray, and Palmerston, Dallas looked further ahead than most men. He foresaw the problems of democracy; and like Macaulay, he feared the crises 'in which it may be necessary to sacrifice even liberty to save civilization'.

As a practical critic, as a metaphysician, as a student of immediate politics, he may have been less important than Matthew Arnold, Walter Bagehot, John Stuart Mill; but in principles of criticism, and in general insight into modern political tendencies, his work is no less acute than theirs, and no less valuable today.

It may have been thought that in what I have said of the obsolescence and humbug of Scottish philosophic writings I have implied that these can safely be disregarded now and need not be read. Nothing can be further from my contention. They must be read if only as a clue to thoughts and feelings still widely prevalent amongst our people although under a variety of disguises nowadays which may make it difficult to identify them with these earlier manifestations. Again careful study of them may help us from falling into similar traps. But above all with our new resources of interpretation we can also find fresh and useful meanings in much that taken in its conventional acceptation would be hopelessly out-of-date. Scottish artists have not written much. They have been unfortunately free from the habit of issuing manifestoes. Few of even the most interesting of them have been Boswellized at all. There are scanty records of their conversations. Yet it is surprising how much could be drawn from their autobiographies, biographies, letters, and occasional writings. That has yet to be done. In passing I will only give one or two illustrations of what may be come upon in even the most out-of-the-way quarters of our national literature. Sir R.G. Stapledon in his book on *Ley Farming* shows how the results of the most recent experimentation in this matter were anticipated long ago by Aberdeenshire farmers and refers to the valuable material to be found in books and articles written by these men and long lost sight of. In the same way discoveries are to be made in old literature in matters of art. At a time when there is a tendency to dismiss modernist artists with a jeering comment that they haven't even begun to learn how to draw properly and an insistence in many quarters on thorough training, it is, I think, useful, or at least entertaining to come across a description of a well-known artist's actual methods and to reflect that the slap-dash paint-pot-flinging ways ascribed to certain experimentalists today are by no means so new as is generally imagined. I cull the following from a little book entitled *Reminiscences of Eighty Years* by John Urie, published in Paisley in 1908. 'It was about this time,' he says,

> that I first came into contact with Sam Bough, the famous artist. A great burly bearded fellow, speaking with a broad Lancashire

> accent, Sam was a rough diamond — but a diamond he was, and no mistake. There was nothing about him that was not genuine. When I first knew him he had just given up his job as a scene painter at the theatre, and was painting scenes and doing other pot-boiler work. But the mark of his genius was on all his pictures, and it was not long after this till his art brought him both fame and fortune. I had frequently seen Sam at the Garrick Club, sitting with a pint of beer and a long clay pipe, before I had the opportunity of speaking to him. Sam had been painting a panorama entitled 'The Overland Mail to India', which was to be exhibited in the City Hall. The man who was to run the show came to me and wanted me to prepare some wood engravings of the scenes for advertisement purposes. I asked him how I was to get them, and he told me to go along to a certain address in Bath Street and Mr Bough would let me know how he wanted them done. I accordingly went up to the address and knocked at the half-open door. The big cheery voice of Sam bade me enter. On pushing the door open I saw the floor covered with a piece of canvas. The artist, with a pot of paint in one hand and a brush in the other, was walking over the canvas, giving a swish here and a splash there at what seemed a chaotic mess of paint. I said, 'I am afraid I will spoil your picture!' 'Not at all,' he said, 'Come in; you will just give it a little extra effect!' I remember afterwards going to the City Hall to see that panorama, and being amazed at the wonderfully fine effect produced by what at close quarters seemed exceedingly rough work. Once when Sam Bough was painting a scene illustrating 'The Lady of the Lake' for the Theatre Royal, Mr Glover came into the room. 'Sam, Sam, that won't do,' he exclaimed. 'Won't it,' answered Sam, 'Then how will this do?' and he dashed a pail of whitewash on the picture. Mr Glover fled in hot haste but a few touches of Sam's deft brush turned the mass of whitewash into a foaming cataract. Sam Bough was a remarkably quick worker. I have seen him set up a number of pieces of cardboard, and then go round them, making a dash with his brush at each in succession. In this way he rapidly sketched at the same time half-a-dozen different pictures in less time than an ordinary man would have taken to paint one.

I was delighted the other day when I found a companion piece to that description of Mr Urie's. It refers to the sardonic creations of Edward Burra, with particular reference to his picture 'Gorbals, Glasgow', painted years before Burra did his famous design for

Arthur Bliss's ballet, *Miracle in the Gorbals*. The technique for these diabolical incantations, I learned, is simply to lie down on the floor with a pencil in your claw-like hand covering sheets of cartridge-paper with meticulous drawings which you afterwards reinforce, still on the floor, with water-colour. If the paper isn't big enough you simply pin the separate sheets together.

Whistler's mother, Anna MacNeil Whistler, was a Scotswoman, and in Elizabeth Mumford's biography of her, published in 1940, I was interested to come across the following passage which brings out so clearly the Gaelic spirit in her. 'She had,' says Miss Mumford, 'a kind of aesthetic craving for perfection in her everyday life that came out in her son's passion for art in its purest essence; and if he arrived at his ideal by eliminating unessential detail, she approached hers by finding no detail unessential.' As soon as I read that I recalled how John Tonge writing on 'Charles Rennie Mackintosh, Celtic Innovator', in *The Scottish Arts Review*, had remarked that

> for most historians he is the master of *Jugendstil*, above all the *Innenarchitekt* who, agreeing with Muthesius that 'a room should be a work of art in itself, not the result of artistically worked pieces joined together', designed everything from the front-door handle to the contents of the cutlery canteen.

While the genius of Mackintosh and his great influence on modernist developments in architecture have now been widely recognized, it is typical of the tremendous amount of study and critical examination that remains to be undertaken in every aspect of Scottish art — as in all other spheres of Scottish life — that his work raises big questions in certain directions which are far from settled. Mr Thomas Howarth, who has recently lectured and broadcast a good deal on Mackintosh, sums up this divided character of his achievement when he says:

> Mackintosh is now acclaimed a pioneer of the modern movement in architecture and the decorative arts. He remains, nevertheless, something of an enigma — the man largely responsible for an abortive outburst of *art nouveau*, a designer of tea-rooms and of absurdly high-backed chairs; and yet one who appears to have held in his hand the key to modern architecture.

In his range of reference and brilliance of unexpected but convincing analogies, and comparisons and cross references drawn from all the fields of human thought and activity, the ecological approach of which I have spoken — the taking in of all the connections between works of art and the thought, history, and physical features of a country — is shown by Mr Ian Finlay as clearly as by Mr Tonge. Mr Finlay always considers a work of art in relation to the life and ideas of its time — and in relation, too, to the minor crafts. Examining Raeburn's 'Macdonell of Glengarry', for instance, he makes use of the fact that the pistols are English-made in order to emphasize the decline of Celtic Art after the Jacobite risings. He points out the connection between the Highland evictions and Horatio MacCulloch's grandiose landscapes, and between the creative vigour of Glasgow's industrialists and their support of the Glasgow School. There is a particularly brilliant juxtaposition of George Henry's 'Galloway Landscape' and the fifth-century Burghead Bull, with the same flowing rhythm perceptible in each.

Other contemporary Scottish writers who are doing the same sort of thing are Mr Robert Melville, Mr John Grierson in his writings on the documentary film and on the arts of the cinema in general, Mr William Power in an interesting book in which he correlates Scottish literature and painting with the landscape — and when the restless and dynamic character of Scottish painting compared with English is being discussed it is certainly necessary to remember with Dr Henry Meikle how sharp the transitions in Scottish scenery are, and what astonishing diversity our country packs into even the smallest regions.

It should always be borne in mind that while it is true, as a recent writer has said, that 'twenty-five years after a book has been published is an awkward age, at which unintended "period effects" begin to show themselves, and when ideas have been aired long enough for some of them to have gone bad', and most of the books on the Scottish aesthetic philosophers are much older than that, and have suffered far more from that kind of deterioration, so that only a very few elements in any of them retain any useful applicability today, it is also true that after such a passage of time they acquire other values in comparison with today's fashions in exposition, criticism, and taste, which may make them a useful corrective or standard of comparison. It is a very great mistake to allow an excessive contemporaneity to make us contemptuous of or indifferent to the very different standards of previous periods. There is also the fact — and this is especially true of a country like Scotland where the national tradition has been hopelessly fragmented or driven underground and very few people, if any, possess a complete knowledge of it, that the kind of reading I am recommending is likely to bring to light again all sorts of people of whom sight has been undeservedly lost and who ought to be kept in mind and esteemed at their true worth. There is, for example, although his tribute is too highly-pitched, a great deal of truth in what Mr Millar in his *Literary History of Scotland* says of a man of whom I suspect exceedingly few people today have ever heard at all, namely R.L. Stevenson's cousin, Robert Alan Mowbray Stevenson (1847-1900), the 'Spring-heel'd Jack' of R.L.S.'s *Memories and Portraits*, and, *omnium consensu*, a master of the art of conversation. W.E. Henley's account of him, published in the *Pall Mall Magazine* of July, 1900, is well worth hunting out and reading. 'Bob Stevenson,' says Millar,

> was anything rather than an easy or prolific writer. But when he did write, it was to some effect, for he wrote exclusively on the subject he knew best and had most at heart — pictorial and plastic art. An essay on Rubens, an all-too-brief treatise on *The Art of Velasquez*, published in 1895 and reprinted with some additions under the title of *Velasquez* in 1899, and the letterpress for Mr Pennell's *Devils of Notre Dame* (1894) comprise the whole of his work that is accessible or that is not fragmentary. Yet small as is its bulk, its value is inestimable. The critic is never pugnacious or provocative; but what he conceives to be error is rebuked and refuted the more forcibly for the calmness and dignity of his manner. Here you feel instinctively is a man who really cares for painting *qua* painting, and not merely because he can connect it with some sentiment or anecdote or can deduce from it some moral lesson. To pass from Mr Ruskin to Mr Stevenson is to pass from thick darkness, illuminated by dazzling flashes of rhetoric, into the peaceful radiance of a summer's morning and a clear sky. What was revolutionary doctrine when Mr Stevenson commenced critic is probably rigid orthodoxy now. Rarely do we hear Rembrandt or Rubens or Velasquez denounced as 'lost souls'. The tombs of the prophets have been piously ornamented by those who would have been the first to stone them; and the President of the Royal Academy is fain to admit that Alfred Stevens was an eminent sculptor. This may not mean very much; and the traditions of two or three generations are not easily subverted. But if the art-criticism of today is, upon the whole, more intelligent than the art criticism of twenty or thirty years ago — less dull, less perverse, less obstinately blind — it is perhaps to R.A.M. Stevenson more than to any other single man that the improvement, such as it is, must be ascribed.

A recent talk in the Third Programme by Mr John Steegman on 'The Eastlakes and Lord Lindsay' recalled another nineteenth-century Scotsman, who deserves to be given his place in such a survey, namely Lord Lindsay, who later became the 25th Earl of Crawford. As Mr Steegman said:

> He is one of the most important of the writers on art in the immediately pre-Ruskin generation, though he is hardly ever read today. Lindsay's great work was his three-volume *History of Christian Art* published in 1847. It is in fact a history of art from the early years of the Byzantine Empire, in the sixth century AD down to the High Renaissance. Calling it a history of *Christian* art was bound to excite controversy, at that particular time, and of course it did: there were attacks on it from the strictly Protestant historians such as Palgrave; from Ruskin to whom at that time the term 'Christian' inevitably implied a hatred of Rome; from those who regarded Renaissance Art as Pagan and not Christian at all; and from those who regarded pre-Renaissance art as merely barbarous. The work, however, was widely accepted as the great achievement which it undoubtedly was. To us it reveals Lindsay as being in the small advance-guard of critics beginning to understand and love the Early Masters. When he stated, for instance, that the fountain-head of all Florentine art was Giotto, he effected a revolution in criticism by putting back that source from its previously accepted place at the end of the fifteenth century to the end of the thirteenth. In another direction Lindsay took a far more seriously considered view of Byzantine art and civilization than was then generally held.

Reference should also be made here to another great Scottish virtuoso — Sir William Stirling Maxwell (1818-1878) whose works, including *Annals of the Artists of Spain*, published in 1848, and whose collection, including works by El Greco and Blake, is still to be found in Pollok House.

In another Third Programme talk, on Palladianism in England, this time by Professor Wittkower, the Durning-Lawrence Professor in the History of Art at London University, we were reminded of two other Scots of whom perhaps we know too little. 'The genesis of this eighteenth-century Palladianism is well known to us,' said Professor Wittkower.

> The crucial year was 1715. In that year appeared in London the first volume of Colin Campbell's *Vitruvius Britannicus* as well as the first instalment of Giacomo Leoni's English edition of Palladio's book on architecture. In their prefaces both Campbell and

> Leoni pay tribute to the genius of Palladio. Campbell attacked the licentiousness and extravagance of the Italian baroque and singled out the great Palladio who has exceeded all that were gone before him and surpassed his contemporaries.

'And indeed,' he continues, 'this excellent Architect seems to have arrived at a *ne plus ultra* of his art. With him the great Manner and exquisite Taste of Building is lost.' Colin Campbell went from Scotland to London, perhaps in 1712 or 1713. His age, as well as his Scottish beginnings are shrouded in mystery, but Professer Wittkower adduces facts to show that the old and often repeated legend of Lord Burlington as patron of Campbell's work as well as Leoni's must be dismissed.

> Burlington House was the first building of the new style in London. It opens an architectural era which, one can safely say, changed the face of England. But in spite of careful research into the history of Burlington House, some questions have so far evaded solution. The mention of the rebuilding in Gay's *Trivia* is proof that the new structure was well under way in 1715. The architect in charge was James Gibb — another Scotsman, an Aberdonian who had studied under Fontana in Rome, and who designed St Mary-le-Strand, St Peter's Vere St., and St Martin-in-the-Fields; part of the Senate House and of King's College, Cambridge; the monuments of Ben Jonson, Prior, and Newcastle in Westminster Abbey; the quadrangle of St Bartholomew's Hospital, and the Radcliffe Library, Oxford, as well as publishing several books on architecture and translating foreign books on the subject. Gibb however did not proceed very far with Burlington House. It would appear that Burlington first took him on as the architect who had the best Italian schooling and who, having recently returned from Italy (in 1709) after a long stay in Rome, would build for him something thoroughly Italian. But after the publication of the first volume of *Vitruvius Britannicus*, the Earl, suddenly converted to Palladianism, switched over to Campbell, leaving only the execution of the forecourt in Gibb's hands. Colin Campbell erected some of the most important neo-Palladian buildings between 1715 and his premature death in 1729. His first great country house commission was Wanstead House, built between 1715 and 1720, and demolished in 1822. The commission from the Prime Minister, Sir Robert Walpole, for Houghton followed in 1722. From Houghton onwards the most important country house commissions went to the Burlingtonians.

> Campbell himself built Mereworth Castle in Kent between 1723 and 1725 in close analogy to Palladio's celebrated Villa Rotonda. When the second half of the century opened most architects of the Burlington group were dead or in retirement. The stars of William Chambers and Robert Adam (two other Scots whose names remain better known) were rising, and neo-Palladianism as an architectural style was succeeded by neo-Roman, neo-Greek, and neo-Gothic tendencies.

I would also mention the French philosopher, Professor Denis Saurat's article 'Scottish Intellectualism: William Johnstone' which appeared in *The Studio* of August, 1943 and discussed the work and ideas of Mr Johnstone, a Scottish artist, who has published two books, *Creative Art In England* and *Child Art to Man Art*. Since Scotland lacks a centre and shows no thrift in dealing with its men of talent but disperses them to the ends of the earth and fails to claim them and build their achievements into the records of our national accomplishment, it is excessively difficult to get an all-in view. I imagine that it will come as a surprise, for example, to be reminded that Lady Mendl — Miss Elsie de Wolfe — the great international de luxe decorator of millionaires' mansions had a Scottish mother, Georgina Copeland, the daughter of a chaplain at Balmoral.

> One of the last big American places she decorated was Gary Cooper's at Brentwood, California. Here the Elsie-de-Wolfe — Lady Mendl modern style is as recognizable as a signature, with its dramatic use of black and white, Zebra skins, Venetian starred mirrors, and its cardinal colours in upholstery against near-white walls or near-white upholstery against coloured walls. In the summer of 1936 she came again into the decorating news when it was reported that she was about to modernise Buckingham Palace for King Edward VIII. This she denied, stating that she had merely executed models, which had pleased His Majesty, for the redecoration of three rooms at Fort Belvedere. The official entertaining by Sir Charles and Lady Mendl is done in her Paris flat on the Avenue d'Iena, which is a sumptuous formal residence. Its salon is decorated with fine pieces of the French haute epoque. There are excellent boiseries throughout; chairs, signed by Cressent, covered with sixteenth-century blue velvet, and a small highly personal collection of eighteenth-century *grisailles* and wash drawings by Boucher, Watteau, Fragonard and Carmontelle. Her Villa Trianon, however, is her real pride. Its property deed, dated 1750, reserves a right-of-way for all time for the King of France.

Lady Mendl spent thirty years and a considerable fortune restoring the place, which had formerly belong to King Louis-Philippe's son, the Duc de Nemours and she made it a model of perfection in period furnishings, terraces, gardens, and the landscape perspectives so precious to the old French ideal. The Savonnerie carpets, the Louis XV marquetry, General Murat's iron camp bed, a Clodion nymph and faun, and copies of the famous Mille Graces curtains (whose originals she possessed till they dropped to dust) are some of the house treasures. I should not be surprised to learn that Miss Elsa Maxwell is half-Scottish too.

I would like to refer also before I close to Sir Eric MacLagan's Memorial Service tribute to D.S. MacColl, 1858-1948. 'As of Browning's poet,' said Sir Eric,

it may truly be claimed that MacColl lived 'through a whole campaign of the world's life and death'. Never has a man plunged with greater gusto into controversy. London is dotted with his battlefields — St Paul's, Westminster Abbey, the Royal Academy, the Tate Gallery, Waterloo Bridge — not all of them, alas!, scenes of victory. And his opponents, even when they were skilled masters of fence like Roger Fry, could hardly have denied that his sword was as formidable as his nose. He often fought on the friendliest of terms; I remember him saying to me some twenty-five years ago, when he proposed to attack an acquisition of which I think we were justly proud at the Victoria and Albert Museum: 'You won't mind me alluding to your new bust as an unclean bird's nest'. But his convictions were theologically adamantine; he was not a son of the manse for nothing, though he carried his passionate orthodoxy and his heresy-hunting into another field. On some subjects, such as English prosody, he would hardly admit that anyone else was to be saved; like the legendary Scottish lady, he had his doubts about John. 'MacColl, you're too dialectic,' were the last words his friend Tonks spoke to him — indeed he is said to have expressed himself more strongly still, viz. 'If MacColl met God Almighty, he would criticize Him to His face'. Generous as his admirations were, criticism was certainly his first instinctive reaction, and it was with pardonable exaggeration that Robbie Ross once suggested: 'MacColl loves art so much that he hates all works of art'. Yet when he did applaud he applauded with his whole-heart, and it is now fifty years since the great Glasgow Exhibition of 1900 gave him the opportunity to open the eyes of a whole generation, to the glories of the French Impressionist

School. We remember him for such characteristics as these; but we remember him too as a painter whose sensitive water-colours won the praise of artists whom he acknowledged as his betters — and that was the praise he really cared to win; as a poet, ranging from the uproariously comic to grave and solemn harmonies that were all his own; as a critic whose main fault was that he wrote far too little. We remember him as the head of two great London galleries, a colleague whose work was an inspiration to many younger men; and as one who played no small part in the creation of the New English Art Club and the National Art Collections Fund and the Contemporary Art Society. But most of all we remember him here as a friend; friend of many great men who have gone before him into another world, and of whom he had so much to tell us, Beardsley and Conder and Bob Stevenson, York Powell and W.P. Ker and Oliver Elton, and in a later vintage Tonks and Rothenstein and Wilson Steer... It is that larger assembly of the dead whom MacColl himself has now joined, the last, one would say, of a mighty generation, his own life prolonged beyond any normal span of years.... And he has left us too his message. In the words with which only a year or two ago he concluded his book on Wilson Steer: 'The battles of Beauty are never finally won; in each generation they must be fought afresh; it depends upon a few voices in each of them whether Titian counts as a master. Let us not be missing among "Knights of the Holy Ghost".' From the roll of that order the name of Dugald Sutherland MacColl is not absent; in it he lived and fought and died; may he rest in peace.

Another implacable fighter whose autobiography and correspondence — both of which he was preparing for publication before he died — was the sculptor, James Pittendrigh MacGillivray, whose colleagues in the Glasgow School had good reason to distort his surname into MacDevilry! I do not know what happened to his papers, but he figured in many famous rows, and compiled racy accounts of them. I hope they may yet be published, and add another notable volume to the all-too-few records of the sort that have been penned by Scottish artists — a companion volume, by a man of very different temper, to Sir John Lavery's autobiography, *The Life of a Painter*, published in 1940, and telling of his Glasgow days, when he was without board or lodging, sleeping on benches in Glasgow Green, picking up food that had been thrown away, and washing in the fountains when daylight came.

In conclusion, I want to say that I agree with Herbert Read when he says:

> It is the practical men of affairs who have solved the problems of art. It is the engineers who built the Forth Bridge and the Crystal Palace, who have more recently evolved the form of the automobile and the aeroplane, who first unconsciously suggested the elements of a new aesthetic... a new tradition, based on practical realities, was formed.

In commenting on this Mr Ian Finlay quotes something I wrote over twenty years ago, as follows:

> What has taken place in Scotland up to the present is that our best constructive minds have taken up engineering and only sentimentalists have practised art. We are largely (the world has assessed us rightly) a nation of engineers. Let us realize that a man may still be an engineer and yet concerned with a picture conceived purely as a kind of engine which has a different kind of functional power to an engine in the ordinary sense of the term. Here then is what we Scots have — a terrific vitality combined with a constructive ability unequalled by any other nation. What more do we need? — merely sufficient analytical power to clear away the maze of sentimentality and accepted 'artistic' values which obscure our ideas of Art.

All the things by which Scotland has captured the world without losing its own soul, have been its most indigenous, exclusive and inimitable things. I mean on different levels such things as Scotch whisky, our tartans, our traditional Scottish dances, and our pipe-music. True some of these are still inadequately or wrongly appreciated. Piping, for instance, not only amongst foreigners, but amongst most of our own people knowledge of piping is limited to strathspeys and military marches and to 'smart fingering' and far too little is known of one of the greatest glories of Scotland, the *Piobaireachd*. All that means is that there is in these matters room to grow — room for creative developments, better informed appreciation, and fundamental exposition.

I mention the value of these peculiarly native things which carry both the credit and the cash — they are among our greatest dollar earners — not only for that reason, but because I do not think there can be any better description of any work of very high artistic value in any medium than just to be able to say of it with truth that it is *mar a tha e* as good whisky is — a Gaelic phrase meaning not only neat, clear-run, pure, or, in Rainer Maria Rilke's words, 'filled with itself alone', but meaning all that is meant by achieving artistic unity. It is, however, in another homely illustration here in Glasgow with its great tradition of shipbuilding that I think I can come still closer to a definition of what we mean by art and should strive for and look for in all creative productions submitted to our judgement. No one has ever been able satisfactorily to explain — probably no one ever will be — the exact nature of that subtle process by which some man-made structure of iron, wood, or steel, is changed from a mere mass of inanimate and unresponsive matter into a thing with a character, a disposition, almost a personality of its own. Yet that some such transformation does sometimes occur cannot be denied explanation apart — most frequently, perhaps, where its subject is a ship. More than one notable instance come readily enough to the mind. The Cutty Sark had that quality of personality. The Thermopylae had it. The Mauretania — for it is by no means confined to sailing craft — had it, while the Lusitania had not, though they were like as two peas from one pod. The Queen Mary probably has it, though she has not yet had quite time enough to prove it in her sea-going career. And in her own particular class the King's Britannia — as her skipper, Commander Irving, aptly termed the famous old cutter in the book he wrote about it — possessed it as possibly no other yacht, large or small, has ever done. Of course in large part she owed her popularity, a popularity which extended far beyond the ranks of those usually interested in the technicalities of yacht design and racing, to her Royal ownership. But that by no means accounts for the quality with which I am concerned. One July day in 1936, forty-three years after she left the Clyde waters whence so many of the great 'personality' ships, both sail and steam, have come, she was launched once more from the ways at Cowes for the last time. 'Requiescat Britannia! Your memory will live.' Assuredly the remembrance of the great old cutter is one which a far wider world than the inner circles of yachting will not willingly let die. Just that capacity for a man's work to leave his hands and sustain a 'life' of its own is what is required of anything that deserves the name of a work of art, and if we Scots can achieve it in shipbuilding and engineering, we ought to be able with a very slight alteration of the direction of our energies, just the matter of putting the emphasis in a different quarter, to do it in painting and sculpture too.

The Scottish dichotomy between experience and consciousness — the dissociation in our midst between energy and sensibility, between conduct and theories of conduct, between life conceived as an opportunity and life conceived as a discipline — cannot be healed in the Edinburgh Festival way. Our national culture suffers from all the ills of split personality. The Edinburgh Festival's high prices excluding most of our people, together with its importation of foreign arts and artists and the virtual exclusion of our own, simply accentuate this schizophrenia. The dissociation of mind from experience in our midst has resulted in truncated works of art, works that tend to be either naive and ungraded, often flat, reproductions of life, or else products of cultivation that remain abstract because they fall short on evidence drawn from the sensuous and material world. It would seem now that some of our better-off people, in compensation for backward cultural conditions and a lost religious ethic, are developing or pretending to develop through this Festival a supreme talent for refinement just as a certain type of Jew, in compensation for adverse social conditions and a lost national independence, developed a supreme talent for cleverness. The one must inevitably be as flashy and meretricious as the other has been. This peculiar excess of refinement is bad in these Edinburgh Festival patrons, and not to be equated with the refinement of artists like Proust and Thomas Mann, as in the latter it is not — as it is in the former — an element contradicting an open and bold confrontation of reality. The explanation of the commodity-fetishistic attitude behind these Festival programmes is not difficult to discern. Artemus Ward wrote that 'the Tower of London is very popular with people from the agricultural districts'. In the same way the Edinburgh Festival is very popular with our cultural provincials. Its borrowed plumes are designed to dazzle our wealthier yokels.

In what I have said of engineering and the possibility of a redirection of our principal aptitudes into modern artistic channels lies perhaps our best chance of development today. However that may be, let me summarize the actual aesthetic position of Scotland up to the present date. The distressing thing about early Scottish aestheticians has been their poor fruits. Their immediate successors were more arbiters of good taste than philosophers. As philosophy in Scotland came more and more to mean only Moral Philosophy, the divorce between artist and thinker became more complete than ever, and when the revival of aesthetic studies came on the Continent Scotland had no equivalent, however small, of Baudelaire, Hanslick, or even Pater. From the consequences of that we still suffer.

The Scottish artist has had little time for aesthetics, sometimes to his advantage sometimes not. There is the letter Sir Walter Scott wrote to the Duke of Buccleuch when asked to look over some paintings belonging to Stuart of Dunearn. After studying the most important, Hobbema's 'Avenue at Middelharnis', Scott decided it was

> fitter for an artist's studio than a nobleman's collection. Your Grace may be reconciled to it by the figure of a shooter and a Spanish pointer who are coming down the road in quest of waterfowl. It is the last thing I would buy for my own taste.

In the practice of the arts, the Scot has tended to eschew aesthetic theories, has usually been content to be a traditionalist like Burns, and always at his best has been a realist. Theories of painting up to a century ago hardly affected Scottish painting. John Pope-Hennesay said at the time of the Burlington House Exhibition of Scottish Art (1938) that of the 550-odd paintings in the Exhibition 'a bare dozen make any predominantly aesthetic appeal', but by 'its healthy philistinism' Scottish painting 'had escaped the hideous falsity of much English painting'. Realism, in that statement, would have been a better word than 'philistinism'. The achievements of Scottish painting have all owed much to realism — Gesses's grand portraits, Ramsay at his best (his prettinesses have blinded people to his asperities), the wonderful intimacy with his sitters that enabled Raeburn (so little an aesthetic painter compared to Reynolds) to overcome great technical shortcomings, the brand of impressionism to which McTaggart came by way of realism. On the other hand, the Italianate classicisers of the eighteenth century and the romanticists of the nineteenth (such as the pathetically Anglicized Wilkie) never pulled their proper weight.

This realistic tradition of the Scot is obscured when Scottish art is considered as part of English art (as when Lord David Cecil recently ranked Scott as a great historical novelist and then proceeded to praise him above all for characters like Jeannie Deans and Edie the old beggar, who to Scott were not history but real people!). This realism has, of course, often, too often, become mere matter-of-factness, incapable of being a vehicle of the imagination, of rising to heights of realistic fantasy. And when Scottish painting became aesthetic, the Glasgow painters, rebelling against the matter-of-factness and its complementary sentimentality, fell for mere decoration. Now MacBryde and Colquhoun have won through Cubism to a new realism combined with deep emotional content and in this way can be reckoned traditionalists.

This takes us far enough away from the Scottish aestheticians who are my concern. It would require careful research to determine to what extent the Rule of Taste that prevailed by the time of Blair and Christopher North was, like other rules of the time, English rule. The philosophical movement that produced Hume's 'Of the Standard of Taste', Alison's 'On the Nature of Taste' and so on sprang from much deeper sources than the latter-day good taste of the bourgeoisie. ('On the credit side, no good taste is anywhere discernible', said Wyndham Lewis of Léger the other week.) It is to Hume, of course, that most importance must be attached. The decline within the next century was catastrophic. Just as philosophic poverty is reflected in Scottish political thinking, the neglect of aesthetic studies is evident every day in what passes in Scotland for criticism. How many averagely-educated Scots can speak intelligently (as a Frenchman might) of, say, the differences between Celtic art and post-Reformation art, between the Old Town of Edinburgh and the New, between the ballad of Gil Morrice and the *Douglas* Home derived from it, between a pibroch and a hymn, between an English pre-Raphaelite and a Scottish genre-painter.

It's not just an academic issue. Clearly, for example, political and other expediencies determine that James Bridie and Eric Linklater will be produced at the Edinburgh Festival, instead of Ewan MacColl and Robert McLellan; but how have the pundits decided on Home's *Douglas*? In the past day or two I've heard the play dismissed as trash and praised to the skies, but not a single comment indicating a real awareness of its kind, its excellence or otherwise of its kind, the place of its kind in Scottish literature, and the desirability of considering carefully what future that kind can and should have in comparison with other kinds in relation to the future of Scottish drama.[2]

*

Since the above was written there have been considerable developments in the arts in Scotland, but few of these have been Scottish and most of them negative. By the last-named I mean that recrudescence of philistinism that has characterized public discussion of the Edinburgh Festival programmes, and to a considerable extent also public criticism of sound radio and TV programmes — almost always opposed in the crudest way to new and experimental work, and dominated by the vociferations of purblind members of the Moral

[2] The 1950 typescript ends here, but with rather different final sentences: 'In the past day or two I've heard the play dismissed as trash and praised to the skies, but not a single comment indicating a real awareness of its kind, its excellence or otherwise of its kind, the place of its kind in Scottish literature, and the desirability or otherwise of encouraging that kind. We are a breed of critical simpletons.' — Ed.

Rearmament Movement. In all of this little indigenous Scottish work has been involved — though developments of abstract painting have shared in this orgy of vicious disapproval. The establishment of a Gallery of Modern Art in the Botanic Gardens, Edinburgh, has hardly helped matters, since the Scottish element included is extremely small. There has nowhere yet been a thorough cleansing of the Augean Stables, and the appearance in the Scottish Press and other quarters of new writers on Aesthetics, concerned with the Scottish position in the arts, has so far been very sporadic and partial. Even an admirable innovation like the Traverse Theatre Club in Edinburgh has relied mainly on kinds of work not yet — or ever likely to be — naturalized in Scotland; the folk-song movement is bogged down in senseless repetition and a hopelessly sentimental attitude to an irrecoverable past, and only occasionally shows signs of coming alive in our own time and addressing itself effectively to current issues, as in some of the admirable anti-Polaris songs of Thurso Berwick and his friends, and the earlier achievements of like kind occasioned by the Coronation Stone episode. In the articles of *The Scotsman* drama critic, Mr Ronald Mavor (son of the dramatist, 'James Bridie'), in the propaganda for realism of Alan Bold and his artist friends in *Rocket*, in the continued writings of William Johnstone and William McCance, there are signs of a genuine advance, but these are still very fragmentary and of little effect in offsetting the general Philistinism. Worst of all is the continued absence of competent modern philosophizing in Scotland, and above all the absence of aesthetic thought of any such value as might realign Scotland with other Western European countries and induce aesthetic developments based on Scottish roots and yet able to withstand comparison with the contemporary aesthetic thought of other countries. The omens are not auspicious. All we can hope for, it would seem, is, as in the past, an occasional voice crying in the wilderness, while the increased facilities given by the great increase of public leisure and affluence, the easier access of foreign arts of all kinds, the work of the Scottish Committee of the Arts Council and of the BBC and BBC-TV in Scotland lead only to a monstrous babble of incompetence as in the 'Arts Review' feature of the Scottish Home Service of the BBC and to only a slightly less appalling state of affairs in the 'Scottish Life and Letters' Programmes of the same body.[3]

---

3 The final paragraph was probably added in 1965. — Ed.

Cunninghame Graham:
a centenary study

Foreword

Although as a young man the writer of this Foreword spent several years in the Argentine and Uruguayan Republics about the same time as the subject of this biography, R.B. Cunninghame Graham, who also spent many years in South America amongst the Gauchos, roaming over the Argentine Pampas enjoying the care-free life of an Estanciero, it was after the first world war ended that the writer came into personal contact with that remarkable Scot, a traveller, writer, and socialist propagandist, and latterly a full blooded Scottish Nationalist. It was in Glasgow as a result of some talks with him that he expressed his desire to join the Scottish Home Rule Association and he did so in August, 1920. Although Cunninghame Graham had been a member of the earlier Scottish Home Rule Association which had been established in 1886, it was not until he joined the second Scottish Home Rule Association, of which the writer was Hon Secretary, that he took an active interest in the movement for Scottish self-government. Soon after he became a member he was elected President of the SHRA and although he spent much of his time travelling abroad, he was usually able to attend Wallace Day Commemorations at Elderslie as well as the Scotland's Day functions held in the King's Park, Stirling on the anniversary of the Battle of Bannockburn. During several years before the National Party of Scotland was formed he spoke at Elderslie. Speaking in 1925 at the Wallace Day Commemoration he commenced by saying,

> Friends, Fellow-Scotsmen, we are assembled here today to celebrate the 620th anniversary of the martyrdom of William Wallace. Six hundred and twenty years ago Wallace laid down his life for the cause of Scottish Home Rule. Six hundred and twenty years is a considerable interval to wait for the crowning of his work. Until we have Scottish Home Rule in a Scottish Parliament in Edinburgh we may say in a measure that the work has been left unfulfilled and that it wants a coping stone.

In 1928 the National Party of Scotland was formed by the Scottish Home Rule Association, the Scots National League and the Scottish National Movement joining together under the title of the National Party of Scotland. Cunninghame Graham was elected President. The following year, 1929, at a by-election in North Midlothian where for the first time a Scottish National candidate stood, Cunninghame Graham gave good assistance, speaking at several meetings. During the same year Cunninghame Graham stood as a Scottish Nationalist candidate at the Glasgow University Rectorial Election. Although Mr Stanley Baldwin the Prime Minister won by a few votes, the majority of male students supported Cunninghame Graham. It was really a great moral victory for the Scottish National candidate, and for Scottish Nationalism. Cunninghame Graham speaking at the Wallace celebration at Elderslie in 1932 giving his views on the form Scottish Home Rule should take, said,

> I would repeal the Union, then I would make a solemn declaration of Scottish sovereignty, and in the third place I would enter into a Treaty with England, the terms would be arranged by High Commissioners, by two contracting parties;

and he proceeded,

> Scotland should have her own territorial force and her ships to protect her fisheries on the sea. She should also have her own coinage, and her own postage stamps and be able to send ambassadors in the same way as Southern Ireland does to foreign Courts.

At the 1933 Wallace anniversary at Elderslie Cunninghame Graham brought as Guest of honour the Spanish Ambassador Don Ramon Perez de Ayala and his wife. Cunninghame Graham told of the singular circumstances of the Spanish Ambassador's visit. The first Ambassador from Spain to Scotland bore the same name as today's visitor, he was Don Pedro de Perez, Spanish Representative at the Court of King James the Fourth of Scotland. Mr Cunninghame Graham paid a tribute to the young and flourishing Spanish Republic which he said was showing her determination to put herself in her rightful position as one of the great nations of Europe.

In the following year, 1934, the National Party of Scotland became amalgamated with a recently formed Scottish National body called the Scottish Party under the title of Scottish National Party of which Cunninghame Graham was elected Hon President and he retained that office until he passed away in 1936.

The last Wallace Demonstration celebrated at Elderslie which he attended was in 1935, at which the writer presided and at the close Cunninghame Graham said, 'I here and now rededicate myself to the cause of Scotland's freedom. So long as my strength lasts I shall continue to advocate an independent Scotland.'

Early in 1936 he was in the Argentine at the invitation of the Argentine Government, who had invited him to be present at the naming of a new town called 'Don Roberto' in his honour. While on this visit he caught a chill and died in Buenos Aires on 20th March, 1936. His remains were brought to Scotland and now rest on the Isle of Inchmahome by the side of his wife who was buried there in 1906. A memorial to Cunninghame Graham was erected on a site at Castlehill on a portion of ground which he had previously given to the National Trust for Scotland. It is situated between Dumbarton and Cardross.

The Memorial was unveiled in June, 1937 by his kinsman, the Duke of Montrose for Scotland, Dr Alberto Guani for Uruguay, and A.F. Tschiffely for Argentina. Cunninghame Graham was a Scot of the Scots, an able and artistic orator, a sparkling wit, and his rich voice added to his noble presence which never failed to impress his hearers. Truly he was an aristocrat of aristocrats and a democrat of democrats.

January, 1952

R.E. MUIRHEAD,
MEIKLE CLOAK,
LOCHWINNOCH.

I

I was introduced to R.B. Cunninghame Graham by William Archer in London in the early 1920s. My decision to make the Scottish Cause, cultural and political, my life-work dates from that moment. It is true I had been moving towards it before that — and along a similar path to his own, since I had been an active Socialist for over a dozen years. But unlike Cunninghame Graham I belonged to the working-class and through John MacLean had had a thorough indoctrination in Marxism. I doubt if Cunninghame Graham ever met John MacLean. If they had met it is unlikely they would have got on together, but, leaving such personal issues aside for the moment, it is unfortunate that Cunninghame Graham's Socialism was not based on an adequate theory of social causation. He was 'one of these damned *aristos* who had embraced the cause of the people' — and as a consequence fell between two stools. He might have worked along with men like E.D. Morel, H.N. Brailsford, and Victor Grayson, but the future of the Labour and Socialist Movement lay with a very different type with whom he could not have worked and from whom he could not have disguised his contempt. He did not suffer fools gladly, and so far as the main and growing body of the Movement was concerned the hatred of intellectual distinction, the actual hostility to literature and the arts, and the fine presence of the man — a very peregrine — ensured that he would have no influence with them but be subjected to their vicious rancour. They knew — and could know — nothing of his writings; their pabulum was of a very different kind — and these two are mutually exclusive. Not only so, but a kind of Gresham's Law was operating — the level was already being dragged down by the worse element. The growth in electoral support of the Movement involved a progressive deterioration of mind and spirit. Though it was soon to command an overall majority of the voting electorate at successive general elections, the Labour and Socialist Movement in Scotland was unaccompanied by any counterpart of the slightest consequence in literature and the arts and failed even to yield any book that influenced the general development of British, let alone European, Socialism, while the majority of the MPs it returned to Westminster were mentally negligible. Even when I met him first Cunninghame Graham was concerned with the failure of the Movement, in its concentration on what it conceived to be internationalism, to reckon with our intranational problems. He was soon to throw himself more and more actively into the Scottish Nationalist Movement which was now developing. It was in that connection that I became more closely connected with him — that, and a little later, his keen and helpful interest in the first stirrings of a Scottish Literary Revival and his Presidency of the Scottish PEN Centre which with Sir Herbert Grierson and Mr William Power, and the effective help of Mr H.W. Nevinson and Colonel Arthur Lynch, I was instrumental in establishing. (Subsequent developments have given me cause for bitter amusement that the hopeless 'mothers' meeting' into which this Scottish PEN Centre has fallen should have owed its birth so much to men like these, and above all to one who, the last-named, was an out-and-out Irish Republican and had been condemned to death for fighting against England with the Boers.) At that time the Scottish Nationalist Movement was largely led by writers — Lewis Spence, Neil M. Gunn, the Hon Ruaraidh Erskine of Marr, William Gillies, Eric Linklater, and others, above all, a little later, Compton Mackenzie. Cunninghame Graham could get along well enough with men like these, but they were soon to give way, just as had happened in the Labour and Socialist Movement, to a gang of dullards with no cultural interests and certainly no personal intellectual or artistic gifts. Yet he kept up his interest and activity in the Scottish Cause to the end and one of the last times I met him we both spoke at an open-air meeting in the St Rollox Division of Glasgow on a cold wet night.

Mr Green in his book on the late Earl Baldwin joined issue with the commonly-entertained idea which Mr (as he was then) Baldwin had expressed in his Rectorial address on 'Truth and Politics' in Edinburgh, when he said that the chief export of Scotland, measured in values, had at one time been metaphysics, and that 'the penetration of English practice by Scottish reflection was one of the most fruitful results of the Union'. Mr Green dissented. The Union of Parliaments, according to his view, was only a secondary disaster to the Union of the Crowns. He saw England's natural Toryism continuously subjected to 'dangers from Celtic reason since the connection with Scotland in 1603'. He made no bones about his distaste for 'Whiggery', and, in a striking phrase, described the *a priori* mind in politics as 'the death-watch beetle that is always ticking in the rafters of tradition'. He defined Toryism as 'the philosophy of political integration', and argued that Mr Baldwin had devoted his energy to 'preventing the final stages of disintegration', or, in other words, that 'since 1923 his outlook has been purely negative'. Mr Baldwin, he said further, has broadened the basis of Conservatism, which after Mr Balfour's leadership was already too wide. 'So broad has become the faith of the party,' he added, 'that it has lost the criterion by which to differentiate a Whig from a Tory, or a careerist from a patriot.' He accused Mr Baldwin of flirting with the ideas of the Left when he should have been reinforcing the dogmas of the Right, and described as 'the most incredible dictum of his career' Mr Baldwin's statement — 'Democracy is the most difficult of all forms of government, and, therefore, it is the more worth our giving our lives to make it a success'.

I, of course, agree with Mr Green, but, while I remember with joy the scorn Cunninghame Graham used to pour on British Imperialism, and while men like Erskine of Marr, William Gillies, and Compton Mackenzie believed, and were determined, that the 'penetration of English practice by Scottish reflection' was working out, and would work out very much more disastrously for England and British Imperialism than even Mr Green imagined. I doubt if Cunninghame Graham realized anything of the sort or would have lent himself to it if he had (though he must have seen the anti-English element strongly enough in Erskine of Marr and in myself, while others among the more active Nationalists with whom he associated at this time were equally uncompromising Gaels like William Gillies, Angus Clark, and Hugh Paterson, some of whom had served the Irish Sinn Fein cause, along with our friend, Art O'Brien — afterwards Eire's Ambassador to France — as a clearing-house in London).

I am sure he could have said (if he had closely examined his mind and put aside for a moment his wonderful courtesy), of almost all those with whom he came into contact in the Scottish Labour and Socialist Movement, that (as Nicolas Berdyaev said of the exiled Social-Democrats with whom he had to associate in Vologda when he was exiled there):

> I liked them; they were fine people, wholly devoted to their idea or ideals. Yet in their company the atmosphere became jejune and oppressive — an atmosphere which seemed to force one into a strait-jacket and made it impossible to breathe... Moreover I came into conflict with a phenomenon, long before it made its appearance in the open, which might be called their totalitarianism, and which demanded the unreserved subjugation of personal conscience to the conscience (if any) of the group or the collective.

What Cunninghame Graham really hated was the bourgeois spirit, and he knew well that the bourgeois spirit is 'no mere sociological phenomenon characteristic of capitalist society (although there it is particularly prominent), but, in fact, may attend socialism and communism, Christianity and Atheism alike'.

Mr W.M. Parker, in the chapter he devotes to Cunninghame Graham in his *Modern Scottish Writers* (1917) says:

> In many of his South American sketches, and particularly in the ones called 'Success' and that merciless piece of irony called 'Calvary', his attitude is the kind of full-blooded defiance in which that other modern Elizabethan, Henley, used to revel. Again his irony towards humanity finds outlet in his denunciation of missionaries sent out to convert the heathen of savage lands and in his contempt for the material success of modern civilization; the wonderful preface to 'Progress' expresses his views on progress and success. 'Failure alone is striking.' His friend Conrad called this 'the philosophy of unutterable scorn'.

It was this irony and scorn towards humanity that caused him to be regarded in many quarters as anti-democratic. It is curious to reflect that in this he suffered in much the same way as another great Scottish writer (albeit of a very different order to Cunninghame Graham), namely Thomas Carlyle. I agree entirely with the late Professor Harold Laski when he said of the latter:

> On the question of admitting Carlyle into the ranks of the Great Democrats there is likely to be a division of opinion. If democracy means (1) universal suffrage (2) *plus* the decision of all national questions by majority voting on that basis (3) *plus* the leadership of parliamentary orators, then Carlyle must be classed as an anti-democrat of the most pronounced and uncompromising type. But if the above system is not what 'the people' really desire, but only what they have been 'enchanted' (Carlyle's word) into believing they desire, their real and deeper demand being not for 'representative' self-government but for *good* government by competent rulers — does it not then follow that a prophet who voices this deeper thing would be a truer interpreter of the popular will than an advocate of the sort of democracy so bitterly denounced by Carlyle? And might we not on that ground acclaim him as the better democrat of the two? And if we find him consistently advocating drastic reforms of democracy all in line with the deeper will of the people thus interpreted, and if further he himself is essentially a man of the people, a peasant by heredity and a worker by habit, not a lover of luxury and pleasure, not a seeker of 'honours', but toiling through a long life to free his fellow-workers from the foul 'enchantments' practiced on them by speech-making demagogues, is not this an additional reason for putting him with the people's side? So far as democracy connotes a real friendship for the people as distinct from a desire for their votes, the present writer thinks it is. He thinks that on all *human* grounds Carlyle's claim to the democratic mind is fully as strong as, if not stronger than, that of many persons who, on the grounds of academic definition, claim to be better entitled to it.

I can certainly make a similar claim for Cunninghame Graham, though he was not a 'man of the people' in the same way, and in so far from being 'a peasant by heredity', his was an assured position, as, on his father's side, one of the most direct descendants of the Cunninghames, Earls of Glencairn, and the Grahams, Earls of Menteith, whom some considered to have a better claim to the Scots throne than the later Stewarts. According to Andrew Lang, indeed, 'he could claim the crown of Scotland by descent from Robert II'. But he would certainly have agreed with Carlyle that the people are (in the latter's phrases) 'mostly fools' to the extent of being 'mere mesmerized cattle' under the malign influence of the political cant and claptrap abundantly poured forth by 'stump orators of every denomination, all intent on getting their votes'. He would have been quite at one with Carlyle in not believing in democracy, conceived as a method of settling all questions by the counting of heads — a thing which Carlyle fiercely and continuously denounced as 'the high way to anarchy and the Bottomless Pit'. Nevertheless, Carlyle regarded his country and Europe generally — the Europe of his day — as irrevocably committed to Democracy of that sort. He called it 'Shooting Niagara', not to be avoided when once you have got into the swirling current above the Falls, as England then was; and he predicted that the swift sequel of it would be a ruinous plunge into the whirlpools below, or, as we now call it, a world crisis. 'Inexpressibly delirious seems to me', Carlyle wrote in 1867, when extension of the franchise was in the air (a trifle in comparison with what has happened since),

> inexpressibly delirious seems to me the puddle of Parliament and Public upon what it calls 'The Reform Measure', that is to say, the calling in of new supplies of blockheadism, gullibility, bribeability, amenability to beer and balderdash, by way of amending the woes we have had from our previous supplies of that bad article...It accelerates what I have long looked upon as inevitable — pushes us at once into the Niagara Rapids; irresistibly propelled, with ever-increasing velocity, we shall now arrive — who knows how *soon*?...For one's own poor share, we would rather have men shot than concerned in it. And yet, after all my silent indignation and disgust, I cannot pretend to be clearly sorry that such a consummation is expedited. I say to myself: 'Well, perhaps the sooner such a mass of hypocrisies, universal mismanagements, and brutal platitudes and infidelities *ends* — may it not be for the better? A superlative Hebrew Conjurer spell-binding all the great Lords, great Parties, great Interests of England, and leading them by the nose, like helpless mesmerized somnambulant cattle, to such an issue — did the world ever see a *flebile ludibrium* of such magnitude before.'

Cunninghame Graham would, I think, have shared that view. I am certain at all events he would have admired and greatly enjoyed Carlyle's expression of it. As I will show, he did not fall short of such expressions himself at times. I know that he hated commercialism so much that he was delighted and shouted his agreement and patted my shoulder once when I quoted to him from some unremembered source:

> England can sink beneath the sea for all I care. Indeed, I wish it would. Forty-six million people with the obligation to export their pots and pans and cutlery and coal, or die... is that a life, is that something to be proud of?... England is the great anachronism, my friend; the Dodo who survived because twenty miles of sea protected it from a just retribution... No, wait! Wait! Of course we still have our culture, our ninety-nine ways of patting a ball about. If England sinks, how should we send a Test Team to Australia? Nevertheless, I prefer that solution to the new war which will soon come because we must sell our hideous egg-cups in the Balkans.

Although what has been called the extremist element or 'lunatic fringe' of the Scottish Movement had scarcely emerged before Cunninghame Graham died — and equally the developments of increasing Londonization and the increasing mismanagement of Scottish affairs which might have elicited stronger expressions from him than any on record had not yet taken place — his knowledge of Spain must have put a fine edge on his appreciation of the position of Scotland and Wales under the Westminster Government, for, as Mr Alan Houghton Brodrick recently pointed out, Spain is like England, not only in the sense of Joseph Bonaparte's famous cry, 'l'Espagne n'est pas un pays comme les autres', but also in the absence of any widespread culture, its 'cultural void'. On the other hand, since the Spanish privileged classes remain, in effect, privileged, and have not yet assumed 'the manner of men who are trained in a caricature' (Mr Brodrick's apt stricture on the English public school system) there is in Spain no machinery for turning out social pretence.

In his volume of reminiscences, *Bohemia Junction*, Mr A.F. Tschiffely (whose book abounds in vignettes of Scots far more interesting than almost any to be found in Scotland itself — for example, Violet Hume, born in Buenos Aires of Scottish-French parents, a talented musician and linguist who, under the stage-name of Violet Marguestia (given to her by her singing teacher, Mme. Blanche Marchesi), played the part of Lucy Lockit to Sir Nigel Playfair's original production of the *Beggar's Opera*, and later, ever since the early days of broadcasting, took part in many broadcasts both in English and Spanish; or, again, Mr Colin Paterson, the Scotsman who was in charge of the Argentine Embassy and through whom Mr Tschiffely first met Cunninghame Graham) — tells how in Mrs Dummett's drawing-room, at No 17 Walton Place, near Harrod's Stores, which had for many years been the meeting-place of famous men of letters, and artists of all nationalities, where, amongst others he met Sir Max Beerbohm, H.G. Wells, Dr Axel Munthe, Compton Mackenzie, Dr Cronin, Ramón Perez de Ayala, General Rafael de Nogales, Segovia the world-famous guitarist, Sir John Lavery, Lady Benson, Maude Allan, and a host of others, 'no matter who happened to be in Mrs Dummett's *salon*, whenever Cunninghame Graham was present he overshadowed the company, not only with his hidalgo appearance and manners, but also with his inimitable wit and grand sense of humour'.

But Scotland is not like Mrs Dummett's *salon* in the least and Cunninghame Graham's attributes were no asset among his countrymen but were generally resented as a sort of insult to their own irremediable medicrity and lack of *panache*. It was no wonder that he did not win the Lord Rectorship of Glasgow University though his election would have conferred a far greater honour on it than it on him. He was in better company among the rejected than he would have been among most of those who have held that post. That Compton Mackenzie later won it was a virtual miracle, and, after his term of office, it speedily reverted to dullards. The 'drift South', so far as Scots of outstanding brilliance are concerned, is not due only to ambition for professional and financial success. There is the need for the company of their own kind and these are seldom indeed to be found in Scotland. Scotland's 'freemasonry of mediocrity' forces them out — and in this process our Universities play their ignoble part. Witness their treatment of Carlyle, Stevenson, Thomas Davidson, and Sir Patrick Geddes — or the Scottish teaching profession's treatment of John Maclean and A.S. Neill. But, however stupid and spiteful and generally ill-conditioned the general attitude to brilliance, and more particularly to versatility (since to achieve distinction in any direction is hard enough, but to achieve it in several directions at once is not to be tolerated at all by the general run!) may be in Scotland, at least we do not have, what another Scottish writer (Mr Cecil Gray) has called the

> spirit of smug, pharisaical gentlemanliness, complicated with social snobbery, which permeates every aspect of English cultural life.... The present circumstances and conditions are uniformly propitious to creative activity in this country (England), save only one which, unfortunately, also happens to be a very important one: namely the attitude of mind and code of aesthetic values which largely dominate English life today, and are mainly responsible for all its worst features and for our complete inability to

> induce other nations to take us seriously in music and the other arts — the cult of the English Gentleman. It is not, of course, confined to music and the arts, but permeates every aspect of the national life. It may well be true that our military triumphs have all been won on the playing-fields of Eton, but it is very certain that most of our artistic failures have been sustained there. This spirit which stunts or oppresses or forces into a pusillanimous compromise every potential native talent; this spirit which is the absolute antithesis of everything that we call art, and which must be fought as one fights the devil, without rest or quarter.

Yet Scotland has its own serious problems for any artist, different though they are from those encountered in England and under the English influence everywhere, and there is every justification to feel as, Miss Agnes Ethel Mackay tells us in her fine book on him, the Scottish Impressionist, Arthur Melville (1855-1904) felt; 'Already he felt the restraint of his native city (Edinburgh). He needed a wider horizon and longed for the freedom of a larger outlook on art.'

That is *au fond* what has led so many Scottish artists and authors South and overseas. The need to escape from the intolerable anti-cultural, anti-intellectual atmosphere of their native country and go where they could find and fraternize with people of their own kind and enjoy the clash of like minds and the active co-operation and competition of men and women with similar creative abilities. And it operated in Cunninghame Graham's case as in that of so many others. It is only necessary to think of his best friends — men like Wilfred Scawen Blunt, Edward Garnett, W.H. Hudson, Joseph Conrad, Bernard Shaw. What had Scotland to offer in comparison?

It was Edinburgh that Arthur Melville rightly revolted from. Glasgow, however, rather than Edinburgh, concerned Cunninghame Graham, and I know that he saw it, as I did and do, in the words of Hölderlin I once adapted and quoted to him in this connection:

> Barbarians of old, grown more barbarous still by their industry, their learning, even by their religion, impervious to every devout feeling, corrupt to the very core, insulting every well-fashioned spirit by the degree of their exaggeration and meanness, dull and discordant, like the fragments of a bowl thrown aside. It is a hard word, and yet I say it because it is the truth: I can think of no people more divided and torn. There are artisans but no human beings, thinkers, priests, but no human beings, masters and servants, old and young, but no human beings — is not that like a battlefield where hands and arms and limbs of every kind lie

> about in shreds while the living blood trickles away into the sand? ... But they like to stick to the most material and necessary tasks, and that is why there is amongst them so much bungling, and so little really free and joyful activity. But even that could be overlooked, if only such men were not so insensitive to all beautiful life, if only the curse of god-forsaken unnatural life did not rest everywhere on such a people.... Everything on earth is imperfect? If only someone would tell this god-forsaken people that things are so imperfect amongst them only because they do not leave purity uncorrupted and sacred things untouched by their coarse hands; that nothing flourishes amongst them because they do not heed the roots of growth, divine nature; that amongst them life is empty and burdensome and too full of cold mute conflict, because they scorn the spirit, which infuses vigour and nobility into human activity and serenity into suffering and brings into cities and dwellings love and brotherhood.

While the living blood trickles away into the sand! I remember how horrified I was when I addressed the students supporting Cunninghame Graham's candidature for the Lord Rectorship of Glasgow University in October 1929, and found that they knew nothing or next to nothing of his writings. Even to this day he can have found only a pitiful handful of readers in the whole of Scotland. His books are not to be found in the majority of our public libraries. Yet Mr Tschiffely tells us that, when Mr Colin Paterson first suggested that he ought to meet Cunninghame Graham; 'Of course I had read a number of this famous author's books and therefore, in a sense, he was no stranger to me.' Francis Parkman, the American historian, said that 'one of the commonest disguises of envy is a preference for the inferior' — and modern Scotland has certainly rejected all the best work its sons have produced and acclaimed only what was comfortably low-brow enough. Thus Cunninghame Graham has been rejected along with Norman Douglas, 'Saki' (H.H. Munro), Francis Grierson and Richard Curle. Nearly every Scottish writer of any consequence at all suffers in fact precisely as Christian Morgenstern has suffered in Germany. As has recently been said of Morgenstern only the less essential, less important and less original part of his work is widely known, so that there is some danger of getting a distorted view — the view held, in fact, by very many of the beautiful and deep in German poetry. Yet it is writers like these, and not the popular writers, Kailyaird or otherwise, who are in keeping with and carrying forward and enriching our best national traditions, and in particular the tradition of the Wandering Scot, the combination of scholarship and adventure.

As the late Mr William Power says in his autobiography:

> Cunninghame Graham had the natural pride of fine race, superb manhood, and mental independence. Those who imagined he had the less pleasant kind of pride should have seen him, at a private literary function in his honour, going round the room talking delightfully with every one he thought was in the slightest danger of being overlooked. It was all the finer since he had, in mixed company, the shyness of the man of action who is also something of a literary recluse. He was too big a man to be afraid of appearing 'faintly absurd' in the eyes of conventional snobs; he espoused struggling causes that appealed to his chivalrous and patriotic instincts, and lent them the *aegis* of his own prestige. He gave loyal service as President of the Scottish National Party. He was never finer than in his annual addresses — the last of them delivered not long before his death — at the Wallace Commemoration at Elderslie. No writer makes less parade of literary knowledge; yet as chairman at the first two of the Makars' dinners when Lewis Spence spoke on Dunbar and Professor Sir Herbert Grierson on Henryson, he showed an intimate appreciation of old Scots poetry. Always when I met him he spoke of some recent book by a Scots writer. Acknowledging a reference to him in my *Literature and Oatmeal*, in which I had remarked on the Spanish inspirations of Smollett, who was born only a few miles from Cunninghame Graham's estate of Ardoch, he wrote: 'I often pass the monument to Smollett, in Renton, or, as we say, "the Renton". Smollett, they say, was the only man that Johnson was afraid to tackle. Had he done so, it would have been a battle of giants, but I would have put my money on the Vale of Leven. I know Cartagena very well, and Smollett must have known it too. I passed three months there in 1916...I agree with your criticisms on most of our writers, especially that on "Fiona Macleod", who was a bit of a mystery. As you say, his Gaelic was inadequate and his characters shadowy. He used, I am told, to pass the summer often on the Gareloch, only six miles from Ardoch. No one speaks Gaelic there now.'

I can testify too, like Power, to Cunninghame Graham's knowledge of Scottish literature, his keen interest in our linguistic and other cultural problems, the sympathy and encouragement with which he watched the developments towards a Scottish literary

Renaissance which were proceeding during the decade before his death, and the avidity and hopefulness with which he pounced on new books by Scottish authors. Yet he remained caviare not only the general but even to the small better reading public in Scotland, the reason being as I have suggested and as Mr Power somewhere said, that

> the vein of cynical humanism that runs through all his books is as different as possible from the cosily insular sentiment of the Kailyairders. It is the expression of the knightly sympathy with the underdog, and with the victims of fate or fortune, that made Cunninghame Graham a militant Socialist, and that drew him to the service of Scotland in her economic adversity and cultural strivings. For the blatantly selfish and self-satisfied type of vulgarian who was rampant in the days of her prosperity he has a withering contempt. The country of his Scots essays and sketches is a twilight Scotland, ennobled by tragedy and defeat. The Scotland of his dreams, which he is valiantly helping to create, is a Scotland nobly self-reliant and bravely idealistic, worthy of her own finest social and cultural traditions. His self-sacrificing devotion to her interests and prestige strikingly exemplifies the fact that national feeling is strongest in the cultured and travelled internationalist.

Both Cunninghame Graham and John Buchan thought very highly of Neil Munro. I could never see why and I think that time has proved me right and showed they were hopelessly wrong in accounting him, as they did, a writer of European consequence, or even, as was perhaps generally believed, of Scottish consequence. Anyhow, as Power says, Munro had just the opposite attitude to Cunninghame Graham's. Munro

> seemed to believe that the day of the Celt as a living force was long over; there was nothing for him but to lose himself in the big, brutal, stupid world of hucksters, climbers, stunters, and Blimps, consoling himself by returning now and then into his dreamworld and by making sport of the sorry scheme of things about him.

No! There was nothing defeatist about Cunninghame Graham, but, as I remember someone saying,

> Don Roberto has played many parts — so many that he is not to be identified with any one mode of living. By what category of his doings did the public know him best? 'Adventurer' suggests itself

as a label, for it was not only in Spanish America that he welcomed hazardous experiences — in some of which the object was the making of money. But it must be discarded for the implication in it that he had his way to make. His was an assured position. While it pleased him to attribute certain actions and renunciations to his being without money, he could always have put a term to his impecuniosity if he saw fit. Of the many acres that he inherited he was at the time of his death still in possession of 'the valuable Ardoch estate on the Clyde'. So secure was his social standing that even in Victorian days it was so little prejudiced by a sentence of imprisonment for his share as an agitator in a riot in Trafalgar Square that the Lord Salisbury of the day, meeting him immediately after his release, treated it as a joke and greeted him with, 'Well, Mr Graham, are you thinking where to put your guillotine?' But in spite of the escapade that brought him to Pentonville, 'Politician' has to be rejected equally with 'Adventurer'; his incursions into politics, though vigorous, were too desultory. Writer? He wrote many books, which certainly found favour with the elect, but he would have repudiated the designation. 'Think,' he wrote, 'what an uneventful life a man who lives by literature condemns himself to pass. Others are preaching, praying, cheating and lying, fighting, exploring, inventing, risking their lives, and sailing on the sea. Whilst they are up and about the writer sits at his table cudgelling his brains!'

In the many photographs included in Mr Tschiffely's book[1] he figures as so conscious of his superb appearance and as wearing his clothes with such an air that we are put in mind of the theatre; nevertheless we cannot do his ghost the wrong to consider 'Play-actor', for his label; he was too formidable. The obvious theatrical element in him is thus discounted by Mr Tschiffely: 'His poses were so natural to him that on better acquaintance with the man they became part of him'; and with that hint we come to the compromise that Don Roberto in his long active life played — and perhaps overplayed — many parts, but that in all these parts he played that unique person himself. How did he conceive this person? For his nearest approach to criticism, Mr Tschiffely offers a caricature of his own in which Don Roberto figures as Don Quixote — without, however, satisfying us that there was any

---

1 *Don Roberto. Being an Account of the Life and Works of R.B. Cunninghame Graham, 1852-1936*. By A.F. Tschiffely (Heinemann, London, 1937).

cause for which his hero would have exhibited himself on Rosinante as described by Cervantes. While there is nothing in his story as narrated to throw doubt on the sincerity of his championship of innumerable underdogs he presents himself primarily as a challenger of other top dogs. We write 'presents himself' for Mr Tschiffely would have himself regarded as the editor of an autobiography for which the writings and correspondence of Cunninghame Graham supplied the material.

I have little fault to find with that. My own answer would be, I think, 'Aristocrat'. He sat lightly to life and to literature. As he says in 'Bopicuá':

> It is not given to all men after a break of years to come back to the scenes of youth, and still find in them the same zest as of old. To return again to all the cares of life called civilized, with all its littlenesses, its newspapers all full of nothing, its sordid aims disguised under high-sounding nicknames, its hideous riches and its sordid poverty, its want of human sympathy, and, above all, its barbarous war brought on by the folly of its rulers was not just at that moment an alluring thought, as I felt the little 'malacara' (white faced horse) that I rode twitching his bridle, striving to be off. When I had touched him with the spur he bounded forward and... the place which for so many months had been part of my life sank out of sight, just as an island in the Tropics fades from view as the ship leaves it, as it were, hull down.

So Cunninghame Graham rides off, leaving us with the enigma of his personality unsolved, (and who after all wants a man reduced to a label?) with these characteristic words: ''Tis meet and fitting to set free the horse or pen before death overtakes you, or before the gentle public turns its thumbs down and yells "Away with him!" ... Hold it not up to me for egotism, O gentle reader, for I would have you know that hardly any of the horses I rode had shoes on them, and thus the tracks are faint.'

Instead of wishing to reduce him to a label then, (I do not like 'the last of the Caballeros' 'a modern conquistador' or any of the other journalistic inventions), we may rejoice in the contradictions which were the man, and which were so brilliantly summarized by Bernard Shaw (whose Moroccan play, *Captain Brassbound's Conversion*, was based on Cunninghame Graham's book *Mogreb-el-Acksa*) when he wrote:

> Cunninghame Graham is the hero of his own book; but I have not

made him the hero of my play, because so incredible a personage must have destroyed its likelihood — such as it is. There are moments when I do not myself believe in his existence. And yet he must be real; for I have seen him with these eyes; and I am one of the few men living who can decipher the curious alphabet in which he writes his private letters.[2] The man is on public record too. The battle of Trafalgar Square, in which he personally and bodily assailed civilization as represented by the concentrated military and constabular forces of the capital of the world, can scarcely be forgotten by the more discreet spectators of whom I was one.... He is a fascinating mystery to a sedentary person like myself. The horse, a dangerous animal whom, when I cannot avoid, I propitiate with apples and sugar, he bestrides and dominates fearlessly, yet with a true republican sense of the rights of the four-legged fellow-creature, whose martyrdom and man's shame therein he has told most powerfully in his 'Calvary', a tale with an edge that will cut the soft cruel hearts and strike fire from the hard kind ones. He handles the other lethal weapons as familiarly as the pen: mediaeval sword and modern Mauser are to him as umbrellas and kodaks are to me.... He is, I understand, a Spanish hidalgo; hence the superbity of his portrait by Lavery (Velasquez being no longer available). He is, I know, a Scotch laird. How he contrives to be authentically the two things at the same time is no more intelligible to me than the fact that everything that has ever happened to him seems to have happened in Paraguay or Texas instead of in Spain or Scotland. He is, I regret to add, an impenitent and unashamed dandy: such boots, such a hat, would have dazzled D'Orsay himself. With that hat he once saluted me in Regent Street when I was walking with my mother. Her interest was instantly kindled; and the following conversation ensued. 'Who is that?' 'Cunninghame Graham.' 'Nonsense! Cunninghame Graham is one of your Socialists: that man is a gentleman!' This is the punishment of vanity, a fault I have myself always avoided, as I find conceit less troublesome and much less expensive. Later on somebody told him of Tarudant, a city in Morocco in which no Christian had ever set foot. Concluding at once that it must be an exceptionally desirable place to live in, he took ship and horse; changed a hat for a turban; and made straight for the sacred city,

---

2 His handwriting was the worst I have ever seen — far worse even than Compton Mackenzie's which is appallingly bad.

via Mogador. How he fared, and how he fell into the hands of the Cadi of Kintafi, who rightly held that there was more danger to Islam in one Cunninghame Graham than in a thousand Christians, may be learnt from his account of it in *Mogreb-el-Acksa*, without which *Captain Brassbound's Conversion* would never have been written.

II

Born in London on May 24, 1852, Robert Bontine Cunninghame Graham was the eldest son of the late Mr William Cunninghame Graham Bontine of Ardoch and Gartmore, and the Hon Anne Elphinstone Fleeming. As was the custom in his family, he changed his name when he succeeded to Gartmore. On his father's side he was one of the most direct descendants of the Earls of Menteith and of Glencairn, and his mother was a member of the noble family of Elphinstone. Robert Graham of Gartmore, the author of the poem entitled 'If doughty deeds my ladye please', was his great-grandfather, and this laird's father was one of the few men who owned land on the Highland line and refused to pay blackmail to Rob Roy. It is said that he once had the famous freebooter under lock and key, but he escaped.

Robert, who was brought up mainly by his Spanish grandmother (whose influence remained with him throughout his life), was sent to Harrow, but his independent spirit chafed at the restrictions of an English public school. In 1868 he first went out to South America, and he found the free life of a cattle rancher rather more to his taste than anything he could find at home. The long days and nights on horseback on the Pampas before the Gaucho were extinct were among Mr Cunninghame Graham's most vivid and pleasant memories, and in after years he was to write about his experiences. He came to know the Argentine pampas better than the natives themselves, for, unlike them, he continually travelled. He came to ride like a Gaucho, and threw a lazo and the bolas with the best of them. As a sign of the honour in which he is held in Argentina, the Government decided to call a new town after him, and he went out to attend the ceremony.

In 1879 he married a Chilean lady, Mlle. Gabriela, daughter of Don Francisco José de La Balmondière. She herself was an authoress, and besides was something of a mystic. Her husband was rarely without her help in his later political campaign, and it was a sad blow to him when Mrs Cunninghame Graham died in 1906. She is buried on the Island of Inchmahome, on the Lake of Menteith. He himself dug her grave in the grounds of the old Augustinian Priory on the peaceful little island.

Mr Cunninghame Graham's father died as the result of a fall from his horse in 1883, and the young cattle rancher became Laird of Gartmore, an extensive estate in Perthshire which had been in the family since 1680. He came home and settled down to the life of a country gentleman, and tried to wipe off the debt of over £100,000, which had been incurred by his predecessors. He worked hard, and soon became recognized as the best farmer in the district. The burden proved too heavy, however, and in 1898 he had to part with the property, which was bought by the late Sir Charles Cayzer, founder of the Clan Line, in whose family it remains. It was a tragic disappointment both to Mr Cunninghame Graham and to his tenants, but his memory is fragrant still in the district of his fathers.

When he inherited the family estate he began to take an interest in public affairs, and his thoughts soon turned to politics. 'Doughty Deeds' Graham had been in the Reform Parliament, and Mr Cunninghame Graham determined to try and emulate his ancestor.

He made his political debut at the General Election of December 1885, when he stood as Liberal candidate for the North-West Division of Lanarkshire. His opponent was a Conservative, Mr John Baird, of Lochwood and Knoydart, an ironmaster, whose family had done much to benefit the district. Although a personally popular candidate, Mr Cunninghame Graham's advanced opinions were too much for the electors, who returned the Conservative with a majority of 1104 votes.

The tables were turned in the following summer, however, when there was another election following the Liberal split over the Irish Home Rule Controversy. There was again a straight fight between Mr Baird and Mr Cunninghame Graham, but this time the latter was elected as a supporter of Mr Gladstone with a majority of 332 votes. At first a keen Radical, the new MP soon developed into an extreme Socialist, and he was one of the founders of the Scottish Parliamentary Labour Party, of which he was appointed the first chairman. His activities led to a clash with those in authority.

Severe criticism was not lacking at the time, but there can be little doubt that it was an effort, however misguided, to protect the rights of free speech which led to the episode known as the 'Battle of Trafalgar Square'. In November 1887 the Metropolitan Radical Federation called a meeting in the Square, to demand the release of Mr William

O'Brien, MP, who had been imprisoned for causing trouble with his demands for Irish Home Rule. The Chief Commissioner of Police (Sir Charles Warren), in view of recent political disturbances in the city, decided to prohibit the meeting, which had been called for Sunday the 13th. On 'Bloody Sunday' — as it was afterwards called — the Square was occupied by the police from an early hour, and in the afternoon the approach of organized processions led to serious conflicts between the people and the police. The Foot Guards and the Life Guards came to the support of the latter, and Mr Cunninghame Graham and Mr John Burns, who led a charge which tried to break the police cordon, were alone able to force their way into the Square. The two leaders were arrested, but not before Mr Cunninghame Graham — who was hatless — had been struck on the head with a police truncheon. They were kept captive at the base of Nelson's Column while the Riot Act was read. Before order was restored two men had been killed and about 100 injured.

Graham and Burns underwent a three days' trial at the Old Bailey in the following January, when the former was defended by Mr Asquith (Lord Oxford) and the latter conducted his own defence. Both were found guilty of inciting to unlawful assembly, and sentenced to six weeks' imprisonment without hard labour. Mr Cunninghame Graham found solace in Pentonville by reading the Book of Job, and when they were released they were the centre of a joyful demonstration outside the prison gate.

Another distinction he achieved during his brief Parliamentary career was that of being the first MP suspended from the House of Commons for saying 'damn!'

He continued to exert himself on behalf of the working man. This led to a further clash with the police, this time in France. His indignation had been aroused when, during a May Day demonstration at Fourmies in 1891, fifteen people had been killed by the troops, which had been called out to quell the riot. He went to Calais soon afterwards to speak at a Socialist demonstration held in honour of the victims, and his speech was considered so inflammatory that he was arrested and expelled from France.

Parliament was dissolved in 1892, and in the General Election which followed Mr Cunninghame Graham contested the Camlachie Division of Glasgow. He had at first been adopted as Liberal candidate, but his criticism of Mr Gladstone turned the local Ministerialists against him, and he stood as a Socialist in the end. He had the support of his wife, Mr Keir Hardie, and Mr John Burns, but he came in third of a quartette, with the Unionist at the head of the poll.

It was about this time that Mr Cunninghame Graham began to write. He himself once said he wrote 'largely for amusement', and Mr Morley Roberts once called him 'our greatest amateur writer'. He wrote, in all, close on thirty volumes, but because he never attempted to write best sellers, their names and contents are known to comparatively few. Their deep sincerity, original philosophy, and distinctive style mark their author as one of the foremost present-day exponents of the art of essay-writing. All his books were introduced by a foreword or preface, which was often the best part of the book.

In his spare time, one of Mr Cunninghame Graham's chief recreations was travelling. He often visited Morocco, and in 1897 his adventurous nature made him attempt to visit the city of Tarudant, which Europeans were forbidden to enter. He travelled through the Atlas Mountains disguised as the Sheikh Mohammed-el-Fasi, but he was captured by the Kaid of Kintafi when only a day's march from his goal. He languished for almost a fortnight in the mountain fortress of Thelata-el-Jacoub, and when eventually Kintafi set him at liberty it was with a polite refusal to allow him to continue his journey towards Tarudant. The whole adventure provided material for his most characteristic book, *Mogreb-el-Acksa*, one of the best books of travel ever written.

During the war Mr Cunninghame Graham spent eleven months in the Argentine, buying horses for the War Office, and nearly a year in Colombia examining the cattle resources for the British Government. At the first General Election after the Armistice — in December 1918 — he fought his last Parliamentary contest, having been adopted as Liberal candidate for the Western Division of Stirling and Clackmannan. His opponents were Mr (later, Sir) Harry Hope, who was successful, and Mr Thomas Johnston. On the eve of the poll Mr Cunninghame Graham wrote a letter to his friend, the late Neil Munro, in which he confessed that he was 'sick of this infernal folly of elections'.

Since then Mr Cunninghame Graham had practically dropped out of party politics. In a subsequent speech he spoke of his attitude to the two parties with which he had been identified so closely. The Socialist party — once the party of his dreams — he described as 'merely a third party struggling for place, for office, and for the fruit of government, all their high ideals lost, and all their aspirations locked away in some dark corner of their souls'. He went on to compare the Liberal party to a bullock bogged in the mud.

From the early days of his political career Mr Cunninghame Graham had been a strong advocate of Home Rule for Scotland, and he now felt that the time had come to sink party differences and work for a Scottish Parliament. He became president of the Scottish Home Rule Association shortly after its inception, and when conditions led to the formation of its successor, the National Party of Scotland, in 1928, he was elected its president. At the Glasgow University Rectorial Election of 1929, while the party was still in its infancy, Mr Cunninghame Graham stood as the first Scottish National candidate. It is no discourtesy to him to say that it came as a surprise to everybody when he nearly defeated Mr Stanley Baldwin, who was Prime Minister at the time. In the four male 'nations' — as the polling divisions are called — Mr Cunninghame Graham did actually defeat Mr Baldwin by 712 votes to 501.

Mr Cunninghame Graham was one of the prime movers in the fusion of the National party with the Scottish party in 1934. He held the office of honorary president of the united organization — the Scottish National party — after that, and up to the end he took an active share in the party's propaganda. For almost ten years he regularly addressed the two chief nationalist demonstrations at Stirling and Elderslie.

He was a magnificent orator, and could speak in French and Spanish as fluently as English. His sparkling wit, and the rich voice which never lost its power, added to his noble presence, never failed to impress his hearers.

Other occasions which brought Mr Cunninghame Graham before the Scottish public in his latter years were functions connected with the Scottish Centre of PEN, of which he was honorary president. At the time of the International Congress held in Edinburgh in 1934, he presided and spoke at a banquet which was attended by some of the most famous writers in the world — men who, as he remarked, were in their common calling slaves and martyrs of the pen.

After the sale of Gartmore, Mr Cunninghame Graham's unpretentious Scottish home was the cottage of Ardoch, beautifully situated on the shores of the Clyde between Dumbarton and Cardross. From 1884 he was a Deputy Lieutenant of Dumbartonshire, and he was a JP of that county, Perth, and Stirlingshire. He also had a house in London and another in Bute. His heir is Admiral Angus Cunninghame Graham, lately Flag Officer, Scotland.

In the political chapters of Mr Tschiffely's *Don Roberto*, Mr Cunninghame Graham in his capacity as Socialist MP is to be found challenging authority in every form. He quelled a disturbance at a meeting by telling the audience that he had had the doors locked and displaying a dummy revolver which he had found among the belongings of a theatrical company in the ante-room:

'I am going to speak for half-an-hour,' he announced, 'and then I shall introduce my friend Keir Hardie, and until he has finished his address not a man will interrupt him or try to move unless he wishes to be carried out of the hall a corpse.'

In discussing his books Mr Tschiffely is in a position to quote letters and tributes from writers whose names read like a list of an academy of men of letters. Conrad acclaims his 'magnanimous indignations': of his answer to the Speaker of the House of Commons, 'I never withdraw', Mr Bernard Shaw writes: 'I promptly stole the potent phrase for the sake of its perfect style, and used it as a cockade for the Bulgarian hero of *Arms and the Man*'.

At the age of eighty-four, he left again for the Argentine, where he died in Buenos Aires, after a short illness of pneumonia, on March 20, 1936. He was buried beside his wife on the island of Inchmahome. If, as Mr Power has written, there was little official representation at his funeral, there was a large gathering of writers, artists, and other people whom he would most have wished to be there, and Mr Power himself delivered an excellent *éloge*. At the inaugration in the autumn of 1937 of his memorial, near Dumbarton, stones from Argentina and Uruguay were unveiled by his friend and biographer, Mr Tschiffely, and by the Uruguayan Minister, Dr Guani; and the memorial itself, with Alexander Proudfoot's vivid medallion, was unveiled by the Duke of Montrose, who paid a moving tribute to his illustrious fellow-clansman.

It is in keeping with the apathy and indifference, and often petty jealousy and spite, of Scotland in such matters that the finest collection of Cunninghame Graham's books, autographed letters, MSS and corrected proofs and other material is to be found, not in Scotland, but in the United States of America. This is the Herbert Faulkner West Collection, which Professor Faulkner West presented in memory of his friend to the Dartmouth College Library, Hanover, New Hampshire. Professor West, whose wife is a Swedish lady with ancient Scottish connections, first saw Cunninghame Graham at the funeral of his friend Joseph Conrad in Canterbury in 1924. He did not actually meet him until five years later, but from then on their friendship was steadfast up to Cunninghame Graham's death and they corresponded frequently and met on various occasions in London and at Ardoch. Professor West's biography of him — the first that had been published up to that time — appeared in 1932, being published by Messrs Cranley and Day, London. (Other books with material bearing on Cunninghame Graham are *An Artist's Reminiscences* by Walter Crane; *The Last Years of H.M. Hyndman*, by

Rosalind Travers Hyndman; *The Death of Yesterday*, by Stephen Graham which contains a seventeen-page chapter entitled 'Laird and Caballero; Cunninghame Graham'; *Conversations in Ebury Street*, by George Moore; and *Contemporary Portraits (Third Series)* by Frank Harris, which has a sixteen-page essay on 'Cunninghame Graham', which Professor West reports as having been declared untrustworthy by Cunninghame Graham himself.

The Dartmouth College Collection, according to the privately printed catalogue issued in 1938, then contained 138 separate lots (but I understand that several rare and early pamphlets and other material have been added since it was printed). The value of the Collection can be realized from the fact that in addition to all the first editions, and association books and other material of all kinds, one lot comprises no fewer than one hundred and thirty letters from Cunninghame Graham to Professor West, all but four of them being in his handwriting and covering the amazing number of six hundred and sixty pages. The four typewritten letters cover eight pages. This Collection is of course indispensable to any one who wishes to make a study of Cunninghame Graham's work and contains many items which could not be found anywhere else or could only be hunted out with great difficulty. There are, for example, thirty-four books (many of which would now be difficult to procure elsewhere) by different authors, containing prefaces by Cunninghame Graham. One of the rarest items is *The Imperial Kailyaird, Being A Biting Satire on English Colonisation* by Cunninghame Graham, published by the Twentieth Century Press, London, in 1896.

A Bibliography of the First Editions of the Works of Robert Bontine Cunninghame Graham, compiled, with a foreword, by Leslie Chaundy, was published by Messrs Dulau and Co Ltd, London in 1924. But the Faulkner West Collection has the further advantage of including cuttings of book reviews and other contributions to periodicals at home and abroad, a great collection of reports of Cunninghame Graham's speeches on Scottish Nationalism, and a splendid series of photographs of him at all ages from seventeen onwards.

As I write I am glad to know that an *Essential Cunninghame Graham* — a selection from his work, chosen and edited by Mr Paul Bloomfield — is about to appear. But neither in the Faulkner West Collection or anywhere else will you find the book I always hoped for, namely that a collection of the best of his amazingly vivid tales of South American men and horses should be illustrated by the equally truthful and virile drawings of Alberto Guiraldes, famous for his eloquent line drawings of horses and gauchos, who illustrated Juan Martin d'Estrada's collection of prose-poetical descriptions of pastoral life, *Campo*, and did the spirited chapter-headings for Walter Owen's English translation of José Hernandez's famous epic poem of the pampas, *The Gaucho — Martin Fierro*, whose hero, like Paul Bunyan in America or in Russia Ilya Mourometz, called Solovey-Razboinik (the 'Nightingale Bandit'), one of the greatest of the bogatyrs (folk-lore heroes), became a fabulous folk-figure — as in Scotland, too, Cunninghame Graham himself might well have become since he sank more Spanish gold amongst us than ever the Armada 'skailed' round our coasts. Cunninghame Graham — *El Rey de Escocia*!

III

Cunninghame Graham not only incarnated again the tradition of the Wandering Scot and of all the best features of that Scottish Internationalism which differentiates us so markedly from the English, but he counterbalanced that with his fervent Scottish Nationalism and thus realized to an unusual degree that ideal Count Keyserling described when he wrote that

> the real goal of progress is then on the one hand a total lived experience of the whole of the real, and on the other such a deeply rooted fixation in spirit, that thanks to it, man can by the function of comprehension, and by spiritual initiative acting through it, make the entire universe his own.

Interest in him has remained the badge of an *élite*. His astringent tonic work is far removed from popular taste. But it can be claimed for all his writing, as Carew claimed for Donne, that he had

> ... opened us a Mine
> Of rich and pregnant fancy, drawn a line
> Of *masculine* expression.

Most even of the small company of his readers know only a portion of his work, but it is necessary to read it all, and preferably in the order in which it was written, to come by a proper appreciation of his literary achievement and the astonishing range of his interests and experiences.

In the Festival of Britain Exhibition of 20th Century Scottish Books at the Mitchell Library in Glasgow he was poorly represented, a mere tithe of his output being shown, though he fared better than other distinguished Scottish writers of the non-popular sort. In the published catalogue of that Exhibition, a special section was given to what were called 'Four great 20th Century Scotsmen', namely John Buchan (Lord Tweedsmuir), Sir Alexander Fleming, John Logie Baird, and Lord Boyd Orr. Only one of these, of course, was a literary man; the other three were scientists and technicians. But if such a section were to be given, there is no excuse for failing to include Cunninghame Graham in those thus specially singled out. Even that small portion of his output shown in the Exhibition necessitated entries in the catalogue under six different headings, namely 1. lives of Scots Men and Women 2. History and Biography 3. Scotland's Towns and Countryside 4. The Scot as Geographer and Traveller 5. Natural History 6. the Novelists. And if there had been a full representation of his publications it would have been necessary to add to these six writings on art, literary criticism, and politics.

His first book was on a Scottish subject, and he kept coming back to Scotland and in the later years of his long life he was increasingly involved in the Scottish literary and political movement. Yet, as Professor West has said, 'He maintained two homes, one in Cardross, Scotland, and one in London. Every winter he travelled. It might be to the Canary Islands, Mentone, Venezuela, Tangier, or South Africa, but always where there was plenty of sun. His favourite Spanish saw was *No hay sabor sin sol*, which means "There is no savor without the sun".' But this love of the sun is an old Celtic characteristic, too, and in all his writing Cunninghame Graham belonged not to the Celtic Twilight but to the Gaelic sunshine.

As Professor West remarks, Cunninghame Graham's first book 'remains one of his most charming efforts'. This is a gray paper-covered book, called *Notes on the District of Menteith*, published in 1895. Three other editions of this have appeared (one of them a *de luxe* edition, illustrated by Sir D.Y. Cameron) and with the exception of *Mogreb-el-Acksa* (1898) this little volume has been reprinted more than any other of his works.

In 1896 Cunninghame Graham collaborated with his wife in a book of sketches entitled *Father Archangel of Scotland. Aurora la Cuziñi, a Realistic Sketch in Seville*, was published as a pamphlet in 1898 by that famous publisher of the 'Nineties, Leonard Smithers. In 1897, Cunninghame Graham went to Morocco and, disguised as a native doctor, attempted to get to the forbidden city of Tarudant. The account of this journey is perhaps his best and most enduring book, *Mogreb-al-Acksa* (1898). He did not reach Tarudant, having been taken prisoner by a Kaid, but his journey, though technically a failure, was such as to give this book a reputation as one of the great travel books of the century, as Joseph Conrad declared it to be.

The Ipané, 1899, is a book of short stories and sketches, which includes not only 'Un Pelado', a revision of his first story published in the San Antonio newspaper of 1886, but three of his most famous stories, namely 'Bristol Fashion', a gruesome sea story of the African Coast and the slave trade, 'Snaekoll's Saga', the story of a cannibalistic horse in Iceland, and his ironic satire on the Aryan Myth, entitled 'Niggers' — a sketch which aligned him politically with the anti-Imperialist Wilfred Blunt with whom he had been on terms of friendship since 1887, when both suffered imprisonment for defending the rights of free speech on unpopular subjects.

The following year (1900) William Heinemann became his publisher and issued *Thirteen Stories*, tales reminiscent in tone and partly autobiographical of Cunninghame Graham's life in South America and in Northern Africa. In 1901, while Cunninghame Graham was negotiating the sale of his estate in Perthshire, came one of his finest books, *A Vanished Arcadia*, being an account of the Jesuits in Paraguay from 1607 to 1767. This was the first of a long series of historical and biographical studies to come from his pen.

Recreations and Reflections, composed of material reprinted from the *Saturday Review*, was published in 1902 and contains four original essays by Cunninghame Graham, three by Max Beerbohm, and one by W.H. Hudson. The titles of Cunninghame Graham's articles are 'Buta' and 'A Triptych' (1. 'My Relative', 2. 'The Colonel', 3. 'The Admiral'). The same year appeared perhaps his best known book, *Success*. 'Readers,' as Professor West says,

> are especially referred to the sketch, *Might, Majesty and Dominion*, which may be taken as the epitaph of the Victorian era, and which describes the funeral of Queen Victoria; *Sursum Corda*, which describes the author's days in Pentonville Prison as one of Her Majesty's guests; and *Beattock for Moffat*, one of the finest stories in English that I know, which tells of the return of a dying Scot to his native land, and *The Impenitent Thief*, which has always reminded me of Anatole France's *The Procurator of Judea*. I can think of no book, more neglected by the reading public, which is of such fine quality. The point of view is ironic and pessimistic in the sense that the author recognizes the ultimate

futility of endeavour, and it seems to re-echo Anatole France's succinct philosophy of life: 'We are born, we suffer, and we die'.

1903 brought *Hernande de Soto: Together with an account of one his captains, Gonçalo Silvestre*, and 1904 *Progress* dedicated to Joseph Conrad who had previously dedicated *Typhoon* to Cunninghame Graham. Professor West's collection includes a presentation copy of *Progress* signed 'from Mrs Bontine, London'. Mrs Bontine, Cunninghame Graham's mother died in London in 1925 at the age of ninety-seven. Cunninghame Graham was then seventy-three.

His People was published by Messrs Duckworth in 1906, dedicated to Edward Garnett. In this volume the author, in an *Apologia*, gives his credo as a writer. 'Still I believe,' he says,

> that, be it bad or good, all that a writer does is to dress up what he has seen, or felt, or heard, and nothing real is evolved from his own brain, except the words he uses, and the way in which he uses them. Therefore it follows that in writing he sets down (perhaps unwittingly) the story of his life, and as he does so, makes it worth reading only by chronicling all his impressions of the world quite honestly, as if he were alone on a desert island (as in fact he is) and he were writing on the sand.

The reader should mark well the author's words on Hulderico Schmidel, the first historian of Buenos Aires and Paraguay, for he will hear of him again in a later book, and note also the author's tribute to one he knew in Parliament, Parnell.

Faith, published in 1909, contains amongst other stories, 'A Silhouette', a tale, unforgettable for its grim and stark realism, of a man having his throat cut on the pampas of South America, and the sketches 'Sor Candida and the Bird', 'An Arab Funeral', and 'In Christmas Week', showing the wide range of the author's sensibilities.

In 1910 came the second of his trilogy. First *Faith*, now *Hope*. The outstanding stories in this volume are 'Un Monsieur', told in the words of a French prostitute, which has always been one of their favourites among Cunninghame Graham's readers, a little ironic masterpiece which made the feminists hail the author as one of their own, and 'Mirahuano'. The third volume, *Charity*, followed in 1912 dedicated to his old friend and fellow-artist, Sir John Lavery. In this book is reprinted 'Aurora la Cujiñi'. Then came *A Hatchment* in 1913, dedicated to Walter Harris of Tangier, who died in 1934 and was for many years the London *Times* correspondent.

El Rio de la Plata, published in 1914, contains translations by various Spaniards of some of Cunninghame Graham's stories and one story, 'La Vieja de Bolivar', originally written in Spanish by Cunninghame Graham himself. This handsome volume which contains a frontispiece of the author in sepia, was issued as a Spanish tribute to the excellence of Cunninghame Graham's works about Spain and Spanish America.

Scottish Stories was published in 1914, too, and brought together the stories laid in Scotland which had appeared in previous books. Some of the sketches concern the author's family.

During the First World War Cunninghame Graham published his second long biographical study, *Bernal Diaz del Castillo*, based on Castillo's own *True History of the Conquest of New Spain*. The author was an eyewitness of Cortez's famous Campaign, 'one of the strangest and most interesting in all history. Diaz was an unusual historian in that he wrote down only what he saw, and manufactured nothing from thin air. The facts, as they usually do, speak eloquently enough.' Cunninghame Graham finds that Castillo's style fulfils the requirement 'that the first essential of a good style is to be natural, and that his own style (Castillo's) had a peculiar charm in its simplicity'.

During that War, Cunninghame Graham bought horses for the British Government in South America. Always a lover of horses, he well knew the fate which was to be theirs when they reached the Western Front, and yet he was no sentimentalist, and as horses for ages have partaken of whatever glory wars have had in the past, he went about his duty with knowledge and acumen. He describes the choosing and shipping of the horses for the far-off fields of carnage in one of his best and most poignant stories of horses, 'Bopicuá', which may be found in his book *Brought Forward*, published in 1916. The title story is one of the very few war stories the author ever wrote, and tells of the enlistment of a Scotsman after he hears that his friend Jimmy has been killed.

In one of his letters to Cunninghame Graham, Theodore Roosevelt wrote:

> What you and Hudson have done for South America, many have done for our frontiersmen in Texas, Arizona, and New Mexico. Others have written of the Mexican frontiersmen, and written well about them. No one, as far as I know, has touched the subject of the frontiersmen of Brazil. Why don't you do it? For you have been there, know them, and speak their lingo. The field is open to you.

Not until the War, when Cunninghame Graham went to Uruguay, and en route entered the harbour of Bahia on the Brazilian coast, did he really get down to work, and decide to write on the strange doings of a religious fanatic, Antonio Conselheiro, of the Jagunços, who lived, fought, and died in the Sertão, a high scrub plateau lying between the States of Pernambuco and Bahia. This is one of the great stories of the world and makes Cunninghame Graham's book not only unusually interesting but the most fascinating of all his historical works. It appeared in 1920 with the title, *A Brazilian Mystic, Being the Life and Miracles of Antonio Conselheiro.*

Next he wrote a history of Cartagena, the Columbian seaport, once sacked by Drake and later raped by Alonso de Heredia. *Cartagena and the Banks of the Sinu* was published in 1921 with a fine equestrian portrait of the author as a frontispiece.

The Conquest of New Granada, being the life of Gonzalo Jimenez de Quesada appeared in 1922. In *The Dream of the Magi*, a little 44-page story, published in 1923, Cunninghame Graham, says Professor West, 'returns to a reverential mood, which he always held for the simple religion of the heart, and from viewing a picture of the Magi in the church of Sant' Abbondio at Coruo he has evoked a vision, or a dream, concerning the Three Wise Men'.

Hulderico Schmidel figures again in Cunninghame Graham's history of the country of the River Plate where, in his varied eventful career, Cunninghame Graham had spent the happiest days of his life. This was *The Conquest of the River Plate* (1924). 'The author's unique position of having known the country personally before "progress" struck it, of being as familiar with Spanish as with English, of having a flair for history and biography,' we are told, 'makes his South American studies especially valuable to lovers of unusual books. The personality of the author, one of the most remarkable of his time, illumines every page, and there is no one better able to understand and appreciate the rare quality of Hulderico Schmidel. This is a book to treasure and to read and re-read.'

Also in 1924 appeared Cunninghame Graham's free translation of Gustavo Barroso's (a Brazilian writer, who used the pseudonym of João do Norte) story of the Sertão, the country of Antonio Conselheiro, entitled *Mapirunga*.

After the funeral of Joseph Conrad his friend Cunninghame Graham wrote one of his finest pieces of prose, often quoted (for example by Christopher Morley in his lectures at the University of Pennsylvania on the Rosenbach Foundation lectures in 1932): 'Inveni Portum'. Reprinted in permanent form in America after its original publication in the *Saturday Review*, this has become one of the most expensive of Cunninghame Graham's books. A copy brought forty-eight dollars in New York in 1936. The text of 'Inveni Portum' appears, however, in a latter collection, *Redeemed*, published in 1927.

In 1925, following the death of his mother, Cunninghame Graham turned to his own family history and wrote *Doughty Deeds, An Account of the Life of Robert Graham of Gartmore, Poet and Politician, 1735-1797, drawn from his Letter-Books and Correspondence*. This book bears the Graham coat-of-arms, with its motto 'For Right and Reason' in gold on the front cover.

Pedro de Valdivia, Conqueror of Chile was published in 1926. I have already mentioned the collection, *Redeemed*, published the following year. In addition to 'Inveni Portum', it contained 'Wilfred Scawen Blunt', a great piece of writing describing the funeral and grave of that doughty Englishman at Newbuilding's Place, Sussex. Another characteristic piece is 'Long Wolf', an essay on an American Indian, who died in London far from his native plains when on tour with Buffalo Bill and was buried in the Brompton Cemetery.

Three books were published in 1929. The first of these was *José Antonio Páez*, a biographical study, the result of a visit to Venezuela in 1927, of a Venezuelan cowboy, who headed with General Bolivar the revolt against Spain and who became the first President of the Republic of Venezuela. Next came *Bibi*, a biographical sketch, being reminiscences of old days in Tangier with a group of friends, among them being El Moro Valienta, a brigand; the painter, Joseph Crawhall, a little-known genius who drank his life away; Bernardino de Velasco; Mohamed-el-Wad, a cattle stealer; and Bibi (Oueld-el-Haram, literally 'son of the illegitimate'). The third book was a very fine selection of Cunninghame Graham's sketches and stories (the cream of eleven books), made by his old friend Edward Garnett, who contributed an admirable appreciative preface on Cunninghame Graham's writings.

In 1930 appeared *The Horses of the Conquest*, and two years later another book of sketches, *Writ on Sand*, which *inter alia* includes his tribute to the remarkable feat of A.F. Tschiffely and his Creole horses, Mancha and Gato, in their epic ride from Buenos Aires to Washington DC, one of the greatest feats of horsemanship in history, and 'Creeps', a very moving sketch of Joseph Crawhall. 'Although the author was eighty years of age,' says Professor West, 'when this book was published it was vigorous in style and characterization. The same ironical philosophy of life, tinged slightly with a melancholy sadness mingled with an unquestionable *joie de vivre*, if such a combination is possible — and it is! — characterizes this book as it does all his others.'

The author's last biographical study, published in 1933, was a portrait of the bloodthirsty, greedy, and cowardly Lopez, dictator of Paraguay, and his French-Irish mistress, Madame Lynch, and covers the years 1865-1870. Cunninghame Graham knew many of the Paraguayans who survived those bloody and wasted years, and knew, too, the country the story covers. This book is entitled *Portrait of a Dictator*.

Mirages appeared just at the time of his death and is his last collection of fugitive pieces.

In addition to all these titles are many pamphlets, innumerable book reviews, and prefaces to books by other writers. Frank Harris said that Cunninghame Graham was 'an amateur writer of genius'. Well, he did pretty well for an amateur alike in quality and quantity. Heaven knows what he might have produced if he had been a professional. Few professionals in Scotland at any rate have ever had a richer and more varied tale of work to their credit or sustained it at a like high level throughout. A whole world of manifold interests, and valiant spirit, lies awaiting those for whom the field of Cunninghame Graham's literary activities is still a *terra incognita*; and there is certainly no field in the whole range of Scottish literature less known or better worth exploring. He was indeed a prince and paladin of our people and will, at all events, never lack his share among readers of rare discernment. There is no finer figure in all the millenary pageant of Scotland's writers. Nor any who, in all he did and was and wrote (and most conspicuously in his Scottish Nationalism), was more scrupulously faithful to the family motto — 'For Right and Reason'.

Francis George Scott:
an essay on the occasion of his seventy-fifth birthday, 25th January 1955

I

Just as Judge Ferdinand Pecora, in *Wall Street Under Oath* says, 'the laxness of the State Authorities borders on the fantastic', so in every direction in which we can turn today we find equally fantastic spectacles which like short selling, are, as the late Otto Kahn stigmatized that operation, 'inherently repellent to a right thinking man', and it is in this general milieu of unsanity that one makes one's friends — and finds them (and oneself) so riddled with absurdities that a decent human relationship is seldom possible, and the best friendship like the curate's egg — only good in parts.

My relations with my friends may be explained if I recall how Major Yeats-Brown on one occasion tells of his impressions of a French cavalry-officers' mess. The talk was infinitely more intelligent than one would ever hear in any British officers' mess, but Major Yeats-Brown was distressed by the absence of the *camaraderie* characteristic of the latter — 'there was no cosy intimacy, apparently these French officers had little or no genuine liking or respect for each other...'

I am with the French all the way in this respect as against the British. I can dispense with any amount of jolly good-fellowship for the sake of a little additional intelligence and a somewhat higher level of conversation. But my general position can be better shown perhaps by saying that I am at one with Lao Tzu when he says:

> To speak of loving all is a foolish exaggeration and to make one's mind to be impartial is a kind of partiality. If you indeed want the men of the world not to lose the qualities that are natural to them, you had best study how it is that Heaven and Earth maintain their eternal course, that the sun and the moon maintain their light, the stars their serried ranks.... the trees and shrubs their station. Then you too shall learn to guide your steps by Inward Power, to follow the course the Way of Nature sets; and soon you will reach a goal

> where you will no longer need to go round laboriously advertising goodness and duty, like a town-crier with his drum, seeking for news of a lost child. No, sir! What you are doing is to disjoint men's natures!

As I have said in one of the poems in my autobiography, *Lucky Poet*, apropos of a Berwickshire friend, I think the Scots when they are good talkers are the best talkers in the world. With F.G. Scott and Neil Gunn, the novelist, in particular, both of whom have a Russian-like capacity for long-sustained talking, not at random but to a purpose — a thorough threshing out of ideas — I have many and many a time talked from supper time the one night till breakfast time the next morning — ten or twelve solid hours of it — and these spates of talk have released a lot of our best work. (As Logan points out in *The Scottish Gael* the pre-Union Scots were, like the Russians great talkers, and all-night 'cracks' were nothing out of the common. The later reputation of the Scots for being dour, taciturn, and limited in conversation to a few Ayes and Umphs is purely a post-Union product, as is the loss of the old gaiety and abandon and the development in lieu thereof of our appalling modern dullness and social *gaucherie*.)

Living for long periods as I have done in out-of-the-way places, I have sometimes gone for months at a time without seeing anyone with whom to exchange a word, outside my own household. Yet, what I missed most was not company and the conversation of my fellow-men (which, except in about one case in every half-million perhaps I would, if I had it, find for the most part only a maddening waste of time, a mud-bath of ignorance) but a heartening professional chat. But that is difficult to find anywhere — almost as difficult in Edinburgh or Glasgow or London as on a little Shetland island; and for the rest I become increasingly impatient with the waste of time 'bunkering up' to amateurs, and experience more and more in all my contacts the utter exasperation of the professional faced with the amateur. I want (and can never content myself with anything else) a thorough mental appreciation and the stimulus of a good argumentative brain.

I was extremely fortunate, however, at the very outset of my work in getting into close touch with a number of men of very exceptional brilliance — Denis Saurat, Patrick Geddes, R.B. Cunninghame Graham, Compton Mackenzie, and others — with some of whom I have retained close friendships ever since. Of all of these men, Denis Saurat, Kaikhosru Sorabji, F.G. Scott, and the late A.R. Orage are,

I have no hesitation in saying, by far the most remarkable of all the men I have had the pleasure and privilege of knowing and associating with. To each of them may be applied the *Bhagavid-Gita* phrase — 'blazing with spiritual energy', and what Ramiro de Maeztu said of Orage in the Literary Supplement of *La Prensa* of Buenos Aires is certainly true of these four. 'Alfred Richard Orage,' he said, 'was one of the most influential spirits in England although not one Englishman in ten thousand would know his name — because Orage only influenced influential people. He had no other public but writers.'

In this connection I agree entirely with what my friend J.S. Collis says in the 'Tribute to Havelock Ellis' in his book *Farewell to Argument.* Calling Ellis 'the greatest living English writer; one of the greatest since Beowulf up to the present day', he says: 'By all the laws of life that we know of intellectually or by intuitive grasp, it is impossible that in occupying that position his stature could be generally recognized; for to be greater than the great and lauded ones calls for the possession of qualities that cannot even be seen by the multitude.'

So, naturally, Orage is known to only a few, while people like J.B. Priestley, Herbert Morrison, or Lord Beaverbrook are known to almost everybody, and, in Scotland, F.G. Scott is virtually unknown while Tom Johnston is regarded as 'perhaps the greatest Scotsman of his day', and, in music, while people like Benjamin Britten have an international vogue, and people like Ernest Newman and Percy Scholes are accounted great commentators on music and profoundly informed musicologists, Kaikhosru Sorabji goes for nothing at all; and, in philosophy, no one hears a word about Denis Saurat and the names of Sir James Jeans and the late Sir Arthur Eddington are almost household words, and even men like Earl Balfour and Lord Haldane win a wide repute as philosophers. And, as soon as one begins to 'distinguish and divide' and claim that a man like Scott is not to be grouped with so-and-so as one of 'our contemporary Scottish composers' but holds a plane apart and far above the others, and that, indeed, with Saurat and Sorabji, his place is so high that he is out of sight of the mob altogether and cannot possibly have the widespread recognition accorded to a whole host of 'famous' composers, none of whom are fit to tie the latchets of his shoes, one is on that deadliest of all grounds of contention which is also in such connections the only one worth fighting on, and has against one all the cohorts of mediocrities, led by all the serried ranks of those practitioners of 'the good which is the worst enemy of the best'.

For it is precisely what these four friends of mine have in common

— an inability to suffer fools gladly or at all; an utter incapacity for the brainless chit-chat which passes almost everywhere else for an 'interest in' literature or music or philosophy or what not, and is in fact intolerable to anyone who has a real interest in these matters or indeed in anything, just as most writers and speakers on spiritual matters may begin well but slump swiftly into platitude and commonplace, and, to be precise, it is these commonplaces that are utterly intolerable in the treatment of any higher human activity; a concentration on their own creative processes which insulates them from the majority of people whenever they encounter it, just as household pets are apt at time to resent people who are always reading or writing or playing the piano, instead of paying attention to *them*.

It is therefore not in the least surprising that four such very different men should have been great friends of each other. Saurat was one of the editors (along with Sir Herbert Read) of Orage's posthumously collected *Selected Essays and Critical Writings*, and he has been one of F.G. Scott's closest friends for many years; Sorabji contributed a great deal of music criticism to Orage's two papers, first *The New Age* and then the *New English Weekly* for nearly twenty years, and he, too, is one of F.G. Scott's oldest friends — though neither in Saurat's case nor in Sorabji's was Orage the catalyst who brought the others into contact: Scott's friendships with them were independently formed, and mine with them were formed *via* Scott, though I had met Sorabji independently before. After an intermission of about fifteen years — from my schooldays until the end of the 1914-18 War; a period during which I had lost contact with Scott altogether — I got into touch with Scott again; but in my case I certainly knew *of* Sorabji first (a different matter from knowing him) through Orage's *New Age*, of which I was a regular reader from 1908 onwards and, later, a regular and voluminous contributor. But it is certainly no mere chance that there should have been these interrelations between these men; they are, in many ways, of a kind. And it was precisely on the same grounds that I met most of my best friends — Æ, and Will Dyson, T.S. Eliot and Augustus John were also all friends of Orage's (though, except for the last-named, I did not meet any of them through him, but quite independently). But, indeed, my best friends are all part of an intellectual *élite* whose members are nearly all known in some degree to each other.

Of Saurat, Sorabji, and Scott, each working in a very different field, related to each other only by the fact that each of them work on the same exceedingly high plane, I have no doubt whatever that they are three of the finest minds Great Britain has had in my lifetime and stand on an altogether higher level than all the other men I know or have known except T.S. Eliot whom I would put along with them, antipathetic to me as much of his writing (his *prose* writing) is. It will no doubt seem incredible to many of my readers that I, who have known them both personally, can seriously contend that F.G. Scott is — but what is the phrase to be? A greater man, a finer artist, a more distinguished personality than, say, W.B. Yeats, or that Kaikhosru Sorabji is a greater musical genius than, say, Delius or Elgar, or that Saurat is a greater philosopher and literary critic (or rather critic of writers' ideas, of the philosophy involved in their work) than anyone who is at all well-known or known at all to any considerable fraction of the British reading public, either as a philosopher or literary critic today. But my reply is simply that I am certain of these three propositions and the reason why these three great men are comparatively little known is precisely that which is given by De Maetzu with regard to Orage, and by Collis with regard to Havelock Ellis.

To F.G. Scott's position and work as a composer of song-settings, I devoted a long essay in my *Contemporary Scottish Studies* (1926). He has an immense musical and general background, and if he had followed the customary practice of brainy Scots and devoted himself to anything but Scotland he would undoubtedly have won recognition a decade ago and more as a great composer. Happily he took the opposite course, and has paid for it by being unable to 'get his work across' save to an infinitesimal public, even in Scotland itself. And yet his work is essentially popular — and should take, or should have taken, the Scottish public by storm. But as matters stand the Scottish public has been so debauched and distorted by English over-influence that the very qualities that have been most typically Scottish all through the centuries, and that characterize all the best work in our national cultural heritage, now seem to them un-Scottish, and in one of my poems on Glasgow I have to cry:

> Scott popular? — Scott, whose work is *di essenza popolare*,
> This popular not meaning plebeian or poor in content
> But *sano, schietto, realistico,*
> *E religiosamente attinente al profondo spirito della razza*!
> Scott popular... in Glasgow?
> What a place for bat-folding!

It is impossible for so distinguished and dynamic an artist to win the hearing he deserves in the infernal babble of a country of whose people today it has been well said that:

> Even the most striking of them are lacking, in a very Scottish fashion, in any real originality. The fact is that Scottish individualism, about which we hear so much, is not so strong a trait as Scottish democratic feeling. (The Scottish Churches, for example, had no use for hierarchy, and the levelling down has been pretty thorough.) Self-assertiveness has taken the place of individuality, and in these days when the problem is one of the free personality, every other little Scot is either a Liberal capitalist or a state-obsessed Socialist.

Scott is the outstanding exception to this general state of affairs in Scotland today.

'Mr Scott,' says Mr James H. Whyte in the anthology, *Towards a New Scotland* (1935),

> was at work on his songs long before the war, and to his stimulus and encouragement — he is a splendid literary critic — more than to anyone else are directly and indirectly due most of the conscious endeavours to bring about a revival of the Scottish arts similar to the revival enjoyed in Ireland in modern times. In emulation of him, a whole group of Scottish artists are attempting to express themselves as Scots and as modern Scots, as opposed to the old-fashioned hacks who exploit a debilitated Scottishness that is their only pull on the Scottish masses.

Apart from a host of part-songs, Scott's published work is contained in five volumes of *Scottish Lyrics Set to Music*. The choice of these shows the impact of a first-class critical mind on the whole corpus of available Scottish song, with the important exception of Gaelic song. It is true as Mr Whyte says that

> there is a very rich folk-music in Scotland, and a musical literature bequeathed by composers for the bagpipe — a classical music more akin to Byzantine music than any contemporary European music, marvellously rich within certain narrow limits. Francis George Scott has mastered this old music, and subsumed it in a markedly modern idiom, in which he has set some of the finest of Scottish lyrics, old and new.

But the fact is that although he has made a thorough study of the music of the pibrochs (about which even among pipers little is known — and that mostly a mass of misconceptions), Scott has found little to his purpose owing to the paucity of good translations of Scottish Gaelic poetry. Writing to me of his latest (the fifth) book of his song-settings, he said in this connection:

> I have, I think, managed 'to sing a song at least' — in fact not only sung, but printed musical settings of some sixty Scottish poems. I'd say of this latest batch your own '*Watergaw*' and George Campbell Hay's '*Fisherman*' are the best, though not likely to be the most popular. Hay's poem has been treated in a pibroch-like fashion — very restrained, mystical, and, with a voice like Paul Robeson's behind it, should be something of a knock-out. I've always wanted and especially of recent years, to work along this contemplative, transcendental line, but unfortunately (owing to the rarity of the material) have only Jean Lang's *Brendan's Graveyard* in Book III and this Hay setting to show for it. It may be that what I'm after is intrinsically Gaelic in flavour and in a long conversation with Hay in Taynuilt we discussed this point and he promised to send along anything he can manage either of his own or in translation.

After working through Burns and the old Scots poets, especially Dunbar, Scott was at a loss for lack of suitable material until I began publishing my earliest Hugh MacDiarmid lyrics, which fell upon him like manna in the desert. He has set over seventy of them, but my own development during the past few years has made me confine myself to kinds of work not suitable for his purposes, and he has been increasingly sorely put to it to find the kind of lyrics he needs. He has happily found a few in modern German poetry, one of the best being Heinrich Lersch's poem, *Bruder*, a grand bit of lyrical expression Scott's setting of which is a very powerful bit of music.

A glance at the sources of Scott's settings in these five published collections is interesting; twenty-six are to Burns's words, four to Dunbar's, ten to mine, and William Drummond, John Imlah, Jean Lang, Mark Alexander Boyd, Patrick Birnie, Sir Walter Scott, William Creech, Allan Cunninghame, and George Campbell Hay account for one each. In addition to these there is his *Renaissance Overture*, rendered by the Scottish Orchestra, conducted by Issy Dobrowen, in January, 1939 (it has not been published yet) and symphonic settings of Dunbar's *Seven Deadly Sins* (this has neither been published nor rendered in public yet). Of the former — the *Renaissance Overture* — I wrote at the time of the Scottish Orchestra's performance:

> The crown of Scott's work to date — which is to say far and away the finest composition by any Scottish composer (for there is no comparison between Scott and any other composer Scotland has ever produced; he stands on a plane of his own immeasurably

removed from theirs), this great overture is a magnificent challenge to all the suppressed and latent potentialities capable of creating a distinctive culture in Scotland on a level in keeping with all the best traditions in the whole range of our national history and the relative status any true Scot must covet as Scotland's due. It is an immensely exciting work, dynamic to a degree, even dynamitic; a superb summation of all the vital elements in our national past, ordered in the most masterly fashion and projected vertically into the future by a single horn on its topmost note — symbolic of the passionate spirit of the composer himself, his relative position to all other contemporary Scotland composers and to the whole range of Scottish music to date, and of his rousing indomitable realization of the unparalleled spiritual impetus which alone can redeem Scotland from its present woeful floundering in the Slough of Despond and encompass the supreme realization of our undoubted potentialities. In its own field the evocative and challenging quality of this work is irresistible; one would fain hope that it might prove so in relation to Scottish life too and communicate in actual fact the superb impulse which is at once its theme and its nature — but will the fat ears of our people hear, or must Scott say too, 'I have piped, but ye have not danced'?

The reception of Scott's *Overture* by the newspaper critics was, of course, precisely as might have been predicted. It seems to have shocked most of them by its sheer din and ferocity. Some of the church mice tried to exonerate themselves by putting some of the blame on the conductor, Issy Dobrowen, for being too slap-dash in his methods, but Scott wasn't long in identifying himself with the conductor's reading — much to the annoyance of these precious gentry! The real trouble, of course, was just the hatred and fear of all dynamic which characterizes these eunuchoid creatures. It was amusing to see how all of them sang dumb about the music's significance — not a word about its implications. A Scottish renaissance is the last thing they want. Where would they be then, poor things? In the meantime they are doing all right — financially, which is the only way they are interested in or capable of conceiving anyone else being interested in. The level of Scottish criticism is the lowest in the world. No wonder a correspondent writes us: 'We've had the contemporary art show (organized by the Saltire Society in Glasgow) and some damnable attempts at criticism in the newspapers — so bad that I've been tempted into saying that all art ought to be incomprehensible, after listening to other folks' ability to comprehend!'

With the substitution of the word Scotland for Norway, the lines Henrik Ibsen addressed to the Norwegian composer, Edvard Grieg (who was partly of Scottish descent, and from earliest youth a zealous republican — in the battles in Norway over the union with Sweden he was always to be found on the extreme Left, and so it was one of the happiest days in his life when Norway won her independence in 1905) might well be addressed to Scott, viz:

> Orpheus woke with crystal tones
> Souls in brutes; struck fire from stones.
>
> Stones there are in Scotland plenty;
> Brutes far more than ten or twenty.
>
> Play, so stones spark far and wide!
> Play, to pierce the brutes' thick hide!

Scott was a schoolteacher of mine at Langholm Academy when I was a boy of 14 or 15. I lost touch with him completely from about 1906 to 1922, when he happened to see one of my early MacDiarmid lyrics in *The Scottish Chapbook* and wrote to me, not knowing, of course, that the pseudonym of 'Hugh MacDiarmid' covered an old Langholm pupil of his. We met, found that I had reached independently (for up to then I knew nothing of Scott's work as a composer, though he had already been setting Scottish songs when he was one of my teachers in Langholm) a position very close to his own with regard to Scottish Arts and Letters, and found we had a great deal more in common — a deep community of insight. We were both Border men — Scott belonging to Hawick, only twenty miles from Langholm. Since then we have been the closest of friends and there can be few cases of closer collaboration between a poet and a composer. We would undoubtedly have done a great deal more together if it had not been for the fact that circumstances carried me first away to London and then located me in the remote Shetlands, and never through all these years enabled us to be in each other's company for more than a few consecutive nights in any year. Scott is one of the few men, perhaps the only man, I have known for whom I have an unqualified respect. Simply because he so clearly and completely understands that ability of any kind depends upon self-respect and is incapable of losing his on any account. I think the world of him and his work seems to me of superlative importance to Scotland. I have said that in the last few years my work has not been of a sort that was suitable for his purposes. I have regretted this very deeply indeed, and would have done anything I possibly could to have met his requirements — if I could have done anything at all. But these matters do not arrange themselves in that fashion. It has at any rate been a weird experience to have so many of my principal associates in the Scottish Literary and Political Movement quite incapable of appreciating Scott — and, though my own standards were much easier, of such a sort that Scott would not have tolerated their company for a moment. The Scottish BBC, of course, has all along treated Scott very shabbily, not because his quality was not fully realized, but on the contrary, because he was clearly so infinitely better than the run of Scottish contributors on whom the BBC depends, and whom it consequently could not afford to have put out of countenance. Scott blew the gaff on all their pretensions too conclusively.

Out-Haydn'd, out-Grétry'd, out-Handel'd, out-Rossini'd
By mannikins a million times pettier still
Than any of these were to their hated betters.

And I am forced to cry to him (thinking in particular of Glasgow):

Who knows in this infernal broth-like fog
There may be greater artists yet by far than we,
Unheard of, even by us, condemned to be invisible
In this Tarnhelm of unconscionable ignorance
Where 'everybody is entitled to his own opinion'?

Glasgow, which in another verse I have depicted as follows:

Where have I seen a human being looking
As Glasgow looks this gin-clear evening — with face and fingers
A cadaverous blue, hand-clasp slimy and cold
As that of a corpse, fingernails grown immeasurably long
As they do in the grave, little white eyes, and hardly
Any face at all
Cold, lightning-like, unpleasant, light and blue,
Like having one's cold spots intoxicated with mescal.
Looking down a street the houses seem
Long pointed teeth like a ferret's over the slit
Of a crooked unspeakable smile, like the Thracian woman's
When Thales fell in the well; and the smell reminds me
Of the *odeur de souris* of Balzac's Cousin Pons,
Or Yankee adverts about halitosis, and underarm odour.
All the strength seemed to leave my body as I looked.
It sucked the blood from my brain and heart like a vampire.

'A hag whose soul-gelding ugliness would chill
To eternal chastity a cantharadised satyr.'
And a deadly grey weariness fell over my thoughts like dust,
A terrible shadow descended like dust over my thoughts,
Almost like reading a *Glasgow Herald* leader
Or any of our Scottish papers,
Smug class organs, standardised, superficial,
Unfair in the presentation of news, and worse than useless
As interpreters of the present scene or guides to the future,
Or like the dread darkness that descends on one
Who, as the result of an accident sustained
In the course of his favourite recreation, tricycling,
Suffers every now and then from loss of memory.

It is in keeping with my general attitude — and with the fact that my best friends are all of the type of great artists whose value is 'invisible to the mob' — that I should not only denounce all 'witch-doctors, chiselers, lookers-under-beds, local Solons, bourgeois bonzes, trained seals, and back-street Bourbons', but that, on the occasion of the International PEN Congress in Scotland in 1934, I should in a rhymed welcome to the foreign delegates, describe the prominent Scots they would meet in the following lines:

As when tempestuous Nature in a torment
Pours out her prodigies and Heaven is rent
With fearful glories, Scotland here emits
In speedy sequence to your gaze her wits
(Nitwits!) and seers, lords, priests, and business-men....
Nonentities in everything but name.
And, above all, her potent *pisseurs d'encre*
Who, subs and copy-boys, rank on (more) rank,
Thunder in cubby-holes....
Do not commit the pardonable mistake
Of slighting them, for, though you know them not,
Their backstairs powers must never be forgot.
Their weasel minds the least of them quintuple
By underhand intrigue and lack of scruple,
And like a weasel pack they always go
Wriggling like one though twenty form a row.

One critic referred to this as an example of 'the famous MacDiarmid invective and ability to make ridiculous a humbug or lambast a time-server, for which we are eternally grateful'.

But apart from the unscrupulous money-grubbers who scoop the pool, and the solid phalanx of mediocrities in Scotland in whom it is impossible to awaken any interest or appreciation in Scott's work, the other great overriding factor that seems to me to have far too narrowly restricted Scott's output is his lack, due to his age and the very different generation most formative of him, of that mental resilience to which Sir Winston Churchill referred when he said: 'It requires not only courage but mental resilience for those whose youth lay in calmer and more slowly moving times in order that they may adjust themselves to the giant outlines and harsh structure of the twentieth century.'

II

In December 1945, I published the following article which is in place here since the situation has not changed in the interval except for the worse, and for a long time now Scott's work has been kept off the air, while singer after singer of Scottish songs has given programmes confined to worthless arrangements by Mansfield, Diack, Moffat, Stephen, Cedric Thorpe Davie, and others, while a member of the BBC staff, Mr Ian Whyte, has used his position to secure the inclusion in the programmes of an altogether disproportionately great — and indeed, egregiously obtrusive — number of his own compositions. Scotland is worse than any other country in the so-called civilized world in respect of that tyranny of the repetition complex of which Mr Michael Tippett recently complained when he wrote:

> We all know that the big public is extremely conservative, and willing to ring the changes on a few beloved works till the end of time. So that our concert life, through the taste of this public, suffers from a kind of inertia of sensibility, that seems to want no musical experience whatever that it does not already know. When this taste is indeed the national taste, the art of the nation certainly dies. But the creative artist is passionately determined that it shall not die. In fact totalitarian societies, which are pathetically conformist and afraid of the new, have had to stamp him out. They are afraid; even of the struggling composer with his tiny public. And what are they afraid of? I think they are afraid of his passion, of his violence, of his unaccountability. For it is a fact of musical history (and this goes for the other arts as well) that during the

> last half-century, or even earlier, every major composer has at the outset found the taste of the big public and its consumer point of view unacceptable.

So it is true of Scott, as Mr Tippett says it was of Bartók, that the big public

> instinctively hated his creative integrity, and no doubt he, for all his courage, was hurt and haunted by this hate. The dilemma is not a conspiracy but a fact. Why does the big public hate extreme artistic integrity? How can a great composer go forward at all in what looks like a voluntary cul-de-sac? Surely the matter is that the very big public masses together in a kind of dead passion of mediocrity, and that this blanket of mediocrity, whether communist or capitalist, is deeply offended by any living passion of the unusual, the rare, the rich, the exuberant, the heroic, and the aristocratic in art — the art of a poet like Yeats. While it is clear from Yeats' life and writings that in this very passion of defiance an artist can find both material for his art, and vigour for his despised activity. But he may starve.

The Edinburgh International Festival has done nothing to remedy this state of affairs. Its promoters do not care if every Scottish composer dies of starvation. The native contribution to the arts is almost wholly excluded from the Festival programmes. The article is as follows:

> The mistake of preferring Barabbas is nowhere so prevalent as in Scotland today; the injunction, 'Seek ye first the Kingdom of Heaven...' more universally neglected than in any other European country. A little country like Finland can produce a man wholly dedicated to his art like Sibelius. And not only so, but a sufficient number of people to recognize the stand he has taken and the incomparable national importance of it — and, accordingly to insist and ensure that he be given his proper place and that whatever encouragement and facilitation, financially and otherwise, lesser spirits can give him in his high task shall be his.
>
> In Scotland alone there is no such incentive to, or encouragement in, serious creative effort in any of the arts. On the contrary! Even the St Andrew's Night programme of the Scottish BBC was a shameful *exposé* of our national atimy and amentality. It was a ludicrously undignified melange of worthless 'arrangements' by Sir Hugh S. Roberton and Mr Ian Whyte, crowned by the participation of the unspeakable buffoon, Mr Will Fyfe. Nobody is allowed to participate in these ceremonial displays of Scottish

bad taste and stupidity who has ever given any evidence of any serious purpose except the snapping up of whatever fees are going. But, you say, it is the kind of entertainment the public likes. No doubt. The unfortunate Scottish public has been thoroughly conditioned to like nothing else. The fact that they like it all right does not alter the fact that it is just as entertaining as Hell!

And on top of that Edinburgh's Lord Provost and his associates are going to have a great International Musical Festival in Edinburgh, and imagine that Edinburgh will as a result come to rival Salzburg! Timbuktoo or Kalgoorlie would have as much chance of doing anything of the kind. Every distinguished composer and executant might be attracted to the Festival; the more they came the more they would emphasize the absence of their peers in Scotland itself and the better the programmes the more ghastly would yawn the abyss between them and the utter inability of the Scottish people to assimilate and profit by anything of the sort, let alone be stimulated even to try to produce anything of comparable worth on their own part. None of these things is, of course, the aim of the Festival. It has commercial, not aesthetic, aims. All that is desired is (1) to get some useful publicity, (2) make money, and (3) jack up a little the general illusion that the Scots are really a cultivated people with an interest in the arts. In short it is just another lousy racket, typical enough of a so-called capital city whose principal daily paper is mean enough to refuse to notice an exhibition of the works of the principal sculptor resident in Scotland on the ground that to do so would partake of the nature of a free advertisement! *The Scotsman* 'reviews' books, of course, but then the publishers can send in free copies of the books; the sculptor can hardly present *The Scotsman* with copies of his works in return for a write-up!

That's all that interest in the arts amounts to in Edinburgh. But this Festival will, of course, allow the Lord Provost and the Bailies and all the rest of the nitwits to strut about airing a lot of quasi-musical jargon just acquired *ad hoc*, and posing as cognoscenti, patrons of the arts, and what not, for the benefit of the dazzled citizenry, while anybody who really does know anything about music in Scotland, and above all, the very few who have done anything worth doing about it, will be kept well and truly in the outer darkness by their successful and self-satisfied inferiors, while the cream of Europe's music-makers are 'enjoying' an indescribable series of encounters with village idiots, characters with cleft palates, and strangers to the district.

I know Edinburgh only too well. I am not, I tell myself, a slave to snap judgements. I try to be broadminded and forbearing; I try to find in even the most repulsive creatures some redeeming spark that would allow my heart to warm towards them. But even with the most noble effort, it is becoming cumulatively plain to me that nobody in Edinburgh who has anything to do with the arts — and above all nobody connected with the BBC — and I can be brothers. Least of all, one who will almost inevitably cut a very prominent figure in the Festival; if that orgy ever comes off.

I mean Mr Nobody, who has just been appointed, by the BBC Director of Music in Scotland, at a salary of some £1,250 per annum. Now Mr Nobody has no right to accept that appointment. To supplant another and better man in the place that is rightly his and appropriate the reputation and influence that ought to be his, is a far more serious felony than any the law punishes, because far deadlier in its effect on the community.

The Press notices of Mr Nobody's appointment list all the busybodyish quasi-musical things he has been doing during the past twenty years. It is a long sad tale of irrelevant jobbery. It may have benefited Mr Nobody's pocket, but it has certainly served no creditable public purpose. And it has nothing whatever to do with music in Scotland. Mr Nobody is a musical nonentity without one jot or tittle of creative ability. Nevertheless he is one of a small group of moronic mediocrities who have literally had a corner in everything lucrative in connection with Scotland during the past quarter of a century. Not one of them has done anything at all for music in Scotland. They have simply jointly and severally succeeded in accentuating the contemptible pass to which Scotland has been reduced in this respect. There was never anything with which they could meddle that they could do other than still further degrade. They are destitute of aesthetic standards; the idea of selfless devotion to a great cause is completely foreign to their natures: their public performances and the pap they spew up in their Press statements and occasional speeches show them to be quite incapable of any high and serious concern with any of the arts. But they have never lacked the colossal crust to assume the role of leading composers in our midst and by their sheer effrontery block out the few men who have a high devotion and genuine creative abilities, and deny any chance of performance to their work in favour of their own piffling productions. The latter few have never had a chance of securing any post of influence or financial value. All such posts are monopolized by this small clique.

It is inconceivable that any of these men could for a moment have been taken seriously or given any of the posts they occupy in any other European country, except Scotland. Mr Nobody would never have had a ghost's chance of securing his new appointment in any other country. And since he must know perfectly well that the whole thing is a ghastly farce — that he has no real qualifications for the job — that it is monstrous to expect any composer of genuine ability, no matter how small, to submit his scores to such a 'judge' — and that he is usurping the place and the power which belong to other men (men with real gifts, and with records of integrity and disinterested service, which entitle them — and not him! — to every possible consideration), his acceptance of the post is neither more nor less than professional hijacking with a vengeance! One such real musician — the best of the few such Scotland has ever possessed — was actually an applicant for the post Mr Nobody now occupies, but the BBC had the incredible gall to turn him down on the pretext that he was too old. Actually he is about the same age as Mr Nobody. As to their relative qualifications there is no need for me to advance my personal opinion. The volume of *Grove's* may be consulted instead, and if consulted will show no mention whatever of Mr Nobody, a brief paragraph devoted to Mr Nobody's predecessor, and — in contradistinction — a lengthy entry dealing with Mr Francis George Scott, not listing a lot of egregious activities pursued with an insect-like industriousness, but treating seriously of his output and quality as a Scottish national composer of outstanding — and almost solitary — importance.

That goes for nothing in Scotland, however. The whole field is monopolized by the monkey tricks of creatures like Nobody, Roberton, Offwhite and the rest; and that must not be attributed simply to the irrepressibility of their simian activity — but to the fact that it pays! That is the crux of the matter. The other principal factor in producing this situation is simply the hatred of men of, it may be, in their own way, no little cleverness, yet essentially uncreative for their superiors — those who really possess that which no application or ambition can acquire for those born without the gift!

But when it comes to the Scottish Musical Advisory Committee of CEMA Mr Scott, of course, is the only Scottish composer on it. The others are all incomers like Professor Bullock and Newman and Dr Hague.

Even more appalling than the impudence with which these

'helot usurpers of the true kingdom of awareness' monopolize the posts which should belong to other, and better, men, and, in so doing, check and stultify every creative effort made on behalf of music and the other arts in Scotland, is the fact that such a state of affairs is accepted without protest by the associations in our midst which ostensibly exist to promote the interests of the arts in Scotland. Not a cheep of protest from the Saltire Society, the Dunedin Association, the Scottish PEN, the Scottish Convention, or even the Scottish National Party! Why? Simply because these bodies too have no real, but only a professed, concern with the arts, and are composed of precisely the same sort of phoney people as those I have been describing. Some of them already hold positions in which they could, if they would, do a great deal to advance the arts in Scotland. But do they utilize their positions to do anything of the kind? Of course not! Instead of that they form or join associations which have no earthly chance of doing as much as they themselves could easily do in their own individual capacities if they cared. But it is much simpler to join associations to foster the arts in Scotland than actually do anything towards that end in one's own personal position. And you can trust the Scottish Press not to make any reference to such a glaring contradiction. And so the old game of mindless grab and mean intrigue, and empty lip service to the arts, goes on, and the arts in Scotland remain in the horrible gutter to which they have been so long confined.[1] And that is precisely what England's *haute politique* requires. And the only ones who suffer are the few who are mugs enough to be genuine creative artists and men of principle and integrity.

Of course, Mr Nobody, Sir Hugh Roberton, and the rest of the gang are all very charming men, so amiable, so refined, so unassuming, so full of fun — but try to screw the blighters down to first principles, and you will notice the change in their tone at once, the steel showing through the whipped cream, the spikes under the feathers.

---

[1] The most distinguished music critic Scotland has ever produced, the late Mr Cecil Gray (not to be confused with C.G. who is *The Scotsman* 'musical critic'), found this situation in Scotland so appalling, that he became completely denationalized and even anti-Scottish, any attempt to interest him in any professed or possible development of music in Scotland evoking from him thereafter only the most blistering fury. I should like to have heard him on the present incumbent of Mr Nobody's post.

TAILPIECE

Having regard to their personal attainments, I would suggest that Messrs Nobody and his like would have been wiser never to have attempted the musical modes in which they have tinkered, but confined themselves instead to that older practice Weldon describes in his *Secret History of the Court of King James* (supposed — probably rightly — to have been edited by Sir Walter Scott), in the passage which runs as follows:

> Sir Thomas Monson was a great lover of musick, and had as good as England had especially for voyces, and was at infinite charge in breeding some in Italy. This Symon was an excellent musician and did sing delicately, but was a more general musician than ever the world had: but in one kind he surpassed all. He had a *catzo* of immense length and bigness; with this being his tabor-stick, and his mouth his pipe, he would so imitate the tabor-pipe as if it had been so indeed. To this musick would Mrs Turner, the young ladies, and some of that gang dance ever after supper. The old lady, who loved that musick as well as her daughters, would sit and laugh: she could scarce sit for laughing; and it was believed that some of them danced after to that pipe without the tabor. His master coming to hear of it turned him away, but was infinitely importuned to take him again, but would not. He could not have wanted a service elsewhere but he never durst use his pipe amongst them for their dancing recreation however he might for any other!

I should add that this is not a whine — not a cry on my part (let alone on Scott's) as in the hymn:

> And is thy table all in vain
> Before unwilling hearts displayed?

But, so far as the people of Scotland are concerned, a cry of woe to those who have heard the trumpets sounding and failed to respond.

A recent writer on Moussorgsky (with whose work, especially the two cycles of his songs — *Without Sunlight* and *Songs and Dances of Death* — Scott has marked affinities, especially in that union in his songs of the tone and innermost colour, nuance, inflection of the text; the union of the two things which are equally indispensable in a master composer of songs — endless and unfailing invention, and, as the supreme guidance for his genius, the meaning and very aroma of the poem itself: his aim always *verismo*, all musical and other means directed uncompromisingly to the expressive end) has said that in almost all his work he was 'saved by the power and authenticity of his musical inspiration, and reinforced, indeed protected, by an armour mightier than perhaps he always knew, the probity of the Russian folk-spirit which permeated his art'. Russian folk-music is woven into every inch of Moussorgsky's creative fabric. There is no half-way process about this either. It is the shape, the sound, and the musical instinct of his people which always affects him. He speaks with their voice and he is incorruptible. He was eternally concerned and absorbed in the human lot, but the prating of internationalism as the necessity of an art which has universality would have found him entirely cold. He comprehended as a seer, but he spoke in music his native speech, heightened and strengthened by the individual powers of his mind and spirit.

It is true in some measure of Scott as of Moussorgsky that he was

> shattered and broken by reactionary forces in art opposed to him. He is one of the spirits of whom it was said by somebody that 'one forsook, and one denied, and the lonely man of destiny went on his way'. In his last years Moussorgsky was unaccompanied, and at a time when he was in greatest need of the comprehension that even Stassof was unable to extend. It is now evident that as Moussorgsky became always clearer sighted and more uncompromising in his quest of truth, the lesser ones, even the most faithful and well-meaning, dropped away.

Our unthinking conventionalists of Scots, terrified of anything with life in it, will, of course, have no more to do with F.G. Scott's resettings of Burns's songs than the Swedes would tolerate the taking of any like liberties with Carl Michael Bellman, the famous Swedish poet and singer of the eighteenth century, although his drinking song, 'To The Galatians', for example, ambles along as amiably as a glass of milk, and has no kick in it whatever despite the allusions in the text to 'rich brown ale' and 'Swedish punch', and it would be easy to think of this song with a different rhythmic emphasis, a brisker tempo, a sensation of the swing and vigour of the quick dotted eight, and not the lilting, languishing beat of the pastorale, six-eight time. Similar strictures must be passed on many more of his songs, though Bellman (the type of man I like best, for, like Mr E.M. Forster, I am 'with the old Scotsman who wanted less chastity and more delicacy' all the time) lived recklessly, with a God-given abhorrence of the smug, secure, and systematic, wasted his substance, consorted on equal terms with scholiasts and tavernkeepers, nobles and lights-o'-love of high and low degree, yet looking to him for the vigorous racy semi-Rabelaisian semi-Robert Burns sort of thing we legitimately expect we are woefully disappointed; he is betrayed by a bad musical tradition — as Burns's poem was betrayed by the utterly alien traditional setting of 'Scots Wha Hae', against which nevertheless, Scott's infinitely better re-setting can make no headway.

III

I think it may be said of my own songs which Scott has set as Peter Monro Jack (himself a Scotsman, and former student under Sir Herbert Grierson at Aberdeen) has said in *The New York Times Book Review* of Garcia Lorca:

> The specific recurrent imagery of olives, jasmine, fig trees, salt pits, the smell of the Sierra, the little squares of the towns, the ponies in the mountains — all this will be for most of us a dream landscape. What makes it *seem* so real to us is that Lorca, without being a storyteller, constantly gives the sense of life in his pictures: men riding, women on the balustrade, gypsy girls dancing. In effect it is what Burns does so easily and simply in his Scots poems, as in 'I'll aye ca' in by yon toun, and by yon garden green again' — and the feeling of Scots life is there. So Lorca will write 'Through the arch of Elvira... I want to see you pass', or 'Although I know the road... I'll never reach Córdoba', or 'You leave us singing... in the little square', and in the same way he savours and sweetens a people and landscape that he loved deeply and intimately. But though like Burns in his realism and his nature-sense and like him also in his musical knowledge (he composed, sang his own songs, had the respect of de Falla), Lorca is far beyond in linguistic sophistication. He uses every effect of symbolism, fantasy, super-realism, and he has the astringent difficulty and corresponding pleasure of solution that most modern verse has, and that Blake, rather than Burns, had.

It was for such a development of Scots song that F.G. Scott was waiting, and supremely fitted to deal. If circumstances had allowed us to live in the same town and be constantly in touch over a considerable period, we would, I think, have performed the necessary long-overdue audit and working-over of the whole corpus of Scottish popular song which would at once have been most beneficial to our respective gifts and would have enabled us to carry with us the great mass of the Scottish people. What I am thinking of is such a procedure of study, analysis, imitation, and adroit variation as the young Maurice Chevalier carried out on the repertoires of the then popular café singers and music-hall artistes in Paris and elsewhere — as when he tuned in for example to Dranem's supreme success, 'Ah, les p'tits pois, les p'tits pois' — watched Mistinguet tackling such songs as 'Coeur en Feu' and 'Mon Petit Watman', music by Lestac — picked up new physiognomical and grotesque tricks and sang 'Les foies gras', 'Sale voyou bonsoir', and on to 'Allume, Allume!', 'L'Omnibus', 'Le Beau Mome'; proceed to Marseilles and sang 'J'aime les fleurs, j'aime les fleurs parce qu'elles ont un bouton' and then sang the same number in the style of Mayon and Dranem, singing as they would have sung it and mimicking their mannerisms; on to 'Ta Bouche' and 'Il faut savoir tout prendre avec le sourire'; and later, showed himself quick to perceive that there was too wide a gulf between the popular American songs of, say, Winnie Lightner, and the free-and-easy ditties of the essentially French 'Dédé'; then, back to France again sang 'La petite bête qui monter', 'La Chanson du Rugby' and 'T'en fais pas pour le chapeau de la gamine' — songs that were

> just street incidents transferred to the stage, complete with words, twists, and gestures. That is what made them so successful. The market-place and the Champs-Elysées were portrayed with equal felicity. Maurice was quite as much at home in the one as in the other...Dressed up as a Breton peasant Maurice asked his audience naïvely: 'Savez-vous planter les choux?' He said it in a way to make them feel as if they had never heard of cabbages before, leave alone how to plant them....Then even that great establishment of which Maurice had become the rage, when he introduced his world-famous song 'Valentine', proved too small for the crowds that rushed to see him. By means of those songs, which seemed to have been transferred straight from the streets of Paris to the stage, Maurice could stir the hearts of the crowd. The fundamental reason of his success lies in that his listeners, especially those of simple heart, get the impression that this popular singer is the interpreter of their own feelings. So sincere and realistic are his renderings of those typically Parisian songs that most of those present think they could express them just as well, if they took the trouble. Of course, that is only an illusion on their part, for it takes a sort of genius to succeed in this difficult art.

What I commend to younger Scots writers is the patient hard work, the acute analysis, based on a thorough knowledge of popular types, local dialects, slang, and a profound love of the streets and all sorts and conditions of people, which are necessary for success of this sort. Scottish life has never been studied to artistic purpose in this way. Our Scottish music-hall artists have no wit whatever to put an edge on their native humour. But to reachieve a body of popular Scottish song that will really capture the public is the great task confronting Scottish poetry today, and apart from that lively affection for the Scottish people, and a good background of knowledge of the Scottish popular tradition down the centuries, few studies would help anyone tackling this great task better perhaps than a study of French popular songs, and of the training in observation and the methods of artistry whereby such singers as Chevalier secured successful additions to their repertoires. That F.G. Scott and I have been unable to do a great deal more in this direction is a great pity, since it is seldom that a poet and a composer with so much community of insight and capable of such an exceedingly close collaboration come together, and the things that have prevented our much more effective conjunction have been so exasperatingly unnecessary. Still that we came together as we did at all has been a bit of supreme good luck, and indeed in itself amply justifies the title of my autobiography, *Lucky Poet*.

'He analysed,' we read of Chevalier,

> the talent of fat Vilbert, that bluff actor from the south who invaded the Paris stage with his wit, his mocking jokes, and his badinage, his breath still smelling of garlic, he having overlooked the fact that he had left Marseilles. Maurice had studied his effect on the spectators. Some shouted with delight; one of them managed to insert a spicy wisecrack in the accent of the south, which made the audience rock and which revealed that the spectator was a compatriot of the artiste. Maurice studied the moment when Vilbert's jokes extracted the maximum of laughter from the audience. He analysed him, just as he had previously analysed Mademoiselle Polaire and Paulette Darty, and as he had analysed the anatomy of his recent colleagues, the crowd-workers, appraising their make-up and the different angles of their legs when at work. Always very observant, he made great strides....

The Scottish Movement will make great strides too when our young writers begin to study Scottish life, and the work of our Scottish comedians and other artistes, with a like thoroughness. And not till then! The only good essay towards beginning an effective analysis of this sort that I have so far encountered is that on 'The Glasgow Comedians' by Colm Brogan in the symposium *Scotland 1938* edited by John R. Allan. And, as he says,

> The stoutest fortress of a grand tradition (*i.e.* among the Glasgow theatres) is not the Princess or even the Metropole but the Queen's. The Queen's is in Watson Street, behind Glasgow Cross. It is a small theatre without a bar.... The pantomime is a twice-nightly show, and its principal comedian is Sam Murray. By instinct and tradition the pantomime is unrefined, and it would be foolish to pretend that Sam Murray does anything at all to raise the general tone.... Next to Sam Murray in distinction is Doris Droy. She is full of life and fire and she is as honest as the day is long. Her voice is wonderfully strong. Her top notes are a punch on the ear. She is never tired.... The pantomime is one solid chunk of 'Glesga'. But even the Queen's is threatened with danger. Treachery is unthinkable; the danger comes from outside. It is impossible to imagine Sam Murray keeping right on to the end of the road or Doris Droy being winsome in the steamie. But they are in danger of having their audience diluted. Half the enjoyment of a Queen's pantomime is the simple but Aristotelian pleasure of recognition, and it is impossible to guess how much encouragement the performers derive from a perfect community of thought and feeling with the audience. That is in danger of being lost, because the clients of more fashionable houses are beginning to discover the Queen's. The Queen's may become a fad. If it does, Genius and Art will take wing and they will not perish in flight. There are haunts as yet unsuspected by the bourgeois. Somewhere or other, honesty will find a home.

Instead of adopting a Kelvingrove snobbishness and despising its 'atrocious garble' of a dialect it would say a great deal more for Glasgow if it threw up a poet of the kind of Jehan Rictus (who, indeed, lived for a time in Edinburgh), or, still better, Jean Richepin of whom, apropos his 'La Chanson des Gueux', 1876, 'Les Blasphèmes', 1884, and other poems, it has been said: 'Il n'y reculait ni devant la grossièrte, ni devant le cynicisme.... Richepin a chanté les loqueteux, les chemineaux, les misérables.... Sanguin et bruyant, mais ayant à son service un vocabulaire extrêmement riche, aussi pittoresque et aussi varié que celui d'un Rabelais, il possède à la fois la couleur et la force.' But Glasgow, alas, has produced backward-looking ruralists, spineless triflers, superior persons insulated from the life of the city in petty suburban snobberies, all utterly incapable of catching the real rhythms of Clydeside at all and all hopelessly at variance politically and in every other way with all that was really significant, really alive, in their area, or, indeed, elsewhere. A Richepin among the members of the Glasgow Ballad Club would, indeed, be a cat among the sparrows, or, rather, the budgerigars. All these Glasgow singers — and, indeed, all the Glasgow intelligentsia — are shut away behind a thick frosted-glass wall of respectability and at the furthest possible remove from realizing joyfully (at least in respect of Glasgow itself) with Maurice Chevalier that in this life 'Faut pas s'en faire'. What an accumulation of hypocrisy, affectation, claptrap, hooey, and anti-vital rubbish of all kinds will be blasted away if ever the dynamite of this realization is put to work by any Glasgow writer!

One of my hopes in organizing the Scottish Renaissance Movement was that such enterprises might be tackled in a co-operative way. Creative work by committee may seem a pretty hopeless proposition, but in fact there are many instances in literary history which show that in this respect, as in others, two heads are indeed better than one, and, as Orage once pointed out to me, one of the greatest undertakings in English literature was carried through in this way — the authorized version of the Bible. The hope proved vain, however; the younger Scottish writers were not prepared to merge their personal efforts in this way and had an incapacity for co-operation resembling that, in another sphere, of the Scottish farmers. Few of them shared my realization of the need to get back to anonymity in creative work. Moreover, they were at far too many disparate stages of development to make it easy or possible to mobilize them for joint efforts in this way. I am convinced, however, that it is only in such a co-operative way that many of the greatest tasks confronting us will or can be tackled, and that the time is coming when they must be so tackled. In Walt Disney's work we are told that 'from fifteen to twenty conferences are held for each sequence in the picture. The artists have found that approximately 20 per cent of the basic structure is retained.' In precisely the same way I am convinced that of all literary work no higher percentage could possibly be retained if a sufficient collaboration of other minds was enlisted. I remember in this connection that when I wrote the *Drunk Man*, working on my own I had got to the point when I had ceased to be able to see the forest for the trees. I found the necessary imaginative sympathy in F.G. Scott and handed over the whole mass of my manuscript to him. He was not long in seizing on the essentials and urging the ruthless discarding of the unessentials. I had no hesitation in taking his advice and in this way the significant shape was educed from the welter of stuff and the rest pruned away. I am not ashamed to make this confession, which so exposes my inartistry, since, if small things may be compared with great, it reminds me of how even while working on the first allegro Beethoven still suspected, so little, what mighty significance the sonata was eventually to assume that he used one of the principal themes in a chorus for four voices sung at some trifling celebration in honour of the Archduke Rudolph. For that matter, after the work was completed he still seems to have been in doubt as to the importance of the masterpiece he had created. He actually wrote to Ries asking the latter, if he chose, to suppress the largo, which forms a bridge between the adagio and the fugue and constitutes one of the most original pages he ever wrote. 'A new and seizing witness,' Romain Rolland, in that commanding addition to Beethoven literature, *Le Chant de la Résurrection*, calls this and similar facts, 'of the power and superior logic of the subconscious in Beethoven.' And Rolland makes the point that Beethoven himself repeatedly failed to realize (sometimes for a long period) that certain ideas belonged not to this or that work for which he had conceived them but quite somewhere else, that in the course of time, by some mystic process, they found their proper path, and their musical association. It is Rolland's opinion that in the course of the *Missa Solemnis*, Beethoven was led to another close than he had conceived at the outset. For this he finds diverse reasons — the long space of time (five years) he spent on the mass, the crises, physical and moral, he passed through at this epoch, and the passionate eagerness with which, when he emerged from the blackest abyss of suffering, he set about to explore new horizons for new worlds to conquer. The greater part of the work profited by the recuperative period that followed the sombre period of 1816-1818. But with 1820 came another bad year, with illnesses, a lawsuit with the publisher Steiner (for a back debt of 4,000 florins at 6 per cent interest), and similar tribulations. In the first sketches of the 'Dona' there is no indication of the sounds of war and the accents of mortal terror which we know from the finished work. Not long ago, Georg Schuenemann discovered in the Berlin State Library a sketch in which the chorus prays — in minor — for peace, whereas the orchestra responds in major 'as if peace were already there'. But the mass was to turn out differently. Beethoven did not find that peace he probably envisaged in his first conception of the work. 'It would be misunderstanding the *Missa Solemnis*,' declares Rolland,

> to regard it as a monument completely planned from the first and

> realized in exact accordance with this scheme.... It is a work which evolved five years long, with the soul of the composer stirred by a flood of emotions which succeeded one another.... But the one certain thing is that hardly had Beethoven finished with the mass, on that anguished appeal to the peace that eludes him, than he threw himself into the idea of the ninth symphony.... By another road the genius of Beethoven hastens in pursuit of the same golden apples of the Hesperides — Peace, Joy, and Divine Fire of the inaccessible Eternity.

But the Hymn of Joy is another matter, and Romain Rolland finds that type of super-earthly peace which Beethoven sought and failed to achieve in the *Missa Solemnis* perfectly encompassed elsewhere — in the variations of the last sonata, Op. 111. My experience in this connection was like that of Disney's staff, and I cut out and consigned to the fire forthwith a high percentage of what I had written — with incalculable gain to the whole. Drastic treatment of this kind is particularly necessary in literary work. Musicians and artists do not require it to the same degree, but in writing it is fatally easy in the absence of such consultative and co-operative correction to forget that the essence of art is presentation. I was, of course, particularly lucky in having at my elbow such a determined artist as Scott who in his own practice is wont to eliminate to the last degree and concentrate, at no matter what sacrifice of pet material, upon the highest ordering.

If F.G. Scott can 'hardly find anyone to talk to' in Glasgow, Kaikhosru Sorabji is in at least as lonely a plight in London — especially in musical circles (saving the mark!). A writer in *The Modern Scot*, reviewing his book, *Around Music*, in 1933, described his work and personality very clearly and concisely in the following paragraphs:

> There are many who, unable to enter into the mind of Mr Sorabji the composer, yet read all that he writes about music, for he is one of the most scholarly and original of critics in Europe, and his *Around Music* contains enough intellectual pabulum to set lesser commentators up in business for life.
>
> The attitude of Mr Sorabji to the heterogeneous mob, of widely differing degrees of culture and completely lacking in common standards of criticism, that is the British musical public is indicated in the lines from Milton which he prints after his title page:
>
> And what the people but a herd confused,
> A miscellaneous rabble who extol

> Things vulgar, and, well weighed, scarce worth the praise?
> They praise and they admire they know not what
> And know not whom, but as one leads the other;
> And what delight to be by such extolled,
> To live upon their tongues and be their talk,
> Of whom to be dispraised were no small praise?

Mr Sorabji is no demagogue, and he never loses an opportunity of belabouring British music-makers for the manner in which they pander to popular taste; hence his repeated criticism of concert programmes, his scotching of the equating of artistry with simplicity, his onslaughts on the teachers of 'musical appreciation', his plea for the performance of neglected masterpieces by Busoni, Mahler and others.

The independence and originality of Mr Sorabji's thought are nowhere more clearly evidenced than in the works he recommends for performance in place of some of the more trite items that clutter up the average programme. A conductor or other artist, in search of novelties, would find attention drawn to a whole literature of neglected music, in different parts of Mr Sorabji's essays — Schumann's *Faust*, Liszt's Fantasia in F on B-A-C-H, Reger's setting of the 100th Psalm, Busoni's Piano Concerto, the Ravel trio, Florent Schmitt's Quintet, Szymanovsky's violin concerto, Debussy's ballet, *Khamma*, the Van Dieren quartets, Lord Berners' *La Carrosse du Saint Sacrement*, Delius's *Songs of Sunset*, etc, etc. No other British critic has more assiduously pressed the claims of unknown masterpieces that clamour to get past the bar of lethargic concert promoters and performers.

Mr Sorabji's own compositions,[2] of such scale as to be all but

---

2 Only Mr Sorabji has performed his major piano works. Disgracefully little is heard of them. His Michael Angelo Sonnets, too, are shockingly neglected. Mr Edward Clarke Ashworth who says that the *Opus Clavicembalisticum* is only to be compared with Bach's *Art of Fugue*, Busoni's *Fantasia Contrapuntistica*, and the Diabelli Variations of Beethoven, adds that it is also far beyond the capacity of any but the supreme masters of the piano to play, and Mr Bernard Bromage says: 'It is probably literally true, as it has often been said, that Mr Sorabji is the only man living who can play his works *as they should be played*.' Mr Ashworth adds:

> Publication of any new work by Mr Sorabji or any of the very (and far too) rare performances of his compositions is invariably a signal for an outburst of abuse and malice on the part of the generality of critics that is in itself, to a discerning mind, a sign of the startling importance of his musical contribution. But this is poor consolation to those who, like the present writer, have learned to know

unplayable, indicate in what directions his musical likes and dislikes lie. He has excellent pages in *Around Music* on Mahler, Medtner, Reger, Busoni and other modern composers whose profundity of thought, expressed in music of an architectural grandeur, commands his admiration. And when Mr Sorabji admires, how generous his praise, how warm the expression of his humble gratitude! The most severely intellectual and inaccessible of composers, whose intolerance of fools is a by-word, is also a hero-worshipper, so that he frequently passes from the extreme of abuse to the highest pitch of praise in the scope of a sentence. Yet it is not the case, as is sometimes held, that there are no shades in his criticism: his all too brief note on 'Pachmann and Chopin', for instance, proves the contrary.

Not only does Mr Sorabji show a wide-ranging knowledge of modern music, as well as old, in such essays as 'The Modern Piano Sonata', 'The Modern Piano Concerto', 'The Voice in Contemporary Composition', but (himself a pianist of extraordinary resources) he is an excellent judge of executants of music. No other critic writing in English today knows more about singing: he is almost the only British critic who writes as if he knew the full requirements of *fioritura* singing. He will have none of the 'intelligent vocal noises' offered as a substitute for the line-drawing in terms of tone of Calve, Tetrazzini, Melba, Battistini, and Gilly. 'What is singing?' he asks, and answers his own question:

> ...it is astonishing that it should be necessary to say it, but it is a stream of vocal tone, even, pure, homogeneous, free, bright, clear and steady — and that it is necessary to define it, Sir Henry Wood's admirable *Gentle Art of Singing* amply demonstrates.

---

and appreciate the supreme qualities of his work, which, as a great critic and writer has said, 'To those who *know* ranks among the greatest work of our time'. But our time does not mean much perhaps. I would put Sorabji's work higher than that. Without a word of exaggeration, in fact, Sorabji reminds me of that character of Beachcomber's who could sing the 'Hiawatha' oratorio and the 'Revenge' oratorio in alternate bursts; yodel the 'Elijah'; sing 'Du Bist So Alsgespruchtengebirgenzuzammenspielenschaftgewohl' backwards, play the whole of Boccherini on a triangle, hum the overture to 'Fidelio' and the overture to the 'Rosenkavalier' at one and the same time, whistle 'Eugene Onegin' through his teeth, and snore the trombone part in 'Amspucci'. Why, stap me, he could imitate the oboes in the 'Danse des Blanchisseuses' and the French horn in the 'Dido and Æneas' aria in Act I, and with cupped hands bawl Senta's ballad from the 'Flying Dutchman', (Dick Wagner up) as loudly as any stevedore or prima donna!

> But to such a pass have things arrived that one asks oneself how often does one actually hear this stream of pure, steady, bright, clear tone? Or if the singer does succeed in emitting it for a few notes, how long can he or she keep it up without letting it drop and sag in the middle after about a couple of bars? The still more monstrous consequence of this inability to stay the course is the wobble. That is not, as it is so often miscalled, *vibrato* or *tremolo* — two totally different things, legitimate and established musical devices...to such an extent have ears been corrupted by this universal and ubiquitous vice that its absence — the most elementary requirement of good singing — is actually regarded as a fault, and voices which are very properly without it will be called unsympathetic or some such nonsense.
>
> Similarly, that pestilent atrocity, the fresh, unspoiled young voice, as the veiled, woolly, wheezy noise is called, is beloved of our public because that is the sort of noise their female relations make. But what salvation or regeneration of the art of singing is to be hoped for, when critics will actually praise a singer whose singing exemplifies this vile fault and abuse another, like Toti dal Monte, who is free from it, and whose tones are bright, clear, firm, clean, pure, and steady, and which they will call hard?
>
> Coming now to physical defects: the present mania among women for the figure of a half-starved and consumptive hobbledehoy may or may not be aesthetically defensible, but it is an utterly impossible physical equipment for a singer. The poor thin, cottony little thread of sound that will issue from such might get across a drawing-room sixteen feet square, but as a vehicle for the interpretation and execution of great music it is impossible....

That is Mr Sorabji in a fairly mild vein: when he goes all out, one is near to echoing, 'Zounds! I was never so bethumped with words'. He piles up abuse or praise until it all but topples over. For Mr Sorabji's criticism is not the work of a writer laying up a store of fine-writing against his name, using criticism as a vehicle of self-expression, but the often impatient proclamation, by a composer and executant of nothing short of genius, of where the good is to be found and what bad ousts it from its rightful place. It is *impromptu* criticism, written nevertheless, by a scholar and artist, equipped — to the regret of many a mediocrity — with 'language at large'.[3]

---

3 Sorabji's splendid essay on 'The Songs of Francis George Scott' appears in his second volume of essays in musical criticism, *Mi Contra Fa* (Porcupine Press, London, 1947).

(With regard to Sorabji's nationality I quote what he says himself):

> I am not an Indian. I belong by race to the ancient Iranian colony of Bombay, commonly known as Parsis, who under the influence of the Iranian *risorgimento* accomplished by Riza Shah Pehlevi are becoming more Iran-conscious, if I may so describe it, and as much object to the description of themselves as Indians as the Scots or Irish object to being called 'British'.

His political attitude is indicated by the following:

> I admit that landlordism (used as a pejorative) is, probably, as bad in India as elsewhere. But in spite of landlordism, what India *was* before empire building began (empire building *à l'anglaise* that is to say) is known. What India *is* after 200 years of it is also known. The full horror of it is on record in Gangualee, *Poverty and Malnutrition in India*, and *Poverty and un-British Rule in India*, by Dadabhai Naoroji (bless his simple heart! He little realized how authentically British it was!), to mention but two. Can you wonder that Indians become sarcastic when they hear about 'freedom and democracy' for everyone but themselves and openly derisive when England announces herself as the Joan-of-Arc thereof?

In a typical letter to me Sorabji says:

> Since *Opus Clavicembalisticum* (1930) there have been completed an immense Piano Quintet (a 400-page work, dedicated to our mutual friend, Professor Saurat), two shorter piano works (each of a total of some 160 pages by the way) and the Fifth Piano Sonata, that is half as long again as *Clavicembalisticum* and sub-entitled *Opus Archimagicum*. This I regard in all ways as the equal even of *your* opus (*i.e. Opus Clavicembalisticum*[4]). At the present moment I am engaged upon another tremendous work, going to take me some years, as I am only just over half-way through the enormous piano part. The work falls into three great sections, each of which will occupy the best part of a programme to itself. Small work I have put entirely behind me, I think. I have moved further and further away, both in my work and my feelings, moods, and thoughts from our crapulous and more than semi-imbecile contemporaneity, and if it were not that I greatly love some few superb human beings who are life itself to me, I should welcome the *pralaya* of this swinish civilization, with its

[4] *Opus Clavicembalisticum* is dedicated to Mr MacDiarmid.

> packing-case architecture, its Tate-sugar-box furniture, and its nickel-brains masquerading as intelligence and its insect-itch masquerading (foulest and worst of all this) as passion; its Hitlers and Mussolinis, Baldwins and Thomases, its Bertrand Russells, posing as the light of the World...had they said light of the demi-monde one might be disposed to agree. You know that is the foulest of all, the foulness of *les clercs*, the stench, physical as well as moral that emanates from the gods of Bloomsbury. Sooner give me the frank philistinism — hard-hearted and within its limits acute intelligence — of the average Glasgow citizen, any day sooner than *THAT!*...To return to myself, about which you are kind enough to ask me, your estimate of my work, expressed with so much touching warmth years since in *The New Age* (*in re* the 'Faitcha' controversy which perhaps you will remember) has been confirmed in a very important Dutch periodical devoted to music, in a long article it gave to my (and your) *Opus Clavicembalisticum*, wherein it was stated this work could only be compared with the very greatest things ever written for the piano — the Bach Art of Fugue, and the Diabelli variations of Beethoven. This opinion has also been expressed by one or two people even in THIS country, so things are not altogether too hostile.

In so far from indulging any 'world-beater' illusions I have only to think of Sorabji's work to feel *my* gas turned down to a peep!

I have referred elsewhere in my writings to Professor Denis Saurat's very remarkable book — doing high honour alike to his heart and head — *La Fin de la Peur*. It is a work of profound imagination and most powerfully concentrated expression. His greatest and much too-little-known work is *The Three Conventions*, which Orage declared had no rival for concentration outside certain untranslatable Sanskrit works. Other important books of his are *Literature and the Occult* (an extraordinary demonstration of the extent to which all great European poetry derives a high proportion of its greatest stuff from little-known occult and anti-Christian writings — to which the sequence of great poets with whom he deals had not themselves direct access, but which they inherited from each other without first-hand examination at all, and thus we have the amazing fact that all the greatest European literature is really a vehicle for the uninterrupted transmission of a body of ideas alien to European civilization as generally understood, and at complete variance with all the Christian and other beliefs most Europeans have professed throughout the centuries) and *A History of Religions*. A reviewer of the latter says:

His writings on the esoteric elements in European literature have shown his tremendously wide knowledge of the by-paths of religious history; he has read prodigiously; and he knows the boundary between knowledge and guesswork. His faculty of condensation is remarkable, as a glance at his footnote references brings home. He does not write popular history, but popularizes history. His *précis* of the historical evidence bearing on the origins of Christianity, for example, is a model of care and concision. He has a mordant, incisive style, and it is interesting to compare — rather, contrast — his method with H.L. Mencken's. Whereas the American is shallow, angry and facetious by turn when writing on the Gods, the Frenchman wastes no time in abuse, and allows himself only an occasional excursion into irony, never a guffaw. 'The Roman... had the feeling that the gods had taken an advantage of a contract that was unfair.... The Sibylline books demanded that two young couples should be buried alive: Greeks and Gauls were chosen: no great loss.'

Professor Saurat treats philosophies as fragments of religious systems, and we can recall no more clear-headed account of the philosophical pre-occupations of post-renaissance times than his. Looking to the future, he foresees a certain progress in philosophical thought, since, for the first time since the Greeks, philosophers are tackling their problems with no presuppositions. 'A first-rate philosopher like the German Husserl, for instance, does not even consider religious probabilities at all.' As for religion, he sees no more intellectual future for the off-shoots of Protestantism than he does for occult pantheism, the 'wisdom of the east'. While recognizing the unlimited intellectual resources of the east, he sees them burdened by the false cosmology, the false history and false anatomy of the eastern religions. 'We can do nothing with oriental religions. The more the east will become civilized, the more it will rid itself of the religions which... contradict its own natural impulses by negating life.' In the west, Catholicism is the only remaining virile religion. 'It has adapted itself to so many changes that it may adapt itself further.' And looking into the remote future:

> One cannot escape the thought of God: one escapes only this or that form of it.... Flowers, and even trees, are still growing on the ruins of religions and philosophies. That is all the historian can tell, on reaching the verge of the present. He cannot but see, besides, that, in the human soul, round the ruins and the flowers and the trees, there is the menace of desert.

Saurat is one of the most delightful men I have met. A terrifically hard worker, he has always time for everything, and he has not only the great French gifts of '*netteté, clarté*, and *ordonnance*' but is full of *bonté*. We have been great friends for over twenty years. Incidentally in an early essay on my work he coined the descriptive phrase, 'The Scottish Renaissance Movement' which has been so persistently gibed at by small minds affecting to believe that it represented an inordinate claim as to what the group associated with me had actually already achieved, whereas, of course, it only defined our general hope and purpose. Saurat, too, did me a high honour by being one of the earliest translators of my Scots lyrics, half-a-dozen or more of which he did into French very well indeed.

What if all the public for a Scottish Renaissance Movement established on such a basis are as few as those who heard Chaliapin on the occasion of which one of his friends told me? 'Shortly after dinner we all adjourned,' he said,

> to the drawing-room overlooking the beautiful Bay of Biscay. Chaliapin seated his daughter (on a visit from Moscow) in the centre of the room and placing a guitar in her hands announced that the evening's grand concert was about to commence. He seated the members of the family and himself in a circle surrounding his visiting daughter and then from 9.30 o'clock till about 11.30, the entire family joined in singing one Russian folk or gipsy song after another to the accompaniment of the guitar, with Chaliapin singing along and at the same time acting as conductor. These were songs which Chaliapin had known and sung as a boy in Russia; still closest to his heart, they ran the entire gamut of elemental human emotions, from those of wild rustic hilarity to those of truly tragic import. This extraordinary performance wound up with 'The Song of the Volga Boatman', encores of which were demanded by the various players themselves — nor was I any less insistent. As may well be imagined this was an unforgettable evening in which the nostalgic atmosphere created by this informal family reunion enhanced to the greatest degree the beauty of the music itself. It is my feeling that the singing of the great Chaliapin has never been more inspired or more truly from the heart than it was this evening.

This is the sort of concert I and Francis George Scott and our friends have been giving in Scotland for the part thirty years. If it is difficult to secure an audience in Scotland today for such a concert, Scott and I and our friends have little more need to worry about the lack of human auditors than had Chaliapin himself on another occasion, when Chaliapin and his family were summering in another part of the south of France and he had ordered a piano to be sent to his villa. Out for an afternoon stroll along the country road with his faithful accompanist Rabinowitz and Mme Chaliapin, he saw approaching a truck upon which was loaded a piano. As the story is told by Mme Chaliapin, Chaliapin's face lighted up; accompanied by a little twinkle in his eye, a sudden great inspiration had come to him. He signalled the truck to stop and asked whether the piano was intended for Chaliapin, and, on being told it was, he instructed that the piano be unloaded and placed on the road. This being done he commanded Rabinowitz to seat himself at the keyboard, and then, with great assumed formality, announced in stentorian tones: 'I shall now give a magnificent concert, not for you who happen to be here, nor for mankind in general, who have heard me sing so often, but exclusively for the birds and the rabbits which are flying and scampering all around us.' Thereupon in the middle of the hot, dusty, country road he rendered a complete concert programme, giving his best to what he termed nature's true, best, and most deserving audience.

Against this background must be placed the distinguished citizens — ministers etc — who at the Burns Suppers in January 1939, drunk with the communion wine of Munich, proclaimed (*vide* Press) that if Burns had been alive at that time he would have found Neville Chamberlain a man after his own heart! But the proportion of the population of Scotland than whom an audience of rabbits or sparrows would be infinitely preferable is steadily increasing. That is why the Edinburgh International Festival has been so successful in attracting hordes of tourists.

Certainly so far as a Scottish programme akin to the Russian and gipsy song concert described in the first of my Chaliapin stories is concerned in Scotland today, the 'few but fit' hearers are a mere handful; and no one can be as intensively concerned with Scottish arts and affairs as we have been in the past two or three decades, so saturated in a knowledge and understanding of the whole of the Scottish past, and so compassed about by a great cloud of witnesses as we are in our intimate and exhaustive knowledge of thousands of the most distinguished men and women of our nation's history without feeling in pretty much the same position as Ossian when, out hunting, (a tale older than Christ) a beautiful girl called Niam, astride a white steed, drew rein beside him and in the moment of their meeting Ossian forgot the high halls of his father and the great feasting and story-telling and deeds of valour. She made room for him beside her on the steed which neighed three times and carried them over the plains and rocky paths and the spray of rolling billows to the Land of Eternal Youth. Niam gave him herself and all else his heart could wish for. But at the end of three hundred years the old reasonless spirit in him began to live and fret, and when Niam in tears questioned him she discovered he wanted to see just one more glimpse of hedge and hill and falling leaves, wanted to feel one small touch of the common earth. Full of pity for the man in him, she set him astride the white steed and warned him not to dismount or touch the earth. Arriving in Ireland he found to his dismay that all the great race of warriors and heroes had disappeared and that the land was now inhabited by a swarming race of little black-haired men. Broken-hearted, he encountered St Patrick who warned him that all his pagan forebears were now deep in Hell, and that the same fate awaited himself unless he repented. A quarrel followed and the defiant Ossian, choosing a Hell full of gallant warriors rather than a Heaven of little black men, wandered disconsolately over the land.

That is the position. Scott and I have not repented. We have not descended from the white steeds of our respective arts — but rather have we like Ossian been tempted by coming upon many hundreds of the despicable little black-haired men vainly trying to raise a great block of marble, and, contemptuously leaning from his horse, seizing the marble and hurling it far into the air — in doing so smashing the saddle straps and falling from the white steed, so that, immediately he touched the earth hundreds of years fell away from him and he withered miserably away.

For, indeed, an authentic expression in poetry or music (such as in the latter case Scott and in the former I myself might have found if we had lived in times when it was possible to achieve 100 per cent work in big forms along the autochthonous lines on which circumstances as they are have only permitted us to effect a few small-scale achievements — though that statement is hardly fair to Scott's latest, and still unpublished work, his symphonic settings of Dunbar's 'Dance of the Seven Deidly Sins', which emerge triumphantly on that major plane with which I am concerned — a worthy service to our Scottish Muse, *Historia Abscondita*) would have resembled the work of the Brazilian composer, Villa-Lobos, whose works are legion and a great number of them still unpublished. Of his chorus No. 8 it has been well said that a first impression is of something tremendous and of harmonies very harsh in places ('Maurice Lindsay, art thou sleepin' there below?') put down with a frankness and conviction that make one think of some aspect of tumultuous, oppressive, mysterious nature. One could call this almost a 'Sacre du Printemps' of the Amazon forest. His chorus No. 10, for full chorus and orchestra, is a perfect beauty, and fascinating in its colour, native eloquence, and evocative power. It is sung in large part, over an Indian chant of the savage and roughly rhythmical sort. The text discourses of the aching heart, the burning sun, the cross of suffering. It implores the singing birds to intercede with God for that heart, and in the orchestra is such a warm and ecstatic trilling and piping as nobody else ever thought of in terms of instruments. It is and is not, imitation. It is rather an impression inseparable from the thought and the word. The instrumental combination includes high wind instruments, as, of course, flageolet tones of the 'celli, and relative devices. It vividly communicates the sensation of something tropically natural, impassioned, and 10,000 miles away from a modern or urban civilization. So, one would say, a savage would sing with all his heart, with no difficulty in finding a melody or accompanying device to convey his responses to the natural world about him and his complete unconsciousness in community with its god. To this fundamental *naïveté* and spontaneousness in these choruses of Villa-Lobos are added an admirable technical address and a form consummately adapted to the expressive spirit, so that we have in him what Scotland so badly needs — if it is to be creatively rehabilitated and to supply, as civilization becomes more world-wide and international, what Scotland's history richly fits it to provide, one of those sources of fresh racial power so vitally necessary (and nowhere in the world more than in English literature, arts and affairs!) when the true creative spirit is so imperilled by those hardening arteries of national consciousness which have had far more to do with present European complications and explosions than we may realize.

The subterranean persistence of unchanged Scottishness under official Anglicization and apparent acquiescence in assimilation to English standards occasionally (if seldom, save in Melville's *Moby Dick* and R.L. Stevenson's *Weir of Hermiston*, so violently as Brazil breaks through in Villa-Lobos's work) rises to the surface in more significant forms than 'legislation by appendix' makes inevitable every now and again in every practical connection; and I believe that the whole hidden Scotland will soon break through the dismal crust of Englishry. The change that is coming over Scottish Gaelic poetry in the work of Somhairle MacGilleathain, George Campbell Hay, and one or two others — redeeming it from the ruts of *bardachd* and making it once more fully alive in its own time — can best be appreciated by comparing MacGilleathain's 'An Cuilithionn' with that '*failte*' in which the late Neil Macleod extols the wild beauties of Skye, recounting the warlike deeds of Skyemen in the past, the joys of the days gone by, now gone with the companions of his youth never to return — all this is fondly dwelt upon: but yet while the people are gone, the poet insists that 'the history they have left behind is such that it will remain forever and the praise of the island's sons will be told and retold till earth decays and until the clouds are folded away in eternity'. There is no hint (amidst all this acquiescent sentimental wallowing) in such previous work, as we find in MacGilleathain, 'Chuireadh Gaidheal cruaidh so dheth fathast', (a hardy Gael would shake this injury off him yet). To bring about that change from defeatism to militant Scottish radicalism and a determination to throw off as quickly as possible now the injuries to which Scotland has been so long subjected has been the work to which Scott and myself have devoted ourselves unremittingly for the last thirty years and there is ample evidence now that a thorough Scottish national awakening is possible — and not a moment before 'time up'.

IV

I have certainly not ceased to hope that Mr Maurice Walsh, in his *Sons of the Swordmaker*, has truly prefigured the coming triumph of Gaeldom, when he tells how, when the Battle of Actium had just passed into history, and Cuchulain was a short time dead, the five sons of Orugh the swordmaker set out one by one, upon their bloody adventures. Urnaul's great cross-hilted sword came home to Long Baravais, delivered by the hand of a friend with a challenge from Fergus of Running Water. The sword came home a second time and Fergus's second message ran: 'Cond was a good man but you'll have to send a better.' Flann of the harsh tongue and the soft heart did as custom dictated. He was not so great a fighter as his dead brothers, but Fergus was in a lenient mood. Flann came home with the sword in his left hand, and afterwards wore a bronze hook where his right hand had been. This left only Delgaun, the eldest brother and a man of peace, and Maur, the stripling and maker of songs, to take up the challenge of Fergus. The clangorous climax from which Delgaun emerges as a heroic and dominant figure, completes what may be called the first movement of Mr Walsh's story.

My hope is that I and Scott conjointly will be remembered as in some measure the Maur to the Delgaun of the renascent Celtic elements in what is still the United Kingdom but will surely become a USSR of Scotland, Wales and Cornwall, a federation of independent Celtic workers' republics.

Our service to Scotland has been similar, I believe, to the service to French Canada of Jean-Charles Harvey's *Les Demi-Civilisés* (translated into English with the title *Sackcloth for Banner* by Lukin Barette). Harvey's dislike for any but a republican form of government, his daring to characterize his fellow-countrymen as 'half-civilized', and to head a passionate crusade against the mental lethargy and submission to regimentation that have, he declares, resulted in French Canadians having 'one of the most backward civilizations among all white races', his persistent denunciations of the censorship exercised in French Canada over art of every sort, his realistic picturing of Quebec's slums, his satirical unmasking of the Tartuffes of his day and city, his scorn for the 'pontiffs of Quebec letters', and for French Canadian education, and his plentifully expressed belief that most of his people's lawyers and politicians are on the make, all these are identical with my own attitudes and actions with regard to Anglo-Scotland, and if it is not difficult to see why constituted authority and vested interests have branded Harvey as a hot-headed iconoclast rather than a reformer, neither are the victimization and obloquy to which I have been subjected any harder to understand. Harvey was dismissed from his editorship and obliged to resign from Quebec Civil Service; every channel by which I might earn a living in Scotland has been closed to me, and I have likewise been forced out of all the associations, political, literary and social (many of them created by myself) to which I have belonged. Harvey wants less wealth, less ceremony, a going back to Galilee; my desires are very similar, but I cannot call the way of life to which I would fain see a return by a name with any Biblical associations. To me as to Max Hubert — the book's protagonist, Harvey's other self — liberty means everything. No smug prosperity can compensate if liberty is being undermined and as Max Hubert wanted to have French Canadians share in the ultimate findings of the highest present attainable civilization, so I with the Scots.

Here then in this essay is a rough outline of the relationship and purposes F.G. Scott and I have had. Readers will understand how bucketing through the Pentland Firth, perhaps the most villainous stretch of water in the world, I will never be found thinking about White Supremacy or the Defence of the West (which I deem as much beneath my attention as any dog-fight in some street through which I happen to be passing), believing as I do that the vast majority of West European peoples are perfectly characterized by Dante in the 3rd Canto of the *Inferno* when he sees upon a Dark Plain, *la buia campagna*, 'a vast multitude of spirits running behind a flag in great haste and confusion, urged on by furious wasps and hornets. These are the unhappy people, who never were alive, never awakened to take part either in good or evil.'

> ...che non furon ribelli
> ni fur fideli a Dio, MA PER SE FORO.

i.e. nor rebels, nor faithful to God, *BUT FOR THEMSELVES!*

'But,' I seem to hear a chorus of protesting voices cry, 'Scott's accompaniments are far too difficult. They are not for the like of us. He is a highbrow, and consequently cannot expect to set the heather on fire.'

There are a few final things I would say in reply to that.

With all the gifts that he had, Yeats lacked — and in the long run fatally — that power of winning through to, and enlisting the attention and interest, not to say passionate enthusiasm, of the common people, which the technically intricate and learned poetry of the Gaels always had. A letter I have from Glyn Jones, the Welsh poet and novelist, says in this connection:

> I think one of the most remarkable things about the culture of Wales is the extent of its diffusion, the way it has escaped becoming the exclusive possession of a district or a class. There is no intellectual counterpart of Cambridge or Bloomsbury in our country, and you will find many Welshmen of considerable intellectual attainments doing all sorts of odd jobs and even living on the dole. Dr T. Gwynn Jones in his *Culture and Tradition of Wales* has quoted many pieces of evidence which support this view and which show the intense intellectual activity which often exists among such people as quarrymen and farm labourers, and when I recall my own early life I realize how natural and how widespread an active interest in some art or in religion or in politics was to the colliery workers amongst whom I spent my boyhood. I recall now such small but illuminating indications as the pictures which hung in the kitchens of these men, the frequency with which one saw the photographs of Ruskin and Keir Hardie and Henry Richard and William Morris. I remember the common interest in music too; in particular I remember a drunken collier

> who used to sit singing on the wall outside his house on Saturday evenings — and his song was something from 'Semele' perhaps, or Mozart's 'You who have knowledge', with the voice of a tenor angel.... I remember the magnificent singing by choirs of miners and their families of choruses by Beethoven and Handel. I remember hearing a young pit-worker replying in public to the criticism a professor of Celtic had levelled against a poem of his written in a classical Welsh metre, and forcing upon the genial scholar a discussion on the nature of poetry....

The same was true of Scotland and of Ireland, and gradually lost there as in Wales — and a gulf allowed to develop between author and public — as a result of the English Ascendancy; but this community with the working class in Ireland was something Yeats never secured in his work. He was more English than Celtic in this respect. I can see little future for his work. Yeats may have been an unearthly customer; I wish he had been a good deal more un-English.

It is of special interest to reflect in this connection of bridging the gap between the people and the arts on the experience of those responsible for the Orquesta Sinfonica de México today in presenting concerts for workers and peasants to whom the world of music has previously been almost wholly inaccessible. Painting has been the forerunner and from the first towering figures of Diego Riviera, José Clemente Orozco and David Alfaro Siqueiros went for inspiration to the art of the people — to the ancient manuscripts and monuments of the Aztecs, Mayans, and other Indian peoples, to the popular wood-cuts of Posada, the Goya of Mexico, and to the paintings on the walls of the pulque shops (saloons) everywhere in Mexico. 'We musicians of the younger generation,' writes Carlos Chavez, 'sought to create a vigorous art that would stem from the people and would reach out to the people. We felt that we had to restore the heritage of honest feelings[5] to our own popular songs, marches, and dances such as "Adelita". At the same time we had to reveal the universal repertory of Beethoven and Bach and Wagner and others.' And what did they find? The following is especially apt to my argument here.

> The music that moved them to applaud and the music that left them unmoved were both surprising. We played once a Haydn

---

5 Precisely what F.G. Scott has been doing in Scotland with his resetting of 'Scots Wha Ha'e' etc, and what is above all necessary in relation to pipe music.

> symphony that to most experienced ears is charming and irresistible in its lightness, simplicity, and gaiety. Our audience in the park on the outskirts of Mexico City behaved as if poor old Papa Haydn were a long-winded soporific orator. Another time we played Stravinsky. His music is difficult, so I thought, in its intricate rhythms and harmonies. But our surprising audience behaved as if they had been brought up on nothing but a diet of dissonance, atonality, and rhythms that changed with bewildering uncertainty. They were delighted with Stravinsky.

Of course! So will the workers be everywhere when they are set free from the strait waistcoat of bourgeois education, patronization, and obsession with 'peace', the easy, the accepted, and generally with what Gorky calls Philistinism. (I have mentioned elsewhere Burns's ability to write his poems undistracted in the most chaotic domestic setting, and here too in Mexico the people listened — 'their eyes were fixed on the orchestra; their heads and bodies barely stirred. They were not uneasy about their children, who wandered among them. They seemed not at all disturbed by the noises that active youngsters will generate, wherever their home.') And beyond that point, the true way everywhere is that to which they proceeded in Mexico — research in the music and instruments of the early Indians and the formation of an orchestra particularly suited to Indian and Mexican music, with a specially balanced group of conventional instruments, plus huehuetls, teponaxtles, chirimias, water drums, rasps, etc., thus 'developing in the average Mexican a broad cultural understanding of his own roots' — a living comprehension of the musical tradition of their own country — balancing native music with the classics of the world and so building a well-rounded, well-educated audience in the land, an audience that cuts through all social strata and is truly democratic.

In Mexico, in contrast to what I have said of the position in Scotland and Sweden, it has been with the dance as with music (only the stage, held in the fetters of old Spanish tradition, has failed to come abreast of the new day). Emmanuel Eisenberg reports that Anna Sokolow in introducing modern methods of choreography and novel dance techniques for the first time into Mexico, found that working class pupils in that stronghold of folk-lore and ritual took to them readily and without any difficulty of adjustment.

It is exactly what the group of intellectual girls defying tradition and founding an association called Anggana Raras in Java with R.M. Kordat as leader have (in dancing) done in another part of the world, influenced, as their spokesman R. Abdul Latief says, by what he calls the 'new and young idea: back to your own culture, developing it in modern direction' — exactly, in fact, what the Scottish Renaissance Movement set out to do.

Even when F.G. Scott's work is performed (this is true of Sorabji's too) it is always subjected to horribly laggard tempi, in flagrant disregard of the composer's directions, just as Furtwaengler in Zurich simply *would* not observe that at the curtain rise in the second act of *Die Walkuere* Wagner has explicitly written '*dasselbe Zeitmass*', instead of slowing down the tempo by one-half!

As Carleton Beals has said many of the better Latin American writers have suddenly become aware of a race bloc of about fifty million people (to whom nearly all of them belong) which for the most part previously, South American Literature, chained to European models, has largely ignored. This rich indigenous field is now beginning, under the influence of intensive study and revolutionary activity, to produce a fine crop of creative work, especially in the work of the young Ecuadorian novelist, Jorge Icaza; Alejo Carpentier's famous *Ecue-Yamba-O*; Romulo Lachatafieré's *Oh, mio Yemayá*; Lydia Cabrera's *Contos negres de Cuba*, a fine collection of folk-lore, mythology and social legend, largely of *Yorubà*, or, as known in Cuba, *Lucumí* origin; and the essays and educational work of Moisés Saenz, Mexican ambassador to Peru, for example, his latest book, *México Integro*, a volume of essays, cultural interpretations, and personal experiences while travelling through remote indigenous areas of the country — Quintana Roo, the mountain settlements of San Luis Potosi in the north, the Island of Janitzio in Lake Patzcuaro on the Day of the Dead, and the mountains of Puebla.

What all this comes back to is simply Justice Brandeis's conclusion that 'ordinary men and women can grasp the essentials of any situation, no matter how involved its details, if the facts are adequately presented to them' and his belief, which I share to the full, that the most important natural resource of any country is the people who live in that country, that the creative and constructive possibilities of the mass of our people have not yet been realized, that these possibilities are great, and that it is the business of democracy to develop them. And like him I would always put guidance ahead of arbitrary authority, and would have discipline come from the inside of a man's character, not be imposed from outside by someone else. Observed facts lead me to believe that the key to democratic progress is the full development of all the capacities of every individual; that institutions and practices which promote this are good and those that hinder it are bad; that centralized power of any kind, whether political or economic, is among the bad influences. 'Bigness' is not primarily an economic question with me. I may have admitted that it sometimes cheapens products, but I distrust it because I think it also cheapens human beings. I see in our life a tendency to throw too much responsibility on a few men and allow too little to a great number of men. I would like to see that tendency reversed. As Dr Barzun says in his splendid book, *Of Human Freedom*: 'A man should not say, "I live in a democracy", but, "I experienced democracy last Tuesday afternoon".'

I must leave it at that. I cannot, of course, presume to identify Scott with all the complexities of my own position. I had the advantage over him that there is a place at Langholm called the Curly Snake where a winding path coils up through a copse till it reaches the level whence, after passing through a field or two, it runs on into the splendid woods of the Langfall. It has always haunted my imagination and has probably constituted itself the ground-plan and pattern of my mind, just as the place called the Nook of the Night Paths in Gribo-Shov, the great forest north of Hillerod, haunted Kierkegaard's. Hawick has no counterpart to that!

The way I most frequently see Scott and myself nowadays, however, reminds me of the worst storm I ever knew at sea. Notwithstanding oil bags swung over both bows, the seas continuously swept the ship and eventually carried away the after wheel and binnacle, and everything movable, as well as flooding the cabin. The navigating and binnacle lights were put out and the logline was snapped by the whirling water astern. Through the whole night the steamer was steered by the direction of the smoke from the funnel.

In much the same way, perhaps, Scott and I have steered throughout our lives, I by the smoke of my good drawing pipe of thick black tobacco and Scott by the smoke of his, the tobacco in his case, however, being thick brown.

Burns Today and Tomorrow

I choose the title *Burns Today and Tomorrow* for this bicentenary essay because, having proposed the chief toast at several Burns Suppers annually for the past thirty or forty years, I have always made a point of proposing not 'The Immortal Memory' but 'The Future of Robert Burns', since immortality is something outwith our comprehension, whereas the future esteem and influence of Burns's work is at least to some extent within our own control.

Over a quarter of a century ago I said, concerning the world Burns cult,

> Scotland will signalize that it has come to itself again and resumed its proper attitude to world affairs when it makes a bonfire of all the worthless, mouldy, pitiable relics that antiquarian Burnsians have accumulated at Mauchline, Dumfries, and elsewhere, and reconcentrates on the living message of Burns's poetry the world-wide attention devoted today (at least once a year) to the mere man and his uninteresting love affairs and the ramifications of the genealogies of his quite insignificant acquaintances and the poor bric-a-brac of his *lares* and *penates*, and the witless lucubrations of the hordes of bourgeois 'orators' who annually befoul his memory by the expression of sentiments utterly antipathetic to that stupendous element in him which ensured his fame — an element, it cannot be overstressed, utterly and forever irreconcilable with the political, religious, social, and all the other bearings and elements of the personalities and lives of 99.9 (repeater) of his yearly panegyrists. Burns cult, forsooth! It has denied his spirit to honour his name. It has denied his poetry to laud his amours. It has preserved his furniture and repelled his message. It has built itself up on the progressive refusal of his lead in regard to Scottish politics, Scottish literature, and the Scottish tongue. It knows nothing about him or his work — or the work that should be done in continuance of his — except the stupid and stereotyped sentiments it belches out annually. It is an organization designed to prevent any further renaissance of the Scottish spirit such as he himself encompassed, and in his name it treats all who would attempt to renew his spirit and carry on his work on the magnificent

> basis he provided as he himself was treated in his own day — with obloquy and financial hardship, and all the dastardly wiles of suave Anglicized time-servers and trimmers. It has produced mountains of rubbish about him, but not a single good critical study, not a single appreciation above the literary level for which a first-year Higher Grade schoolboy would be thrashed if he so dealt with some petty English novelist or poetaster. It has failed (because it never tried — it has been numerically ample to succeed if it ever had) to get Burns or Scottish literature or Scottish history or the Scots language, to which Burns courageously and rightly and triumphantly reverted from English taught in Scottish schools.

Almost the entire personnel of the Burns Movement are, in my opinion, in Sean O'Casey's phrase, 'drawn away from the sensitive extension of the world', and I think that is largely Burns's fault and a valid criticism of a very great deal of his work — his peasant conceit, his inverted snobbery, his 'nostalgia de la boue'. I agree with what Robert Graves says in 'The Common Asphodel':

> Poetical ideas and poetical technique have always been class institutions and poets from the labouring or shopkeeping classes have with few exceptions tried to elevate themselves by borrowing ideas and techniques to the enjoyment of which they were not born. Even revolutionary ideas are, by a paradox, upper-class ideas, a rebound from excesses of decorum. Burns's romantic sympathy with the French Revolution in its earlier stages could be read as a sign of natural good breeding, the gentlemanly radicalism of the literary *Jeunesse*; the social gap between the crofters and the gentry was, moreover, not so wide in Scotland as in England, and he soon learned the trick of drawing-room writing. The Romantic Revivalists were all spoiled as revolutionaries by their gentility. Blake was not one of them; he was a seer and despised the gentry in religion, literature, and painting equally, which is why there is little or nothing of his mature work that could be compared with that of any contemporary or previous writer. He never forfeited his personality by submitting to any conventional medium, nor complained of the neglect of his poems by the larger reading public.

Cleanth Brooks in *Modern Poetry and The Tradition* echoes and emphasizes Robert Graves. 'Robert Burns,' he says,

> will illustrate the extreme to which emphasis on the materials of poetry had been pushed by the end of his century. For Burns's

popularity represents, in large measure, an interest in local colour and picturesque primitivism — interests not foreign to our own civilization. And Burns himself was not unwilling to play up to this interest. His frequent apologies for his ignorance and unconventionality fall somewhere between honest naiveté and knowing irony. Burns is never either the simple peasant on the one hand, nor, on the other, the craftsman who is ironically attacking the reigning conventions. There is a certain self-consciousness about his work that is perhaps not to be completely detached from shrewdness. It is an impurity which injures some of his more serious work. The strongest element in Burns is to be found in his efforts to absorb the conventionally unpoetic in to poetry. But the attempt is not made in his more serious poetry.... If this praise of Burns as a satirist and writer of light verse seems wilfully perverse in view of Burns's reputation as a simple, artless poet, the poet of the heart, one must simply call for inspection of the poems in question. Ironically, for those who insist on 'nature', it was not the romantic ploughman who restored liberty to the imagination, but the cockney Blake. Blake represents, as Burns does not, the return to the daring of Elizabethan metaphor, to the use of serious irony, to a bold willingness to risk obscurity, and even to something very close to metaphysical wit.

The Burns legend is largely dependent on a complete misprizal of Burns's work — a determined 'preference for the inferior'. As Cyril Pearl says:

> Despite the scholarly revaluations of Burns that have taken place in the last half-century — from Henley to De Lancey Ferguson — it seems that a contemporary survey of bardolaters celebrating 'The Immortal Memory' on January 25 in any part of the world would show that most still think of Burns as the author of 'The Cottar's Saturday Night', 'Scots Wha Hae', and 'Auld Lang Syne' rather than as the author of 'The Jolly Beggars', 'Holy Willie's Prayer', and 'The Rantin' Dog'. Burns would have enjoyed the irony of it.

Burns Clubs are still multiplying in number. But Burns himself could never have imagined that his 'immortal memory' would today be toasted so vociferously by hosts of celebrants who care nothing for the continuance, in poetry or politics, of the great causes to which he devoted his genius.

Burns knew that a nation's literature and its other arts can never rest on past achievements, but must go ever forward to cope with new needs and new difficulties.

Yet the Scots poetry that has been written in the last forty years by the so-called 'new Lallans poets' has been cold-shouldered by the majority of Burnsians, who have shown a disposition lamentably different from that of Burns himself.

Because it expresses other ideas than Burns expressed, because it embodies a different attitude to the Scots language itself, it seems to challenge Burns's supremacy — and consequently gives offence to those mainly non-literary and mostly very parochial-minded people who regard Burns as the be-all and end-all of poetry.

Instead, they would do well to consider his 'Prologue to a Play at a Dumfries Theatre', in which he urges that young Scottish writers should be encouraged, and prophesies that if that were done, Scotland would continue to produce writers worthy of their greatest predecessors in the Scottish tradition.

In poem after poem Burns expressed his concern to ensure that future Scottish poets should continue to celebrate the national muse 'in nobler style, with more poetic fire' and 'Burnses spring, her fame to sing, to endless generations'.

Keir Hardie was a great lover of Burns songs and poems, as were his father and mother before him, and many of his happiest recollections of his childhood days were of hearing Burns's works recited or sung round the domestic hearth.

Alas, later on when he was in the House of Commons, on his flying visits home to Ayrshire, he was bitterly grieved to find that his own children could not appreciate Burns, because they did not understand the Scots words.

Standard English is insisted on in Scottish schools. A virtual monopoly is given to English literature and practically no place at all in the curriculum accorded to Scotland's own very different literature.

It is thus not surprising that real knowledge and understanding of Burns is declining — even though annual lip-service to his name is still increasing.

This is only one of the great contradictions inherent in the Burns cult.

Another is the fact that all the principal Burns clubs are middle-class institutions, into whose midst few genuine members of the working class would enter — even if they could afford it, which they can't.

From this point of view, the Burns movement largely represents a filching away of Burns from the people of whom he was the incomparable spokesman, and hypocritical homage to him by the very types whose pretentions, were he alive, he would flay with his satire.

Burns, in fact, has fallen into the hands of the Philistines, who exalt his name, but deny in practice, if not in precept, all the values he stood for.

A strange side-light is thrown on the whole business when we find that the School of Scottish Studies, established in Edinburgh a few years ago, has made tape-recordings of thousands of Scots songs and ballads from people (mostly old people) to whom they had been transmitted orally down the generations.

It does not look as if Scotland's vaunted pride in its great treasury of folk songs is justified when such a wealth of material has remained uncollected until the very eleventh hour, when the last heirs of the old tradition must, but for the tape recorder, have died out ere long.

It is the new movement in Scottish literature of the past half century — and not the Burns movement — that has led to the establishment of this School of Scottish studies, as also to a lecture-ship in Scottish literature at Glasgow University, the only one of Scotland's four universities which has yet made any such provision for the subject.

It isn't only the language difficulty, and the fact that they are taught nothing at school of the whole sequence of Scottish poets, that accounts for a lessening knowledge of Burns's works among broad masses of the population, but the fact that Scotland has changed out of all recognition in the interval since Burns died.

It is now one of the most highly industrialized nations in Europe. Two thirds of its population are packed into a narrow belt, while hundreds of thousands of acres are depopulated and derelict.

Burns wrote of the old rural Scotland which has almost wholly disappeared. The psychology of the people has changed accordingly and the strong rustic humours which fill Burns's songs and poems are nearly unintelligible to the bulk of the population.

Scottish poetry obviously needs to be brought into keeping with the urban civilization, and the scientific knowledge, of the present time.

Above all, its content must be squared with our political position and our requirements. Burns was a poet fully 'alive in his own time'. Scotland needs poets equally alive to the problems and prospects of today.

It will be lucky indeed if it gets another such as Burns, but if it did a lot of people would not recognize him.

The newcomer, if such there were, would at first glance seem very different from Burns, because there could be no mere repetition or imitation of Burns.

There has been far too much of that already. The result has been that, until very recently, Scotland has had no genuine continuators of Burns's work at all, but simply a host of doggerel-mongers.

The belated appearance of new departures in the Scots language, and with a content and concern as bound up with the working class interest as was Burns in his own day, has nonplussed his purblind idolators, but it is a healthy and long overdue development.

Scotland must recover the spirit of Burns. 'The letter killeth but the spirit gives life.'

What would Burns have said about the proposed siting of Yankee-controlled rocket-launching sites in Scotland? That is the sort of question to which Scottish poets today should address themselves.

At long last they are beginning to do so, and recent gatherings in Glasgow and elsewhere — and also genuine working-class Burns clubs like the Bowhill People Burns Club in Fife and the West Calder Burns Club — show that they are beginning to prevail over the stick-in-the-muds and have an adequate mass support behind them.

Fortified by a thorough understanding of social causation they can usher in a brilliant new phase in Scottish literature, built on the splendid foundations Burns laid but did not live to complete.

In the last half-century there has been a great decline in the general use and understanding of the old Scots language.

This is a consequence of the fact that only Standard English is permitted in our schools, which, when you think of it, is an extraordinary state of affairs since Standard English is not spoken anywhere in England itself. It is largely an educational fiction, though there is an accepted usage of English generally characteristic of certain social levels. There has been a good deal of controversy recently about 'U' and 'non-U' ways of using English. This snobbery in regard to particular usages of the language is a peculiarly English phenomenon and is not found in other great world languages. It corresponds, of course, to the social stratification of the English people, which is much greater than anything of that kind Scotland has ever had, and is, indeed, quite foreign to our national tradition. The great bulk of the English people are, however, not affected in this way so far as their speech is concerned.

In different parts of the country they speak a great variety of dialects, some of which are virtually unintelligible to people from a different district. Many dialects are spoken in Scotland, too, but they are neither so numerous, nor so far removed from each other, as the English dialects are. The strong centralizing force in English literature and education has always refused to give due recognition to these dialect differences, which, duly recognized, could have enriched English literature with a fine variety, as well as having the realistic value of catching and reproducing the actual tone of local life inseparable from a genuine portrayal of the different characteristics of the people. Even so, there is quite a volume of excellent poetry in Cumbrian, Dorset and Yorkshire dialects and societies exist to maintain and encourage their knowledge and use.

The revival of old folk-songs in recent years has also stressed the value of these dialects since the old songs are written in dialects for the most part. As the County Quiz feature on the BBC has shown, a knowledge of local dialects is the key to an understanding of many place-names, traditional customs, and aspects of history and social life, all which would become a closed book if the dialect words ceased to be appreciated.

In Scotland, however, the case is far more serious. For centuries, Scotland had a distinctive literature of its own, quite different from that of England, and much of it was written in Scots. Scots is the language of our great Border ballads and of a great proportion of our songs. Many of our best writers have continued to use Scots right up to the present day, not only in songs and poems, but also in the dialogue parts of novels and short stories and plays. It continued to be used not only by the working class but by ministers, judges, and the upper class generally until less than a century ago. Its general popularity even yet is amply attested by the fact that it is used by our comedians and other variety artistes. Nevertheless, owing to the lack of systematic instruction in Scots in our Schools, it is ceasing to be spoken to anything like the same extent as even a few years ago, and the danger is that just as with Keir Hardie's children a great part of our national treasure of balladry, song, and folk-tales will soon be irretrievably lost to our people.

The only two thorough scientific enquiries conducted into the linguistic situation in Scottish schools (leaving the Gaelic-speaking area out of account) found that while Standard English was insisted on in the class rooms, the children lapsed into Scots as soon as they were out into the playgrounds or the streets again, and it was thought that this duality of language had a retarding effect on Scottish children. Is it not a good thing therefore if Scots is dying out and English securing undivided attention? What is the point of trying to insist upon a separate Scots literature at this time of day? One of the greatest literatures of the world is accessible to us in English. Is it not simply trying to 'put back the clock' to revert now to a literature in Scots? These questions remind me of how, during the war years when butter was in short supply, we were urged to use margarine instead and told that it was just as good, if not better. The fact is, of course, that the imitation can never compete with the genuine article.

That is why, though the majority of Scottish writers have written in English for four centuries, most critics have agreed that they have not succeeded in contributing anything of first, second, or even third class value to English literature and that the course of English literature owes nothing really vital and indispensable to any of them. In other words, if Scottish writers use English, they must be content to play a subordinate role. Yet Scottish brains are in no way inferior to English brains. Why, then, should they be placed at such a disadvantage? Schoolmasters know that the same thing happens in relation to all sorts of appointments. A pronounced Scots accent is a handicap, Scottish pupils are said to lack the address, the social graces, of their English counterparts. After four hundred and fifty years, when the English language and English literature have had a virtual monopoly in Scottish schools and colleges, surely the matter has been adequately tried and if failure has been registered there is little hope that further effort along the same line will ever yield better results. The fact is that despite surface assimilation the Scottish people and the English are utterly different in their deepest promptings, likes, dislikes, aspirations and potentialities. The highest Scottish faculties may be driven underground by the English overlay, and if the latter is allowed to thicken and harden sufficiently, our creative powers may be inhibited altogether. In any case, no other country has ever allowed its own language and the literature in it to be virtually excluded from the schools and place given instead to the very different language and literature of another people. Even in the relatively simple matter of song, Scottish song owes its richness to the broad vowels of the Scots language and England is comparatively impoverished in this respect because of its narrowed, clipped vowels. Creative work proceeds from below the threshold of consciousness and the reason why Scots is not less important but more important to us today then ever, is that it covers, as English does not, the whole field of our sub-conscious.

There has been a little improvement in recent years. Some leading English critics have realized that it is to the advantage of English literature itself that there should be alongside it a flourishing literature in Scots too. Even in some of our schools there has been a little improvement. But to teach a few of Burns's songs and poems is not enough. Burns cannot be properly appreciated unless he is seen in relation, not only to Allan Ramsay and Robert Fergusson, but to the great fifteenth and sixteenth century 'makars' to whom he owed so much; and this is only one facet of a much greater requirement. Scottish children ought to be put into full possession of the national heritage. That is not being done, and the consequence is that the present writer finds in Adult Education classes that his pupils have no background of knowledge on which he can rely — name after name of famous Scots in different departments of science and the arts is quite unknown to them — and as a result it is very difficult to elicit from them Scotland's distinctive contribution and to show how in vital respects it differs from the English. Scotland contributed more than England to the Industrial Revolution and to the building of the British Empire, and is again contributing more to the so-called Second Industrial Revolution as the mention of key-names like those of James Clerk Maxwell, Lord Rutherford, and J. Logie Baird shows. Why? Questions such as these cannot be answered unless we are in full possession of our native tradition. They cannot even be asked. And it is vital that they should be asked and answered if Scotland is to continue as it should to deserve the tribute paid to it by the historian Froude when he said: 'Except the Athenians and the Jews, no people so few in number have scored so deep a mark on the world's history as the Scots have done'.

As Fletcher of Saltoun said: 'No inclination is so honourable nor has anything been so esteemed in all nations and ages as the love of that country and society in which every man is born'.

In modern times Scots have paid homage more vociferously than most to that principle, but they have betrayed it in practice to an unparalleled degree, as is borne out, for example, by the fact that for generations we have boasted of the glories of Scottish song, yet it has been left to the School of Scottish Studies in Edinburgh University in the last year or two to tape-record thousands of Scots songs and ballads (and Gaelic songs and tales) handed down orally through the generations — an immense treasure of which until lately we were totally ignorant, and which would have perished if it had not been recorded now just in the nick of time, since all this wealth of song and story only lingered on the lips of old people and in the nature of things ere long it must have perished with them. Is this the true measure of our love of Scotland and our response to the injunction to know ourselves?

I have had no cause in the interval to change my opinion (especially since, as Dr Kurt Wittig points out, Burns, little suspecting that he himself was destined to become one of the curio-hunters' chief victims, laughed at an antiquarian's treasured finds as 'a fouth o' auld nick-nackets'), and in an article published this year in *The Daily Worker* (23/1/58) and in *Lion Rampant (An Leomhan Arronta)*, the organ of the London Branch of the Scottish National Party, I described some of the aspects of the present position as follows:

Mr J.R. Campbell incited the fury of many typical illiterate Burns sentimentalists a couple of years ago when he said:

> Is it not humbug when Burns clubs meet year after year to extol the poet and yet have done nothing to make the immense majority of Burns's songs, together with the traditional music to which they were written, accessible to the people of Scotland? I repeat that there are no more than a dozen songs (some of them not sung to the traditional airs) at this moment recorded for the gramophone. Burns is beyond doubt the greatest figure in Scots literature, which, however, did not *start* with him, and thank heavens, did not *end* with him. He wouldn't have wished it otherwise. Yet the mere mention of any twentieth-century Scots literary figure always provokes outpourings of hatred, ridicule, and contempt from large numbers of Burnsians.

Mr Campbell is, of course, right when he complains of the neglect of most of our great treasury of Scottish songs and the endless repetition *ad nauseam* of a few favourites. Scotland is, indeed, worse than any other country in the so-called civilized world in respect of that tyranny of the repetition complex of which Mr Michael Tippett complained not long ago when he wrote:

> We all know that the big public is extremely conservative, and willing to ring the changes on a few beloved works till the end of time. So that our concert life, through the taste of this public, suffers from a kind of inertia of sensibility that seems to want no musical experience whatever that it does not already know. When this taste is indeed the national taste, the art of the nation certainly dies. But the creative artist is passionately determined that it shall not die. In fact totalitarian societies, which are pathetically conformist and afraid of the new, have had to stamp him out. They are afraid, even of the struggling composer with his tiny public. And what are they afraid of? I think they are afraid of his passion, of his violence, of his unaccountability. For it is a fact of musical history (and this goes for the other arts as well) that during the last half-century, or even earlier, every major composer has at the

outset found the taste of the big public and its consumer point of view unacceptable. It is true of Bartók, for example, that the big public instinctively hated his creative integrity, and no doubt he, for all his courage, was hurt and haunted by this hate. The dilemma is not a conspiracy but a fact. Why does the big public hate extreme artistic integrity? How can a great composer go forward at all in what looks like a voluntary cul-de-sac? Surely the matter is that the very big public masses together in a kind of dead passion of mediocrity, and that this blanket of mediocrity, whether communist or capitalist, is deeply offended by any living passion of the unusual, the rare, the rich, the exuberant, the heroic, and the aristocratic in art — the art of a poet like Yeats. While it is clear from Yeats' life and writings that in this very passion of defiance an artist can find both material for his art and vigour for his despised activity. But he may starve.

The Edinburgh International Festival has done nothing to remedy this state of affairs. Its promoters do not care if every Scottish composer dies of starvation. The native contribution to the arts is almost wholly excluded from the Festival programme. The mistake of preferring Barabbas is nowhere so prevalent as in Scotland today; the injunction 'Seek ye first the Kingdom of Heaven...' more universally neglected than in any other European country. A little country like Finland could produce a man wholly devoted to his art like Sibelius. And not only so, but a sufficient number of people to recognize the stand he has taken and the incomparable national importance of it — and, accordingly, to insist and ensure that he be given his proper place and that whatever encouragement and facilitation, financially and otherwise, lesser spirits could give him in his high task should be his. In Scotland alone there is no such incentive to, or encouragement in, serious creative effort in any of the arts. On the contrary! Even the St Andrew's Night programme of the Scottish BBC was a shameful *exposé* of our national atimy and amentality. It was a ludicrously undignified melange of worthless 'arrangements' by Sir Hugh S. Roberton and Dr Ian Whyte, crowned by the participation of the unspeakable buffoon, Mr Will Fyfe. Nobody is allowed to participate in these ceremonial displays of Scottish bad taste and stupidity who has ever given evidence of any serious purpose except the snapping up of whatever fees are going. Government and municipal grants to the Arts in Scotland are less than in any other European country — Edinburgh, for example, only gives the proceeds of a ¾d rate whereas it has the power to give a 4⅘d rate, and while other countries and/or municipalities build theatres, opera houses, and art galleries Edinburgh fails to do anything of the kind. The Act of Parliament permits Scottish local authorities to spend up to four and four-fifths pence on the rates in promoting 'artistic enterprises'. In England it is 6d. Not one local authority in Scotland spends anything like the sum. Which explains why Scottish towns are such cultural deserts, while, apart from the generous subsidies of the arts east of the Elbe, the Danish Government, for example, subsidies the Copenhagen Royal Theatre to the tune of £400,000 annually. In Scotland the Government gives the Scottish Committee of the Arts Council only £86,000 to spend on all the arts in Scotland — less than the price of one single fighter aircraft!

With that brief detour, I return to the question of Burns's songs. Our unthinking conventionalists of Scots, terrified of anything with life in it, will, of course, have no more to do with F.G. Scott's resettings of Burns's songs than the Swedes would tolerate the taking of any like 'liberties' with Carl Michael Bellman, the famous Swedish poet and singer of the eighteenth century, although his drinking song, 'To The Galatians', for example, ambles along as amiably as a glass of milk, and has no kick in it whatever, despite the allusions in the text to 'rich brown ale' and 'Swedish punch', and it would be easy to think of this song with a different rhythmic emphasis, a brisker tempo, a sensation of the swing and vigour of the quick dotted eight, and not the lilting, languishing beat of the pastorale, six-eight time. Similar strictures must be passed on many more of his songs, though Bellman (the type of man I like best, for, like Mr E.M. Forster, I am 'with the old Scotsman who wanted less chastity and more delicacy' all the time) lived recklessly, with a God-given abhorrence of the smug, secure, and systematic, wasted his substance, consorted on equal terms with scholiasts and tavern-keepers, nobles and lights-o'-love of high and low degree, yet looking to him for the vigorous racy semi-Rabelaisian semi-Robert Burns sort of thing we legitimately expect we are woefully disappointed; he is betrayed by a bad musical tradition — as Burns's poem was betrayed by the utterly alien traditional setting of 'Scots Wha Hae', against which, nevertheless, Scott's infinitely better re-setting can make no headway. No wonder even the former is now being supplanted by the worthless 'Scotland the Brave'!

Every Scotsman is faced with just the same position as in Russia faced Chaliapin. It was Dmitri Andreivitch Ousatov who at Tiflis gave Chaliapin his first insight into musical characterization, and he did so through examples from Moussorgsky's *Boris Godounov*,

'Now,' he would say, 'You see how music can react on the imagination. You see how silence and a pause are able to give the subtle effect of characterization.' This was the lesson which invoked in Chaliapin the qualities which made his art unique. 'Don't take any notice,' the other singers of Ousatov's class said, 'all he says may be true but *La donna e mobile* is the right stuff for singers. Moussorgsky with his Varlaams and Mitiouks is literally poison for the voice and singing.' Chaliapin declares that he was torn in two. 'Sometimes I was so racked with doubt that I lay sleepless. Which should I choose — *La donna e mobile* or *In the big town of Kazan*?' This was the one critical moment in his career, the one moment when he had to choose his party. Beside it all the later adulations of the great, the angling for his adherence, the fawning of the crowds, and the police warrants out against him, were of no importance whatsoever. Which should he choose? If he had chosen 'The right stuff for singers', there would have been, no doubt, one more highly successful singer in a world full of them, but there would have been no Chaliapin — none of that secret of his art, a secret which everyone knows but no one else can possess. So far Scotland in every connection has chosen 'the right stuff for singers', and the whole influence of our Anglo-Scottish newspapers (whether they favour or oppose 'some measure' of devolution), all our MPs, all our ecclesiastical leaders, most of our writers and other cultural figures, and even the Scottish Nationalist organizations themselves is on the other side and against any attempt at inducing Scotland to realize its *Ur-motives*. If the so-called Nationalists among these succeed there will be a measure of autonomy, and a somewhat better, but not essentially different, administration as a consequence, but Scotland will again betray its native genius and fail to make that unique contribution which it ought to do, and beside the mere possibility of which nothing else it can do is of the slightest consequence. It will not have the excuse that the alternatives were not clearly and persistently put before it. So far as music is concerned Scott is the only one who has chosen as Moussorgsky and Chaliapin chose.

One of the best living Scottish poets, Mr Norman McCaig, provoked a tremendous uproar this year when he declared: 'Burns's scope is narrow, his vision small, his intelligence not large and his imaginative grasp superficial. He could never make up his mind whether to write in Scots or English. I don't think he was a great craftsman.'

Among the monstrosities of irrelevance, incomprehension, and sheer fatuity this drew forth a high place must be accorded to the declaration of Sir Patrick Dollan, a former President of the World

Burns Federation, 'Burns was one of the best-informed politicians of his day. In his *Lines To a Gentleman* he showed he had a good knowledge of 14 different countries.... There are three continuous best-sellers in Britain today — the Bible, Shakespeare, and Robert Burns — in that order.' Sir Patrick had, of course, immediate recourse to the old device of 'No case — abuse plaintiff's attorney' and asked — with great scorn and shabby cheapness — 'Who is Norman McCaig?' I was not surprised in the least that Sir Patrick did not know the name of one of the best poets using the English language, Scotland has ever had and a scholar and gentleman of a kind never likely to be found in his (Sir Patrick's) company. I remember Ramsay MacDonald pontificating about contemporary Scottish literature and mentioning as outstanding among living authors James Welsh and Joe Corrie. I wrote to him and pointed out that these were writers of little or no consequence at all and that he had preferred them to others of far greater stature. Mr MacDonald had the grace to apologize and say that in his position he was naturally far too busy to keep abreast of our literary developments. Recently another Labour MP — no less than Mrs Jean Mann — shook a sorrowful head over the sad decline of Scottish literature and looked back to the great days — and wished we had them again — when we had such a towering genius as John Buchan in our midst. I did not write to Mrs Mann. I knew it wasn't worth while. She forgot, of course, — if she ever knew — Buchan's vicious travesty of the Socialist movement in general, and John MacLean in particular, in *Mr Standfast.* Our Labour MPs have betrayed everything true Socialism implies, their so-called policy in every vital respect is practically indistinguishable from that of the Tories. Mrs Mann may have been speaking well within her book when she longed to have our literature dominated again by a rank Tory Imperialist. More probably her remarks showed partly that, but mainly just that, like most of her kind, she is only minimally literate and far fonder of her own voice than she is of any literature.

While stressing the continued demand for Burns's works in this way Sir Patrick might well have considered the fact that, as Dr Kurt Wittig points out,

> the *Poetic Gems* of the Great William MacGonagall, Poet and Tragedian, and shabbiest of public-house rhymesters, are still reprinted almost every year; and their continuing popularity would indeed be an interesting problem for a psychiatrist to study. It is not rock-bottom we touch here, that would suggest something solid; with him, poetry is irretrievably sunk in mire.

Much of Burns's work is of just this sort, and led directly to this degeneration of the Scots tradition — not only in MacGonagall, but in most of the post-Burnsian bards, the 'Scotch coamics', much of the material on the Scottish BBC, like the late Helen Pryde's 'McFlannels', and it is, indeed, just this sort of thing that most Scottish people regard as being synonymous with Scottishness and as constituting the very essence of the Scottish tradition alike in literature and in life.

What Stephen McKenna, the Irishman who translated Plotinus, said about modern Irish Gaelic literature in one of his letters, is even more applicable to Scots and Scottish Gaelic writing, and to the effect Burns has had on subsequent authors, viz:

> Get a blue pencil and make two re-writings per page on Patrick O'Conaire's stuff and you have the only thing of modern Ireland that could be written by a French, a German, a Russian, a Swedish novelist or playwright or essayist.... Patrick is often grammatically careless and inconsistent, sometimes confused, a hundred faults; but he belongs to the European kind; compared with any other Munster writer he stands about as a rather crackedly crotchety university don to a schoolgirl: he is mature though faulty, he has range; the Munsterites are bright limited childishness. I don't know one Munsterite that has any notion of literature whatever... no notion of literary congruity, no sense of literary architecture or carpentry, no sense of depth or range, no notion of true observation or of significant selection, no spiritual emotion, no nothing that makes literature.... I maintain that with all Patrick O'Conaire's little flaws he's such that an imaginary non-English-speaking Irishman steeped in him would be prepared for all European conversation and literature; no Munster writer prepares the mind for anything but a Munster cabin or old Irish story life.

He adds that O'Conaire, speaking not of his mental value but of his range and language, goes very close to Maupassant, whereas 'Munster keeps to the *Aonach* and to *cro na muc*' (*i.e.* to 'the fair' and 'the pigsty')!

Even so Munster Gaelic writing is richer and livelier than most modern Scots or Scots Gaelic writing which keeps for the most part to far duller things than the fair or the pigsty, namely, the kirk and the kailyaird.

McKenna raged against those who thought of Irish as a patois for peasants, 'who in grotesque ignorance or lying malice assert that the Irish of so much poetry is fit only for discussing the feeding of pigs and the promise of cows. A man could do anything in Irish,' he wrote to a friend in 1914, 'say and express anything and do it with an exquisite beauty of sound.... I consider it the flaw and sin of my life that I didn't twenty years ago give myself body and soul to the Gaelic to become a writer in it as some — God forgive me! — some Conrad in English or some Flem flammanding in French, and help to make the literature that would reroot the language.'

How he hated the contemporary fiction and poetry that was beginning to be written in Irish as 'narrow in range, tenuous in substance, and too often childishly sentimental' — almost exactly the terms Norman McCaig used of much of Burns's work, and terms applicable enough certainly to most of our post-Burnsian verse and fiction. This is the curse that has fallen even more heavily on modern Scottish Gaelic letters and Lowland Scots writing. And the cause of it all? McKenna puts it splendidly, and for the Scots and the Welsh as much as for the Irish, when he says: 'We never did fry our own fish, but did always be jumping into the fire to yank out the herrings for the other man — and small leavings to ourselves when that one had them gozzled!'

Burns led directly to this sorry pass through his anti-intellectualism and his xenophobia. It is nonsense to say that he embodies all the great elements of the Scottish tradition when in these two main respects he in fact completely betrayed it. Pasteur, the great French scientist, praised Scotland because 'it was the first nation to link its destiny with the development of the human mind' and, later, Edinburgh was widely acclaimed as the intellectual capital of Europe. All that Burns wanted, however, was

> ae spark o' Nature's fire
> That's a' the learning I desire.

Well, it is not enough and less so today than ever. It is a betrayal of Dunbar and Gavin Douglas and the other great *makars* to whom Burns owed so much, and it has been largely responsible for landing the Scottish Muse in the horrible mess it has occupied since. Mr Ivor Brown in his obituary of Colonel Walter Elliot was right in pointing out that that great Scotsman had no need to echo Burns's wish for a spark of Nature's fire — he had *that* all right — but could never have subscribed to the following line. And as to Burns's chauvinism and aversion from what was foreign, that again is a betrayal of one of the greatest impulses the Scottish people have shown all through their history — that internationalism which stands in such contradistinction to English insularity.

That is why thirty years ago I had to write — and have had no occasion to modify the passage since: The Burns Cult has been, and is being, used almost wholly as a psychological 'compensation' for a sense of disloyalty to Scotland's — and Scottish literature's — real interests. All the staple claims of Burns devotees vanish immediately on critical inspection. Burns was not a representative Scotsman; economic and other limitations restricted him for the most part to certain relatively unimportant aspects of Scottish life and letters. It is a gross misunderstanding to suppose that he touched our national being at every point and voiced the whole range of our traditions and aspirations. Only those who know little of these, and next to nothing of Scottish history and literature, and care less, can contend anything of the sort. We can pass over the fatuous people who contend that he was 'greater as a man than as a poet' — a mere reflection of their own ignorance and incapacity for literary matters; just as we pass over the declaration of people like the late Lord Sands that Scotland is not declining, since, even in his own day 'Holyrood House has been put in order as a King's residence, a chapel established for our order of chivalry and the finest War Memorial in the world ensconced in Edinburgh Castle' — three matters that should not, and I think, do not matter a brass farthing to more than a small fraction of one per cent of the Scottish people. It has been said that repetition of the same lines or phrases accounts for seventy-five per cent of Burns's work; certainly his great work is a small portion of the remaining twenty-five per cent — and not the portion generally known. Most of his work has dated very badly; it is full of eighteenth-century conventionalism and the minutiae of dead and even at the time very local controversies. It marked the end of a phase — not a fresh start in Scots letters. It contains surprisingly little description of Scottish scenery, little concern with Scottish history, little sense of Scotland's destiny, and as to his love-songs they might all have been written to the same lay-figure, for any particularity they contain. He has the typical voluptuary's aversion from realism in this respect. Lord David Cecil has quoted, apropos Scott's conventional heroines: 'Very nice young ladies,' as Admiral Croft said of the Misses Musgraves, 'I hardly know one from the other.' Burns's are completely indistinguishable.

Mr T.S. Eliot is right when he says, 'I suspect Arnold of helping to fix the wholly mistaken notion of Burns as a singular untutored English dialect poet, instead of a decadent representative of a great alien tradition.' Precisely. *A decadent representative*! This is the force of my old dictum in *Albyn* (1927): 'Burns betrayed the movement Ramsay and Fergusson began.' And quoting this in *Lucky Poet*, I continued:

> The term 'betrayal' is not one to be used lightly about Burns in any connection, but my whole attitude has been based on the realization that Burns's poem of which 'a parcel of rogues in a nation' is the refrain was applied to this tiny class of England's lackeys who have oppressed Scotland in England's interests ever since the Union. Further, a study of Burns from the Marxist angle shows that the poem in question (1794) was, like 'Scots Wha Ha'e' (1793) inspired by Thomas Muir's movement — which Burns himself lived to betray and attack (*vide* 'Does haughty Gaul invasion threaten?'[*sic*] 1795). I also think that Burns betrayed his keenest realizations of the kind of poetry he should write, lapsing back on too easy models and compromising too much with English standards, since, as Mr J.B. Caird has pointed out, 'Burns's remarks on the song "The Mill, Mill O" show that he had reached conclusions regarding poetic rhythm, without endeavouring to work them out systematically or to put them into practice, which in some respects anticipate those of Gerard Manley Hopkins.'[1]

To undo that betrayal, to get back to and move forward from the previous position, and to succeed where the two former attempts to revive Scots as a medium for the full range of literary purpose failed has been the aim of the Scottish Renaissance Movement which is now widely held to have succeeded far better than its predecessors and to be capable of leading now to the greatest phase in Scottish literary history. This Movement (though Stevenson and others had been moving in the same direction before that) began in 1920, and as Sydney Goodsir Smith has said,

> In the early days there were only a few adherents to the cause. Today there are hosts of them. They are not all of the first flight, of course; many a crow squawks among our nightingales. But there are seldom more than one or two first-class artists, in any line, in one generation. What *is* a healthy sign, and a sign that this time the revival, the newly recaptured tradition, is not so likely to prove a nine day's wonder, is that the general *idea* is accepted by so many — the idea that the soul of Scotland can only be revived by a return to our true tradition — the idea that Scots is a language

---

1 Hugh MacDiarmid, *Lucky Poet* (1943; Carcanet , 1994, p.205) – Ed.

> and not merely a hotch-potch of dialects (or even *one* dialect, as the foolish say); that it's a language capable of coping with any subject in heaven or earth or hell; the idea implicit in this belief that Scotland has a part to play in Europe as it had before, and the realization that Scots is a more expressive and potent medium for a Scottish Writer than is English or American or Esperanto.

So, just as my friend, Saunders Lewis, considers the Welsh National Eisteddfod artistically dull, yet thinks its social and national importance immense, so I with the Burns Movement, though it is the potentiality of the latter, rather than its present actuality, I have in mind.

The whole raison-d'etre of the Burns cult is to deny that Burns was Burns — and to make him instead acceptable to conventional standards that would have found in him (in so far as he was able to be true to the best in himself) their most powerful and persistent enemy, and to middle-class 'buddies' whom he would have flayed alive.

What an organization the World Federation of Burns Clubs could have been — could even yet become — if it were animated by the true spirit of Burns and fulfilling a programme based on his essential motives applied to crucial contemporary issues as he applied them while he was living to what, according to his lights, were some of the crucial issues of his own day and generation! What a true Scottish international that would be for the 25 million Scots and 3000 Scots Societies abroad — what a culmination and crown of Scotland's role in history, the role that has carried Scotsmen to every country in the world and given them radical leadership wherever they went! 'You may dislike the English,' it is frequently claimed, 'but you cannot deny that they have produced the greatest body of poetry in the world.'

The claim is seldom made except by those who know little or nothing of any other — except the 'classics'. It is true that one of the greatest bodies of poetry in the world has been produced in the English language, but not by the English people. The great majority of its producers have been wholly or partly Celtic. Even so, since Shakespeare and Milton, I am disposed to say that English poetry is 'great unfortunately', as the Frenchman said that the greatest French poet was 'Victor Hugo — unfortunately'. It is not my purpose to deal with these particular issues here, but I would add that I believe it is the recoil of the Celtic spirit — its desertion of English literature for a renewed concern with Irish, Welsh, and Scottish literature, and the Gaelic languages, I hope and believe, in the long run, which largely accounts for the insignificance and anaemia of modern English poetry.

Whatever the explanation, however, this relative triviality (the fact that, as Mr J.B. Priestley has said, English literature today is at a lower ebb than at any time since the fourteenth century) is one of the reasons that make it deplorable that English poetry (which is likely to have as poor a future as it has a rich past) should occupy so disproportionate a place in Scottish education and Scottish reading generally.

It would be ludicrous, in considering the novel, to promote English fiction to such a role and ignore Dostoevski, Tolstoy, Stendhal, Balzac, and a score of other Europeans whose work must be known to anyone whose opinions on the subject are of the slightest value, but these are never ignored as European poets of similar status are. It would be grotesque to discuss the drama in terms of the English theatre (forgetting that less than 2 per cent of the population has ever been in a theatre or seen a dramatic production of any kind) and not realize the far greater importance of Ibsen, Strindberg, Pirandello, and others. It is equally, and even more, absurd in poetry. Just as with past poetry an insular dismissal of Homer, Vergil, Dante, and other great European poets would be absurd, so it is with contemporary poetry.

There might be good reasons for confining our schoolchildren first of all to the Scottish poets (but not to most of those poets of whom they are at present taught anything!) no matter how poverty-stricken the course of Scottish poetry may be to that of many other countries — even countries with much smaller populations and poorer in other respects — but it is ridiculous to bring them up on Walter de la Mare and other recent English poetasters, or even on Tennyson, Browning, and Mrs Hemans not only in preference to our own very different writers, but to far more important European figures, and especially to those elements in European poetry which have a far greater bearing on the position and potentialities of Scottish poetry than almost any English poetry has. Much European poetry has positive bearings on Scottish poetry; most English poetry has only negative bearings; and an over-concern with the latter is likely in the future, as in the past, to be extremely misleading and unprofitable. The relative Continental significance of three Scots — Byron, 'Ossian', and Carlyle — to that accorded to them in English estimation is a valuable 'pointer' in this connection. They are not all out of step except 'our Jock' (*i.e.* England or Anglicized Scotland).

I was, I think, fortunate in being not only an omnivorous reader determined to get into touch with vital contemporary poetry no matter in what country or language it was being produced, but from the beginning, instinctively 'cool' to English literature, which has never had any disproportionate place in my reading, and which I have all along recognized as far less closely related to my own spirit than many elements of European literature for which English literature has, if not an actual distaste or constitutional incapacity to assimilate, at least no equivalents. But as a Scotsman under our deplorable modern dispensation, I was naturally unduly influenced for a long time by types of poetry which, if I have not yet outgrown them in my actual practice, I now set aside critically as far less worthy of study and emulation with a view to the ultimate realization of any of the greater latent potentialities of the Scottish genius than certain other types.

Broadly, if I were asked what kind of poetry young Scots seriously concerned with this matter ought to concentrate upon, I would quote Professor Faesi's general description of Carl Spitteler's qualities: 'Certainly love is not the basic feeling of Spitteler or the *primum mobile* of his self-created world. Courage, patience, self-assertion, unyieldingness, energy, and (above all) a steel-like and combative virility are the most important sources of his inspiration.'

The almost superhuman problem of creating even yet a worthy Scottish poetry demands like qualities — a similar conjunction of daemonic will with poetic genius. Or, as I have written elsewhere of our Gaelic poet, Uilleam MacDhunleibe (William Livingston);

> He did not write 'love poetry'. He did not address himself to any of the infantile themes on which ninety per cent of versification depends. He stood clear of the tradition that insists that the substance of poetry must be silly vapourings, chocolate-box-lid pictures of nature, and trite moralizings; penny novelette love is all right, but not politics, not religion, not war, not anything that can appeal to an adult intelligence. He is a splendid masculine poet, who 'put away childish things'. The irresistible verve of his utterance, the savagery of his satire, are abhorrent to the spineless triflers who want pretty-prettifyings, and not any devotion to matters of life and death.

One of the most difficult things is to get Scots to understand that the English language is not omnicompetent — that any language is not only a medium of expression but a determinant of what can be expressed in it.

In his essay on Racine, dealing with Mr John Bailey's book *The Claims of French Poetry*, Mr Lytton Strachey had things to say of particular consequence to Scots who remember the 'Auld Alliance' and know how much it influenced the Scottish mind and the Scots language.

> 'L'épithète rare,' said the De Goncourts, 'Voilà la marque de L'ecrivain.' Mr Bailey quotes the sentence with approval, observing that if, with Saint-Beuve, we extend the phrase to 'le mot rare', we have at once one of those invaluable touchstones with which we may test the merit of poetry. And doubtless most English readers would be inclined to agree with Mr Bailey, for it so happens that our own literature is one in which rarity of style, pushed often to the verge of extravagance, reigns supreme. Owing mainly, no doubt, to the double origin of our language, with its strange and violent contrasts between the highly-coloured crudity of the Saxon words and the ambiguous splendour of the Latin vocabulary; owing, partly, perhaps to a national taste for the intensely imaginative, and partly, too, to the vast and penetrating influence of those grand masters of bizarrerie — the Hebrew prophets — our poetry, our prose, and our whole conception of the art of writing have fallen under the dominion of the emphatic, the extraordinary, and the bold. No one in his senses would regret this, for it has given our literature all its most characteristic glories, and, of course, in Shakespeare, with whom expression is stretched to the bursting point, the national style finds at once its most consummate example and its final justification. But the result is that we have grown so unused to other kinds of poetic beauty, that we have now come to believe with Mr Bailey, that poetry apart from 'le mot rare' is an impossibility. The beauties of restraint, of clarity, of refinement, and of precision we pass by unheeding; we can see nothing there but coldness and uniformity; and we go back with eagerness to the fling and the bravado that we love so well. It is as if we had become so accustomed to looking at boxers, wrestlers, and gladiators that the sight of an exquisite minuet produced no effect on us; the ordered dance strikes us as a monotony, for we are blind to the subtle delicacies of the dancers, which are fraught with such significance to the practised eye.... Similarly when Mr Bailey, turning from the vocabulary to more general questions of style, declares that there is no 'element of fine surprise' in Racine, no trace of the 'daring metaphors and similes of Pindar and the Greek choruses' — the reply is that he would find what he wants if he only knew where to look for it. 'Who will forget,' he says, 'the comparison of the Atreidae to the eagles wheeling over their empty nest, of war to the money-

changer whose gold dust is that of human bodies, of Helen to the lion's whelps?...Everyone knows these. Who will match them among the formal elegancies of Racine?' And it is true that when Racine wished to create a great effect he did not adopt the romantic method; he did not chase his ideas through the four quarters of the universe to catch them at last upon the verge of the inane; and anyone who hopes to come upon 'fine surprises' of this kind in his pages will be disappointed. His daring is of a different kind; it is not the daring of adventure but of intensity; his fine surprises are seized out of the very heart of his subject, and seized in a single stroke. Thus many of his astonishing phrases burn with an inward concentration of energy, which, difficult at first to realize to the full, comes in the end to impress itself ineffaceably upon the mind.

C'etait pendant l'horreur d'une profonde nuit. The sentence is like a cavern whose mouth a careless traveller might pass by, but which opens out, to the true explorer, into vista after vista of strange recesses rich with inexhaustible gold. But, sometimes, the phrase, compact as dynamite, explodes upon one with an immediate and terrible force —

C'est Venus toute entière à sa proie attachée! A few 'formal elegances' of this kind are surely worth having.

But what is it that makes the English reader fail to recognize the beauty and the power of such passages as these? Besides Racine's lack of extravagance and bravura, besides his dislike of exaggerated emphasis and far-fetched or fantastic imagery, there is another characteristic of his style to which we are perhaps even more antipathetic — its suppression of detail. The great majority of poets — and especially of English poets — produce their most potent effects by the accumulation of details — details which in themselves fascinate us either by their beauty or their curiosity or their supreme appropriateness. But with details Racine will have nothing to do; he builds up his poetry out of words which are not only absolutely simple, but extremely general, so that our minds, failing to find in it the peculiar delights to which we have been accustomed, fall into the error of rejecting it altogether as devoid of significance.

In the same way the supreme power of Burns's finest line —

Ye arena Mary Morrison —

may easily fail to impress. But why should I bother even to cite it when such misconceptions of the poetic are rife as that voiced the other day on STV when I quoted Hölderlin's statement that 'love poems are a tired affair' and contended that Burns's 'To A Louse' was one of his greatest poems. 'What,' said another member of the panel, 'Do you mean to say that a poem to a louse could possibly be as good poetry as one to a bonnie lassie?'

Incidentally, a BBC feature showed by tape-recordings that a random number of Glasgow citizens failed completely, given a line from one of the most hackneyed of Burns's songs, to give the following line, and all those interviewed admitted that they knew little or nothing about anything Burns had written. I am sure the great majority of Scottish people today are in like case. Keir Hardie, a great Burns lover, on returning home to Lanarkshire from Westminster, was appalled to find that his own children did not understand Burns's words. They had been taught 'standard English' — that pedagogic fiction only taught in Scottish schools, but to be heard nowhere in England itself. The Scottish genius is far closer to the French than to the English, and our best poetry is classical, not romantic. It is certainly at the furthest remove from the English tradition. Even today despite the progressive Anglicization of our people and the worthlessness of almost all they regard as poetry, it can never be said of Scottish poetry (and this is what we owe to Burns — and his defiance of the Edinburgh *Literati* with their sedulous aping of English models and their pathological fear of Scotticisms — The so-called Golden Age of Scottish literature was, of course, nothing of the kind and clamantly calls for revaluation as a Quisling conspiracy against the Scottish genius) as Lord David Cecil in his essay on Dante Gabriel Rossetti has so well said of modern English poetry:

> There is no doubt that the nineteenth century, which witnessed progress in almost everything else, witnessed a decline in poetry. It began, indeed, with a great outburst of it, the Romantic Movement. But that very Romantic Movement bore within it the seeds of poetic decay. For it marked the beginning of a fatal division between poetry and life. A poet, like anybody else, is not a completely self-dependent individual; he is also a member of society. And like any member of a society, he must partake of its general life if he is fully to develop his talents, must draw nourishment and stimulus from its common interests and enthusiasms if he is to maintain the vitality needed to make him create. But he can only do this in a society that appeals to his sympathies, one whose institutions and preoccupations and underlying values have that ideal justification, and can be regarded in that romantic aspect

> which can give them significance or attraction in the eyes of one whose ultimate standard of values is aesthetic. Now the life of England up till the nineteenth century did have such an aspect and such a justification. The religious questions which dominated the interests of the average man of the seventeenth century were also some of the dominating interests of Milton and Herbert; the social and political causes which stirred the enthusiasm of the average man of the eighteenth century stirred equally the enthusiasm of Addison and Swift; Addison was even a member of the Government. But by 1880 the Industrial Revolution had broken up the fabric of common belief and institutions, and put no other new one in its place; so that in order to find that background of moral and intellectual values necessary to stimulate them, the poets had to turn to the unorganized certainties provided by their own experience: Wordsworth to his own personal response to nature, Keats to his personal response to sensuous beauty, Shelley to his personal response to the calls of love and liberty, and to construct from these a moral and intellectual background of their own. But though in varying degrees they succeeded in doing this for themselves, they did not do it for anybody else.... With the consequence that artists grew steadily more indifferent to the religious or political questions that agitated the men of action of their day; till today they are two nations which hardly know each other's language. One would as soon expect a poet to be an engine-driver as a member of the Cabinet. Abstracted from that soil of common life which alone could generate the sap necessary to keep it alive, it was inevitable that the flower of creative inspiration should wither. And it has withered. There is no living tradition of major poetry in England today: such genuine poetry as there is can be divided into fragmentary and plaintive dreams of a never-never land of poetic fancy to which the poet escapes for a moment from the prosaic reality which imprisons him, and fragmentary and incoherent imprecations against his chains.

The same thing must have happened in Scotland tethered to and dominated by England but for Burns, and that character of democracy in Scotland which is utterly different from the bogus 'democracy' of England, since Scotland happily lacks England's snobbery and social stratification — but for these two things (which are really one, since Burns was pre-eminently the voice of that Scottish democracy), and the third fact that Scottish poetry is largely a poetry of song (and consequently nearer the people), whereas English poetry is practically destitute of song — since the broad Scots vowels lend themselves to song in a way the clipped English vowels can never do. Hence, distorted as it has been and largely wrested away from the working-class by business and professional men, the Burns Movement was initially a sound impulse, and even the form of the Annual Suppers — the haggis and mashed neeps, the whisky, and the songs — was on the right lines and infinitely preferable in almost every way to formal commemorations of poets' anniversaries in other countries, and I would certainly be the last person in the world to wish to modify the gorging and the boozing, since these create an atmosphere Burns himself would have been at home in, and consequently an appropriate setting for his songs and poems — only (and this is my sole reservation) the fact that Burns was primarily a poet should never be forgotten, nor the fact that his work cannot be properly appreciated unless it is seen in its proper historical context, nor, again, that there can be no real homage to Burns unless it is part and parcel of a vital concern for Scotland and Scots and the present condition and prospects of Scottish literature. But experience has shown that none of these requirements are any better met in blue-nose company than in the most ranting and roaring assemblages of a Burns Nicht. Burns must be seen in proper perspective, however. Professor Barker Fairley has well said that

> Among the least noticed, and possibly the most insidious, of the forces taking, or tending to take, literature out of society is the belief, commonly held and seldom challenged, that an author is a fixed magnitude, not perhaps capable of being assessed in percentages, like examination papers, but nearly so. The belief which tempts us, then, in our weaker moments to give Shakespeare, say ninety-five per cent, taking five marks off for *The Merchant of Venice*, and Milton eighty-five, both first-classes. The belief that tempts us to rank all authors as major or minor without admitting or bothering about a middle stage. When the mood is on us, we ask who are the great English poets, and we count them on our fingers, five, perhaps six.... This is an attitude we have all encountered somewhere in our concern with books, but we seldom stop to ask what it means. If we do stop to ask, we have to recognize that in proportion as we think of an author as fixed in value we are taking him out of society, since we can only fix him by lifting him out of the social environment in which he wrote and by assuming that he will be just the same in any one of countless others. In short, we assume that environment has nothing to do with him.

I don't know where we put him when we take him out of the environment, but we put him there. It must be thought of as a sort of shelf or cupboard where we can find him when we want him and place him back again. We all do this in one way or another. If we discover an author whom we happen to value was less valued in an earlier society — take the poet John Donne now and in the Victorian age — we are much more likely to think of the Victorians as not equal to him than of him as not equal to them. It is so much easier to see them as different than to see differently with them. And it is the same with an author who is less valued now — say Thackeray or Meredith. Here again we are much readier to say that their judgement was at fault than to recognize that their experience was not the same as ours. In other words, we imply that the act of reading a book is the same at all times and that the argument, the thought, the images, the sensations will be identical, no matter who reads it or when. It is only with difficulty — if I may trust my own experience of reading — that we learn how erroneous the implication is. One way to learn — perhaps the only sure way — is for the same person to read the same book after a sufficient lapse of years to enable him to come at it out of a changed world and possibly with a changed self. With luck he will then catch the experience at first hand. But this is a slow business.

(This was what I had in mind when in a speech I delivered some thirty-five years ago I suggested that the best thing for Burns Clubs to do was to forget all about Burns for quarter of a century — and reconsider the whole matter then. This suggestion created a tremendous row. Newspapers in leaders, special articles, and letters to the editor, not only in Scotland but in Canada, Australia, New Zealand and elsewhere, attacked me viciously. I had stacks of letters from incensed correspondents, I was expelled from the particular Burns Club to which I then belonged, and for years afterwards I was treated as a leper in Burnsian circles.)

There are many today who think reading will die out altogether ere long, and all the arts be reduced to the level of mere entertainment, under the pressures of TV and other media catering for that horrifying Admass so tellingly described by Mr Priestley. But the real danger, as Virginia Woolf foresaw, is not the extinction of the highbrow but the triumph of the middlebrow. 'The true battle,' she wrote, 'lies not between highbrows and lowbrows, but between highbrows and lowbrows joined together in blood brotherhood against the bloodless and pernicious pest who comes between.' Most of the Burns orators are middlebrows — what John Buchan stigmatized as 'the interpreting class' — ministers, bankers, schoolteachers, business men, and what not.

I remember a delegate conference of working-class theatre-goers held in the North of England a few years ago to discuss 'What's Wrong With the Theatre?' Delegate after delegate had the same complaint. An engineer said that he had charge every day of very complex machines — the theatre seemed to him a very old-fashioned machine. A weaver said she ran a number of high-powered looms — the theatre seemed to her dreadfully primitive. Almost all the speakers found the theatre hopelessly slow compared with the environment of their working lives. And it was rightly pointed out that all the great theatres from Greek times onward — all the theatres that had really commanded a big public — had been experimental theatres. It is the same thing with modern poetry middlebrows denounce as far too complex, difficult, obscure. If the workers get a chance of appreciating it they will. It is the older stuff — the stuff they got at school or similar stuff — they cannot tolerate, and find hopelessly irrelevant to life as they know it. This was Mr Eliot's point when he said that poetry had been completely changed by the invention of the internal combustion engine.

Milton did not say that poetry should be 'simple, sensuous, passionate'. A great deal of misunderstanding has arisen from the belief that he did, and the misquotation is one of the standbyes of all the platitudinarians who deprecate the increasing complexity of ultra-modern poetry, and think that the poet has no right to demand any intellectual effort from his readers. Such poetry is admittedly difficult — and ought to be. Life is not becoming simpler. Who wishes it was? What Milton did say was that poetry should be more simple, sensuous, and passionate then prose. That is a very different (and, after all, not undebatable) matter, and what Milton meant by these three adjectives is, in any case, sufficiently attested by his own work, but remote from what the platitudinarians in question imagine.

It is time that definite issue was joined, especially in Scotland, with the continual denunciations of modernist poetry and other arts on the ground of their untraditionalism, ugliness and incomprehensibility. I am an unrepentant and militant highbrow and do not believe that the great body of the public needs nothing but 'pap', cold kail hot again, and that simple straightforward diet most of their self-appointed mentors assume is good for them. With all due deference to the poetry of the past, our chief concern should be with contemporary poetry, and, unless we would write ourselves down as lazy, or incapable of mental exertion, or assert our indefensible 'right to be ignorant', with that poetry in its most difficult, rarefied, and experimental aspects. The poetry of the past can only be properly appreciated when it is seen in its proper historical setting. The whole position of poetry has been menaced by the insistence in schools and elsewhere on the poetry of the past, divorced from vital current interests, which is as if children were compelled to learn Sanskrit or Anglo-Saxon before they learned English; and by the insistence that the general public must have things made as simple as possible for them. This, to my mind, is simply not true, and only a 'superior' bourgeois assumption, flattering to themselves, and convenient to their interests as lecturers, teachers, reviewers, journalists and so forth. There is no divergence between the interests of the masses and the real highbrows. On the contrary, what menaces the deepest interests of the masses is all that would 'keep them in their place', spoon-feed them, pretend that certain things are beyond them and that they must be restricted to the conventional, the familiar, the easy. In the last resort this makes for their stabilization — as the masses, in contradistinction to the classes; and, finally, it makes for the short-circuiting of human consciousness, whereas all that is experimental, creative, repudiative of facile simplifications and established modes moves in the opposite direction.

All these falsehoods about simplicity and prejudices against mental strife and experimental work have been thoroughly instilled into the people. They have been assiduously taught that difficult intellectual interests are not for them. They have been demoralized by an incessant spate of mindless rubbish. All this will take a great deal of countering and undoing now. And it can only be done by the poets (and other artists) cutting out the middlemen and going direct to the people. The public are shrewd enough at bottom. Intelligence and receptivity are by no means synonymous with so-called educational advantages. The public know that all manner of dud stuff is foisted on them; that they are systematically talked down to, and made the victims of all sorts of 'popularizations' and simplifications which only falsify and spoil; and that most of the 'interpreting class' who intervene between them and the poets and artists have their own professional grooves, and their own axes to grind, and even at the best are almost always more interested in expressing their little opinions about works of art than simply giving the people the stuff itself. The people do not want inferior stuff; they are no less willing than any other class to make the necessary effort to understand difficult things if they are convinced it is worth while (and they know better than most that nothing worth having is easily got); they are more receptive than those whose saturation level has already been reached by a little superior education.

To try street-corner methods, to go everywhere amongst the people and try to interest them, instead of holding aloof, will do the poets themselves good too. 'In literature,' Yeats has very well said, 'partly from the lack of that spoken word which knits us to the normal man, we have lost in personality, in our delight in the whole man — blood, imagination, intellect running together.' I am convinced that that wholeness, that unity of artist and people, can, and must, be recovered, and that the task will nowhere in Europe be easier than in Scotland. But it cannot be accomplished by simplifying things for the public — and thus subtly insulting their intelligence. We must remember that before the days of popular education, when the masses were far more illiterate, but perhaps no less intelligent, greater poetry than is being produced almost anywhere today had a general currency, and the common folk, in the evenings, after their labours in the fields, had no difficulty in bringing to it an acute understanding and keen appreciation of the niceties of technique and fine points of expression even which is sadly to seek today — mainly, I think, because we artists have ceased to go in and out among the people as our predecessors used to do, and have taken their relative unintelligence and lack of interest in higher things far too readily for granted.

T.S. Eliot is absolutely right when, in his 'The Use of Poetry and the Use of Criticism' (1933) he says:

> When all exceptions have been made, and after admitting the possible existence of minor 'difficult' poets whose public must always be small, I believe that the poet naturally prefers to write for as large and miscellaneous an audience as possible, and that it is the half-educated and ill-educated, rather than the uneducated, who stand in his way; I myself should like an audience which could neither read nor write. The most useful poetry, socially, would be the one which could cut across all the present stratifications of public taste — stratifications which are perhaps a sign of social disintegration.

In Scotland the alienation of poets and people has never developed to anything like the extent experienced in many other countries. Scottish people are still interested in Scottish poetry, and if they, for the most part, only know poor poetry, that is not their blame; our schools are largely to blame; they teach relatively worthless English poets, but ignore the best Scottish poems with the exception of a few staple items like Burns's 'Tam O'Shanter'. What Scottish reader ever heard a word at school of Dunbar's great poems, of Alasdair MacMhaighstir Alasdair's 'Birlinn of Clanranald', or Duncan Ban MacIntyre's 'Praise of Ben Dorain', and of, say, fifty per cent of the poems given in John Buchan's splendidly selected *Northern Muse*?

On the other hand, the bad tradition which has so long dominated Scottish life, and is only now being effectively exposed and destroyed, has given an altogether disproportionate currency to the broken-backed verses of local paper rhymesters and the puerilities of 'Surfaceman' and the Whistle Binkie and Kailyaird Schools.

Of the ill-effects of the Burns Cult in concentrating undue attention on Burns to the exclusion of any appreciation of the Scottish tradition as a whole I need say no more at this juncture. It is rapidly breaking down now in any case. What I am concerned with here is rather the fact of Burns's contemporary popularity (no greater than Sir David Lindsay's was for centuries — a point Burnsians ought to note as a warning, for Burns's acclaim may well disappear as completely as Lindsay's has done, if they do not take heed in time) and the extent to which this was again shown as a characteristic of the Scottish people in the big sales achieved by Charles Murray and Mrs Violet Jacob, and such a predecessor of theirs as 'Hugh Haliburton' (J. Logie Robertson) whose poems as they appeared in the papers used to be clipped out and treasured in cottar houses and bothies all over the country.

My own experience has shown that interest in poetry is as lively in Scotland today as ever it was (evidenced, too, by the fact that national papers knowing the public concern have devoted many columns to articles and letters on the issues raised in the contemporary Scottish literary movement — not a thing that could happen in any other highly-industrialized country today perhaps), and that if the more modernist and difficult contemporary poets are not sharing in it that is largely their own fault.

If the people do not come to us we ought to go to them. They do not prefer poorer poetry to better; demonstrate the difference to them and they will take your points readily enough. Vachel Lindsay (it is significant perhaps that he was of Scots descent) was — whatever we may think of his own verse — on the right lines when he went up and down America declaiming his poems.

Why should we leave it to political propagandists and religious evangelists to proclaim their messages at the street corners? There are, it is true, even yet, always a few tramp poets, but as a rule, the alfresco peddling of poems is left to the lowest kinds of doggerel mongers. Why shouldn't our highbrow poets, who complain of the public's indifference, go into the highways and byways too and explain to all and sundry precisely what they are about and why their activities are more important than those of more conventional bards, and why the public should be interested? I am convinced that they would not carry their message to the public in vain. Against my own 'Synthetic Scots', it used to be urged that 'nobody understands it', but I have tried it on countless audiences and succeeded in getting it through to them all right — discovering as a rule, indeed, that many of those in these audiences knew far more Scots than they knew (or would have believed if told) they knew.

All sorts of anticipated difficulties disappear in the direct contact of poet and people; and I remember being particularly struck by the effect of telling an audience how I worked to get a particular poem — the trial shots I made, the lines I cancelled out, the way I gradually shaped it, and finally secured the effect I was after. I found that the public appreciates being taken thus into the poet's workshop and shown just 'how the wheels go round'.

They should get a great deal more of that. Who can do it better than the poet himself, provided he really believes in himself, understands his own processes, and has the courage to be perfectly frank about them?

Personally I am sure that the future of poetry largely depends upon 'going to the people' in this way, making pilgrimages through the length and breadth of the country, declaiming and explaining poetry at street corners and market squares and in pubs and wherever 'two or three are gathered together' and prepared to listen — as they almost always are.

A host of correspondents to all sorts of periodicals hastened to declare when Mr Norman McCaig ventured to question it, that Burns was the greatest poet Scotland had ever had or ever would have — that every line he wrote was an immortal gem — and so on.

What is the truth? Is Burns a great poet? Edwin Muir is right when he says in one of his essays:

> For a Scotsman to see Burns simply as a poet is almost impossible. Burns is so deeply embedded in Scottish life that he cannot be detached from it, from what is best in it and what is worst in it, and regarded as we regard Dunbar or James Hogg or Walter Scott. He is more a personage to us than a poet, more a figurehead than a personage, and more a myth than a figurehead. To those

> who have heard of Dunbar he is a figure, of course, comparable to Dunbar; but he is also a figure comparable to Prince Charlie, about whom everyone has heard. He is a myth evolved by the popular imagination, a communal poetic creation, a Protean figure; we can all shape him to our own likeness, for the myth is endlessly adaptable; so that to the respectable this secondary Burns is a decent man; to the Rabelaisian bawdy; to the sentimentalist, sentimental; to the Socialist, a revolutionary; to the Nationalist, a patriot; to the religious, pious; to the self-made man, self-made; to the drinker, a drinker. He has the power of making any Scotsman, whether generous or canny, sentimental or prosaic, religious or profane, more whole-heartedly himself than he could have been without assistance; and in that way perhaps more human. He greases our wheels; we could not roll on our way so comfortably but for him; and it is impossible to judge impartially a convenient appliance to which we have grown accustomed.

No criticisms of Burns as a poet, or complaint about his inadequate and outdated 'philosophy of life', or his glaring political inconsistencies really affect his place as 'Scotland's National Bard' at all. It is possible to hold that he was not a great poet but only a popular song-writer, that it is a national misfortune that he has been allowed to overshadow all other Scottish poets and indeed, the whole national tradition in the way he has done and still does, and that he has been such a bad influence on all subsequent Scottish poetry that one can only claim he is our greatest poet in similar terms to those employed by the Frenchman when asked who was France's greatest living poet, replied, 'Victor Hugo — alas', — it is possible to hold all that, and yet agree with Walt Whitman:

> Finally, in any summing-up of Burns, though so much is to be said in the way of fault-finding, drawing black marks, and doubtless severe literary criticism, after full retrospect of his works and life, the aforesaid 'odd kind o' chiel' remains to my heart and brain almost the tenderest, manliest, and (even if contradictory) dearest flesh-and-blood figure in all the streams and clusters of by-gone poets.

In case that pleases too many of those who only laud Burns because he seems to flatter them by expressing thoughts and feelings they have themselves — and gives them the illusion that given a little luck they could almost have written poems and songs exactly like Burns's themselves — I hasten to add that I also agree with Whitman when he says in the same essay (one of the few of the tens of thousands of Burns' Ovations worth reading!)

> I find his most characteristic, Nature's masterly touch and luxuriant life-blood, colour and heat, not in 'Tam O'Shanter', 'The Cottar's Saturday Night', 'Scots Wha Hae', 'Highland Mary' and the like, but in the 'Jolly Beggars', 'Rigs of Barley', 'Scotch Drink', the 'Epistle to John Rankine', 'Holy Willie's Prayer' (to say nothing of a certain cluster, known still to a small inner circle in Scotland, but, for good reasons, not published elsewhere). In these compositions, there is much indelicacy, but the composer reigns alone, with handling free and broad and true, and is an artist. You may see and feel the man indirectly in his other verses, all of them, with more or less life-likeness — but these I have named last [*i.e. The Merry Muses of Caledonia*] call out pronouncedly in his own voice,
>
> I, Rob, am here.

In one of his essays Henley wrote:

> Burns has been the victim of more ignorant and besotted eulogy than any man that ever lived. The Burns of fact, the Burns of history, of life, has disappeared, and in his room there is shown a kind of popular transparency. In the foreground are a Mouse and a Mountain Daisy; to the right a Wounded Hare limps painfully across the muir; to the left are Soutar Johnnie and Tam O'Shanter; in the centre the Poet, the ideal of a housemaid's dream, embraces chastely, his plough laid aside, a lady-like Young Person in short petticoats, conspicuously snooded, hosed and shod; and from the background the Kirk, personified in the Genius of Caledonia, bends in act to crown 'her own inspired Bard' with holly. It is not the least bit like the real Burns or anything real for that matter.... But it serves... to prove that Burns was wholly and sentimentally admirable.

Mr Cyril Pearl, in *Bawdy Burns, The Christian Rebel* (Muller, 1958) says,

> Burns has been the victim, not only of besotted eulogy, but of benighted editing. It is against the law to adulterate food or liquor but apparently anyone can adulterate literature with impunity; no important writer has suffered more than Burns from unscrupulous editors and biographers.

Professor David Daiches says: 'A succession of nineteenth-century editors suppressed, distorted, rewrote and apparently sometimes even destroyed his letters in order to obscure his love of a bawdy song and his frank and robust attitude to carnality'. Again, as Dr Daiches says, 'Burns was a master of bawdry and produced...some of the finest examples of that underground art', and he continues, Burns

> enjoyed sex with a huge enjoyment; it was for him one of the most exciting elements — perhaps *the* most exciting — in human experience, and while he explored its emotional aspects in some of the most tender and passionate love lyrics ever written, he also produced with equal gusto, and with equal skill, remarkable lyrical comments on the purely physical aspects of the relation between the sexes.

The present writer remembers the delight with which W.B. Yeats heard the verses from *The Merry Muses* which include the lines:

> I put my hand atweesh her feet
> And felt her wee bit maukin,

which he declared one of the finest obscene poems he had ever heard, a verdict enthusiastically endorsed by Dr Oliver St John Gogarty.

As Mr Pearl says:

> While English poets, glutted on the *gradus* epithet, were panting in London drawing-rooms for ethereal nymphs in roseate bowers, Burns was enjoying simple houghmagandie in the cowshed, and writing of his Jeans and Bettys in language attuned to their uncomplicated couplings. A few years after Burns's death Hazlitt complained that Tom Moore had turned the wild harp of Erin into a musical snuff-box. With Burns at his best — not Burns writing with one eye on an Edinburgh salon — the wild lyre of Scotland remained always the wild lyre. The real Burns was faithful to the old Scots genius for vigorous, earthy, direct expression. His bawdiness was as different from what Jeffreys called the 'ludicrous twining and panting of Moore's pasteboard lovers', as new-mown hay is from patchouli.

The Kirk, when Burns assailed it so formidably, had already lost some of its virulence. Enlightened Scotsmen, particularly in Edinburgh and Glasgow, were abandoning its implacable doctrine of depravity and damnation for a common sense, humanitarian deism. But despite the influence of these 'generous intelligences' Calvinism still exercised its tyranny in many parts of Scotland, a tyranny, as Henley describes it, 'potent enough...and offensive enough to make life miserable, to warp the character of men and women'. The Kirk, he says, 'was largely occupied with the work of narrowing the minds, perverting the instincts, and constraining the spiritual and social liberties of its subjects'. It still is. Indeed it has recently recaptured some of its evil power, especially in relation to religious instruction in schools. Insolent Sabbatarian demands, objections to Sunday drinking and to dances and games, disgusting Revivalist orgies and many other deplorable manifestations stress the characteristic hypocrisy of the many ministers who take a prominent part in Burns Clubs and show anew how right Burns was when he said that of all nonsense 'religious nonsense is the most nonsensical'.

However, while the Scottish Reformation stifled nearly every form of art, one form was actually stimulated by the persecutions of the Kirk — the folk art of popular bawdry. Robert Chambers thought it was 'a strange contradiction to the grave and religious character of the Scottish people' that they possessed 'a wonderful quantity of indecorous traditionary verse...expressive of a profound sense of the ludicrous in connection with the sexual affections'. The more perceptive Henley, as Mr Pearl points out, realized that this 'large body of lyrical bawdry' had been developed 'by the punitive rule of the Kirk and by the Kirk's discouragement — its prohibition indeed — of every kind of song except the "godly" and of every kind of literature except the theological'.

As Mr Pearl writes:

> There is profound truth in Otto Weininger's observation that 'anyone with so keen a sense of delicacy and subtlety as Shakespeare must also be capable of extreme grossness'. Byron was puzzled by a similar mixture in Burns; after reading some of his 'unpublished and never-to-be-published letters...full of oaths and obscene songs', he wrote to Hodgson, 'What an antithetical mind! — tenderness, roughness — delicacy, coarseness — sentiment, sensuality — soaring and grovelling — dirt and deity — all mixed up in one compound of inspired clay!'

It is certainly not surprising that Mr Notestein could not find 'a single Scottish poem that deals lovingly with the village Kirk', though 'the literature of England is full of allusions to the village church'.

It is typical of the stupidity and confusion and unscrupulousness of many Burnsians that even when Dr Duncan McNaught issued, in vindication of Burns, and on behalf of the Burns Federation, his privately-circulated 1911 reprint of the first edition of *The Merry*

Muses, he could not resist the old game of editorial falsification. Mr Sydney Goodsir Smith, collaborating with Professor J. DeLancey Ferguson and James Barke, in preparing a definitive edition of *The Merry Muses* for the Auk Society, found that McNaught had garbled and partly rewritten the text, though his proclaimed purpose was to rescue Burns from the distortions of previous editors.

However, I myself do not think Burns ever wrote a poem of this kind or achieved such an effect of brilliant sensuality as the Haiti poet Emile Roumer did in his 'Declaration Paysanne', translated by John Peale Bishop in *An Anthology of Latin-American poetry*, edited by Dudley Fitts:

> High-yellow of my heart, with breasts like tangerines,
> You taste better to me than eggplant stuffed with crab,
> You are the tripe in my pepper-pot,
> The dumpling in my peas, my tea of aromatic herbs.
> You are the corned beef whose customhouse is my heart,
> My mush with syrup that trickles down the throat,
> You are a steaming dish, mushroom cooked with rice,
> Crisp potato fries, and little fish fried brown...
> My hankering for love follows you wherever you go,
> Your bum is a gorgeous basket brimming with fruits and meat.

And that seems to me worth far more than any, and all, of Burns's love-poetry.

One prefers to these tricks of those anxious at once to figure in the Burns Cult and remain respectable — and, indeed, to remodel Burns himself in their own likeness — the occasional honest but ludicrous protests voiced against the adulation of 'a scoundrel — a deliberate offender against all decency' which, of course, is just the other side of the Burns Cult medal. A particularly juicy example of this is *The Book of the Century*, by John R. Craig (1952, published by Messrs Alex. Maclaren & Sons, Glasgow), of which the author says in his introduction, 'it is my belief that this first edition shall yet be of more value than the Kilmarnock edition of Robert Burns'. The book is in fact an incredibly illiterate attack on Burns, largely in unspeakably atrocious doggerel, some of it appropriately dedicated to 'the author, Maurice Lindsay, inspired by his four articles published in the *Sunday Mail*, January 9th to January 30th, 1956'. Burns, Mr Craig calls 'The Monster of Mossgiel', and the annual Burns Club toast, '*The Immoral Memory*'. To a man who said Craig was copying Burns, Craig replied:

Copy Burns! Absurd, absurd,
  Tae get me greater laurels,
I've nae mair need tae copy his word
  Than you have tae copy his morals.

and in another poem cries

Can ony man that's no' a fool
Who learned the laws he got at school,
Who conscious of God and better rule,
Has read Craig's rugged letter —
Man, there's nane but what's a stubborn mule
Can say that Burns was better.

One of his chapters tells how he gave a public Anti-Burns address and was 'as popular as a polecat'. No wonder this appalling character, completely out MacGonagalling-MacGonagall, says 'Home Rule humph! It's God's Rule we need, and the nation that's ruled by God does not need any other dictator.' Mr Craig says he has dedicated himself to the task of pulling Burns down. He will neither succeed in that, nor in his allied objective of pulling himself up. To people who said he was jealous of Burns, and to others who said he was 'another Burns', Mr Craig says:

Aye, maybe I am Burns his'sel;
Here to free his soul from hell —
Or better if you're a spiritualist
Do you not think it could be
That it's not Craig that's using Burns
But Burns that's using me.

It is, of course, neither; but there are many anti-Burnsians of Craig's type in Scotland today — fundamentalists in religion and utterly illiterate; a fitting counterpart to the Burns Cult. 'The painter,' he says,

> can paint the face of the dog, of the landscape, and of the woman and still retain his honour and even add to it. Can the poet not do the same? Can Craig not paint the picture in words without perverted minds degrading him to the level of Burns whose brutal brothel morals left the picture of ruin and disgrace behind each painting? Can I not paint the portrait and leave the rose unharmed?

He answers himself in the affirmative, of course, and produces in justification a batch of poems of a badness I would not have believed possible until I read them. They have no redeeming feature.

Ah mother mine, I see thy tear,
Thy last farewell rings in my ear,
With trembling lip and tight teethed jaw,
Farewell the banks of Barbauchlaw.

While only a minority share Craig's violent sectarianism in Scotland today, and fewer still his rancour and overweening and baseless conceit, there are many hundreds of 'poets' whose 'verse' is of the same kind as his, and indeed, a large part of all Scots [poetry] since Burns has been of just this sort, and this is true of much of Burns's own production.

While I am no upholder of conventional morality, and have no use for any form of religion, my objection to much of Burns's work is not its obscenity or its blasphemy, but its vulgarity. Burns's task was perhaps to reveal, with the utmost candour, his own personal lack of decency, not only in thinking and writing, but in living too, and this task on the whole he discharged well, tho' too frequently he loses his power in self-contradictions. The characteristic I have in mind, however, was unfortunately too often superadded to the frank animality and the shrewd and justified self-criticism and well-pointed satire. It is a quality of vulgarity best defined by the Russian term, *poshlost*. What Renato Poggioli says of Rozanov in *The Phoenix and the Spider* (Harvard University Press, 1957) is equally applicable to this element in Burns.

> In plain English *poshlost* means vulgarity, a vulgarity which is not merely a matter of taste but of ethics as well. *Poshlost* rules the minds of men or of a class only when it has already dominated their souls. Thus, at least ideally, *poshlost* means a degeneration and corruption which are accepted with a sense of absolute innocence, as if they were facts of nature or acts of God. In brief, the *poshlost* of the Russian bourgeois or officeholder generally goes without that hypocrisy so highly regarded by their equivalents in the West. As a matter of fact, the Russian bourgeois is characterized by a cynicism not less naive than the idealism of the intelligentsia. Rozanov possesses this kind of cynicism with a peculiar intensity. 'The idea of law as duty never occurred to me. I only read about it in the dictionary under the letter D . . . Any duty at the bottom of my heart always seemed comical to me!' . . . To quote a phrase which Rozanov must have known, we may recall that Dostoievski said once, that 'there are many, even too many, indecent things in the minds of decent people'.

Burns might have written that — it was what he thought, and several times expressed in slightly different words.

Though the Burnsians will not have it, it is necessary to 'distinguish and divide' very carefully — they are wrong when they imagine that all Burns's work is immortally good and fail to recognize that the gems are few and the greater part of his work rubbish. Like Whitman, J.H. Millar was right when he said in his *Literary History of Scotland* (1903): 'The inherent force and overpowering spirit of *The Jolly Beggars* are perhaps sufficient to account for the inferior popularity of that "cantata" as compared with *Tam O'Shanter*'. Had Burns swerved for one moment from the path of true craftsmanship, had he relaxed the severity of the artist and emitted the smallest whine of sentiment, had he dowered any one of his marvellous gallery of mendicants and mumpers with those virtues which draw the tear to the eye and the snuffle to the nose, *The Jolly Beggars* might have stood first in the hearts of its author's countrymen as securely as it does in the estimation of those best qualified to form an opinion. But Burns was loyal to his artistic instincts, and consequently the rank and file of his adorers, while paying the usual quote of lip-service, are puzzled, and do not quite know what to make of a piece which Scott pronounced to be, 'for humorous description and nice discrimination of character', 'inferior to no poem of the same length in the whole range of English poetry'.

As a Communist, the present writer, is pleased to find Dr Millar going on to call attention

> to the extraordinary *crescendo* movement of the little drama as one of its most striking characteristics. From a splendid start, it goes on getting better and better, and wilder and wilder, until at length it culminates in that astonishing finale which fairly takes the reader's breath away. Here, after all, it is impossible to help feeling, is the mood which Burns expresses more adequately, more completely than any other — the spirit of rebellion against 'law, order, discipline', the reckless self-assertion of the natural man who would fain, if he could, be a law unto himself, that violent revolt against the trammels and conventions of society, which may indeed win a temporary success, but is sure in the long run to be extinguished by the indomitable fact that man is a 'social' animal. It is this mood that underlies the spirited piece of inverted snobbery, known as 'A man's a man for a' that'; it is this mood that animates 'McPherson's Farewell' with its glorious refrain —

Sae rantingly, sae wantonly,
Sae dauntingly gaed he,
He played a spring, and danced it round
Beneath the gallows-tree;

it is this mood that breaks out with a cry of fierce defiance in that marvellous glorification of illicit love:

O' wha my babie-clouts will buy?
O' wha will tent me when I cry?
Wha will kiss me where I lie? —
The rantin dog, the daddie o't!
O, wha will own he did the faut?
O, wha will buy the groaning maut?
O, wha will tell me how to ca't?
The rantin dog, the daddie o't.

Finally, it is this mood that finds its crowning and eternal triumph of expression in the conclusion of 'The Jolly Beggars'.

A fig for those by law protected!
  Liberty's a glorious feast!
Courts for cowards were erected,
  Churches built to please the priest.

It is failure to realize with Dr Millar 'the indomitable fact that man is a social animal' that accounts for the claptrap of self-constituted defenders of 'the free nations of the West' as against Communists and of a writer like James Douglas who wrote of these four lines:

> ...in these began the Revolution of Revolutions, compared with which the French Revolution is but a ripple on the sea of change. The revolution of Burns is an insurrection of the naked spirit of man. It goes deeper than the pimples and blotches of wars and legislations, those cutaneous abrasions on the skin of society produced by kings and soldiers, priests and politicians; for it transforms the inner soul of humanity. It affects not merely the physical arrangement of units, but the unit itself....The new revolution seeks to free the personality of the separate man from spiritual and intellectual oppressions. Burns foresaw the future revolt against all the external compulsions of collective opinion. He described the dawn of law that is lawless and lawlessness that is law. He grasped the great principle that each man ought to be law unto himself, and out to do that which is right in his own eyes, regulating his conduct by no outer criterion of corporate conventions, but

> solely by the statutes of his own conscience. He realized that the only moral law is that which is enacted in the parliament of the spirit and that the highest standard is set up not outside but inside the soul. He perceived that there is only one person who can never forgive sin, namely the sinner. He knew that the virtue that is rooted in conformity to external menace is an immoral cowardice and that the free play of the free mind in the free body is the ideal goal towards which man is marching over the ruins of philosophies and civilizations, moralities and creeds.... He challenged everything that speaks with authority, reverencing nothing save irreverence and fearing nothing save fear.

Nonsense! No wonder Dr David Daiches says in a recent article: 'We sympathize with Burns's attacks on the Holy Willies, but have we ever thought what a sad mixture of platitudinous and simple-minded sentimentality is the alternative he offers?'

In the same way the lines

> When man to man the warld o'er
> Sall brithers be for a' that

are quoted incessantly, with little or no realization of their useless non-dialectical World-Stateist character — a mere bit of 'wishful thinking' without any constructive suggestion, any indication of the means whereby it is to be achieved.

Is Burns one of the world's great poets? Is he even Scotland's greatest poet? The answer in both cases must be in the negative. In the essay already quoted, Whitman had perforce to say:

> Burns is not at all great in the sense that Isaiah and Aeschylus and the book of Job are unquestionably great — is not to be mentioned with Shakespeare — hardly even with Tennyson or Emerson, yet he has a nestling niche of his own, all fragrant, fond, and quaint and homely — a lodge built near but outside the mighty temple of the gods of song and art.

It was this feeling that prompted Swinburne's verses in his ode on Burns:

> But Chaucer's daisy shines a star
> Above his ploughshare's reach to mar
> And mightier vision gave Dunbar
> More strenuous wing
> To hear, around all sins that are,
> Hell dance and sing.

And when such pride and power of trust
In song's high gift to arouse from dust
Death, and transfigure love or lust
    Through smiles or tears,
In golden speech that takes no rust
    From cankering years,

As never spake but once in one
Strong star-crossed child of earth and sun
Villon, made music such as none
    May praise or blame
A crown of starrier flower was won
    Than Burns may claim.

In his very next verses, however, Swinburne does his best to redeem what he has just said in qualification of Burns's claims. He goes on to say:

Above the storms of praise and blame
That blur with mist his lustrous name
His thunderous laughter went and came
    And lives and flies;
The roar that follows on the flame
    When lightning dies.

Swinburne's ode like so much of his work is far too long and too wordy, but he was a great poet and every now and again his genius shines unmistakably through the dross, as when he claims for Burns that

Never song took fire from earth
More strong for strife.

or cried that in Burns:

The joyous lightning found its voice
And bade the heart of wrath rejoice
And scorn uplift a song to voice
    The imperial hate
That smote the God of base men's choice
    At God's own gate.

Yet Swinburne's tribute to Burns does not achieve anything like such great poetic utterance as we find in his poems to Victor Hugo or to Baudelaire.

Over quarter of a century ago in my *Scottish Chapbook* I had occasion to write as follows:

> Few poems of the slightest literary merit have been dedicated to Burns. Mrs Isa Knox's 'Ode on Burns on the occasion of his century' which took first place in the competition against 620 rivals and was read by Mr Phelps, with fine effect, to listening thousands in the Crystal Palace had the merits of simplicity and straightforwardness but was commonplace in conception and pedestrian in effect. Wordsworth's 'At the Grave of Burns (Seven Years after His Death)' is a poor affair — not to be compared for a moment with his sonnet 'On The Departure of Sir Walter Scott from Abbotsford to Naples', which begins:
>
> > A trouble, not of clouds or weeping rain,
> > Nor of the setting sun's pathetic light
> > Engendered, hangs o'er Eildon's triple height.
>
> The general run of effusions about Burns is commonplace and utterly unworthy of the poet who in his own addresses to Lapraik and other poets drove so directly to the root of the matter and expressed himself with such incomparable wit, humanity, nobility, and critical understanding.
>
> Cannot the theme of Burns himself be treated without flat-footedness, windy generalizations, and mean moralizing — or does the Muse recognize class distinction and rule out Burns from 'princely praise', precluding him from being made the subject of a poem similar in merit to Wordsworth's 'Milton', Matthew Arnold's 'Shakespeare', or — to cite a contemporary poem — J. Middleton Murry's 'Ode on Dostoevski'.
>
> The best verses perhaps in Wordsworth's poem to which I have just referred are these:
>
> > Fresh as the flower whose modest worth
> > He sang, his genius glinted forth,
> > Rose like a star that touching earth
> >   For so it seems
> > Doth glorify its humble birth
> >   With matchless beams.
> >
> > The piercing eye, the thoughtful brow,
> > The struggling heart, where be they now? —
> > Full soon the aspirant of the plough,
> >   The prompt, the brave

Slept, with the obscurest, in the low
  And silent grave.

I mourned with thousands, but as one
More deeply grieved, for He was gone
Whose light I hailed when first it shone
  And showed my youth
How verse can build a princely throne
  On humble truth.

The difficulty caused by the gulf between Scots poetry and English poetry — and which accounts in great measure for the unsatisfactory treatment of Burns by English poets — is recognized by Wordsworth when, speculating on the fact that he and Burns might easily have been close friends, he adds:

True friends though diversely inclined;
But heart with heart and mind with mind,
When the main fibres are entwined
  Through Nature's skill
May even contraries be joined
  More closely still.

Another great English poet even further removed from Burns in kind who wrote a 'Sonnet On Visiting the Tomb of Burns', was John Keats and in it he shows a worthier sense of significance of the difference between the genius of Scotland and the genius of England. Here it is:

Burns! with honour due
I oft have honoured thee! Great shadow, hide
Thy face: I sin against thy native skies.

Not less poignant and probing to the core of the tragedy is Keats's other sonnet, written in the cottage where Burns was born, in which he shows his sense of the elements in Burns's life equivalent to his own and the fact that future fame is a poor recompense for a tortured life and premature death. It reads as follows:

This mortal body of a thousand days
  Now fills, O Burns, a space in thine own room
Where thou didst dream alone on budded bays
  Happy and thoughtless of thy day of doom!
My pulse is warm with thine own barley-bree,
  My head is light with pledging a great soul,

My eyes are wandering, and I cannot see
  Fancy is dead and drunken at its goal.
Yet can I stamp my foot upon thy floor,
  Yet can I ope thy window-sash to find
The meadow thou hast tramped o'er and o'er
  — Yet can I think of thee till thought is blind,
— Yet can I gulp a bumper to thy name —
O smile among the shades, for this is fame!

The American poet, Longfellow, wrote a poem on Burns which is similar in kind to most of the tributes he has received from his fellow-poets but while uninspired better than most.

In it he says:

...the burden of his song
Is love of right, disdain of wrong;
    Its master chords
Are Manhood, Freedom, Brotherhood;
Its discords but an interlude
    Between the words.

But Longfellow, after commenting on Burns's hard fate to die so young and leave unfinished what he might have achieved, points the moral by exclaiming:

For now he haunts his native land
As an immortal youth; his hand
    Guides every plough;
He sits beside each ingle-nook
His voice is in each rushing brook,
    Each rustling bough.

His presence haunts this room tonight
A form of mingled mist and light,
    From that far coast.
Welcome beneath this roof of mine,
Welcome! this vacant chair is thine,
    Dear guest and ghost.

Many Scottish poets have written poems on Burns but none of these are of the slightest distinction. Whatever the difficulties in English are, it might have seemed that the Scots tongue was the medium in which its great master could best be praised. But all the poems about Burns by modern Scots versifiers I have seen are poor imitations of Burns's own addresses and epistles to other poets and nowhere rise to the height of their theme or express anything of permanent value. William Soutar — who in all his hundreds of poems strangely enough addressed none to Burns — wrote that

> Nae man wha loves the lawland tongue
>   But warsles wi' the thocht
> There are mair sangs that bide unsung
>   Nor a' that hae been wrocht.

So it may be that a truly great poem about Burns in the language he preserved and renewed has still to be written by one of our younger poets. The worst fault of those who have so far essayed this task whether in Scots or English has been empty rhetoric and sentimentality — as when, for example, Jessie Annie Anderson called for

> Endless immeasurable love to him
> Who made our land a lyric for the World!

George Reston Malloch was right when he issued a warning:

> Rasp not a condescending, alien tongue
> With the rugged metre of his favourite song,
> As those who bend a peasant to address,
> By the mere act implying something less,
> In his own dialect. Bards of funerals,
> Abstain beside this grave! And yet they come,
> The corpse has warmth enough in it to heat
> A cold invention.

Scotland has, in fact, produced extraordinarily little poetry — if by poetry is meant something more than verse. The statement holds good both absolutely and in comparing Scotland's achievement in this respect with that of other countries. What little it has produced has been in relatively unimportant categories, and Scotland has had no great poet. It is strange that the etymology of the Greek word — 'A makar', so-called in old Scots — should have been so consistently forgotten in Scotland of all countries. It has been said that in so far as he is imaginative the poet creates what has not been, at all events as he sets it out, and gives it to us as what might have been, or might be going to be. He clothes it in a reality even more convincing than the reality of what we call 'fact'. He is the *maker*, not the *follower*, of fashions. How do the long line of Scottish rhymesters answer to this test? It is a test that cannot be over-insisted upon today, when belated new departures in Scottish poetry are being savagely assailed, or stupidly misprized, by 'stick-in-the-muds'.

Scotland has had no great poet? What is meant by great poet? What combination of qualities constitutes supreme poetic art? It has been said — and I accept the definition — that these qualities are three, viz. (1) Robustness of thought; (2) felicity of expression; (3) comprehensiveness of view. Many poets possess all of these qualities in *large* measure, many more possess one or other of them in *full* measure, but exceedingly few possess all three in full measure. The purely lyric poet, by the very character of his muse, is incapable of excelling in the first quality — robustness. Scottish poetry has been overwhelmingly lyrical and is abnormally destitute of intellectual content. Recent poetry in most countries has suffered the same fate. Writing of contemporary English poetry, Mr H.P. Collins has said that he

> has gone scrupulously through the whole of a widely-acclaimed volume of *Georgian Poetry*, not without pleasure, and afterwards reflected with consternation that never for an instant had he the sensation of being in contact with the serious creative intelligence of a great modern nation. The quality of thought embodied seemed immeasurably inferior to that which goes to the making of a high-class review of letters, or philosophy or scholarship. There was nothing to recall or suggest the impressive intellectual and moral traditions of English literature.

(And who would claim that matters have improved in any way since Mr Collins wrote? Indeed, Mr J.B. Priestley has declared — and I certainly agree with him — that English literature today is at a lower ebb than at any time since the fourteenth century.)

The poverty of Scottish poetry is what one would expect to find in a country that has put on record so incredibly little thinking about poetry? Where are our poetics? Has Scottish poetry, such as it is, 'just growed', like Topsy? The attitude — or lack of attitude in other than a negligible sense of the term — of the entire body of Scottish poets to their art is in keeping with the paucity and low level of their achievement. They did not take it seriously; there is a conspicuous absence of fundamental brain-work throughout. And in the rarest quality of all — comprehensiveness of view — no Scottish poet comes into the reckoning at all. Professor Otto Schlapp in a lecture in Edinburgh reminded his hearers of similar criteria of supreme poetry expressed by Seeley — who, as he said, has the credit for fixing

Goethe for the British reader in the front rank of poets. 'The sovereign poet,' said Seeley,

> must be not only a singer, but also a sage; to passion and music he must add large ideas and abundant knowledge; he must extend in width as well as in height; but *besides this he must be no dreamer or fanatic*; he must be as firmly rooted in the hard earth as he spreads widely and mounts freely towards the sky.

I have italicized one of these clauses in view of certain much-discussed Scots poems. It is well to note in this connection — not only the relationship of *Hymns to Lenin* with Burns's welcome to the French Revolution — but the significance of such an assertion of the Marxian critic, L.L. Auerbach (in connection with the Soviet celebrations of Goethe's centenary) viz, 'our artists need neither the subjectivism of Schiller nor the objectivism of Goethe, neither prejudice nor impartiality, but the Party passion of struggle for communism'. Or, as Lenin himself said, 'Literature must become party literature'.

Even in Burns's day it was difficult to possess oneself, save in discrete bits and pieces, of the very complicated and many-sided body of Scottish history and literature. Burns's requests to his correspondents for books are as numerous as Lenin's, but, owing to his circumstances, he was largely subject to English literary over-influences incompatible with his essential genius. His reading of the *History of Sir William Wallace* had 'poured a Scottish prejudice in my veins, which will boil along them till the flood-gates of life shut in eternal rest', but he was almost completely alienated from his proper pabulum. One reads with horror: 'My reading at about this period was enlarged with the very important addition of Thomson's and Shenstone's Works and a collection of letters of Queen Anne's reign. This last has helped me much in composition. . . .' Even today almost any English reading to which a Scottish writer with the root of the matter in him can turn appears to me (unless he has first possessed himself fairly fully of all the best elements of Scottish literature, alike in Gaelic, Latin, Scots and English) as appallingly unsuitable, as shockingly beside the point, as the stuff mentioned in these hapless confessions from Burns's letters. The curse of fragmentary knowledge (knowledge already largely vitiated by having had to pass through the English filter before being available to our people) of what in all its fullness should have been their birthright has afflicted all modern Scotsmen with any spark of genius. The late Sir Donald MacAlister, Principal of Glasgow University and a great linguist, told in a remarkable passage how it had retarded and mutilated his mental development. Mr Ivan Sanderson, the brilliant scientist author of *Animal Treasure* and other books, testifies to the same effect and wishes he had been able to escape an English education.

Readers who have had just an English education, and have practically no knowledge of anything Scottish except the little — and that often wrong — allowed through the English filter are apt to imagine that I am a solitary Anglophobe. That is not the case. By the death in 1951 of Cecil Gray, Scotland lost (characteristically without any appreciation of the loss) one of her most distinguished sons of the century and her ablest music critic — indeed, the only music critic of any consequence she has yet possessed. While he lived mainly outside Scotland and took no active part in Scottish affairs, it is not surprising that a man of his rich aesthetic sensibilities and great intellectual gifts should nevertheless by an independent path have reached many of the basic conclusions upon which the Scottish Renaissance Movement (begun in 1920 and continuing) was founded.

This was admirably exemplified in one of the brilliant essays in his volume *Predicaments* in 1936, when he wrote:

> Present circumstances and conditions are uniformly propitious to creative activity in this country (*i.e.* Great Britain), save only one which unfortunately also happens to be a very important one; namely, the attitude of mind and code of aesthetic values which largely dominate English life today, and are mainly responsible for all its worst features and for our complete inability to induce other nations to take us seriously in literature and the arts — *the cult of the English gentleman*! It permeates every aspect of our national life. It may well be true that our military triumphs have all been won on the playing fields of Eton; but it is very certain that most of our artistic failures have been sustained there. This spirit stunts or oppresses or forces into a pusillanimous compromise every potential native talent and is the absolute antithesis of everything that we call art, and *must be fought as one fights the devil, without rest and without quarter*. There can be no hope for English culture until this fatal confusion of artistic with false social and ethical values has broken down.

The present writer is not concerned with English culture, but with Scottish culture, but if all the implications of Cecil Gray's statements are understood, it is clear that a complete dissociation of Scottish from English culture is necessary, and an unequivocal declaration to this effect was in fact the basis of the Scottish Renaissance Movement. It is unfortunate that in the subsequent development of that

Movement a clearer realization of the incompatability — indeed, the mutual exclusiveness and actual opposition — of everything English in literature and the arts to everything Scottish has not been developed. Nothing in my controversial career has evoked more opposition from all our over-Englished compatriots in Scotland (cultural Quislings in fact) than my acceptance as my own attitude what Henry Miller says in his book *The Cosmological Eye*, namely,

> as for English literature, it leaves me cold, as do the English themselves; it is a sort of fish-world which is completely alien to me. I am thankful to have made a humble acquaintance with French literature, which on the whole is feeble and limited, but which, in comparison with Anglo-Saxon literature today is an unlimited world of the imagination.

Thanks to the virtual monopoly accorded to English language, literature, and history in our schools — and the unparalleled neglect of our own languages, history, and literature — this point of view is not one that is easily understood by the vast majority of our people. Nevertheless Cecil Gray and I do not stand alone by any means. Professor Denis Saurat wrote that unless the Second World War was to prove to have been fought in vain there must be a profound change in English mentality (and he did not mean that availability to Yankee trash-culture which has developed apace). Professor Saurat used his terms with scrupulous care. He pointed out that he was not referring to Scottish mentality, but strictly to English mentality. Everything that has happened since — and is happening now — has shown how right he was. Sir Maurice Bowra, Vice-Chancellor of Oxford University, has pointed out that the very flower of English poetry consists of lyrics of a kind which are peculiarly English and have no counterpart in any other literature, yet these unique products of English insularity are dinned into our Scottish children as virtually synonymous with poetry itself. Professor Ernst Curtius of Marburg has gone further and remarked that English literature has had virtually no influence on any other European literature, whereas it has been indebted (after a time-lag) to all sorts of European influences which however have always constituted a one-way traffic, with no reciprocal influence from the English having any seminal effect on other literature. Certainly three Scottish writers have had an immensely greater creative influence on writers in almost all civilized countries than any English writer, or all English writers put together. I refer to Sir Walter Scott, 'Ossian' Macpherson, and Byron.

In his autobiography, *Musical Chairs* (1948) Cecil Gray showed that he had thought round the whole problem and arrived at conclusions in keeping with those of so-called 'extremists' and 'Anglophobes' like myself.

'Up to about the age of seventeen or so,' he says,

> I was a complete and intransigent cosmopolitan. If there was anything I detested it was the conventional Scottish racial idolatry of Sir Walter Scott and Robert Burns. I have never been able to endure either of them. At the same time I felt no bonds of attachment to the culture which existed on the other side of the River Tweed. 'Englishness' as such I have always disliked as much as, if not more than, the bastard culture of Lowland Scotland. English art in the Middle Ages, when it was an integral part of the European heritage, and in the time of the Renaissance, when cultural values were largely continental and predominantly Italian, I could and did wholeheartedly appreciate, but the more characteristically English it became, in the 18th and 19th century, the less it meant to me.

This is clearly and courageously said, and he goes on to add something that should be hung up in large print in the vestibule of every library in Scotland, namely:

> Even today the whole hierarchy of the English novelists from Fielding and Smollett, through Dickens and Thackeray up to Hardy and Meredith, means precisely nothing to me. I simply cannot read them. I have tried hard, I have read several books of each, I have given them all a fair trial, but it is no use.

Alongside that should also be hung up in every Scottish library this passage from Thomas Davidson, viz,

> What shall we say of people who devote their time to reading novels written by miserable, ignorant scribblers — many of them young, uneducated, and inexperienced — and who have hardly read a line of Homer or Sophocles or Dante or Shakespeare or Goethe, or even of Wordsworth or Tennyson, who would laugh at the notion of reading and studying Plato or Aristotle or Thomas Aquinas or Bruno or Kant or Rosmini? Are they not worse than the merest idiots, feeding prodigally upon swinish garbage, when they might be in their father's house, enjoying their portion of humanity's spiritual birthright? I know of few things more utterly sickening and contemptible than the self-satisfied smile of Philistine superiority with which many persons tell me, 'I am not a

philosopher.' It simply means this, 'I am a stupid, low, grovelling fool, and I am proud of it.'

I am glad to see the true position of our independent Scottish tradition is at long last being clearly understood in many quarters. Mr George Malcolm Thomson, in his book *Caledonia* described the position it so long occupied excellently when he wrote:

> Such interest in literature as exists finds its expression in a curious substitute for intelligent appreciation, the forming of associations to worship the memory of dead authors and to celebrate their anniversaries with great eating, drinking, and platitudinizing parties. Thus there are Scott Clubs, Stevenson Societies and the all-powerful Burns Clubs. Officered mainly by lawyers, business men and ministers, they exist to prove that the objects of their worship were not only great men of letters but, also and more important, good citizens, pious Christians, and sound anti-Socialists. They have already made Burns safe for hypocrisy. An eminent physician has proved conclusively a hundred and thirty years after the event that alcohol had no part in bringing about the poet's death. In order that the last lingering doubts about Burns's respectability should be dispelled, it only remains for an eminent obstetrician to discover that the ladies who saddled Burns with the paternity of their children were deluded by parthenogenesis, or hero-worship, or actuated by spite.

Again he said:

> The idea of a national genius expressing itself in art, literature, drama, or music may occasionally (at least once a year on Burns's day) entice a leader-writer from serious matters like Trade Union Legislation to the bestowal of a patronizing platitude or two. But any notion that Art may be present and alive; any notion, above all, that it really matters a hang except as a harmless recreation for the declining years of retired business men — all that is respectably absent, as the first man who acts on the assumption that art both matters and is alive will painfully discover. The literary level of the press is low, a circumstance which is to be attributed partly to the fact that Scottish newspaper proprietors do not pay such high salaries to their editorial staffs as they can obtain on London or English provincial papers, and partly to a deliberate policy of stamping out any attempt at original or striking expression which would mark out a journalist of talent from the humdrum routineers. Literary skill is suspect — and this suspicion is a symptom of the

> inferiority complex that is hag-riding the nation.... Literature in Scotland? There is no literature in Scotland.... The publishing of books has been dead in the country for a very much longer period unless the issuing of brochures in tartan covers, containing coloured views of the Trossachs interspersed with excerpts from *The Lady of the Lake* can be dignified with the name. The book-buying public is, as a matter of fact, extraordinarily small. In Norway, which has half the population, an author can live comfortably on cheques from his publisher. In Scotland he could not keep himself in whisky.

Mr Thomson is quite right. It is only necessary to compare Scotland with other small — even much smaller — nations to see the deplorable state to which we have been reduced by the poison of the over-influence of England, what I have called in one of my poems, 'the wandering abscess of the English influence'. There can be no question of the great internationalism of the Scottish compared with the English people, or of the much greater liking for the Scot all over the world compared with the dislike of the Englishman. It should, having regard to all our pre-Union traditions, have been of Scotland and not of Iceland that the following should today be true:

> The Icelanders' command of languages and their passion for translation ensured that they should feel with little delay the main movements in the greater European literatures. More especially, since 1874, a crucial date in the long-continued struggle for Icelandic independence, one sees not only the broad influences of realism, naturalism, symbolism, surrealism, and the like, but the rapid exploitation of new kinds of writing, essays, short stories, novels, and plays. Poetry, of course, is ever-present. The bulk of Icelandic literature in the past hundred years is as astonishing as that of saga times, when one considers that it is the product of a nation which even now numbers fewer than 140,000 souls. Its quality was recognized in the award of the Nobel prize for literature in 1951 to Halldor Kiljan Laxness.

The writer from whom I am quoting goes on to say that Professor Stefan Einarsson, in his *History of Icelandic Literature* (1958) concludes with a chapter on the fairly extensive Icelandic literature of Canada and America. There are over twenty million Scots overseas and less than five million at home in Scotland, but the last thing that would occur to any Scottish literary historian is to include a chapter on, say, the Ulster writers in the Scots Vernacular, or Canadian and

Australian Scots writers. Indeed, reviewers have just been commenting on the novelty of Dr Kurt Wittig in his book, *The Scottish Tradition In Literature* (1958), including a section on Scottish Gaelic literature.

My friend, the late William Power, in his excellent little *Literature and Oatmeal* said:

> Gaelic has had a far bigger and longer run in Scotland than Scots or English. Teutonic speech is still a comparative upstart, and its sweeping victory did not begin till well on in the seventeenth century. A conscientious Chinaman who contemplated a thesis on the literary history of Scotland would have had no doubt as to his procedure. 'I will learn a little Gaelic, and read all I can find about Gaelic literature, from the oldest Irish poets down to Ban Macintyre, and nearly a third of my thesis will be on Gaelic literature.' He would be rather mystified when he discovered that historians of Scotland and its literature had known and cared as much about Gaelic as about Chinese, and that they had gone on the remarkable assumption that the majority of the Scots were Anglo-Saxons and that their literature began with Thomas the Rhymer in the reign of Alexander III.

Very much to the point is what Power says of the Scottish attitude to our literature and history, and the different attitude of the English people to theirs (for, of course, while we accord a virtual monopoly to English literature that is a one-way traffic — there is no reciprocal interest in Scottish literature in England, and if some of us are Anglophobes that is nothing to the continual disparagement and sneering at Scottish literature and Scottish matters generally — and usually on the basis of utter ignorance — in English papers and periodicals.

> In the compartment of the Flying Scotsman, roaring north along the central rock-ridge of the Merse, I began to dilate to a companion on the part that the Canyon of Pease Dean, near Cockburnspath, had played in Scottish history. I spoke of Cromwell and the Battle of Dunbar, Scott and *The Bride of Lammermoor*. A man in a landward corner of the compartment broke in: 'Ugh! That's history. An' literature, I suppose'. He was burly and fiftyish, with a bristly moustache. He wore a good suit of rough brown tweed, and there was a horseshoe pin in his ugly tie. His boots had cost a good deal more than sixteen shillings. I guessed him to be a prosperous contractor and general merchant in a country town, grazing beasts on a couple of 'led' farms. 'Don't the history and literature

of your own country mean anything to you?' 'Not a bit. Just nonsense. The stuff we used to get in school. Ugh!...' His contempt was beyond articulate expression. In the attitude of this man, I reflected, there was more than mere indifference. There was a positive hostility. History and literature, particularly those of Scotland, were somehow inimical to his way of life. He had a bad conscience concerning them. The outlook in such matters that usually confronts one in England is curiously different. It is one of amiable nescience. Anyone who begins to talk of history or literature in a chance company is listened to with polite inattention, as if he were a foreigner inadvertently speaking his own language. The terms seem to have no connotation. But nobody is ever rude about it. A change is going on in England. The younger generation are less oblivious to things intellectual than their fathers and grandfathers were. The whole lump is being leavened. But England has still to depart completely from the old paradoxical position as a mainly unliterary country which produced a great and voluminous literature. Down almost to our own time, English literature was produced and read by about a twentieth of the whole adult population. To the rest of the people it was Chinese metaphysics.

I am not at all sure that Power was right in these concluding sentences, but he certainly was in relation to Scotland. The effect in all connections of the English over-influence has been that which Dr Edwin Muir describes when he says of Sir Walter Scott:

> The eighteenth-century English novel was a criticism of society, manners and life. It set out to amuse but it had a serious intention; its criticism, however wittily expressed, was sincere, and, being sincere, it made for more civilized manners and a more sensitive understanding of human life. Scott marks a definite degeneration of that tradition; after him certain qualities are lost to the novel which are not recovered for a long time. The novel becomes the idlest of all forms of literary art, and by a natural consequence the most popular. Instead of providing an intelligent criticism of life, it is content to enunciate moral platitudes, and it does this all the more confidently because such platitudes are certain to be agreeable to the reader. It skims over every aspect of experience that could be obnoxious to the most tender or prudish feelings, and in fact renounces both freedom and responsibility. Scott, it seems to me, was largely instrumental in bringing the novel to that pass; with his enormous prestige he helped to establish the mediocre

> and the trivial.... All that Scott wrote is disfigured by the main vice of gentility; its inveterate indifference to truth, its inability to recognize that truth is valuable in itself.... Scott was the first writer of really great powers to bow the knee unquestioningly to gentility and abrogate his responsibility.... When we turn to his influence on Scottish literature we find the same story. There were not many genteel Scottish writers before Scott; there have not been many ungenteel ones since.

Mrs Virginia Woolf in her essay 'Gas at Abbotsford' fully showed the necessity and complete justification of The Vernacular Revival Movement when, writing of the Scott and the anti-Scott parties, she asked, 'Is it not the combination in the Waverley Novels of gas and daylight, ventriloquy and truth, that separates the two parties?' and told how, in the course of one of those ghastly nights at Abbotsford,

> There is Lady Scott gossiping with kind Mrs Hughes; there is Scott himself, prosing and pompous, grumbling about his son Charles and his passion for sport. To complete the horror, the German Baron D'Este strums on the guitar. He is showing how in Germany they introduced into guitar performances of martial music the imitation of the beating of drums. Miss Scott — or is she Miss Wardour or another of the vapid and vacant Waverley novel heroines? hangs over him entranced. Then suddenly, the whole scene changed. Scott began in a low, mournful voice to recite the ballad of Sir Patrick Spens:
>
> Oh lang, lang may their ladies sit
> With their fans in their hands
> Or e'er they see Sir Patrick Spens
> Come sailing to the land.
>
> The guitar stopped; Sir Walter's lips trembled as he came to an end. So it happens, too, in the novels — the lifeless English turns to the living Scots.

That is precisely what those of us who initiated the new Scottish literary movement about forty years ago hoped would happen to Scottish literature, and to Scottish life, as a whole. And we have had a certain amount of success and believe that the leaven is working and that we may yet secure what we set out to achieve. As I now go on to show this was what Burns wanted too — it was the very sense and core of what he devoted his life to, and only those who carry on his work, only those who know and share his ideas, can be accounted true Burnsians, and that rules out at least ninety per cent of all who have posed as such. For if one thing is certain, it is that Burns would have approved of practically nothing that has ever been written about him, or said at Burns Summers, but he would have wholeheartedly agreed with D.H. Lawrence who, in a letter to Donald Carswell, said:

> I read just now Lockhart's bit of a life of Burns. Made me spit! Those damned middle-class Lockharts grew lilies of the valley up their arses, to hear them talk. My word, you can't know Burns unless you can hate the Lockharts and all the estimable *bourgeois* and upper classes as he really did — the narrow-gutted pigeons. Don't for God's sake, be mealy-mouthed like them — No, my boy, don't be on the side of the angels, it's too lowering.

If I have approved a passage from the writings of Dr Edwin Muir, I cannot make it too clear that critics of any value are as scarce in Scotland as snakes in Ireland. Our worst enemy is not the English, but the Anglo-Scots, and since literary periodicals are centralized in London, human nature being what it is it is inevitable that Scots with a predisposition to literary criticism should find their market there and trim their sails accordingly. The worst opponents of the Scottish Renaissance Movement have all been Anglo-Scots, while the ablest and most sympathetic writers on the matter have been French, German, Polish, Czech, Americans and other foreigners. This however, does not excuse Dr Muir (who used his influence to stab the movement in the back by denouncing the revival of Scots as a medium for modern literary purpose — and, after the damage was well and truly done, found that he had been mistaken and recanted) saying in his *Scott and Scotland* (1936)

> Scottish poetry exists in a vacuum; it neither acts on the rest of literature nor reacts to it; and consequently it has shrunk to the level of anonymous folk-song. Hugh MacDiarmid has recently tried to revive it by impregnating it with all the contemporary influences of Europe one after another, and thus galvanize it into life by a series of violent shocks. In carrying out this experiment he has written some remarkable poetry; but he has left Scottish verse very much where it was before.

And, almost in the same breath, in an article in the *Scotsman*, entitled 'Literature from 1910 to 1935', he said:

> It is in Scottish poetry, however, that the last twenty-five years

> have witnessed the greatest change. The man who has been the chief cause of this is Mr C.M. Grieve, better known as 'Hugh MacDiarmid'. Apart from his achievement as a poet, which cannot be easily judged yet, he has done something for Scottish poetry of quite unique value; he has made it a vehicle capable of expressing, like English or French, the feelings and thoughts of the contemporary world. He has put into practice more boldly and comprehensively than anyone else the idea of a really modern Scottish literature. In judging his work, one has to take this into account and recognize the service that he has rendered to Scots poetry. If an anthology of current Scots poetry were made I think it would be found to be quite different in spirit from an anthology of Scots poetry written twenty years ago, and the writer who has been chiefly responsibe for this change is Mr Grieve.

What can one make of a critic, with a notable reputation for integrity, who can say diametrically opposite things in this way? Dr Muir is not alone in this, however. The late Mr Lewis Spence now praised me and now denounced me in exactly the same fashion, and Mr Maurice Lindsay is another conspicuous exponent of the art of having it both ways.

As Professor J. Isaacs points out in his *The Background of Modern Poetry* (1951):

> Poetry must always be renewed, and it is the renewal which is always an affront to a public conditioned with difficulty to a previous phase. Shelley put his finger on the essential nature of this process of renewal when he wrote that the language of poetry 'is vitally metaphorical; that is, it marks the before unapprehended relations of things and perpetuates their apprehension, until words, which represent them, become, through time, signs for portions or classes of thought, instead of pictures of integral thoughts; and then, if no new poets should arise to create afresh the associations which have been thus disorganized, language will be dead to all the nobler purposes of human intercourse'. Which is as much as to say that new poetry with a new and direct approach to life is essential if mankind is to remain alert.

In his preface to the pamphlet *Annals of Scotland*, issued by the BBC in connection with a series of programmes on Scottish literature broadcast in the winter 1956-57, Dr Edwin Muir said:

> I shall hazard the generalization — and I know few will agree with it — that the distinguishing mark of Scottish literature is

> conservatism, and of English, innovation. In philosophy, engineering, and medicine the Scots have been great innovators. But in imaginative literature Scotland has drawn its chief strength from the past; it has looked behind it and found there both great treasures and sentimental fancies. Despite an occasional gesture to eighteenth-century enlightenment, Burns's main inspiration was the centuries-old treasury of Scottish song, where he rediscovered a half-buried land. Walter Scott, a more thorough conservative than Burns, remains in spite of this, the chief innovator in Scottish literature, and one of the chief innovators in the various literatures of Europe. He grafted on the flat present of the eighteenth-century novel a sense of a past that lived a clandestine life within it. James Hogg's justified sinner lives both in the present and the past, but in the past more intensely. Stevenson drew his energy from the past; so did Neil Munro; and even the Kailyairders drew what energy they had from the same source. Coming to more recent writers, there are Neil Gunn with his sense of the magical fusion of past and present, Sir Compton Mackenzie with his wonderful sense of period, Fionn MacColla with his evocation of depths beneath the surface; and nobody who savours Eric Linklater's fantastic humour can fail to see where his heart lies — with Dunbar and his friends! Hugh MacDiarmid, it seems to me, is the one deliberate and eminent innovator in Scottish literature.

Dr Muir, however, does not go into the causes (which are mainly political) of this deplorable state of affairs, and what he says about Sir Walter Scott does not affect the fact that John Tonge, in his *The Arts of Scotland* (1938) is right when he says:

> By personal contact in more than one case, and by the pervasive influence of his writings, Scott turned men's eyes to what Stevenson called the background, and in the case of the smaller artists stamped on their minds an utterly false image of Scotland, an image, moreover, which, because it was anachronistic, required constant revivifying from literary sources. For at a crucial moment of her history Scotland's greatest genius was a backward-looking sentimentalist, writing about alchemists and astrologers (as Professor Knott has complained) in the Edinburgh of the anatomist Knox and Burke and Hare, reviving Scottish Baronial in the fantastic Abbotsford, seeing in the Highlands what Karl Marx called 'the promised land' of romantic literature at a time when 'areas as large as German principalities' were being 'cleared'!

Burns was little better. The tremendous changes that had taken, and were taking, place were not reflected in his poetry. He introduced no new initiatives into Scottish literature.

Dr Muir, however, to say nothing of his failure to refer to Lewis Grassic Gibbon, should not have failed to recognize Galt's significance. As Dr Kurt Wittig says in his *The Scottish Tradition in Literature* (1958):

> John Galt's sensitive awareness of contemporary social and economic changes was a new gift to Scottish literature, and his insight into contemporary Scottish life went much deeper even than Fergusson's. But the nineteenth century did not realize the gift. When D.M. Moir ('Delta') dedicated *Mansie Waugh* to Galt, he may have believed he was writing in the same vein, but instead of social changes we find only 'a good few uncos' and other quaint incidents that befell the tailor of Dalkeith. They are broadly caricatured in 'couthie' style, and even where a certain cultural importance might be felt, as in the case of the first playhouse, this leads ultimately to clownishness. In Scotland, as elsewhere, the nineteenth century was a time of violent changes. Ever-sprawling Glasgow had more spindles than Lancashire and built its huge shipyards; the tragic Highland clearances changed the structure of a whole society — but apart from a few political songs the present only speaks in an occasional short poem like Alexander Smith's 'Glasgow', which expresses the sad and stern beauty of the capital of the Clyde, the fiery stream of blinding ore, and says 'Yes' to the city. Of all the major Scottish events of the nineteenth century, the only one that finds its way into literature is, characteristically enough, the Disruption of 1843, when the Free Church seceded from the Church of Scotland. This is the background to Hugh Miller's *My Schools and Schoolmasters* and especially to William Alexander's *Johnny Gibb of Gushetneuk* (1871), an honest and realistic series of sketches of landscape places in the North-East that repeats Galt on a narrower scale. The focus of interest for these countryfolk is the question of patronage and the Free Kirk, but in the bygoing we see real life develop around us, or get some idea how the introduction of some new thing like guano is brought about. The language, the Buchan dialect, is more seriously Scots than Galt's, and we feel that Alexander needs the Scots words to render exactly what he means. Apart from this, the less said about the two generations after Scott the better. The shadow of Burns and Scott had fallen across the path, and minor spirits

> were content to move inside it. Burns had summed up a tradition, but since little was added to it it rapidly became an exhausted stereotype. There are some few good songs, mostly by gentle ladies (Dorothea Maria Ogilvy of Clova, 'The weary spinnin o't'), one or two readable local poets ('J.B. Selkirk', James B. Brown), a few echoes of Gaelic, but more caricature. Otherwise whisky and weaver bodies and bairnies and nostalgia and sentimentality, all gloriously 'successful'. The *Poetic Gems* of the Great William MacGonagall, Poet and Tragedian, and shabbiest of public-house rhymesters, are still reprinted almost every year; and their continuing popularity would indeed be an interesting problem for a psychiatrist to study. It is not rock-bottom that we touch here — that would suggest something solid; with him, poetry is irretrievable sunk in mire.

What would Burns have thought of the Scottish Renaissance Movement? He'd have been with it all the way — and further. He said so again and again in advance of the event.

Would any poet have made poetry his life work if he had thought it would come to an end with him? Have not all poets established a relationship with, and owed much to, their predecessors, and have they not expected to be given their due place in that sequence in animating the poets of succeeding generations? Is it not the case that in all the greater literatures certain authors have a dominant influence for a time, but that, sooner or later, fashions change and the source of influence and inspiration passes to other authors eclipsed for a time by the former? And is that not a healthier state of affairs than that literature should be dominated generation after generation, irrespective of changes no matter how tremendous in all other directions, by one great figure whose overshadowing reputation denies due consideration to all the others, blurs his own relationship to his predecessors, makes it difficult to apply proper literary standards and 'distinguish and divide' among his own works even, but insists that they must all be accepted without criticism as beyond question and justifies their effect in assimilating all else to their own type? How far we are in such a situation (and that has been the situation in Scots literature ever since the death of Burns until quite recently) from any possibility of our young poets acting upon that principle which the poet Gerard Manley Hopkins defined when he said: 'The effect of studying masterpieces is to make me admire and do otherwise. So it must be on every original artist.' Burns himself was not a slavish imitator of any of his predecessors, much as he owed to them; but it cannot be denied that his influence on subsequent Scots poetry has been a bad one. That is scarcely a criticism of Burns himself — though it was weaknesses in him and in his work rather than his strengths that led to such a state of affairs. It only means that he carried the lines along which he worked to such a point of achievement that nothing further could be done along these lines.

'Think of the petty environage and limited area of the poets of past or present Europe,' said Walt Whitman,

> Think of the absence and ignorance in all cases hitherto of the multitudinousness, vitality, and the unprecedented stimulants of today and here. It almost seems as if a poetry with cosmic and dynamic features of magnitude and limitlessness, suitable to the human soul were never possible before. It is certain that a poetry of absolute faith and equality for the use of the democratic masses never was.

It is against this background that Burns must be measured, and, though no poet has done better perhaps, it is a poor enough figure he cuts in the light of this great need and opportunity.

Another writer has said that never before in history could people look round them with eyes that saw so much and minds that grasped so much. It almost looks as though knowledge has ceased to march and has taken to leaping, something Tennyson foresaw in these words:

> Let knowledge grow from more to more,
> But more of reverence in us dwell,
> That mind and soul, according well,
> May make one music — as before,
> But vaster...

It was precisely the same idea — but applied to Scotland in particular — that Burns expressed in *Nature's Law* when he said:

> Auld cantie Coil may count the day
> As annual it returns
> The third of Libra's equal sway
> That gave another Burns
> With future rhymes and other themes
> To emulate his sire;
> To sing auld Coil in nobler style
> With more poetic fire.

Ye powers of peace, and peaceful song,
   Look down with gracious eyes
And bless auld Coil, large and long,
   With multiplying joys.
Lang may she stand to prop the land
   The flower of ancient nations
And Burnses spring, her fame to sing,
   To endless generations.

Again, in *The Cottar's Saturday Night*, he reverts to the same theme:

O Thou! who pour'd the patriotic tide
   That stream'd through Wallace's undaunted heart:
Who dared to nobly stem tyrannic pride
   Or nobly die, the second glorious part;
— O never, never Scotia's realm desert
But still the patriot and the patriot-bard
In bright succession raise, her ornament and guard.

Because it expresses other ideas than Burns expressed, because it embodies a different attitude to the Scots language itself, above all, because by these, and other, differences it seems to challenge Burns's supremacy and consequently gives offence to those mainly non-literary and mostly very parochial-minded people who regard Burns as the be-all and end-all of poetry and are unwilling to contemplate the possibility of other developments utterly different in form and content to anything to be found in Burns, the Scots poetry that has been written in the last thirty years by myself and other so-called 'new Lallans Makars' has been cold-shouldered by the majority of Burnsians who, in this as in many other connections, have shown a disposition lamentably different from that of Burns himself, when, instead, they would do well to consider these lines from his Prologue to a Play at a Dumfries Theatre.

      If a' the land
Would take the Muse's servants by the hand;
Not only bear, but patronise, befriend them,
And where ye justly can commend, commend them.
And aiblins when they winna stand the test
Wink hard, and say the folks hae done their best.
Wad a' the land dae this, then I'll be caition
Ye'll soon hae poets o' the Scottish nation
Will gar Fame blaw her trumpet crack
And warsle Time, and lay him on his back!

Burns knew that a nation's literature and its other arts can never rest on past achievements but must go ever forward to cope with new needs and new difficulties, and as he said, in the same prologue:

> There's themes eneuch in Caledonian story
> Would show the tragic muse in a' her glory!

The Scottish Drama Movement, despite its developments in the past few years, has scarcely touched the fringe of its great possibilities yet. But Burns would never have done the great work he did if he had imagined for a moment that the tradition of Scots poetry would end with him and the Scots language itself die out of use. He looked forward to its continual development and none knew better than he that no matter how great a poet may be it is necessary for subsequent poets not to imitate him but to create something altogether different and vary and enrich our tradition and carry it to new levels of achievement.

Despite the stick-in-the-muds, however, great progress has been made during the past few years. Scottish national consciousness is more intense and determined than it has been for more than a couple of centuries; and this new national awakening is manifesting itself in every department of our Arts and Affairs. For a very long time Scottish schools have tried to impose standard English on our children and any lapse into Scots in the classrooms has been frowned upon. It is significant of the change that is taking place that the Scottish Education Department has recently altered its attitude to this; the pro-English tendency ever since the Union is at last being reversed and Scots speech is not only to be permitted but encouraged in our schools. Whether that decision can be implemented is, however, another question. As an Aberdeen University writer says:

> It was quite obvious at the conference attended by Scottish teachers in November that they were ill-equipped and unwilling to implement the provision made for the teaching of Scottish literature in schools. They did not know if Scottish literature was good. 'Would somebody tell us?' they asked. That is, of course, a reflection on the way they'd been taught literature. They had no critical method or initiative to study what was to them a new literature.

This writer concludes that

> the only means towards the writing of much good poetry or many good novels in Scots is the compulsory use of Scots for all purposes.

> One indispensable requirement for appreciating what has been achieved, for achieving more and appreciating that, is a native academic and reading class.

Surely that is what the Burns Clubs should provide. If they did, and if other Scottish organizations, like the Saltire Society, also contributed, the problem would be solved — a problem which involves the future of Burns himself, as a poet who is read and not merely one to whom lip-service is paid by people to whom poetry means little or nothing and to whom the language in which he wrote is increasingly unintelligible. But even if the Saltire Society, the Burns Clubs and the other Scottish associations cannot be said to guarantee the future of Scots literature in that way, surprising progress is being made in other directions. An American scholar in a recent essay surveying what has been achieved in this field during the past thirty years points to a new political orientation in Scotland and an altogether different prestige enjoyed by the vernacular. 'A whole new official attitude sympathetic to the vernacular has grown up,' he says.

> Since the end of the last war we have seen Edinburgh University establish a new School of Scottish Studies, the phonetics department of which has sponsored delightful recordings of hundreds of bothy ballads from Aberdeenshire, still one of the richest repositories of folk idiom in Western Europe. We have seen a Scots National Dictionary proceeding at Aberdeen University; a new lectureship in Scottish Literature at Glasgow University (the first lectureship in the subject at any of our Scottish Universities); and a whole new literary movement both in Scots and in Gaelic, applying our national traditions to contemporary purpose.

I know too well that Burns, like the Bible and like statistics, can be made to prove almost anything, and that it is easy to forget that, above all, he was concerned with poetry, and, as a poet must be, with language. Poetry means little to the vast majority of people today — but to Burns it was the greatest thing in life and he gave his life to it. That is the greatest difference between the Soviet Union and this country, or any of the other nations of the West. A recent writer has said — and my own experience completely confirms it — that 'the principal and obvious result of the Soviet emphasis on the use of art is that it is really taken seriously'. Is literature really taken seriously in Scotland? Hundreds of books (all the best of them by non-Scots!) have been written about Burns, but very few of them tell us anything about the poet's art, and in the whole lot you could number the pages of really reputable criticism on the fingers of one hand. Although the World Burns Movement is a unique phenomenon, it is necessary to remember that its members have failed to follow Burns's lead in every vital connection. They have failed to follow him in turning from English back to Scots. They have failed to show a like concern to his for Scotland's welfare and independent place (and voice) among the nations. They have failed in politics to maintain Burns's radical spirit, his scorn of hypocrisy, and the empty shows of royalty and rank. They have failed to have Scottish literature and history, and our native languages, taught in our schools and colleges, where, instead, a virtual monopoly has been given to the language, literature and history of our traditional enemy. I fully appreciate, of course, the excellent work done by the Burns Federation's school competitions, but this, after all, merely affects the fringe of the problem; it has little or no effect on the subsequent cultural orientation of more than a very small section of our people. We Scots are apt to boast of our love of country. How does it come about, then, that it is only within the past twelve months that hundreds of Scots ballads and songs, passed down by word of mouth through the generations, have been collected and recorded? The same thing is true of a huge treasury of Gaelic songs and folk-tales. The lack of interest in such matters has been made good at last — but only in the nick of time! They have been taken down from the lips of old people; but if these old people had died before that was done this great folk-heritage would have been irretrievably lost, as so much has already been lost of the literary glories of our people; probably several times as much as we now possess altogether!

The future of Scots poetry lies in the extent to which it can express — as Burns did in his own very different day and generation; and as all our experience and the verdict of all the great critics shows no poetry in English can do for us — the hopes and fears, dreams and desires, and the actual conditions, problems and potentialities of our lives today. Like Burns, we must not be too 'nice' to indulge in political poetry and in satire. We must square our poetry with our feelings and our requirements. And that is precisely what our Scots poets today are doing or trying to do. A great American poet has said that poetry's first task today must be a tremendous effort of assimilation, to bring our means of expression abreast of the immense and ever more rapidly changing developments of modern life. Scotland today is a very different Scotland from that of Burns's day. In keeping with it, our poetry must be largely urbanish. It must express itself in conformity with modern scientific ideas. It must reflect the realities of contemporary life. And there is no reason why it should not do so in an enriched medium of Scots — and every reason why it should do so, since Scottish poets have attempted to contribute to English poetry for over a century and have failed to produce anything of the first, second or third order of excellence in that alien medium, while a consensus of critics affirms that wherever modern Scottish poets have written in the two media — Scots and English — their best work has invariably been done in the former, through which they are, it seems, able to reach and express qualities of their nature inaccessible to, and inexpressible in, English.

That is why the most influential living poet in the English language, Mr T.S. Eliot, has said:

> I am convinced that many things can be said, in poetry, in Lallans that cannot be expressed at all in English. I think that Scots poetry is, like that of other Western European languages, a potentially fertilizing influence upon English poetry, and that it is to the interest of English poetry that Scots poetry should flourish.

A recent writer in the *Times Literary Supplement*, goes even further. 'People,' he says,

> are fond of their illusions, and one of the favourite illusions of the 'educated' Lowland Scot is that the bastard tongue he habitually speaks is English. No Englishman is deceived. The first thing a young Scottish actor, coming to London in search of fame, is told by his first agent is that he must 'lose that Scots accent'. In other words, he must acquire one which has no foundation in his own native tongue (and though, off the stage, a Scottish accent and turn of speech is perhaps less of a bar to social and professional success than an English provincial one, in all successful Scots who have been long enough settled in England their native note tends to be almost rubbed away). Scotsmen, or at least, 'educated Scotsmen, have long forgotten how to write Scots, how to read it properly, and they have even forgotten much of its rich vocabulary; yet the 'auld leid' lives on, at a deep level, as a jealously-guarded emotional attitude and an almost ineradicable brogue. This is not the result of a merely sentimental feeling in Scotsmen for the 'Doric', that 'language of the home-bred slave', though certainly Scotsmen are sentimental enough; it is the result of a profound psychological exigence. The deepest nature of a Lowland Scot is involved in the Lowland Scottish language; he cannot cut himself wholly off from it without maiming his soul.... This is a question

> of integrity. Childhood is the period during which people live closest to the 'collective unconscious', to the soul of the people, and childhood is the period of life therefore that is most receptive to those grand, persistent *motifs* of the race which it is the poet's business to keep viable. This is the main reason for the present revival of the Scottish language, and one main result of this revival has, of course, been a new awareness among Scotsmen of the deep life of their race. It could be argued that similar considerations may well apply to English dialects; William Barnes wrote better poetry in the Dorset dialect than in standard English. The argument that the attempt to keep dialects alive for literary purposes impedes communication (or that nobody can understand a poem in a dialect not his own) is a false one. Poetry, with its traditional themes and images, is itself in a sense 'a language', and the Scot who can genuinely appreciate Burns as a poet — he is not by any means a common phenomenon even today — should be able to appreciate Barnes. Any dialect of English poetry can easily be read by any English reader if he overcomes the prejudice of a stock attitude.

The article goes on to remark on the anaemic character of modern English poetry and contrasts it with the superior vitality of Scots poetry today. All who have written on the subject, from Sir George Mackenzie down to Dr Gregory Smith, have pointed out that Scots is a superior literary medium to English. Its potentialities may be realized in the near future.

The same article in the *Times Literary Supplement* from which I have just quoted went on to dispose of another objection that has bulked largely in the minds of those who object to political poetry unless it expresses their own politics. I will quote it, and then go on to deal with the relationship between poetry and politics in Burns's work and in the work of Scots poets today. The passage is as follows:

> It may be objected that an encouragement of regional, or dialect, poetry must be a sign of, and in any case will encourage, weakness and decadence in the 'central language', the language of the capital. If poets in Edinburgh write in Lallans, in fact that means poets in London are losing their grip. The opposite is true. When the 'central language' (or the official dialect of the universities and the capital) is in a healthy state it encourages commerce not only with its own dialects, but with many foreign languages. This is certainly true of the English of the Elizabethan drama. On the other hand, the fear of such external and internal commerce, the narrow

standardization of the language, — the kind of fossilizing influence which Fowler represents — is debilitating; and in the long run leads to the correct but thin 'mandarin' prose of much literary journalism today and at a lower level to the gobbledegook of Government Departments.

A more recent writer has shown that even the article quoted above deals with considerations which have been superseded already by major developments in other directions. Here is what he says:

The development of an Irish poet like Yeats is revealing. Had he been born a century earlier than he was, had he been a contemporary of Tom Moore, Yeats would either have written within the English conventions or he would have been a much more modest poet than the one we know. He could not have been both an Irish poet and a great poet because there was no cultural context in which a great Irish poet could exist, unless, perhaps, he wrote in Erse. The power of the English language was such that he would have been transformed by it into an English poet who happened to have been born in Ireland, just as Swift and Burke are English writers though they remain Irishmen.

With Yeats, indeed, we can observe the creation of a cultural context, and of a language, large enough to contain a great poet. His early poems are scarcely more ambitious than those of Tom Moore and one of the reasons for their decidedly minor attractiveness is that he was working with much the same material as Tom Moore — the lilting Irishry that Imperial England could accept with a smile of indulgent patronage. Nobody was ever heard to assert that 'The Lake Isle of Innisfree' was written 'for my own race/And the reality' since, in fact, it was written for an alien race and the fantasy. Only a growing realization of the bankruptcy of England herself and the comparative richness of Irish traditions allowed Yeats to assume his later proud disguises. By the time he did so other Irishmen, like Synge and Joyce, Americans like Pound and Eliot, and even an Indian, Tagore, had joined him in the task of enlarging the intellectual and emotional context in which the English language took place and of creating new forms and symbols adequate to express this enlarged vision. A few Englishmen, Wyndham Lewis and D.H. Lawrence among them, added to the richness of the confusion but most of the elder English writers were left, like Robert Bridges, in a position of isolation that they liked to regard as splendid.

The diminished importance of England's contribution to English literature, which is signified by the development of Yeats, has continued and will continue to diminish ever further during the present century. The reasons for this are much bigger than the tiny tidy series of precedents beloved by literary historians: yet there are precedents. Arabic literature would be of limited interest if it were entirely the work of the inhabitants of Arabia and even the purest of classicists would hesitate before depriving us of the prose of St Augustine. Wherever Empire has been established and the subject peoples have learned the tongue of their conquerors there has been a proliferation of literatures within what appear to be the limits of a single language. This proliferation takes place when the material attributes of Empire begin to be dwarfed by its cultural effects, and we are indubitably living through such a period. That is why there is little point in talking about a 'period of consolidation' in our literature. Whether or not we consolidate the experiments of Hart Crane and E.E. Cummings is largely irrelevant since, while we are busy 'consolidating', a brand new 'English' literature will be appearing in Johannesburg or Sydney or Vancouver or Madras. Those who regard such a notion as absurd would do well to examine closely the thesis that Oxford, Mississippi, has given us a more solid corpus of creative achievement than Oxford, England, during the past thirty years.

'The Bankruptcy of England herself' — 'the diminished importance of England's contribution to English literature', phrases such as these lead naturally to the all important matter of Burns's politics and the necessary politics of all who have a like concern with Scotland, all who profess to be true Burnsians. To adapt a phrase from my friend Sean O'Casey I have never been in doubt that: 'To ask Scotland to keep out of politics is asking her to keep out of life; and the only politics for Scotland today is animosity to England, shown by word of mouth and blow from fist!'

As Sir Alexander MacEwan said in *The Thistle and The Rose*:

> It is plain truth that no great national movement was ever founded on caution and half-hearted measures.... The objections to Home Rule are not so much reasoned arguments as vague apprehensions, but fear is often more potent than reason, and must be dealt with.... The answer to all the misgivings as to what a Scottish Parliament might or might not do is that Scotland is a nation of sufficient strength and independence and experience of public affairs to find a solution of her own problems.

The case for Scottish autonomy is so strong — and has been so clearly and incontestably set out in every respect in the wealth of publications on the subject in the past thirty years — that anyone who is not convinced that it is not only absolutely right but urgently necessary should have his (or her) head examined. Burns was never in any doubt on the subject. 'Alas!' he wrote, 'I have often said to myself — what are all the boasted advantages which my country reaps from the Union that can counterbalance the annihilation of her independence and even of her very name?'

The present writer has taken an active part in the campaign for Scottish autonomy for over thirty years but does not belong to any of the organizations existing which claim to promote that cause. He was expelled from the Scottish National Party because he is a Communist. In *The Flag in the Wind*, his story of the developments in Scottish Nationalism this half-century, Dr John McCormick says:

> Although I have no doubt that he has done invaluable work in the whole field of Scottish literature I am certain that C.M. Grieve has been politically one of the greatest handicaps with which any nationalist movement could have been burdened. His love of bitter controversy, his extravagant and self-assertive criticism of the English, and his woolly thinking, which could encompass within one mind the doctrines of both Major Douglas and Karl Marx, were taken by many of the more sober-minded of the Scots as sufficient excuse to condemn the whole case for Home Rule out of hand.

The reason behind Dr McCormick's remarks is simply that I never had any interest in securing any measure of mere Home Rule for Scotland. I objected to the National Party pledging its members to continued loyalty to the Throne, to the autonomous Scotland remaining a member of the British Commonwealth, to the pretence that the Party was open to members of any and every political party or shade of political opinion provided only they believed in Scottish self-determination when in fact they excluded Communists (although many Communists like Willie Gallacher, for example, were out-and-out Scottish Nationalists of the finest type, and the Communist Party of Great Britain is the only party which has the restoration to Scotland of a Parliament of its own as a plank in its platform), and above all I objected to any constitution-mongering which reserved finance, foreign affairs, and the question of war and peace to the Imperial Parliament. I wanted complete disjunction from England and a Scottish Workers' Republic. But Dr McCormick is a lawyer, and the real trouble is that I was never a politician in his sense at all and never wanted to be. Politics is a system of swaps and switches. A man who isn't out for himself and can't be approached on a dicker is (from the point of view of such politicians) nothing but a bottleneck. Certainly in such connections I have never wished to be anything else. I believe with Miss Mary MacSwiney, the sister of the Lord Mayor of Cork who died on hunger-strike, that 'the people have no right to surrender their independence at the ballot-boxes; if you allow that you are raising a situation in which you are appealing to a majority. The people have no right to do wrong.' I am primarily a poet and what I wanted the Scottish Literary Movement to do was to produce a poetry that would be an eternal reproach to every Scot who had in any way acquiesced in English over-control, to all our quislings, recreants and traitors — a poetry of which it might be said as was said of certain Polish poets, viz, 'With the full power of their poetic genius, Mickiewicz, Slowacki, Krasinsky and Norwid erected a chain against the consequences of the defeat by enabling the nation to preserve, even though only in the field of culture and moral ideas, its faith in its own existence. The idea, implied in their philosophy, of the invincible spiritual independence of the nation was a call for heroism in the real struggle for political independence.' Despite what Dr McCormick said, the Scottish students who presented me with the Andrew Saltoun Medal for my services to the Scottish cause, understood this — understood that my name could appropriately be linked with that of the great Scottish patriot who said that he did not care who made the nation's laws so long as he might makes its ballads. And so far as Scottish Nationalism is concerned that has ever been, and remains, my purpose — to keep the way open to an indigenous Scottish future. I owe most of what follows regarding Burns's politics to the research of my friend, Mr Alex McCrindle.

Although the number of people who read — indeed, can read — Burns in Scotland is in decline, there is a vast new audience opening up for Scotland's national poet in the Soviet Union, in China, and elsewhere in the world today.

At a meeting of students and staff of the English Faculty of the Foreign Language Institute a Scottish delegate fifteen months ago talked to them about contemporary Scottish literature. At the end he asked them if they wanted anything read and among other things they asked for Burns's 'Is there for honest poverty?' better known as 'A man's a man for a' that', and for 'On Thanksgiving for a National Victory'.

Ye hypocrites, are these your pranks?
To murder men and give God thanks?
Desist for shame! Proceed no further
God won't accept your thanks for murther.

A greatly-loved Russian poet and playwright, Samuel Marshak, has been translating Burns into Russian for fifty years, and, according to Moscow Radio in a Burns Night programme upwards of half a million copies of these translations have been sold in the Soviet Union.

The significance of Scottish poetry is not simply insular. As the late Professor W.J. Entwistle delighted to illustrate,

> Scotsmen can meet Europe more easily than Englishmen do... and though Scots is only a fraction of English literature, it has exerted something like a parity of influence in Europe. Some of the greatest English writers — *e.g.* Chaucer, Spenser, or Milton — had no European consequence.

Many other countries have recently been furnished with new — and better, translations of Burns. In Peking six years ago the Scottish delegate above-mentioned stood beside the translation of Burns into Chinese and from a book of 'peasant poetry' his interpreter read him, first in Chinese and then in perfect English —

My heart's in the Highlands: —
  My heart is not here.
My heart's in the Highlands a-chasing the deer,
A-chasing the wild deer, and following the roe
My heart's in the Highlands wherever I go.

'My heart's in the Highlands' was the title of the book and it contained no fewer than eighteen poems by Burns.

In the celebration of the two hundredth Anniversary of the poet's birth this process of world-wide dissemination will continue, and must be welcomed. It is the way to save Burns from the Philistines — from those who pay lip-service to his name but whose lives are a repudiation of all that Burns stood for; the sort of Burnsians who at the Annual Supper forget that Burns was a republican and anti-militarist and have on their toast-list not only 'The Immortal Memory' but the loyal toast, and the toast to the armed forces, but leave out one essential toast that used to be included in the early days of the cult, the toast to 'Scottish Literature' or 'Other Scottish Poets'.

Leaving aside the reasons for the decline of the Burns Movement in Scotland itself, and in the reading of Burns by the Scottish people, what is the reason for his continued, and increasing popularity with people of different races all over the world?

According to Maxim Gorki, 'Man only becomes man *as he resists his environment*', and this is perhaps the key to what is most important in Burns — *his lifelong resistance to his environment.*

Consider his station. The son of a poor tenant-farmer, subject to ill-health from his earliest youth, patchily educated, longing for all the delights of a comfortable home with children — yet determined to exploit to the fullest possible extent his great gift for poetry. The courage of the man was unbelievable. The political climate of Scotland at that time was against him too. He was a republican under a monarchy, a democrat under a despotism, a man who believed in the self-determination of nations living in a country that went to war in order to keep its North American colonies.

As a youth in Irvine Burns was under pressure to join the forces fighting against the American rebels, and his reply was typical of him:

> I murder hate by field or flood
>   Tho' glory's name may screen us.
> In wars at hame I'll spend my blood —
>   Life-giving wars of Venus.
> The deities that I adore
>   Are Social Peace and Plenty.
>   I'm better pleased to make one more
> Than be the death of twenty.

Scotland in Burns's day was a poor country. Another John Knox had this to say about the Highlands nineteen years after the Jacobite Rising of 1745.

> A tract of land that comprises one-fifth of the area of Great Britain appeared with some few exceptions to be in a state of nature, a great body of people, and these the most virtuous of our island, dragging out a wretched existence, perishing through want, or forced through wild despair to abandon their country, their kindred and their friends, and to embark moneyless and unknown, the indented slaves to unremitting toil and drudgery at a distance of 3,000 miles from home.

Burns dedicated his searing 'Address to Beelzebub' to the Right Honourable the Earl of Breadalbane, President of the Right and Honourable Highland Society which met to concert ways and means to frustrate the designs of five hundred Highlanders who were so audacious as to attempt an escape from their lawful lords and masters whose property they were, by emigrating from the lands of Macdonald of Glengarry to the wilds of Canada in search of that fantastic thing — liberty! It is a poem not to be missed.

If such was the condition of the Highlands the condition of the Lowlands was not much better. There was a famine in 1782, when Burns was a lad of twenty-three, and in one of the last agonized and agonizing letters he ever wrote he said: 'Hundreds of other families are absolutely without one grain of meal. How long the "swinish multitude" will be quiet I cannot tell; they threaten daily.'

By the time Burns was twenty, Scotland had been without a Parliament of her own for seventy-two years, and so far as the shires went the average number of persons entitled to vote was eighty! No wonder, in his election writings, Burns made use of these occasions to expose their farcical nature. The most important event in his lifetime was undoubtedly the great French Revolution of 1789. Its effect was comparable to that of the Russian Revolution of 1917. Burns's attitude and activities in this connection are too well-known to need elaboration here. It inspired that important poem which it was good to see the late James Barke restore to its proper place in any volume of Burns — namely, 'The Tree of Liberty'.

Heard ye o' the Tree o' France
   And wat ye what's the name o't?
Around it a' the patriots dance —
   Weel Europe kens the fame o't!
It stands where aince the Bastille stood —
   A prison built by kings, man,
When Superstition's hellish brood
   Kept France in leading strings, man.

and so on to

Wae worth the loon wha wadna eat
   Sic dainty halesome cheer, man!
I'd gie the shoon frae aff my feet
   To taste the fruit o't here, man.
Syne let us pray, Auld England may
   Sune plant this far-famed tree, man,
And blythe we'll sing and herald the day
   That brings us liberty, man!

But liberty was not to come to Scotland, despite the efforts of Thomas Muir and his 'Friends of the People' Society. A panic-stricken Government using (as so many successive Governments were to do again in our history) its own agents within the reform movement, brought the ring-leaders to trial for sedition and had them transported across the world for many years.

Burns was naturally in a white heat over these events and they directly inspired what has become Scotland's National Anthem.

> Scots wha hae wi' Wallace bled,
> Scots wham Bruce has aft-times led,
> Welcome to your gory bed,
> Or to victory!
>
> Lay the proud usurper low!
> Tyrants fall in every foe,
> Liberty's in every blow.
> Let us do, or die!

The American War of Independence not only produced the anti-war poem referred to, but a poem in praise of 'General Washington's Birthday' in which he greets the free American people, the former British colonists:

> But come, ye sons of Liberty,
> Columbia's offspring, brave as free,
> In danger's hour still flaming in the van
> Ye know, and dare maintain, the Royalty of Man.

As for other kinds of Royalty, Burns held (and expressed!) views on them that make Malcolm Muggeridge sound like a sycophant:

> For Lords or Kings I dinna mourn!
> E'en let them die — for that they're born!

He wrote in a poem to greet a new year, and on seeing the Royal Palace at Stirling in ruins he was moved to exclaim:

> The injured Stewart line is gone.
> A race outlandish fills their throne,
> An idiot race, to honour lost,
> Who knows them best despise them most!

Burns was moved too by the little incidents and by the pattern of social life around him. His picture of the man

Who begs a brother of the earth
To give him leave to toil

in 'Man was Made to Mourn' is drawn from a life Burns knew intimately and savagely resented.

If I'm designed yon lordling's slave —
By Nature's law designed —
Why was an independent wish
E'er planted in my mind?

What a wealth of observation and social criticism there is in such poems as 'The Twa Dogs' and 'The Holy Fair'! What a blast of iconoclasm in 'The Jolly Beggars'!

So much, then for Burns's attitude to the important political questions of his day. What about his attitude to the cultural questions, for in these, of course, as a poet he was deeply involved?

Sufficient has been said, perhaps, about his work in searching out folk-songs, rewriting them where necessary, and fitting them to old and new tunes. And of course many of his own original songs are among the best in the collections he made first with Johnson and then with Thomson. It is less well known, however, that Burns was fascinated by the theatre too and during his years in Dumfries he was a regular attender there. Actors, like poets, belong to 'the ram-stam boys, the rattlin' squad', and Burns was at home in their company. He wrote a series of prologues for Mr and Mrs Sutherland and for Wood and others who played in Dumfries and taken together these present as good a case for Scottish drama as may be found. In this, indeed, as in all things that men are working for today in Scotland, Burns's great gifts would be of inestimable help.

What would he not say about 'Labour' journalists who take a lot of money from the BBC and Tory newspapers to attack militant trade unionists, or about 'Co-op' viscounts who, in their senility, parrot the battle cries of the equally senile Churchill, or about titled 'Socialist' lawyers with luxury yachts accepting briefs from Copper bosses to keep African miners in slavery, or about the descendant of a Highland crofter who, when the people asked for life and work, offered them a rocket range and further insulted the working class of Scotland by offering them missile ramps instead of factories, schools, homes, and hospitals?

Surely his answer to all this would have been along these lines from 'Why Should We Idly Waste Our Prime?'

The golden age we'll then revive!
Each man will be a brother.
In harmony we all shall live
And share the earth together!
In virtue trained, enlightened Youth
Will love each fellow creature,
And future years shall prove the truth
That Man is good by nature.
Then let us toast with three times three
The reign of Peace and Liberty.

Those who follow today's apolitical fashion, and deprecate political poetry and do not believe that poetry has a public mission to fulfil may well be reminded of a case in point.

The Hornet was a weekly issued in 1893 in Vancouver. The brilliant letterpress was the work of A.M.R. Gordon, an ex-minister from Scotland. The cartoons were by John Innes, the famous Canadian artist. It is specially prized for the first publication of that universally-known skit on the German Emperor, 'Mineself and Gott'. One day there came through the press an account of some characteristic activity of the Kaiser that annoyed Gordon. Going into a saloon in New Westminster, he ordered a glass of whisky, and told the proprietor he 'was going to make that ——— SET UP!' In the back room, between sips, he wrote the first draft of the poem, which, after some revision, he published in *The Hornet.*

Later, the paper folded up, and Gordon went to Montreal, where he republished the poem with some minor changes. It got to New York, and there at a dinner given to Admiral Dewey and his captains fresh from Manila someone recited it to the highly appreciative gathering. The German Ambassador reported the incident to Berlin, and, in the words of Gordon, the Kaiser 'set up!' There were diplomatic exchanges between Berlin and Washington, providing such excellent advertisement for the poem that it travelled all over the world, and became the best-known piece of humorous verse of its day.

The hope of Scotland lies in the fact that many of the younger Scottish writers of significance today have glimpsed the great truth Lenin expressed when he said 'we must utilize every moment in which we are free from war that we may learn, and *learn from the bottom up*', and are possessed with a furious need to make up for the waste of their school and University years, and learn Scotland in that way — Scottish history, Scottish literature, and all the ins and outs of Scottish life, the physical Scotland and the Scotland with all its international contacts, ramifications, and affiliations, the Scotland whose circumference is that of the whole world. And because these younger Scottish writers and politicians recognize as their leader a great murdered, and hitherto most cruelly misprized and neglected Scotsman, John Maclean (1879-1923), and because it is under the slogan of Maclean's name and animated by the example of his incredible energy, and equipped, thanks to him, with the necessary knowledge of Dialectical Materialism the whole movement is at last developing something like the requisite knowledge, determination, and dynamic power.

I have been reproached at times for a propaganda that could only succeed if there were a sudden and profound change in the psychology of the majority of my compatriots, and I have replied that it would be by no means the first time that had happened — and *that it must be made to happen again now*. The choice is between a willed mutation along the lines I want, or the abominable change that is actually taking place and transforming Scots into morons. The great Scottish actor, Duncan Macrae, was right when he said that the majority of theatre-goers in Scotland today are moronic. So are the majority of Scots who are not theatre-goers.

In the latter part of the sixteenth and nearly the whole of the seventeenth century, Scotland was engrossed in questions of theology and politics and war. Then came a sudden change in the direction of the national aspirations — the desire to become colonists instead of soldiers; to become traders instead of theologians.

When discussing this question, Fletcher of Saltoun, writing in 1698, says that by an 'unforeseen and unexpected change of the genius of the nation, all their thoughts and inclinations, as if united and directed by a Higher Power, seemed to have turned upon trade, and to conspire together for its advancement'.

An unidentified pamphleteer, writing in 1696, comments on this change in the Scottish attitude, 'for,' he says,

> the bias of their people seems generally to be another way — yet that is merely the effect of custom and not of nature, and as it would not have been difficult at any time heretofore to have diverted and turned their inclinations and humours from soldiering to commerce, so it is not to be doubted but that upon their being once brought to apply unto it, they would be found as ingenious and brilliant in trade as they have had the character to be skilful and brave in war.

But Burns was right (though even he — fortunately — could not foresee that men of that type would constitute ninety per cent of the membership of Burns Clubs) when he said:

> The warldly race may drudge and drive
> Hogshouther, jundie, stretch, and strive;
> Let me fair Nature's face descrive,
>   And I, with pleasure,
> Shall let the busy, grumbling hive
>   Bum ower their treasure.

I have, therefore, ample grounds for believing it to be far from impossible that the Scottish national genius may yet be turned to Literature and the Arts, and certainly it is urgently in need today of such an application to adult education and to scientific thought and research — and to getting rid of all the incubi of religious superstition — as have been brought about in a single generation in both Russia and Turkey, and I still hope and believe that my lifetime may see such a concentration of Scottish national purpose as is long overdue and most badly needed in these neglected fields. Scotland's sudden switch-over to Trade has in the intervening centuries more than abundantly justified the unknown pamphleteer's prophecy. I have no doubt whatever that if a like switch-over to philosophy and the arts could be effected it would justify itself as completely in its revelation of the national aptitude in departments in which it has hitherto been content to leave the initiatives to foreigners and to play second fiddle to many other European countries really incapable of competing with it at all were it once effectively roused to apply itself in these connections.

That is for the future. But if, among our corrupted people, there is still no more than a tiny minority audience for the truly Scottish, a still better parable for the present state of the arts and affairs of Scotland occurs to me. The 'Dundee bap' — a 3¼ oz roll that is a famed production of Dundee and East of Scotland bakers might have disappeared from breakfast and tea tables during the last War, along with various other tea-time favourites, if Scottish bakers had been able to understand a new Bread Order scheduled by the Ministry of Food. The Order was made to save labour and waste in the bakeries of Britain by abolishing fancy loaves and restricting bakers to only four standardized types of loaf. It also laid down that rolls must not exceed 2 oz in weight — a provision that would have banished the 'Dundee bap' among other forms of rolls. But Scottish bakers continued to make bread and baps, as usual, because they were completely confused by the terms of The Bread Order. They did not know what it meant. A leading baker said: 'We appealed to the Ministry of Food to state in plain language the meaning of the Order, and the reply was that we should merely carry on as we have been accustomed to do.' The bakers themselves agreed that there were too many types of loaf, and wanted to co-operate in the economy move to restrict the range. But their confusion, they declared, was due to the fact that the Order had been framed by English minds to suit English trade conditions. It defined a 'Scotland loaf' as a 'tin loaf of 1 lb 12 ozs' — which is an accurate description of the 'pan loaf', a product that represents only one-tenth of the bread output from Scottish bakeries. Ninety per cent of Scotland's bread, however, is made in the form of the ordinary square or batch loaf. So the bakers, happily, unable to understand what the Ministry of Food wanted them to do, simply carried on with 'business as usual'.

This is typical of English (and English Government) dealings with Scotland in every connection.

This subterranean persistence of unchanged Scottishness under official Anglification and apparent acquiescence in assimilation to English standards occasionally rises to the surface in more significant forms than 'legislation by appendix' makes inevitable every now and again in every practical connection, and I believe that the whole hidden Scotland will yet break through the crust of Englishry. In this sense, the whole Scottish Movement might define its purpose in the lines of Matthew Arnold (himself half a Celt — his mother was a Cornishwoman):

> To see if we will poise our life at last,
> To see if we will now at last be true
> To our own only true, deep-buried selves,
> Being one with which we are one with the whole world.

The curse of Scottish life and literature and the other arts has been an appalling infantilism. A splendid case in point was provided by the late Lord Tweedsmuir (John Buchan) of whom one obituarist told the exact truth when he wrote:

> John Buchan wrote some of the best thrillers ever published in English and some of the best popular historical biographies. Some of his books sold by the hundred thousand, but like some greater men, he always hankered after success in spheres not suited to his talents. Just as Cicero wanted to write poetry so John Buchan wanted to be a statesman. He was obsessed with the idea

> of 'greatness' (*sic*!) Those who knew him will tell that he had no political gifts of any kind. As a result his achievements were mainly ceremonial. When he was Lord High Commissioner of the General Assembly of the Church of Scotland he wore splendid robes and was radiantly happy in their magnificence. The House of Commons led him not to Cabinet office, but to the Governor-Generalship of Canada. Here was the perfect honorific post. If one cannot achieve real political success, to be the King's representative is surely the best possible substitute.

Burns was of a very different cast of mind. On the subject of titles he would have agreed with the Australian paper that wrote 'since St Michael and St George are both dead and buried, to be the companion of two corpses is just about the same as being brother to a quantity of stale fish or uncle to an ancient egg', and he would certainly have treasured the story of how, when a former Governor, Lord Carington returned to England and told the Duke of Clarence that 'Australia would for ever remain loyal to England', the *Bulletin* exploded in a fury of invective, in the course of which it referred to His Royal Highness as 'the flabby little duke, whose face is as expressionless as an African's feet'.

The way in which Scotland must be seen can hardly be better expressed than it is in that fine Aberdeenshire classic, *Johnny Gibb o' Gushetneuk*, when Johnny says to his wife:

> 'The Apos'le speaks o' the life o' man as a "vawpour that appeareth for a little, and then vanisheth awa"; an' seerly there couldna be a mair nait'ral resem'lance. Fan we begood the pilget here the gither, we' three stirks an' a bran'it coo't cam wi' your providin', the tae side o' the place was ta'en up wi' breem busses an' heather knaps half doon the faul'ies, and the tither was feckly a quaakin' bog, growin' little but sprots and rashes. It luiks like yesterday fan we had the new hooses biggit, an' the grun' a' oon'er the pleuch, though that's a gweed therty year syne. I min' as bricht's a pentet pictur' fat like ilka knablich an' ilka sheugh an' en'rig was.'

That is how we must learn to see and know Scotland again. Sir John Boyd Orr and others have made it clear that Scotland is potentially a rich country, well able to feed our population, if proper use is made of our land, which, under the present dispensation, has been abominably wasted and converted to an appalling extent into derelict areas reserved for plutocratic sports. As Sir John Boyd Orr has said: 'Scotland is one of the finest agricultural countries in Europe. It is a rich country. The Clyde Valley has terrific powers of production which are *lying half idle*'. This is true of many other great areas of Scotland. And along with that return to an intimate first-hand practical knowledge of every inch of our terrain, there will be a return to the languages (Scots and Gaelic) which are the proper media for the expression and extension of that knowledge — a purpose (as our devotion to writing in English for the past two and a half centuries has made clear enough) for which English is worse than useless.

It is in keeping with the whole present position — what the late William Power called 'the mystery of Scotland's self-suppression' — that the worst defeatist writings against a return to Scots have been by Anglo-Scottish authors. As I have shown in the introduction and notes to my *Golden Treasury of Scottish Poetry*, Edwin Muir in his *Scott and Scotland* and John Spiers in his *The Scots Literary Tradition*, have not a leg to stand on in their contentions that Scots has lapsed so greatly that its resuscitation is now out of the question. The facts (a great mass of which I cite in the above-mentioned quarters) are all the other way. All over Scotland — in the 'Black Belt' as well as in the rural areas — Scots is still the native speech of the great majority of the people; and the real objection to it is a class objection — for Scots is the language of the working class.

An Inspector of Schools who said he could not see the argument nearly so clearly in regard to words told me he must admit the cleavage between Scotland and England was most marked in regard to music and most important — important practically, *i.e.*, in relation to teaching singing in schools, etc. In this respect, as in all others, the real life of Scotland is being denied. He gave me many striking instances from his own experience of experiments with children in senior classes when pseudo-Scottish work by very competent English or Anglo-Scottish composers was at once spotted by the children as 'not the real thing', and, in one case, though the children could not explain just what was wrong, a setting of Reid's poem, 'Kirkbride', was tried on them in which the first two lines were set in the Scottish folk-song tradition and the next in an English fashion. They felt at once, however, that there was something very queer and not in keeping about this setting — as well they might, since it switched back and forward from one country to another, from one tradition to another radically different one. *Which* tradition made all the difference to the whole-hearted responsiveness of the children — their ability to reach to what, in Jeeves's phrase, is really 'of the essence' — and this difference was *not* in favour of teaching English songs in

Scottish schools. The children could not really enter into the spirit of the former and sing them with any authentic effect. This must be taken as an analogue of what has happened, and is still happening, in all directions in Anglicized Scotland, and a convincing index of the immeasurable loss sustained. Our national life has been reduced to a shadow of its former self, and what little vitality still remains is being continually sapped by the English connection. But under the English Ascendancy the Scots are so subjugated and befooled, so deceived and self-deceiving, that they persist in singing even their great national song, 'Scots Wha Ha'e', expressing Bruce's address to the Scottish army before the Battle of Bannockburn, to a hopelessly inappropriate dirge-like German setting, despite the fact that the only Scottish composer worth a rap, Francis George Scott, has supplied a magnificent resetting in thorough keeping with the spirit of the poem. The poor creatures are so tradition-bound, so spiritless, that they dare not substitute the new for the old setting, although the latter is a lugubrious idiocy in conjunction with the verses in question, and the other dramatic and dauntless in perfect keeping with Burns's immortal words. This is an exact parallel to the plight of the Scottish people — the superficial Anglicization, and, hidden underneath it, and still visible now and again in a man like F.G Scott, true Scotland's *raucle* spirit. They have gelded Burns — Burns of all men! It is only the more innocuous pieces, the silly love-songs, they are concerned with in Burns; they have no desire to remember that

Auld Scotland has a raucle tongue.

They know that if they give *that* a chance it will be turned against *them* with devastating power.

In a memorandum, pleading for the more serious treatment of the Scots Vernacular in our schools, put forward to the Scottish Education Department by a deputation representative of the Burns Federation, the St Andrew's Societies of Edinburgh and Glasgow, the Scottish National Dictionary Association and the Ballad Society, it was rightly declared that 'in spite of some decay in the towns the Vernacular is still the speech of those who do the work of Scotland in field, mine, workshop or fishing boat'. But the campaign of such bodies for the revival of the Vernacular makes no headway. It has not the people behind it. These bourgeois agencies cannot reach the hearts of the workers, who do not trust them and will not follow them. The Vernacular to these people is only a fad, a hobby, a lovable whimsicality of well-to-do business men, their pleasure in occasionally sitting in their shirt-sleeves and hobnobbing with their betters.

The last thing these 'well-to-do business men' want to do is to 'go too far' in the matter — to arouse the genius of the Scots language, and, with it, of the Scots working class. Their job is to divert the people from big social questions to safe channels. So they have no sympathy with recent creative work in the Scots medium — any attempt to use Scots for serious modern purposes and bring it abreast of contemporary requirements. Theirs is entirely a conservative manoeuvre; they think of Scots entirely in terms of the past, and of the worst elements of its past at that. All they want, or want the people to want, is 'the songs my mither used to sing', the toast of 'Gentlemen, the King!' before proposing 'The Immortal Memory', and then 'God Save the Queen' sung as a windup to a concert of Scottish songs. Scots culture must be taken out of the hands of these people altogether.

Cut off from their real life, the Scottish workers cannot be appealed to in a fundamental way by the Tories, the Liberals, the Socialists, or any such agencies as the Burns Clubs or other bourgeois Scottish agencies. They can only be dynamically reached — stirred to the very depths of their beings — through the Scots Vernacular (or, if they are of the Gaidhealtachd, Gaelic), applied to modern purposes and expressly directed to their vital needs. This is the dynamic angle — the only way to get into the hearts of the Scottish people and rouse them.

A mighty force will be generated as soon as that is done. It is worth concentrating all our energies on; it will burst the existing social system in Scotland into smithereens. This is why the English and the Anglo-Scots have sought by every means in their power to isolate the Vernacular from vital expression, to restrict it to the past, and to unreal romantic subjects, and to bourgeoisify and emasculate the Burns Cult until, today, they have made it, and the whole range of Scottish sentiment, describable only in the well-known phrase of Professor Harrower of the Chair of Greek in Aberdeen University — 'isn't that perfectly obscene — perfectly obscene!'

So obscene that our Anglo-Scottish press is constantly filled with the philippics of men like Professor J.L. Morrison of Durham University, who trounced the young intellectuals of the Scottish Movement for the delectation of probably the most suitable audience he ever had — to wit, a lot of Greenock grocers and pettifogging lawyers and assorted 'nyaufs' constituting The Burns Club there — secure in the sense that he was in his proper element at last, and that none of the young intellectuals in question was present to expose (as any of them could easily have done) his (Professor Morrison's) total lack of capacity to discuss the subject at all.

In a word, Scots poets have today regained for themselves — and seek to regain for this misled and mismanaged country as a whole — that lost tradition of Scotland to which Louis Pasteur paid tribute (albeit he associated it with names to which it is impossible now to concede any respect, and impossible to believe that the homage once given was ever in any degree really due) when, on the occasion of the Tercentenary of Edinburgh University in 1884 he said, in a speech to a gathering of students:

> A French writer, one who had carried abroad the philosophy of Robert Reid and Dugald Stewart, addressing young men in one of his prefaces has exclaimed: 'Whatever career you may embrace, look to an exalted goal; worship great men and great things.' Edinburgh students have recently seen such men as are there mentioned, and in Scotland their memories are accorded rightful recognition,

and, again, at the Tercentary banquet, Pasteur said:

> The City of Edinburgh is now presenting a spectacle of which she may well be proud. All the great scientific organizations, assembling here, seem an immense gathering of hopes and mutual encouragement. The honour reflected by this international concourse rightly belongs to you, *for centuries ago the fortunes of Scotland were joined with those of the human mind. She was one of the earliest nations to realize that intellect rules the world.* And the world of intellect, gladly responding to your call, places a well-deserved homage at your feet. Yesterday, when the renowned Professor Robert Flint, in his address to the Edinburgh University from the pulpit of St Giles uttered the words, 'Remember the past and look to the future', all the delegates, sitting like judges at a great tribunal, called forth a vision of bygone centuries and united in a unanimous desire for a still more glorious future.

No one today — except in Scotland itself and especially among ordinary illiterate Burnsians — could possibly say as Dr Hepburn Millar said over half-a-century ago (indeed, leading critics in a score of countries have testified to the very opposite effect in recent years) that

> though vigorous attempts have been made to galvanize the Scottish muse into a semblance of life, it is plain to all with an eye to see or an ear to hear that she is dead as dead can be; and it seems a tolerably safe prophecy to predict that no fruit worth the trouble

> of picking and preserving will now ever be yielded by the fertile and long-lived national tradition of poetry which was summed up and perfected in Robert Burns.

Nor will anyone with any qualification to speak endorse now what he goes on to say:

> Of one thing we may be tolerably confident, and that is that we shall never witness a revival of the old Scots tongue as a medium of expression for serious thought in prose.... Nor is it possible to anticipate a much brighter future for the literary Doric in the region of poetry. Its resources as regards verse appear to be exhausted, and all its conventions have been worn to a thread. Everything has the air of a more or less — and generally a less skilful imitation of Burns. Burns himself was not 'original' in the sense of having founded a new school of poetry. He was rather the consummation of an old one; and for that very reason he presents an insuperable obstacle to the triumph of those who also would fain be his disciples. It was easy for him to borrow from Ramsay and from Fergusson, and to improve upon what he borrowed. It is also possible for later generations to borrow from Burns; but who is to improve upon him? The plain truth is that the language in which he wrote has ceased to be a literary vehicle for intense and genuine emotion. And thus, while his cheaper and more sentimental pieces provide congenial models for those whose feelings have always an infusion of the self-conscious and the second-hand, we may suspect that any modern compatriot with a true lyrical gift would seek some other mode of displaying it than the methods which Burns has made immortal. A clearly marked separation between the current spoken and written dialect of a people may in some respects be a misfortune, but it is a phenomenon which may be remarked in other countries than Scotland, and in other ages than our own.

The work of the last thirty to forty years has shown that Scots is far from exhausted; that it is neither necessary nor in any way desirable to imitate Burns — he can be bypassed altogether; that a different approach to the language and altogether different themes than any previous Scots poets attempted can yield results ranking among the finest achievements of the Scottish Muse at any time. But there are, of course, tremendous difficulties which only one or two can possibly surmount now, or, even if the Movement continues, for a very long time to come.

In endeavouring to recover and develop attributes of the independent Scottish tradition, the Scottish Renaissance Movement's aim included (1) to bring Scots poetry abreast of contemporary intellectualism and as a first step towards that took the slogan, 'Not Burns — Dunbar!' (2) to bring Scots poetry into line again with contemporary political requirements, and give our people a proper appreciation of their literary patrimony, and (3) to get back behind the Renaissance — in other words, to break out of confinement to a mere 'earthly eudaemonism with Christian nuances', that pseudo-religious mental climate which keeps the harmonies and solutions of our writers on so contemptibly shallower a level than the conflicts and tragedies which encompass our lives.

In the light of these aims we see that almost all the poets of the Scottish Renaissance in so far as it has gone have developed two rather intractable defects or diseases, both of which lead to neurosis or worse. Everything depends on these being cured. The first is a sort of osmotic reluctance, on the part of their mental perceptions, to step through the cilia of what *seems* to be, and reach the vital stream of what actually is.

The second is the lack of correspondence or an essential incongruity between the words they try to use, and the way their minds work, so that their verses are afflicted by a species of *aniseikonia*, a word derived from Greek words meaning 'unequal imagery' and usually applied to the distressing consequences that sometimes result from the fact that images carried to the brain by the two eyes are quite different both in size and shape. This defect, amongst other things, prevents some people, even of fair intelligence, from comprehending what they read. It is prevalent among opponents of the Lallans Movement who, even when they have a fairly good knowledge of Lallans, are divided between it and the English to which they are so hopelessly overconditioned. As in the difference between the right eye and left eye images, such readers — and writers — in passing from Scots to English have a violent struggle to equate the two things. It must also be admitted that all of these readers and writers can only be described as hard-of-thinking — which is the main problem confronting our Movement.

As a consequence of these and other ills the results achieved by almost all the Scots poets today remind me of what Dorothea Stanhope says in the following passage:

> The Winter Sports Season of 1931-32 will be remembered sadly by those unfortunates who, owing to a rise in patriotism and a fall

in income, were obliged to forego Switzerland and take their skis and skates to Scotland. Under the circumstances Swiss hotel-keepers were chary of engaging dance bands, so we also went north and accepted a ten weeks' contract at the Fife Arms Hotel, Braemar. Always treacherous and perverse, the Scottish climate excelled itself. It was the warmest winter that had been experienced for years. The sun shone, the birds sang, and the flowers came out weeks before their time. Sometimes it rained gently but firmly and occasionally there were thunder and hailstorms, but the thermometer stayed at summer temperature and even the highest tops of the hills remained a virgin green. Unperturbed by any of these meterological errors the majority of visitors were determined, at all costs, to preserve the Spirit of Switzerland in Scotland. Regardless of the summer-like temperature they elected to walk about the muddy countryside dressed in the very thickest of ski-ing suits and boots, much to the gaping astonishment of the local inhabitants who rapidly became convinced that Braemar had been turned into a northern branch of Colney Hatch. Out of the ten weeks which we spent in that sad little village there were exactly three days on which it was just possible to ski. The excitement was terrific. Skis were waxed and rucksacks strapped on. More and more scarves and sweaters were donned as for a North Pole expedition. Press photographers and the Movietone News came north and drove madly round the countryside trying to get 'shots' before all the snow had melted away. Two practically flat fields were turned into nursery slopes. Herr Schmidt, a ski-ing expert from St Moritz, whose opinion of Scotland does not bear repetition, was heard politely requesting fallen beginners not to lie too long as the heat of their bodies caused ominous green patches to appear through the precious snow. One of these mornings the banjo player and I decided to try a bit of luge-ing. Laboriously we climbed up a steep path above the golf course; groaningly we extended ourselves, stomachs down, on two very small toboggans; majestically we started down the hill at a comfortable twenty miles an hour. 'What a lovely view,' said I, and carelessly took my eyes off the track and admired the surrounding scenery. I shall never luge in Scotland again. While I wasn't looking, the snow came to an end, the toboggan stopped dead, and I went on — face downwards where a cow had lately stood...

That is exactly what happens when one has an insufficient vocabulary and depth of understanding of the language, when one is writing

Scots poetry. Nearly all living Scots poets have had Miss Stanhope's experience. Burns himself, had it very often indeed. But in the intervening quarter of a century since the time of which Miss Stanhope wrote, ski-ing in Scotland has developed splendidly and attracts a great many people. That may be a good omen for the development of a sufficient area and depth of Scots poetry too. I hope so.

Anyhow, contrary to all expectation, Scots has triumphantly manifested in this half-century a renewed vitality when all seemed lost, and demonstrated a vitality that has led to quite unforeseen and very valuable achievements bound to modify valuation of all former work in this medium — and a vitality the further literary products of which, while certain and assuredly of importance, are as yet unpredictable in kind but almost certainly not inferior to those likely through any other language in the world. A new departure has yielded splendid results with which Burns had nothing whatever to do. His influence is not in the least susceptible of affecting the subsequent outcome in any way. He will be completely outgrown, or rather, the growth will be into a dimension to which nothing he was or did has any relevance, and, indeed, although he will always hold his place in the history of Scots poetry and be honoured for the stand he took and the revolutionary ideas he expressed in the context of his own day and generation and particular circumstances, his work and personality are not likely to be much admired but rather to be regarded with aversion and avoided by subsequent Scots poets, who will all be psychologically, and in their exceptionally highly educated quality, so different from him and all his imitators and admirers as to seem — and perhaps actually to be — of a different species of human being altogether. It is true, as Dr Wittig says, that

> the brunt of Burns's ferocious attack on Calvinist orthodoxy fell on the reactionary party popularly referred to as the Auld Lichts; Burns rarely attacked the Kirk or Christianity as such. Dunbar's 'anti-clerical' poems had been travesties of Holy Offices or sacraments; they were full of gusto, but contained little thought. Burns, too, could strike a hymn-like note or parody a prayer, but he had to reckon with a Kirk in which ritual had been suppressed, and its place taken by rationalistic dogma, predestination, Sabbatarian zeal, rigid severity, and stern disapproval of worldly joy. With quasi-Satanic passion Burns traces out the consequences of accepted orthodoxy until it stands fully revealed in all its inherent logical and moral absurdity. Holy Willie's abstract theological premises are entirely orthodox, but as they are set against the

realities of life, we behold his cunningly worming mind wresting them to his own purpose — and orthodoxy is blasted to pieces.

But future Scots poets of any value whatever will have got rid of the incubus of superstition altogether and no hangover of orthodoxy will adulterate their work. They will not be 'Christian rebels', but completely 'Christless' to use Willie Nicol's mistaken adjective for Burns, whereas, Mr Pearl's sub-title — 'Christian rebel' — is unfortunately accurate. That is Burns's funeral.

'Scotland,' says some moronic Town Councillor, 'is still looked upon as having a background of stability. That would be lost if we opened cinemas on Sundays.' A Communist councillor retorts: 'We are here to serve the public, not to dictate to them. I claim I am a democrat, but you people want to dictate to the public.'

In the meantime the only element directly in the Burns tradition that still appeals to any large public is 'Scotland Aye', followed the advertisement tells us, by 'a strippingly saucy Nite revue', and to all appearances it won't be long now before the Church follows its evening services with entertainments of that sort. Already less than a third of the Scottish population have a Church connection of any kind, while the BBC persists in giving an altogether disproportionate amount of its programmes to bolster up this minority, and the Capitalist press is, of course, its unscrupulous ally — but all that is unlikely to last much longer.

The vulgar seaside postcards issued by a Scotsman and sold in enormous numbers — the subject of one of George Orwell's best essays — is for the time being the heir and successor of the really popular element in Robert Burns, while the big circulation Women's Journals find millions of feet to try on the 'auld bauchles' of his love-songs. These are the paragoges of Burns's work and it is only through such that it has any — however indirect — potential of continued acceptance.

David Hume: Scotland's Greatest Son
a transcript of a lecture given at Edinburgh University, April 1961

If anything could have added to my pride and pleasure four years ago on receiving the Honorary Doctorate of Laws from this University, it would have been the fact that in the citation my name was coupled not with Robert Burns or William Dunbar or any other poet but with the names of David Hume and Thomas Carlyle, and it was stated that 'it is with such Scotsmen that he must be ranged'. I fully appreciate, of course, that this was meant simply in kind, and not at all in degree.

In my opinion David Hume is the greatest Scotsman who has ever lived. Most people who know any of their names at all would, I suppose, think Robert Burns or Sir Walter Scott occupy that position. Scott knew better; he knew — and said — and he was right — that nothing would flourish in his shadow. Burns knew that he was addicted to idle slapdash rhyming that for the most part wasn't poetry at all — and he was right: he was anti-intellectual and often xenophobic, thus opposed to two of the greatest Scottish traditions; and in consequence his influence on subsequent Scottish life and literature has been almost wholly bad. As Mr T.S. Eliot has said: Burns was the decadent representative of a great alien tradition — the independent Scottish native tradition, that is, alien to the English literary tradition. Burns's work inevitably paved the way for the stages of progressive degeneration which led through the Kailyard School and the Whistle-Binkie School to Sir Harry Lauder and the Scotch coamics, and which via the variety theatre and the recent folk-song revival has such an appalling grip on most of our people. Neither Scott nor Burns were seminal; their work has no unexhausted evolutionary momentum. I agree with Hume's great biographer Professor E.C. Mossner that 'thanks largely to the stimulus provided by Edinburgh's own late Professor Kemp Smith shortly before the turn of the century, Hume's thought is more alive today than before' — but not in Scotland. It is true, too, as Professor Isaiah Berlin has recently observed that Hume may claim to be the greatest and most revolutionary of British philosophers, and furthermore that 'no man has influenced the history of philosophical thought to a deeper and more disturbing degree'.

Hume was at the beginning of what can now be seen to be 'the general show-up of man's thought through the ages' —

> the astonishing and perturbing fact that almost all that has passed for social sciences, political economy, politics, ethics, in the past may be brushed aside as mainly rationalizing. When we are offered a penny for our thoughts we always find that we have recently had so many things in mind that we easily make a selection which will not compromise us too nakedly. On inspection we shall find that even if we are not downright ashamed of a great part of our spontaneous thinking it is far too intimate, personal, ignoble or trivial to permit us to reveal more than a small part of it. We find it hard to believe that other people's thoughts are as silly as ours, but they probably are.

Two hundred and fifty years is a long time and a great deal has happened in the interval, while these past few decades have shown an unprecedented acceleration of change, yet re-reading Hume startles one every now and again by showing how up-to-date he remains — how much he says that is apt and vital to our concerns today.

What I propose to do in the present talk is to ask why then Hume is a live influence in the thoughts and actions of so few of our people? What is the force — or are the forces — that continue to prop up the positions Hume demolished, and still constitute a cabal of obscurantists to occlude Hume from due influence in much the same way that a clique of ministers prevented his securing the Chair of Ethics and Pneumatical Philosophy in this University?

Scotland has continually preferred — and still prefers — Barabbas in this way, and it seems to me that there would be little or no point in celebrating this 250th Anniversary of Hume's birth unless with a determination to continue his work in the most explicit, not to say aggressive, way. Louis Pasteur, the great French scientist, speaking at the tercentenary of this University, said that Scotland was one of the first nations to link its national destiny with the powers of intellect. Nobody can contend that it has continued to do so. At a tercentenary banquet he said:

> The City of Edinburgh is now presenting a spectacle of which she may well be proud. All the great scientific organizations assembling here seem an immense gathering of hopes and mutual

> encouragement. The honour reflected by this international concourse rightly belongs to you, for centuries ago the fortunes of Scotland were joined to those of the human mind. She was one of the earliest nations to realize that intellect rules the world.

As McDougal said, Hume initiated developments in psychology to which no one has yet seen the final issue. A very great deal has been done since to carry on that great work, but most Scottish people have remained quite unconscious of it and still conceive of themselves and others in an utterly fatuous and quite indefensible way. A little leaven leaveneth the lump: why have Hume's ideas failed to do so, so conspicuously in his own country?

Another great Scot, rejected like Hume — and several other great Scots — by the Establishment, Thomas Davidson, has said:

> What shall we say of people who devote their time to reading novels written by miserable ignorant scribblers, who have hardly read a line of Homer or Sophocles or Dante or Shakespeare or Goethe, or even of Wordsworth or Tennyson, who would laugh at the notion of reading and studying Plato or Aristotle or Thomas Aquinas or Bruno or Kant or Rosmini? Are they not worse than the merest idiots, feeding prodigally upon swinish garbage, when they might be in their father's house, enjoying their portion of humanity's spiritual birthright? I know of few things more utterly sickening and contemptible than the self-satisfied smile of Philistine superiority with which many people tell me, 'I am not a philosopher.' It simply means this, 'I am a stupid, low, grovelling fool and I am proud of it.'

Davidson also wrote — nearly three-quarters of a century ago —

> I think the time has come for formulating into a religion and rule of life the results of the intellectual and moral attainments of the last two thousand years. I cannot content myself with this miserable blind life that the majority of mankind is at present leading, and I do not see any reason for it. Moreover I do not see anything really worth doing, but to show men the way to a better life. If our philosophy, our science, and our art do not contribute to that, what are they worth?

That incapacity for, and hostility to, intellectual distinction has intensified greatly in our population in the interval. Our education system has been sabotaged. We are told there are two cultures — science on one hand, and literature and the arts on the other. Our

Universities are in danger of being degraded into technological training centres: it is not a question of making men scientists — ninety per cent will only be technicians. Simultaneously all our arts are in danger of being reduced to the level of mere entertainment. The distinguished Scottish actor, Mr Duncan Macrae, not so long ago complained that the majority of Scottish theatregoers are morons. I think he is right and that this is by no means confined to the theatre, but is equally true of every department of Scottish life. The abandonment of a broad general cultural basis in our educational system in favour of premature specialization will only greatly worsen this deplorable and inexcuseable state of affairs.

Over thirty years ago I confessed that I was very young when I arrived at the position — which I have never abandoned since — which Professor Kemp Smith defined when he said:

> Hume's attitude to true religion can therefore be summed up in the threee-fold thesis: (1) that it consists exclusively in *intellectual* assent to the somewhat ambiguous, at least undefined proposition, 'God exists'; (2) that the 'God' thus affirmed is not God as ordinarily understood and (3) as a corollary from (1) and (2) that religion ought not to have, and when 'true' and 'genuine' does not have, any influence on human conduct — beyond that is to say, its intellectual effects, as rendering the mind immune to superstition and fanaticism.

It is a very different state of affairs that the greatest agencies in our midst are persistently inducing and intensifying. I defined it as follows in one of my poems:

> The illiteracy of the literate! But Glasgow's hordes —
> And the same thing is not less true of Edinburgh's hordes —
> Are not even literate save a man or two;
> All bogged in words that communicate no thoughts,
> Only mumbo-jumbo, fraudulent clap-trap, ballyhoo,
> The idiom of which constructive thought avails itself
> Is unintelligible save to a small minority.
> All the rest wallow in exploded fallacies
> And cherish for immortal souls their gross stupidity,
> While in the deep layers of their ignorance who delves
> Finds in this order — Scotland, other men, themselves.
> Consequently we have a Jeans accommodating the stars

And against this state of affairs I have set out what I think ought to be our aims — a campaign that cannot be better conducted than under the great name of David Hume, and represents the only way in which we can truly pay tribute to him:

> To traditional superstitions, and a Barnes who thrids
> Divers geometries — Euclidean, Lobatchewskyan, Riemannian
> — yet stubbornly heads
> (Tho' he admits his futile journey fails to reach
> Any solution of the problem of God's relation to time)
> Back to his starting point — to a like betrayal
> Of the scientific spirit to a dud sublime
> This is the lie of lies — The High Treason to Mankind.
> No one but fritters half his time away.
> It is the human instinct — the will to use it — that's destroyed
> Till only one or two in every million men today
> Know that thought is reality — and thought alone —
> And must absorb *all* the materials — their goal
> The mastery by the spirit of all the facts that can be known
> (Leaving only that irreducible minimum of alogicality
> To which scientific explanation is always asymptotically tending.)

It is easily seen then that I owed a great deal to Hume when forty years ago I included in the statement of aims of the Scottish Renaissance Movement my friends and I were then launching, the declaration that one of our aims must be 'to break out of confinement to a mere earthly eudaemonism with Christian nuances, that pseudo-religious mental climate which keeps the harmonies and solutions of our writers on so contemptibly shallower a level than the conflicts and tragedies which encompass our lives'.

Since then religion has by the most unscrupulous means staged a very considerable come-back — in influence if not in church membership. We had gone a long way prior to the first World War to secure a secularized educational system. Now so-called religious instruction has invaded our schools very strongly again. We have industrial chaplains and the horrors of the Tell Scotland Movement and a readiness to lower standards to any depth to welcome an abomination like Billy Graham, as if the dire results of the never-to-be-forgotten Moody and Sankey campaign were not still confining a large proportion of our people in a ghastly rut.

I am opposed to Sunday schools — and religious instruction in day schools — for the same reason that I am opposed to brain-washing or to the hidden persuaders and subliminal propaganda. The great obstacle to the spread of Humian ideas and to intellectual and aesthetic development in Scotland generally can be exemplified in what happened to the genius of one great Scotsman — and has, I am sure, happened and is still happening to the minds of most Scots. The great Scotsman I refer to is John Ruskin, and Mr R.H. Wilenski said that Ruskin largely failed in his life's endeavours for the simple reason that he could not write. And he continued:

> When I say that Ruskin could not write I do not mean, of course, that he could not produce literature, or strike out an arresting sentence, or charm, interest, and stimulate his reader. Everyone who has ever opened any volume of his writings knows that he could do any of these things, and that it would scarcely be an exaggeration to say that he never wrote a page in which he did not do them all. But it is, I think, accurate to say that he could not write, because all through the years of his maximum activity he was incapable of using language as a precise means of communicating ordered thought. For 35 years from 1843 to 1878 he played a part of consequence in the life of his day, in spite of this inability to write; when finally he arrived at real control of language he was an exhausted organism with nothing to communicate but the gossip of a tired old man. The trouble was that he was a victim of a vice. He was addicted from childhood onwards to a drug which he was forced to take in daily doses in the nursery until he acquired the taste for it. In youth and maturity he fought against the abuse of the drug, but he fought in vain; when at last he was immuned by satiety, his power of action was all spent.
>
> The drug of course was the emotive language of the Bible. Ruskin, as everyone knows, was made to read the Bible *aloud* every day in childhood and early youth. He was started at the beginning, taken through to the end, and then taken back to the beginning again. He was also made to memorize long sections of the text. This continued till he went to Oxford. He even knew *by heart*
>
> Exodus, Chapters 15 and 20.
> Deuteronomy, Chapter 32.
> 2 Samuel, Chapter 1, from v. 17 to end.
> 1 Kings, Chapter 8.
> Psalms 23, 32, 40, 41, 103, 112, 119, 139.
> Proverbs, Chapters 2, 3, 8 and 12.
> Isaiah, Chapter 58.
> Matthew, Chapters 5, 6 and 7.
> Acts, Chapter 26.

1 Corinthians, Chapters 13 and 15.
James, Chapter 4.

And he had thousands of other phrases in his head. He continued to read the Bible as long as he read anything. He was always obsessed with the emotive rhythm, the sonority, the obscurity, the archaism, and awful associations of this living text within his brain. We shall never know to what extent the obsession impeded his power of thinking, but no one who has really studied his writing will, I am convinced, deny that this obsession fatally impeded the precise externalization of his thought. The remembered language continually intervened between the thought and its expression, and often side-tracked the thought itself. Ruskin, it is quite clear, struggled to use language as a means of precise communication. He guessed about the derivations of words in an effort to persuade himself that he was learning to use words with scientific care. But in fact he continually failed to achieve sustained control of his vocabulary. Again and again he began by making sentences in which the words exactly represent the thought; and then some remembered emotive words and phrases would rise to his mind's surface, and he would take at first one sip of the fatal drug, and then another, till finally he would abandon the hard task of precise externalization of thought and yield to the pleasure of 'making some sort of melodious noise about it'. Again and again a paragraph begins as precise writing and ends as emotive rhetoric recalling the Bible. In book after book the words on the first few pages have no power for themselves but submissively obey the thought; then gradually the words become more biblical, and so emotive, till, in the end, the thought is dancing to their tune.

Many of you will remember how to an even more appalling degree the same thing happened in Mr Ramsay MacDonald's speeches. Despite the vast sums we spend on education today, and the emphasis publicly placed on the importance of science, we allow thousands of ministers, themselves addicts of the same mass drug to contaminate the minds of their hearers Sunday after Sunday: and although the membership of all churches in Scotland is less than one-third of our population — and less than one-fifth of the English population — we allow to this minority far too large an element in our radio and TV programmes, a legacy of the anti-social arrangement made in the early days of the BBC by a notorious Scottish bigot and carried on since by sedulous officers of the organization.

Professor James Harvey Robinson in his wonderful little book *Mind In The Making* was right when he said that thinking was an extremely rare, and very painful and unnatural process, and that all but a tiny minority never engage in thought but only in rationalization.

When in my opening sentence I mentioned Carlyle as well as Hume there did not perhaps seem to you to be any real reason for dragging *his* name in this address. But I would remind you of what he says of the 'so-called Christian clerics' in the Seventh of his Latter-Day Pamphlets:

> Legions of them in their black or other gowns, I still meet in every country, masquerading in strange costumes of body and still stranger in soul; mumming, grinning, grimacing — poor devils, shamming and endeavouring not to sham; this is the sad fact. Brave men many of them, after their sort; and in a position which we may admit to be wonderful and dreadful! On the outside of their heads some singular headgear, tulip-mitre, felt coal-scuttle, purple hod; and in the inside — I must say, such a theory of God's Almighty Universe as I for my part am right thankful to have no concern with at all! I think, on the whole, as broken-winged, self-strangled, monstrous, a mass of incoherent incredibilities, as ever dwelt in the human brain before. O God, Giver of light, hater of darkness, or Hypocrisy and Cowardice, how long, how long!

And in one of his letters Carlyle wrote:

> Theologies, rubics, surplices, church articles, and this enormous ever-repeated thrashing of the straw: a world of rotten straw: thrashed all into powder; filling the universe and blotting out the stars and worlds: — Heaven pity you with such a thrashing floor for world, and its draggled dirty farthing-candle for sun! There is surely other worship possible for the heart of man; there should be other work or none at all, for the intellect and creative faculties of man!

I think Dr Oscar Levy was right when he said in his book *Idiocy of Idealism*:

> Yet if they had been really and truly religious their own faith might have shown them the way out of the wilderness. For the religious conscience begat the scientific conscience, and the scientific conscience ought to produce the intellectual conscience. Of the latter, Puritanism knew nothing; it has stopped at the religious,

> and in a few cases at the scientific conscience. It fought shy of the last step; it did not allow truth to enlighten the intellect; it was not honest enough to criticize moral values, and has thus allowed the world to tumble into chaos, which it tries in vain to organize now by more reaction, by still more religion, by still more morality — that is to say, by still more alcohol for a world of dipsomaniacs.

Our lack of imagination — our lack of innovating ability — our willingness to leave all the initiatives elsewhere, and let ourselves be dominated by an anti-creative repetition complex, leaves us only one way in which we may escape from this sorry pass — and that is to realize the significance of David Hume and adopting his principles apply them thoroughly to our own problems, becoming ever more and more radical in the process, for, as John Cowper Powys says: 'Deep in us is a secret fount from whose channel by a resolute habit of the will we can clear away the litter that obstructs the water of life', or again,

> Most people are not sceptical enough. If you are sceptical enough about all human hypotheses, clear down to the very bottom of the abyss, then, and then only, and not till then, are you in a position to enjoy the significance, not merely of the spiritual atmosphere of the countries through which you travel, but of the great romantic dramas of races, cults, religions, and philosophies concerning which almost every stone in these historic places has its own particular palimpsest. To believe in nothing, to be a Pyrrhonian sceptic down to the very bottom of your nature, and yet to put into practice — if not actually to feel — many of the most subtle emotions which have been from time immemorial linked up with the idea of a saint, does that not strike your mind as having in it not only something for which irony, with all its nuances, is not only a rough-and-tumble synonym, but something which marks a real step forward in that planetary casuistry with the difficulties of which all higher intelligences are forever struggling.

In many ways Hume exercised a caution that is no longer either necessary or desirable — he even repudiated the *Treatise* itself with its systematic approach to the study of human nature, surely, as Professor Mossner says, 'One of the most grandiose works every projected by philosopher'. But circumstances have changed and we have no need to be so circumspect. Society is wont to deal unkindly with those it does not fully comprehend. Hume's life was a constant struggle against odds — against financial straitness, poor health, family ambitions; against the power of names, the inertia of ideas, the forces of superstition and intolerance. Having all Hume's life and work in mind, we must surely agree with Dr Levy on the stand we must take: 'In short,' as Dr Levy says, 'Christ and Christianity can be beaten by its own weapons — the weapons which they have forged and to which they owe their success over what was better, nobler, and higher than themselves.' To the general allure of 'feeling elbows', to the German 'worship in fours', to the victorious clamour of millions in every land, the higher man will reply with a stern SOS — or as he will most certainly be alone and without friends — with a grim but determined SMS — Save My Soul! Only it will not be easy. That way too lies crucifixion. But Christ's was a crucifixion in public, lasting a few hours, sweetened by weeping women, comforted by a sponge of vinegar, or, if desired, by a narcotic, and brightened by the certain hope of being in Paradise. 'This very night.' Ours will be a long crucifixion, lasting for years and decades, without any consolation from man and woman, without conversation with God Almighty, without a drop of water in the desert of silence, calumny, and false applause. And when the final breakdown has come there is sure to turn up a good Christian, or a candid friend, or worst of all the victim's own conscience, grown sick with misery, and telling him: 'It was your pride, that deadly sin, which led you off the path of your ancestors into this hell of isolation, where you now give up, away from man, beast and God, your supercilious and alas! superfluous soul!' No, it is dangerous to save one's soul nowadays; but it is honourable, and in the best religious tradition. And if one escapes, it is also highly satisfactory — if one can convince by word and example that there is a way even today to save one's soul; if one can persuade some men of our time to strive after a Kingdom other than Heaven, to wit, that 'within you' — that which Christ never preached to his slaves, but which will finally conquer for the masters, dechristianized and de-vulgarized, the Kingdom of this Earth.

I do not forget the auspices under which this address is given. So it may interest you to turn to page 229 of Professor Mossner's huge biography of Hume and read how 'Hume's efforts as literary patron to bring about a renaissance of Scottish letters were to form no inconsiderable part of his activities'.

I have spoken of the pressure to conform — the conspiracy against the free mind — the various factors that keep most people in a rut. So I will end by reminding you that the idea of a Scottish literary renaissance is no less difficult than the effort to develop the power to think instead of merely to rationalize, and this is clearly expressed by the late Professor George Gordon, President of Magdalen College, Oxford, when he said — in a book published in 1932 in *Our Scottish Heritage* containing essays by various hands on almost all the departments of our national life; a book which characteristically only accords Hume a single passing mention —

> 'It was only in the age of Sir Walter Scott,' says Mr Trevelyan, 'that England discovered once and for all that she was linked with a partner not inferior to herself.' Might we not have hoped that that late discovery, and the triumph of a time when Abbotsford was the principal shrine of British literature, would stir the young pens of Scotland to a feverish and inspired scribbling for the honour of literature and the north? A little of that there was but it could not hold. Scotland has produced since that time, and continues to produce, its occasional great author, its Stevenson and the rest, but not one has kept his roots there and stayed where he was planted. Like Carlyle, the greatest Scotsman of letters since Sir Walter's death, they all go south, and are numbered with their English brethren. There may be wisdom, as well as destiny in this; but it leaves Scotland bare and the old altars smokeless. Signs are not wanting that these things are understood in Scotland, and that a remedy is being sought. The search will be salutary even if the remedy should not be found. The leaders of the quest have much to hamper them, for Scottish literary tradition is as narrow as it is illustrious. Can it be widened, we must ask, without ceasing to be Scottish? A country which has produced no epic, no national drama, no vernacular or national prose, and which in lyric, where it is strongest, has never cared to attempt those elaborations of art which distinguish the highest performance of other nations — such a country is ill-equipped for new literary adventures. The ingrained Scottish habit of cultivating the old patch will be hard to alter.

It is not only that in Scotland, as elsewhere, as Kierkegaard reminds us Johannes Muller declared, there are two great powers round which everything revolves: ideas and women. That is quite true. Naturally there is this great difference, that among thousands who run after a skirt there is not always one who is moved by ideas. In Scotland, it seems to me, there is a positive detestation of ideas, a hatred of cerebration, and one does not need to go to the slums of Edinburgh or Glasgow, or a big football match, or a political meeting, to be forced to reflect with D.H. Lawrence,

> I realized with amazement how rapidly the human psyche can strip itself of its awareness and its emotional contacts and reduce itself to a sub-brutal condition of simple gross persistence. It is not animality — far from it. These people are much less than animals. They are cold wills functioning with a minimum of consciousness. The amount they are *not* aware of is perhaps the most amazing aspect of their character. They are brutally and deliberately *unaware*. They have a strange stoney will-to-persist, that is all, and they persist by reaction, because they still feel the repulsiveness of each other, of everything, of even themselves...

So we have the stark reduction to a persistent minimum of the human consciousness. It is a minimum lower than the savage, lower than the African bushman. Because it is a willed minimum, sustained from inside by resistance, brute resistance against any flow of consciousness, except that of the barest, most brutal egoistic self interest. I still think that is an accurate description of about ninety-five per cent of the population of Scotland today.

We are told that at the trial of Eichmann in Jerusalem this week, when Professor Baron spoke of the great names in the arts and sciences among European Jewry, Eichmann leaned back and sucked a finger. One can easily imagine most people in Scotland today if the name of any great thinker were mentioned doing precisely the same thing — if indeed they did not protest vociferously against anything of the sort being mentioned at all. 'Intellectual' — 'highbrow' have become terms of abuse. And yet we are living on the verge of the introduction of automation which will abolish the need for much human drudgery and vastly increase leisure. How is that leisure to be occupied? I think the arts and philosophy and the sciences are on the point of coming into their own — that we are bound to experience shortly an immense liberation of human faculty — that Gurdjieff was right when he said that most people passed their lives more than half-asleep — like hypnotized cattle as Thomas Carlyle put it — and that they are about to be forced ere long to become fully awake. The more or less immediate future promises them a new flexibility, a new freedom of movement in a better-understood world — what Edmund Wilson calls the height and exaltation of the untried, unsuspected possibilities of human thought and art.

More than ever today then our young people should be like Igor Stravinsky who says: 'My childhood was a period of waiting for the moment when I could send it and everything connected with it to Hell.'

As the American poet Wallace Stevens says:

> To say more than human things with human voice
> That cannot be; to say human things with more
> That human voice, that, also, cannot be.
> To speak humanly from the height or from the depth
> Of human things, that is acutest speech.

He goes on to say:

> Perhaps we should like to know what reality would be if we could stop our hearts from beating...and released from destruction be at the azury centre of time: but our affair is with the possible, with a paradise that is, if anywhere, here, with death as part of life. The imagination of the poet deals in the final uncertainties, the 'comparisons of intelligence' — and this places him in total contrast to the priests with their 'ever-living subject'.

There are many signs that this acceptance of the earth as the proper and sufficient basis of our lives is gaining ground among the most significant voices in the world today — André Malraux in France, Harry Martinson in Sweden, Gottfried Benn in Germany. In an age of disbelief, when the gods have come to an end, when we think of them as the aesthetic projections of a time that has passed, men turn to a fundamental glory of their own, and from that create a style of bearing themselves in reality.

Scottish poetry was early at this task. The poets who led the way — and who, not Burns, should have been followed — had of course a very difficult time of it. They had all abandoned Christianity as an exhausted creed. They sought to embrace scientific development — instead of pretty trivialities and childish sentimentalizings they confronted the problems of urban life in a highly industrialized society — two of them committed suicide — another was confined in a lunatic asylum — a fourth died in destitution and despair. The poets I refer to are John Davidson, Francis Adams, James Thomson of *The City of Dreadful Night*, and Evelyn Douglas (alias John Barlas). They are little known in Scotland today where pride of place is given to hopeless infantilists. Scottish literature — and with it Scottish life — took a wrong turning and missed its greatest opportunity.

And Gottfried Benn only echoes again what David Hume said when he confessed that to continue his 'cold speculations' became intolerable, and he went to make merry with his friends instead. But Benn (while shying away also from the abyss, the void, the unsolvable, the inhuman element) was right when he said: 'Once, to be sure, God was the creator of the worlds — but for some time now it has been brains that keep the earth going'. But our attitude should, I think, be that which, following Leo Chestov, I express in these words:

De Profundis

I delight in this naethingness
Mair than ever I did
In the creation it yielded
And has aince mair hid.
Sae an ardent spirit
Should submerge a' it's learned
And enjoyed to the full
Whatna leisure it's earned.
For what is the end
O' a' labour but this?
— Earth's fruits to the flesh:
To the soul the Abyss.

The development I have been sketching should have been easier in Scotland then — Scotland has no religious poetry — any reference to the Kirk has been a sarcastic or condemnatory one, not like the devotion expressed in the English poets — and we have no counterpart to the great lines of English mystics. All that is utterly foreign to the Scottish genius.

The Man of (almost) Independent Mind: Hugh MacDiarmid on Hume

'It is permissible to wonder whether Hume took his scepticism far enough,' ran a sentence in an admirable centre-page article on 'The Philosophy of Hume' in *The Times Literary Supplement* of 22nd July, 1951. I do not consider Hume carried it nearly far enough, but do not think, to quote the following sentence in that article, it is permissible to wonder 'whether, if he had taken it further, taken it, indeed, to the full length of the implications which it carries, he would not have stultified it'. Bien au contraire! Thinking of this matter recently, I remembered a novel I had read lately, about a young woman. It had taken her a long time to realize that her mother was an ignorant, stupid woman. Her mother was well-educated, she practically ran her church, she was considered a fine wife and mother. How was she, a gangling knob-kneed girl, to know that these judgements and opinions were all wrong, were superficial, and were not even believed by the ones who said them; were merely part of the network of lies necessary to maintain the great human conspiracy of importance — the mass blackmarket of you-believe-me and I'll-believe-you. By the time she found out it was too late. Her mind and opinions could be changed, yes, but you could never change the emotions that had been built into her brick upon mortared brick like a wall from the time she was old enough to have an emotion. They were still there. And they would stay there.

Precisely. Hume's enemies have their like by the hundred-thousand in Scotland today. Instead of diminishing, mumbo-jumbo is as rampant in our midst today as ever — and conspiracy to keep it going and constantly renew and reinforce it and seek in fact to give it a monopoly. The brain-washing of religious education is being insisted on more powerfully than ever. The churches are ready to sink to far lower levels to retain or regain their hold on the masses. They have the assistance of the press, radio and television. If the greatest test of normality is how much you can lie to yourself and believe, normality rules the roost in Scotland today to an unprecedented degree. Intellectual integrity is difficult to find anywhere. It is almost as if, in every connection, our people had modelled themselves on the blimp Haig, of whom it has recently been well-written:

> What was it that enabled a man of Haig's uprightness to over-ride not only the code of his class but also the scruples that would have been natural to him? The clue may be found in the blend of a deeply religious trend with an evergrowing self-confidence. As his success grew so did his sense of a special call, culminating in the conviction that he was chosen by a higher power for a great destiny. In reaching it he was not hampered by a sense of humour. We may find cause for amusement, but he apparently did not, in his record of the first of a number of spiritualistic séances which he attended before the war, with his sister: here he received the assurance of his destiny, 'to do much good and benefit my country; and also that the spirit of Napoleon was always near me, and ready to aid'. If there is significance in the seriousness with which he apparently took this communication, there is no less light on his character in the questions on which he solemnly consulted the medium — how to ensure the success of the Territorial Army scheme and whether a company or battalion basis was the better system! The war deepened his religious tendency, and with it grew the sense of divine inspiration. Even when he beat the French generals in an argument he ascribed it to the entry into him of a special power. Sometimes events cast a doubt on his certainty as to the source of his inspiration: above all when he wrote on the eve of the Somme offensive: 'I feel that every step in my plan has been taken with the Divine help'. The tragic opening day of that offensive brought the heaviest day's loss in the history of the British army — 60,000 casualties for hardly any gain... good intentions paved the path to Passchendaele. It is not true to say that he was unreceptive to ideas: he was more open to them than most soldiers, so long as his mind was open, but they made no impression if they conflicted with a course upon which he had determined or if they too obviously deviated from his 'doxy'! Also, contrary to the common opinion, he himself had a capacity for ideas and imagination — until inspiration intervened — which few of his fellows possessed. In his diaries one can trace the evolution of critically inclined youth into pontifically inclined maturity. And in his portraits too, the eyes appear to grow duller and the chin heavier.

In short, a typical Scot.

No wonder I rejoice when I find in Brecht's 'Flüchtlingsgesprache':

'I have never found anybody without a sense of humour who could understand dialectics.'

On the occasion of the Tercentenary of Edinburgh University in 1884 Louis Pasteur said: 'Centuries ago the fortunes of Scotland were joined with those of the human mind. She was one of the earliest nations to realize that intellect rules the world.' That has long been abandoned. No wonder one of the declared aims of the Scottish Renaissance Movement is:

> to break out of confinement and a mere earthly eudaemonism with Christian nuances, that pseudo-religious mental climate which keeps the harmonies and solutions of our writers on so contemptibly shallower a level than the conflicts and tragedies which encompass our lives.

Alas! Billy Graham attracts far more attention than the two hundred and fiftieth anniversary of David Hume. As the late Professor George Gordon, then President of Magdalen College, wrote in 1932:

> 'It was only in the age of Sir Walter Scott,' says Trevelyan, 'that England discovered once and for all that she was linked with a partner not inferior to herself.' Might one not have hoped that that late discovery, and the triumph of a time when Abbotsford was the principal shrine of British literature, would stir the younger pens of Scotland to a feverish and inspired scribbling for the honour of literature and the North? A little of that there was, but it could not hold. It leaves Scotland bare and old altars smokeless. Signs are not wanting that these things are understood in Scotland, and that a remedy is being sought. The search will be salutary even if the remedy should not be found. The leaders of the quest have much to hamper them. A country which has produced no epic, no national drama, no vernacular or national prose, and which in lyric, where it is strongest, has never cared to attempt these elaborations of art which distinguish the highest performances of other nations — such a country is ill-equipped for new literary advances. The ingrained Scottish habit of cultivating the old patch will be hard to alter.

In fact, Scotland is far more hostile to the arts than any other European country, and the term 'intellectual', let alone 'highbrow', is a term of abuse or contempt from which the majority of our people hasten to dissociate themselves. No wonder a *Scotsman* book review said of Hume that: 'despite his atrocious opinions he did no real harm'. This is a characteristic expression of that dead weight of mediocrity which has so long rendered any intellectual or artistic development in Scotland impossible. Hume's two hundred and fiftieth anniversary was very poorly observed. An article or two in the press, three lectures by members of Edinburgh University staff which received less space in even the Edinburgh papers than would have been accorded to a minor burglary or a chimney on fire, another address given by Principal Sir Edward Appleton at a claret party and which, so far as I saw, was not reported at all — that was virtually all. Not much homage to accord to undoubtedly the greatest Scotsman of them all.

The Begum Anwar Ali of Pakistan recently said: 'I have been most impressed with the amount of preservation of historical sites in Scotland, and I find the people very proud and conscious of their history and culture.' Nonsense! Most Scots know nothing worth knowing about their national heritage at all. It is impossible that they can, for English history, language and literature are given a virtual monopoly in our schools and colleges, and practically nothing is given of the corresponding Scottish subjects at all. In the past few years I have lectured to adult evening school classes (composed mainly of teachers) and have found that one can take absolutely nothing for granted. They have no background whatever. One must start from scratch. When I mentioned one of the greatest modern Scots, Sir Patrick Geddes, not one of my pupils had ever heard of him. The only members of the Geddes clan they had heard of were the two nonentities, Eric and Auckland, and, of course, the mythical Jenny who threw the stool in St Giles'. More recently, when I mentioned David Hume and asked what they knew of him, one bright pupil said: 'He's the Foreign Secretary, of course'. This was in Edinburgh, for Peggy Phillips in *The Scotsman* was wrong when she said: 'Only in Glasgow does this cumhoochie — if that is the way to spell it — Haw-Wullishness reach full flower. It may not be a flower that fussier gardeners would choose for their borders, but it is as truly indigenous as the thistle.'

To escape even momentarily from this ubiquitous idiocy in Scotland is no easy matter, but a perusal of the most important Scottish book published this century may help. I refer to George Davie's study *The Democratic Intellect: Scotland and her Universities in the Nineteenth Century*. 'Edinburgh,' says Dr Davie,

> in the decade after Sir Walter Scott's death, was far from sinking into provincial dullness. Thanks to Sir William Hamilton's stimulus, there was a 're-enthronement in the world of speculation of the

> good god difficulty' and in constant debate with him 'the brilliant Ferrier' was redefining the tasks and problems of philosophy with an 'intimate union of clearness and depth' equally rare both then and since. As a result of their joint efforts the commonsense tradition seemed to be undergoing a renovation destined to adapt its sagacity and moderation to the conditions of the modern world, and it worked for a time as if the burning bush of Scottish philosophy might contrive to be a beacon to the nations.

That restatement of the Common Sense principle in terms appropriate not only (belatedly) to: 'the social and cultural complexities of the new age of industrialism and rising democracy', but to the period of vastly accelerated change through which we are now living is the prime matter which should occupy every Scot with a brain in his or her head. It is vitally necessary to recover loyalty to Scottish usage and to be concerned chiefly with the task of effectively perpetuating its values. I recommend amongst recent books: E.C. Mossner's huge biography of Hume and his *New Letters of David Hume*, supplementary to J.Y.T. Greig's *Letters of David Hume*; *David Hume: Theory of Knowledge*, edited by D.C. Yalden-Thomson; *Theory of Politics*, edited by Frederick Watkins, and D.G.C. MacNabb's *David Hume*.

If we Scots have the reputation of being controversialists, radical reasoners, searching questioners, hard-headed thinkers (and if we haven't that reputation it is high time we set ourselves to deserve it), not to be fobbed off with old wives' tales, superstitions and infantilist fancies, then David Hume is our greatest exemplar, and it is high time ninety per cent of our people went to school with him again. As one of the greatest thinking-masters of the human race, it can scarcely be expected that he should have the claim of a star footballer, a champion golfer or a racing motorist. But perhaps we should be beginning to arrange our interests a little more worthily. We have had one or two centuries in which to do it. How much longer are we going to take?

We should all recognize with Gottfried Benn that:

> all the great minds among the white nations have felt only one inner task, namely, the creative camouflaging of their nihilism... not for an instant are they unaware of the essential nature of their own inner creative substance. It is the abyss, the void, the unsolvable, the cold, the unhuman element!

These were precisely the 'cold speculations' from which Hume hastened away to 'make merry with his friends', when all the more it was vital 'in the destructive element to immerse'. Again and again re-reading Hume I am struck by how prophetic he was, how up-to-date, how applicable to all that has happened since and is happening now. In this 'cold speculations' matter, he is precisely re-echoed by the Russian philosopher Shestov who accepts the earth for his body but craves the void for his spirit.

What I have said about the stranglehold of mediocrity in Scotland today — the moronic character of most of our people — Hume anticipated (as did Burns despite his 'A Man's a Man for a' that') when he wrote:

> Think on the emptiness, the rashness, and futility of the common judgements of men: how little they are regulated by reason in any subject, much more in philosophical subjects, which so far exceed the comprehension of the vulgar. 'Non si quid improba Roma, elevet, accedas examenque improbum in illa, perpendas trutina, nec te quaesiveris extra.' A wise man's kingdom is his own breast; or, if he ever looks farther, it will only be to the judgement of a select few, who are free from prejudices, and capable of examining his work. Nothing indeed can be a stronger presumption of falsehood than the approbation of the multitude; and Phocion, you know, always suspected himself of some blunder, when he was attended with the applauses of the populace.

Let us agree with W.B. Yeats that we have only our wills — and must not allow their clearness to be blown upon and dimmed by impure desires. And with Hume remember that:

> Plato says there are three kinds of atheists: the first who deny a deity, the second who deny his providence, the third who assert that he is influenced by prayers or sacrifices... the addressing of our virtuous wishes and desires to the deity, since the address has no influence on him, is only a kind of rhetoric figure, in order to render those wishes more ardent and passionate. Now the use of any figure of speech can never be a duty. Secondly this figure, like most figures of rhetoric, has an evident impropriety in it. For we can make use of no expression, or even thought, in prayers and entreaties which does not imply that these prayers have an influence. This figure is very dangerous and leads directly and even unavoidably to impiety and blasphemy.

We must also remember Hume's concern for literature and his attempts to promote a national rather than a provincial Scottish literary tradition. Recently, J.B. Priestley said that English literature today was at a lower ebb than at any time since the fourteenth century.

But Hume saw this decline and wrote: 'I am only sorry to see that the great decline, if we ought not rather to say, the total extinction of literature in England, prognosticates a very short duration of all our other improvements, and threatens a new and sudden inroad of ignorance, superstition and barbarism'. 'I think,' he wrote in another letter (which might be dated yesterday or today), 'you grow every day madder in England; there is a prospect that that worthless generation will soon bring themselves to ruin, by their own folly.'

For our present purpose the key passage in Dr Davie's great book is that in which he says that in the last century and the beginning of the present one: 'There has been a failure of intellectual nerve among the Scots, and the educated class of the new century, though still loyal enough to inherited principles in a quiet way, had become increasingly chary of public demonstrations of national pretensions to intellectual independence.' And of the universities he says that: 'although the massive sanity of the old Scottish tradition remained fundamental, it was no longer off-set by a social and cultural venturesomeness'. That is what we must at all costs recover, and in addressing ourselves to that task we must remember that since Hume's day there have been great developments in the breaking down of matter (or, sometimes, metaphorically, 'substance') into energy: first by the painters like Manet, van Gogh, Matisse; by the poets like Rimbaud (whose objects are surcharged with energy, but in the process loose their identity as objects); by the musicians like Debussy (who dissolves the solid matter of form and tonality into a vague and luminous energy not unlike that of Monet); and by the more savagely energetic atonalists. At the same time, all the forms, the matter, of nineteenth century social life have been, on the one hand, rigidified by the vested interests and hired liars (historians, preachers, cheerleaders and ad-men) and on the other hand broken down by enlightened criticism, till even the solid mask of personality (the most carefully guarded vested interest of all) has collapsed as depth psychology probes into the sources of energy beneath.

As Mollberg in Malraux's *The Walnut Tree of Altenburg* says: 'The less men partake of their civilization, the more they resemble each other. But the less they partake of it, the more they fade away. The permanence of men can be conceived, but it is a permanence in nothingness.'

Let us remember that Kant, whom Hume woke from his 'dogmatic slumber', in *The Critique of Judgment* defined the 'dynamic-sublime' as 'man's consciousness of the final inability of the power of nature, however menacing it may be, to force him to surrender his humanity'.

the ugly birds without wings

He kept looking at so-and-so's wagging jaw and thinking of the multitude of people like him on the earth, perhaps half the people on earth were of his type, or potentially his type. The ugly birds without wings. The mediocre who perpetuated mediocrity – the resentful, the world-owes-me-a-living face, which was the reflection of the small, dull mind behind it...

— PATRICIA HIGHSMITH in *Deep Water*

He was a man with a mediocre mind and instincts, who had been overshadowed by genius until he was well into middle age, and who, consequently, was never able to accept his own mediocrity. He was a little man who pined to wear a giant's boots.

— MARY STEWART in *Towards The Storm*

Edward Crankshaw in his introduction to *An Essay In Autobiography* by Boris Pasternak (Collins and Harvill Press, London, 1959) points out that while many imagine it meant that there had been a total reversion to Zhadanovism in the cultural life of the Soviet Union when Pasternak's *Doctor Zhivago* was denounced, the facts are that

> until well into 1957 it was still hoped that *Doctor Zhivago* might be published in the Soviet Union.... Even as late as that, *Novy Mir* published more of his poems, and when in the same year the Italian publisher Feltrinelli brought out the first translation of the novel against the express wishes of Alexey Surkov, Secretary of the Soviet Writers' Union, Pasternak was not made to suffer. It was not until the Swedish Academy fatefully decided to award the Nobel Prize to Pasternak that the storm broke loose. Then he was solemnly expelled from the Writers' Union and a number of the most undesirable characters in the land started using the language of the gutter.... Pasternak would not allow himself to be conveniently shipped abroad and then held up as a traitor to his country.... That is important because he has since been accused in the West, either through stupidity or malice, of cowardice in his clinging to Russia, in his refusal, so long as refusal lies in his power, to

> follow so many of his contemporaries from his own and other lands into the bitterness of exile. No charge was ever shabbier or wider of the mark.

Pasternak himself in the same book tells of an evening when the great poet, Alexander Blok, was to give a reading of his poems.

> Mayakovsky, whom I met at the Polytechnic, told me that a plot had been cooked up at the Press Club and that, under the pretext of independent criticism, Blok was to be received with catcalls, whistles and abuse. Mayakovsky suggested that we should go there and try to prevent this infamy....But it was all over by the time we reached the Club. The row had been as bad as we had feared. After the reading, insults had been showered on him; he was even told to his face that he was 'a back number' and 'a living corpse'. And all this was said to him a few months before his death.

The great Rumanian writer, Ion Luca Caragiale, after incredible hardships and after most of his greatest work had been done, was forced to go to Germany.

> Caragiale's departure to Berlin (1904) where he was to remain to the end of his life, was the result of a long series of discontents. His plays had often been subjected to infamous calumny campaigns; petty journalists, great scandal-lovers, envious colleagues, influential politicians attacked directly or indirectly in his plays and pamphlets, formed a real *maffia* which teased him. It was not the desire to seek glory abroad that determined him to take this decision, but a long range of galls and disappointments which wounded his heart. It is important to point out that in these years of banishment I.L. Caragiale remained the man of his time and country.

The history of literature is full of that sort of thing—the little men, the hopeless mediocrities, ganging up against their betters. On the verge of my seventieth birthday, I have been made the subject of a similar attack, or, as Mr Douglas Young has observed in a letter to me, 'You must have been surprised to find yourself regarded as the arch-enemy by some of our younger writers.'

The thing began with the publication of Mr Norman MacCaig's anthology *Honoured Shade*, sponsored by the Scottish Committee of the Arts Council to mark Burns's bicentenary. Any anthology is inevitably a personal choice of the editor's and cannot possibly include every poet writing in the country concerned. Not only so, but the conditions applying to this particular book were that poems to be included should not have been previously published and should have been written within the preceding twelve months. A number of the poets not included started a correspondence in *The Scotsman*. It transpired that a number of them were ineligible because they had no poems available which met the stated conditions. Personally I thought, and said, that none of them had written anything worth including in any case. The allegation was made that a particular clique of poets had been favoured and that they had acquired, and exercised, a virtual monopoly. After this correspondence ceased, a period of silence followed, and then the whole matter blew up again. First in the columns of *The Scotsman*, then in *The Scottish Field, The Manchester Guardian*, the BBC and Granada TV. And in the course of this renewed attack, in terms very similar to those quoted above as used against Alexander Blok, I was informed (by a lady named Jessie McGuffie) that my poetry was hopelessly provincial, that I was quite out of touch with contemporary life, and that all the young people to whom she had talked found my work completely boring. Miss McGuffie, I discovered, was connected with a little enterprise called the Wild Flounder Press, on the point of starting a periodical poetry broadsheet called (appropriately) *The Poor, Old, Tired Horse*, and that her associate and the star author of their publishing activities was Mr Ian Hamilton Finlay, author of a book entitled *Glasgow Beasts, an a Burd, haw, an Inseks, an, aw, a Fush*. I was accused by Mr Finlay, Miss McGuffie, and others of failing to help younger writers, of exercising a virtual monopoly in the field of Scottish literature to their detriment and/or exclusion, and along with these and other associated charges there were bitter complaints that they could not find publishers for their immortal works and the implication was that I and my friends were responsible for that too.

The whole thing was of course a farrago of nonsense. Various writers have testified in published articles to the help I have, over the past forty years, given to many young Scottish writers and I have letters from many of these acknowledging that help in the most grateful terms. These letters, along with the rest of my correspondence, will afterwards be available to students in the National Library of Scotland. The same correspondence will show the global range and multiplicity of my contacts with foreign writers, while any one who consults either Dr W.R. Aitken's or Mr Duncan Glen's bibliographies of my books, articles in all sorts of papers and periodicals at home and abroad, inclusions in innumerable anthologies, translations from German, Russian, Swedish, French and other writers and translations of my poems into Icelandic, Catalan, Chinese, Rumanian, French, German and Czech, will perhaps acquire a different view as to my alleged provinciality.

With regard to the allegation of monopolizing the field of Scottish literature, the fact, which can easily be verified, is that (except for *ad hoc* periodicals initiated and run by myself) I practically never contributed to most of the Scottish papers and periodicals and certainly never for many years unless I was invited to do so — and these occasions were few and far between.

So far as young people are concerned I have for many years been actively connected with student societies in all our Scottish Universities, and the audiences I secured when I addressed them, the tokens of esteem with which they have on four or five occasions presented me, and the tributes paid to me on many occasions in the student magazines lead me to suppose that Miss McGuffie's and Mr Finlay's acquaintance with the young people is either extremely limited or too confined to types of youth to whom I can readily understand I would not be likely to appeal — nor wish to. One only gets from literature and the arts in proportion to what one brings to them, and I have never sought to address myself to the uneducated or undereducated, to juvenile delinquents, to beatniks and the like.

I do know, however, that many writers in different countries have had to keep sending their stuff out, and receiving it back with rejection slips, for a very long time before they succeeded in commending themselves to editors or publishers. I do not believe that the writers of Scotland who allege that their way is hopelessly blocked have given the matter a fair trial. Nor do I think they have sent in (only to be rejected) stuff worth publishing either in quarters to which they submitted it or, indeed, anywhere at all. Their output seems to have been extremely scanty. One of their principal complaints is that they were excluded from the various organs promoted to develop the Scottish Renaissance Movement and, in particular, poetry in Lallans. They allege that these organs were the preserve of a small dominant clique. That is quite true. These organs were formed for an express purpose and were naturally not open to writers who did not share that purpose and manifest it in writings of an adequate quality in the view of the editors of these periodicals. That is not a phenomenon peculiar to the editors of these periodicals. All editors have some measure of editorial discretion which they exercise in accordance with their judgement and the accepted policy of the journal or journals they control. But what these whining *jeunes refusés* failed to recognize is that Scotland has other papers and periodicals to which the aims and products of the Renaissance writers are anathema, and which are consequently closed to these writers. The organs in question comprise almost all those in Scotland which pay for contributions, and also those national dailies reviews in which are likely to give books the best publicity. The remarkable burst of creative activity in the West Indies in recent years, for example, has owed a lot for the encouragement of the local newspapers. In Scotland during the forty years of its development, the Scottish Renaissance Movement has not been encouraged but opposed by the Anglo-Scottish press, which continues to print worthless kailyaird stuff (when it prints anything Scottish at all) but never includes any verse or prose by any of the writers most prominently associated with the Scottish Renaissance Movement. Nor do these papers review the books of such writers in many cases, and when they do it is unfavourably. One national daily was for years the only quarter in which book after book of mine was violently slated when reviews everywhere else were laudatory; and another national daily simply did not review my books at all. All this surely is a strange monopoly.

Stranger still is the monopoly I, and three or four other poets closely associated with me, seem to have acquired in respect of anthologies — not only in this country, but in other countries too. Surely all the compilers of these anthologies were not also in this conspiracy to exclude Mr Finlay, Mr Hugh C. Rae, Mr Tom Wright, Mr W. Price Turner and a few others. It seems extremely unlikely. It is more probable that these anthologists actually thought the poems they included were the best available to them in the contemporary Scottish output. They may have been wrong, perhaps, but the rejected bards have certainly advanced no good reason to suppose so.

Strangest of all is the fact that well-known critics in Great Britain and several other countries kept on writing not merely favourable book reviews but substantive critical studies of the work of these favoured three or four poets. Scores of such articles are now listed in the bibliographies. And the matter did not rest at that. Two books devoted to these writers were published in Germany and two in the United States, while they were the subject also of innumerable theses by Continental students, most of whom, one imagines, were under forty, hardly to be denied the adjective 'Contemporary', and enthusiastic about the work in question instead of being bored.

Another complaint of those (in their own view) frozen-out and frustrated young writers is that they could not find publishers. I had no difficulty in securing one of the oldest publishing firms in Scotland for my first four volumes. My latest three volumes were solicited by well-known publishing firms. It is a very unfair world isn't it? What peculiar influence is it supposed I had with the directors of these firms to induce them to give me not only preference but a virtual monopoly? The thing won't bear a moment's examination.

Or wouldn't — if those who made the charge did not immediately afterwards make claims for themselves quite inconsistent with it, and with any complaint that they have been hard done by.

Mr Hamilton Finlay, for example, follows up his sad story of neglected genius, by saying: 'My first collection of poems was published a year ago in the USA. It is now going into a second edition. It was praised in — among other places — *The National Review* and *The Nation*. A famous San Francisco poetry magazine is about to do a special issue on my poetry. And so on.' In view of all this, what then has Mr Finlay to complain about? What becomes of his elegantly phrased complaint concerning 'shouting poet monopolies'?

Perhaps Mr Finlay will go further and tell us how many dozen copies of his first book of so-called 'poems' were in the edition? I ask because five of my own books have sold consistently for over thirty years and are still selling. Also, the organs in which some of the poems appeared originally included *Botteghe Oscure, The (New York) Nation, The Hudson Review, The Criterion, The London Mercury, The Irish Statesman, The Welsh Review*. Does Mr Finlay contend that 'the famous San Francisco poetry magazine' to which he refers can be mentioned in the same breath as any of these? Or that any critic of established repute has ever praised his 'poems' — or considered them as poetry of any value? A few words of praise from someone whose opinion goes for nothing in any connection, published in a hole-and-corner periodical on paper (appropriately) resembling toilet-paper is scarcely international recognition.

Mr Finlay goes on following the sentences quoted above to refer to my 'anachronistic propaganda'. He presumably means by that my advocacy of Lallans as a medium for modern literary purposes, and also perhaps is referring to my Scottish Nationalism. It is not clear to me why Scottish Nationalism should be considered 'anachronistic', when the like phenomenon manifesting itself in scores of African and Asian countries is one of the burning issues in the world today. Nor is it clear why Lallans is singled out in this way at a time when many lapsed languages have been revived and become the media of lively contemporary literatures. As with many leading workers in the other arts today, my return to primitive and archaic techniques was not inspired by a nostalgia for the past, but by the desire to utilize some already existing method of expression to help towards the expression of my personal conception. This archaism (confined to a matter of vocabulary) is deliberate and self-conscious, 'a necessary stage' (as Jean Metzinger said) 'in the preparation of a new movement'. And so far as my Scottish Nationalism is concerned, not only do nationalities still exist, as a matter of perhaps regrettable and actual fact, but because (I believe with T.E. Hulme) it is desirable even on abstract grounds that they should.

The charges Mr Finlay and others to whom I have referred made against myself and the Scottish Renaissance Movement were based on a tissue of misconceptions and erroneous statements. 'I am a poet,' wrote Mr Finlay, 'who has never been printed in any Scottish newspaper or periodical.' But Mr Warrington Midge of *The New Saltire* replied, 'In the first place this is simply untrue; Mr Finlay has had poems published in *The Glasgow Herald, Gambit, Sidewalk*, and has no fewer than five poems in the current issue of *New Saltire*.'

I myself replied to the correspondence as follows:

(1) That non-Lallans writing poets were never excluded from the periodicals, anthologies, etc, run by myself and others. On the contrary, they always predominated in numbers, if not in quality. It was the stated aim of the Scottish Renaissance Movement to encourage better work by Scottish poets not only in Lallans, but also in English and Gaelic, and there is ample testimony that this was successfully achieved.

(2) Since these publications included poems by over sixty writers, it is absurd to assert that they were operated by an exclusive clique. Writers who failed to secure entry may well reflect that they were simply kept out not because they did not belong to a clique but simply because they were not good enough.

(3) After all, Messrs Tom Wright and Hugh Rae, failing admission to the Scottish Renaissance publications, were not debarred from appearing in the hundreds of English, American and British Colonial organs. Yet the fact remains that Lallans poets like myself appeared in far more of these than Scotland's self-pitying *jeunes refusés*.

(4) Mr Wright may assert that Scottish Nationalism in poetry and elsewhere is out of date, but his mere assertion proves nothing. I am of the opposite opinion entirely, but in reply to what he says about foreign editors (unlike those in Scotland whose first concern is that a piece of writing should be Scottish and its quality as literature a secondary matter) recognizing the worth of a poem *per se*, how does he explain the fact that the work and worth of the Lallans poets has been recognized and highly praised by leading critics and fellow poets of many nations who do not appear to have been at all similarly

impressed by the poems of Messrs Wright, Rae and the other young poets they mention.

I think these four points are relevant and are straightforwardly and politely enough stated, but the guttersnipe character of those who initiated this *brouhaha* is shown unmistakeably in Mr Tom Wright's retort to one defender of Scots: 'I say I do not write for "illiterates" even if they are scientists... Since he expresses fondness for both dialect and open abuse, I combine them in the living Scots tongue, "Gaun, you mug ye",' and Mr Finlay's 'Really, everyone I know under the age of forty is bored stiff by Mr Hugh MacDiarmid'.

That is probably an accurate assessment of the calibre of the people under forty Mr Finlay knows. I think his trouble — and the trouble of very many people today — is just what Thomas Griffiths in *The Waist-High Culture* discerns as the way of modern business, viz,

> As places narrow and the competition increases — out in the big-game waters — the sport gets rougher, and victims are then required. Employees on the outer edge of these treacherous waters become expert readers of the battle communiques which issue from time to time, and know that fulsome praise of some poor fellow in an inter-office memo probably indicates that, whatever his new title, it probably reflects a demotion.
>
> *'Well, you asked for it. I wasn't going to let you have it, but now that you're acting this way, I'll tell you straight out. You've had it, brother. Nobody wants you around any longer. You haven't a friend in the place.'*
>
> And then there are the farewell dinners, those hypocritical occasions when they pass the poisoned chalice and sing of comradeship. After many drinks, a few insincere remarks and a set of golf-clubs, everyone appears equally a good fellow, and the victim may even become convinced that what had to be done probably hurt the other fellow to do it.

There is no virtue in contemporaneity apart from quality, but in any case Finlay's work is all 'old hat'. His *Glasgow Beasts* is dedicated to Kusano, a Japanese poet. This is obviously just a device to suggest a non-existent internationalism, a world scope, which Finlay has not begun to possess. Kusano, we are told, 'began the whole idea of poems in the perpendicular'. Rubbish! The setting out of letter-press in all manner of designs on the page is nothing new, and certainly did not originate with Shimpei Kusano. Finlay intends, it is stated, to have his book translated into Japanese. That will not increase his stature one iota. The poems will not read any better in Japanese or any other language. But the point is that Finlay is not blocked from publication. Far from it. He sees himself as a world figure. His cronies tell us that he is 'an important writer' — a really big figure. Nonsense! We are also told he is 'very ambitious', and my 'bitterest enemy'. But, poems apart, he has had short stories in *The Glasgow Herald*, he has done broadcasts (and complained passionately when his poems were read by a less character than a famous star — I hope the BBC felt suitably chastened by this unparalleled presumption) and has had a play (of sorts!) produced by the Unity Theatre in London. And he and Miss McGuffie and others have been lavishly written up in *The Scotsman* by Magnus Magnusson, as well as having space squandered on them in *The Scottish Field*. Where then is the monopoly against which they are protesting, and what are they themselves trying to do but acquire such a dominant position as they imagine others possess?

Just look at the standards of these young writers. Mr Hugh C. Rae, for example, 'Rather than face the perils, disappointments and labour involved in accepting the high standards set by large publishing houses and magazines of wide circulation', he says, 'they (i.e. too many Scottish literary aspirants) content themselves with the comparative obscurity of small home-grown periodicals and an occasional fêting by groups of local literati.'

The fact remains that little local groups and small home-grown periodicals have done — and are doing — infinitely more for literature than all the big magazines and publishing houses. T.S. Eliot was right when he pointed out, on relinquishing *The Criterion*, that the future of literature lay with very few, and that there would be little or no money in it. Mr Rae and his like can scoop the pool as far as I am concerned. Best sellerdom does not appeal to me; I know nothing of any value in literature that has been achieved by the route he recommends. He and his friends are welcome to take it; their doing so will in no way affect the Scottish Renaissance Movement; but I wish they would get on with the business, compete successfully with pop-singers, rock and roll adepts, twist experts and the rest of it — and not merely advocate such 'success' on the basis of so infinitesimally little production either in prose or verse that their efforts are difficult to discern through a microscope. In short, their achievement is like that at the shearing of the pig — muckle squeal and little 'oo'.

The Scottish Renaissance Movement is, I think, only beginning. The foundation has been laid. When the Movement was initiated in 1920 there were many departments of Scottish Arts and Affairs quite inadequately documented. Our school children and students were not put in possession of our national heritage at all. English language, literature and history were given a virtual monopoly in our educational system. There were no cheap editions of our classics. All these deficiencies have now been made good. The volumes on Scottish literature by Mr John Speirs and Dr Kurt Wittig and most recently Dr David Craig's *Scottish Literature and the Scottish People, 1680-1830*, Dr George Davie's *The Democratic Intellect*, and Mr Moray MacLaren's *The Wisdom of the Scots* mark a tremendous development. The leaven is working in every branch of our national life, and while there has been a little falling off in the production of creative literature since the 'twenties, that can, I think, be better regarded as a recoil to enable a better leap forward. The groundwork for that has now been laid.

Reviewing Dr Davie's book Sir C.P. Snow said:

> This admirable book is an account of how, in the nineteenth century, the Scottish Universities were persuaded, coerced, bullied and argued into something like English *pastiche*. Not that this process was straightforward. It is still not quite complete. Scottish education has taken a long time to become *gleichgeschaltet*, and the Scottish universities preserve vestiges of an intellectual system and policy radically dissimilar from ours. At its core the English policy is (a) to allow very few students into universities at all, (b) to subject those few to courses of intense specialization. The Scottish policy — in this respect like the American or Russian or in fact the policy of all advanced countries except England — is (a) to regard university education as the normal thing for a high proportion of students, (b) to provide courses of considerable generality. ...Dr Davie is sure that, of the two policies, the Scottish one is much more nearly right. I might say I agree with him. For the crude purpose of making our kind of society work, for the subtler purpose of giving it some decent, democratic, spiritual health, I have no doubt that higher education has got to go deeper into the population than the English can even now begin to imagine. Without this, we shall be sick, and the Venetian shadow will deepen. ...Curiously enough, in their criticisms of each other, the English and Scots were pretty near right. On the particular issue of teaching of mathematics they were both wrong. It was, and still is, hard not to be wrong, for we are faced with a conflict or opposition which can by its nature be mediated, but not finally resolved. This being so, an adequately trained mind can do two things. The first

is to follow the *inner dynamic* of a subject as far as the mind can go. This means thinking about one thing in depth for a long time. The Cambridge mathematicians were right in seeing that the inner dynamics of mathematics was going to find its way through analysis, and that a mind wasn't going to get experience-in-depth through a mathematics which creative persons had abandoned (they were wrong in detail, though. G.H. Hardy used to say that the Cambridge mathematical tripos, through its competitiveness and its emphasis on mechanical tricks, killed mathematics in English during the whole of the nineteenth century). The second thing which the mind can do is dramatically opposite to the first. It is the ability not to think of one thing alone for a long time, but of one thing in relation to many others. In training and encouraging this ability, the Scots were dead right, and it accounts for the density and massiveness of the intellectual statements of Hamilton and his friends. In almost all formal English education, it has been similarly neglected: and its absence is responsible for a good many of our faults and mistakes. A foreign friend of mine used to say, rather sadly, 'You are empirical people, and that I like. You are a clever people, at least as clever as anyone else. But so many of your clever people seem to have no substance in their minds. There is less intellectual exchange than in any country I know. Sometimes you think you are exchanging ideas; but all you are exchanging is intellectual gossip. Gossip. Nothing but that.'

What Dr Davie's book marks at this juncture when the nature and purpose of higher education is being debated as never before, and in view of increased leisure and the doing-away of a great part of human drudgery by the introduction of automation, is not less than Scotland once again giving the world a clear lead in education. And as Sir Charles Snow shows the particular requirement of that education is precisely what has been one of the cardinal ideas in the Scottish Renaissance Movement, namely, the Caledonian Antisyzygy.

Those who appreciate that point will have no difficulty in recognizing why, in one of my poems, I crave

A learned poetry wholly free
Of the brutal love of ignorance;
And the poetry of a poet with no use
For any of the simpler forms of personal success.

And in another

Oh, if only ceasing to suffer
They were able to become men.
Alas! how many owe their dignity,
Their claim on our sympathy,
Merely to their misfortune.
Likewise, so long as a plant has not blossomed
One can hope that its flowering will be beautiful.
What a mirage surrounds what has not yet blossomed!
What a disappointment when one can no longer
Blame the abjection on the deficiency!
It is good that the voice of the indigent,
Too long stifled, should manage
To make itself heard.
But I cannot consent to listen
To nothing but that voice.
Man does not cease to interest me
When he ceases to be miserable.
Quite the contrary!
That it is important to aid him
In the beginning goes without saying,
Like a plant it is essential
To water at first,
But this is in order to get it to flower,
And *I am concerned with the blossom.*

And, finally in another I crave the kind of poetry

That like a wrestling bout on a village green
Divides the people and wins only those
Who are honest, strong and true
— Those who admire the man
Who has the faster mind,
The faster, suppler, better-governed body —
For there is not only a class war
But a war in the working class itself
Between decency and self-respect on the one hand
And a truckling spirit, seeking self-gain, on the other.

The work of Mr Finlay and others — notably in that happily short-lived periodical *Sidewalk* — is fittingly characterized by Jacques Barzun in an essay in which he says that the effects of the second World War are ensuring the elimination not only of Romanticist art and its sequels, but of all the high art of the last five centuries. The revolutionary intention is no longer merely to shelve the past but to erase it, and by doing this to produce in man a wholly new consciousness — not a new outlook upon the old makings of life, but a life made of a new substance... The search is for materials absolutely disinfected from Art and ideas. Each kind of artist wants to come upon, overbear, or summon forth something that shall in no way be remembered literature, music or painting. The suspension of intent is to preclude in the 'act' any habitual choosing of the material or censoring of the sensibility. The aim is to flee from the previously actualized and also from the prescient foreshadowing. It is a sacrificial effort, a pure anti-mental education.... They want to carry nothing forward, but to get rid of all their inherited aesthetic and intellectual lumber; they have no public hope, for they feel soiled and guilty from contact with any part of existing society. They want to strip bare and dig down to a hoped-for-bedrock showing no trace of an earlier passage of man. That is what Mr Allen Ginsberg means when he says that man himself is obsolete; this is what Samuel Beckett and others are trying to show us on a stage where no responses are predictable or congenial; this is what Mr Henry Miller is explaining at length in works where visions of love and feasts of sexuality outrank and displace all other concerns; this is what Mr Norman O. Brown theorizes about in *Life Against Death*, which pronounces the doom of mankind unless we return to the indiscriminate self-gratification of the infant: Man is played out, an orgiastic mysticism is in the air, expressive of a search for a total renovation. To such sensibilities, it is clear, the old high Art since Petrarch and Giotto is a horror of childish contrivance and intellectual axe-grinding. The only acceptable art is the art of Unconsciousness, of Accident, of No-meaning, and hence in the majority of artists an obsessive preoccupation with these parts of experience that are forever neutral in themselves and that mean only what the intellect attaches to them by an act of will — sexuality, narcotic visions, or the bare sequences in a stream of images. The germs of this near nihilism existed before the present generation of beat poets and of painters calling themselves Obsessionists or makers of '*art brut*'. We find those germs in the late French Symbolism (Ducasse, Laforgue, Tarry), in Marinetti's Futurism, in the German Expressionists, in the Surrealists, in Kafka who wanted his works destroyed, and in Paul Klee, who said: 'I want to be as

> though new-born, knowing nothing, absolutely nothing of Europe'. Indeed, the first Collage was the first denial of Art. Yet here one feels the difference between words and attitudes directed in the old way, as a criticism of life and a preparation for a new Art (of which these same critics were to be the makers) and the present mode of renunciation which is a calculated, intrepid striving for purposelessness.

However, as a leader in the *Times Literary Supplement* put it recently,

> The Gentility Principle may have had its day, and perhaps it would be tactful of literary historians today to play down the fact that most of the best British poets have been, in some sense, gentlemen. But when the Gentility Principle is finally abolished its place is likely to be taken by some other principle with a different name — the Principle of the Decent Human Being, possibly: a principle different in name but not so very different in essence. No poet, in even the worst of times, has ever merely reflected the world's disorder; the good poets have striven to wrest their own order out of that

— and it can never be done with *Glasgow Beasts, an a Burd, haw, an Inseks, an, aw, a Fush.*

But, no! I am sure Scotland is not going that way, no matter how 'many of the most undesirable characters in the land start using the language of the gutter', but in the way that Sir C.P. Snow indicates in the passage I have quoted, and Dr G.E. Davie fully maps out in his book, and the best work of the Scottish Renaissance Movement despite all the difficulties in contemporary Anglo-Scotland has sought to rediscover and develop. For, as Pushkin wrote, 'Only barbarism, villainy, and ignorance do not respect the past, cringing before the present alone.'

When the Rat-Race is Over:
an essay in honour of the fiftieth birthday of John Gawsworth

It takes the weight of all the waters of the oceans to raise a wave to a crest, and in the same way the great names in literature depend on the labours of the host of minor figures who serve the Muse in many unobtrusive ways. In like fashion, it is a poor lover of Nature who confines himself to the main roads and eschews all the fascinating bypaths and trackless areas. Changes in literary fashion and appreciation there must be, since change is the law of life. It is regrettable nevertheless that some dominant trend (so often not one of outstanding merit but dependent on such extra-literary factors as the log-rolling of cliques, pressure groups of one kind or another, the power of money in buying publicity, and so forth) concentrate the limelight on certain types of literature and certain authors, and occlude other types and other writers. Best seller-dom seldom if ever connotes outstanding quality. Indeed, commercialization weighs the scales in favour of mediocrity against genius. The minority who are not swept off their feet by prevailing currents may well find some happy haven in backwaters and side-eddies. That there is such a constant minority is evidenced not only by the way in which at all times overpublicized favourites have their brief hour of apparent fame but ere long lapse to their true negligibility or to oblivion, whereas constantly in literary periodicals one finds queries from all over the world asking for information, correspondence etc of obscure figures, such material being desired for critical and biographical studies of these 'inheritors of unfulfilled renown'. A year or two ago I saw such a query in the *Times Literary Supplement* and other quarters regarding Father John Gray and André Raffalovitch and others of a now-little-known circle in Edinburgh and I thought at once of my friend John Gawsworth who had expressed an interest in and evinced a knowledge of these men when he (John Gawsworth) and I were in close touch in London thirty years earlier. He was much younger than I, but even then I had cause to envy his generous appreciation and detailed knowledge of many fascinating sidelines of literature. Above all I marvelled at his warm-hearted concern for many writers who seemed to have fallen by the wayside and suffered from unjustifiable neglect. I think especially of his interest in men (caviare to the general) like Theodore Wratislaw, Arthur Machen, Richard Middleton, Hubert Crackanthorpe, E.H. Visiak and M.P. Shiel.

It may be thought that bibliography, anthologizing, the collection of holograph MSS and letters, constitute *in toto* a very subsidiary contribution to literature, but in the last analysis that is not the case. It is all an essential, though poorly rewarded (save in the sense that poetry is its own reward) activity and has the redeeming character of being actuated by pure enthusiasm and devoid of that egocentricity, often paranoia even, inseparable from the exercise of creative faculties.

It is because this unselfishness and generous discrimination characterized John Gawsworth's interest to such an exemplary degree that I am happy to respond to the request that I should pay my tribute to him now — a man who has shown again and again this eagerness to help the too-little-appreciated and taken the trouble to that end to acquire the necessary knowledge — for I feel he should not in his turn be overlooked and refused his meed of praise.

I had lost touch with Gawsworth since he ceased to edit *The Poetry Review*, and was very sorry indeed to learn that he was ill and had fallen upon evil days. For a time in the interval between the wars I owed a great deal to him and saw much of his work. So far as poetry was concerned he was a traditionalist and I in my own practice a follower of the innovators who have created such a division in contemporary poetry. While interested so greatly in what Dr Leavis has called 'new directions' in English poetry I have never thought it impossible to see poets of older schools in due perspective and give them the appreciation they deserve for what they wrote in their own day and generation however far removed the standards and fashions of their period may be from ours. Those who have paid high tribute to John Gawsworth's poems include men of the calibre of Professor G.S. Fraser, the late Roy Campbell, Lawrence Durrell, Kenneth Hare and Austin Clarke. These testimonies are not lightly to be put aside and, if they are, give at least a guarantee of subsequent revival. This may seem poor consolation for present neglect, but I do not wish to make greater claims for my friend's work since we are living in a time of unprecedently accelerated change and modesty is becoming to a prophet in this connection — such a modesty as Gawsworth himself displayed in his editing (and thus giving another chance to) the poems of Theodore Wratislaw, for example. What must be asked, however, is how it comes about that those who praised Gawsworth's poems so highly in former years, and who, many of them, now possess great influence in the literary world, have not ensued their *encomia* but acquiesced by default in the neglect that has overtaken this man and his work. He served others nobly whenever he could, and in turn deserves to be similarly served now by those who can.

The band of younger poets who have come to the fore in the last decade certainly includes no figure who is in many respects as interesting as John Gawsworth. I do not know that like the financier Harmon, who was King of Lundy Island, Gawsworth ever issued coinage and postage stamps of his own, but he is King of Redonda nevertheless and has conferred patents of nobility on some of his friends. He has been garlanded with flowers and hailed as a prince of poetry in India and North Africa by groups of poets there. He visited Croce at Sorrento and Sarojini Naidu in Bombay, and paid fitting tribute to such men as Umberto Fraccacreta, Romualdo Pàntini, and Giuseppe Ungaretti. An account of his friendships, travels, and many-sided literary interests would make a most desirable volume. It is to be hoped that Gawsworth will yet give us his autobiography as befits one who after all is descended in one line from the same stock as Shakespeare's Mary Fitton (the dark lady of the Sonnets) and by another line from the Lords of Annandale.

Good luck then, John, on your fiftieth birthday. May the future hold much that is good in store for you yet. The race is not to the swift nor the battle to the strong. You will not be denied your niche in the great temple of English Literature. Others far less worthy may fill the public eye for the time being; let the rat-race go on. It is what is left when that is over that matters and you will have your place there all right.

Sydney Goodsir Smith

To honour our jest tonight is no onerous task, and I am fully aware that this is not an occasion when it is necessary in any way to attempt to geld the lily.

There are many people amongst us who think that the age of miracles is past. Sydney Goodsir Smith is at least one living refutation of that notion. He is one of a small number, albeit one of the greatest of them, who, in the great desert of contemporary Scotland, continues like the prophet Elijah of old to derive nourishment from his own ravings. If I may be allowed to bring home the bacon I need have no hesitation in claiming that he is one of those writers we should read, mark, inwordly by jest.

I have already made an ornithological reference. I am sure that most of you are very keen bird-watchers, but that kind of bird is not very relevant to our purpose here — at this juncture at any rate, though I may have cause to recur to it a little later in these remarks.

Anyhow I take it that you all know that Mr Gow's avian symbol is the Great Auk, which, like the coelocanth, has far too long wrongly been assumed to be extinct. I am not sure, however, that it is not in this instance a crossbred. He is the solitary specimen of his kind in Scotland today. There are of course plenty of Little Auks and Auklets, but these belong to different genera of the Alcidae family. The cross in Sydney's case is quite clearly one between the veritable Great Auk and the Mynah, which as you all know is one of several sturnoid passerine birds of India. Some nitwits argue from that that Sydney is only a minor poet. Orthography is shockingly neglected in Scotland today. This bird is not spelt minor — still less miner — or mynheer — but simply and effectively mynah. An outstanding example of the mynah died the other day. It was probably the most verbose bird that ever existed, having, the BBC assured me, a vocabulary of over 1,500 words.

Whatever may be said of the Mynah, however, unlike the Great Auk it has not that power of autogeny which is Mr Gow's most important characteristic. Autogeny — a mode of spontaneous generation. Thinking of self-generation, independence, brings us near to an understanding of our guest's significance. Not indeed that like

Melchizadek he is unique — without ancestry or progeny. Far from it. He is the heir and successor of one of the most distinguished and valuable elements in the entire field of Scottish genius. I have only to mention Sir Thomas Urquhart of Cromarty, who had, like our guest, language at large and in his incomparable translation of Rabelais showed a verbal resource and range of vocabulary that in many instances went far beyond that of Rabelais himself. I might mention also Smollett, who anticipated James Joyce. Lady Snow — the novelist Pamela Hansford Johnson — recently contended that Joyce's work was a cul-de-sac — that it led nowhere, was utterly sterile and would — and indeed could — have no imitators. That's no' the case. She has evidently not read Mr Gow's *Carotid Cornucopius*, which I am glad to know is about to be republished with — as is entirely fitting — a whole new fitt. We are drawing near to our great national festival of New Year and I can imagine no better First Fit for any consciously Scottish household than a copy of this splendid work. It is on the contrary the conventional novel that is coming to an end. No intelligent reader can put up any longer with something so utterly false to life. I have observed before that if records could be made of the ordinary course of conversation between human beings they would be quite incredible in their hopeless disjointedness, incoherence, and utter banality. They would, in fact, be unintelligible even to those who indulge in them if they were not eked out with gestures or those ubiquitous assumptions which enable so much just to be taken for granted on the universal ground that it doesn't matter anyway. Above all, these sounds know nothing of sentence formation or other grammatical forms. The whole thing is a tissue of verbal fragments, interjections, expletives, liberally peppered with sniggers, snufflings and other stock aids to mutual understanding. In a few hostelries, however, where men of intelligence foregather — and jukeboxes and television are not allowed to spoil any possibility of 'feast of reason and flow of soul', you do get in sum-effect precisely what the prose of *Carotid Cornucopius* gives in the complex word-play of its prose. That amounts to a sort of composite reproduction of the sound and sense — where any — of normal Scottish intercourse at its best. It used to be said that James Joyce's *Anna Livia Plurabelle* was unpronounceable and meaningless: but you have only to hear the record of Joyce's own reading of it to realize that it contains the very breath and finer spirit of Irish blarney and is, in fact, an accurate exhalation of Dublin speech raised to a level of literary genius. Above all, it is as Irish as Guinness. So it is with our guest's prose in *Carotid* — it is couched throughout in the very quintessence of Scottishness. There is nothing in it, of course, of the tongue-tackit, inarticulate Scot, that English invention which has been so largely responsible for the subversion of our national psychology. The Irish have a way of describing a fellow they esteem as 'a broth of a boy'. There can be no doubt whatever that Sydney is a real Cockaleekie of a lad.

The atmosphere, the tone and temper, in which his great work (*Carotid*) is conceived and carried through is that in which our guest has his life and being. He speaks Carotidese fluently — especially at times when he would have no little difficulty in using at all what is absurdly known as standard English. One of his rarest, most admirable qualities is the way in which he squares precept and practice. He doesn't merely praise Stand-fast. He stands or falls by it with the most commendable consistency. I have long known the howffs he frequents and I can attest that he is one of those people who seem to improve a room just by being in it.

Philology has always been one of the main concerns of great Scots: and if I may refer to the Great Auk again, the name is probably derived from the Icelandic Alka, which happily is near enough to be taken for an abbreviation of alcohol — not that anybody with any sense wants that abbreviated. But the little auk or Rotche — or Rotchie — probably from the Dutch rotje, meaning petrel — denotes sea-dove. Now if our guest substitutes for that Picasso's dove of peace, that is in perfect keeping with the strain of radicalism, of social and political protest, which is one of the leading elements in our independent Scots literary tradition, running through its entire fabric from John Barbour to the present day like a red thread. Red thread! Rotje! There may be ill-disposed persons who are content to use only the first syllable and stigmatize the whole thing as just 'rot'; but the true meaning is *red*; and I am glad to see the colour of heart's blood glinting so markedly in much of our guest's poetry.

As to the other kind of bird to which I promised — and am only too glad — to return. Where else but in Sydney's poetry in all the corpus of Scottish verse, are you so insistently reminded of the ironclad rule that if the ankles are more than half as big around as the calves that settles it and one can no longer maintain any interest whatever? Being trained to observe details even when under a strain, a poet like Sydney catches at a glance the outstanding characteristics of members of the other sex who come under his observation — as few of them can fail to do — and qualities such as youth, shapeliness, and shallow depressions at the temples, which happen to appeal to him, inform his verses to a much greater extent than in the work of any other Scots poet.

You may sit in a cubicle, partaking of, say, a dish of Cassoulettes Castlenaudry — which, as you know, is boiled beans — and if you are privileged to have Sydney's company you will, after a few drinks, be surprised to realize that you could make out a case for calling him handsome. You would say to yourself with proper judiciality, 'They have overdone it a little on the ears perhaps, but on the whole he is at least up to grade if not fancy.' It is well known in such surroundings that he has one of the biggest and warmest hearts on record except in mothers and three characters in books by Dickens.

I hope what I have said will prove a lot of organic fertilizer. I may be pale and not seem any too sure of my leg-action, but I fancy I have reached my objective all right. Ladies and gentlemen, I respect your intelligence and I am sure you will agree with me that if on occasion Sydney's muse leaves her mouth hanging open, still, in spite of that handicap, no one with an eye for essentials can have any fault to find with the outlook, or perhaps I should say the inlook.

Our guest is versatile, and has a multiple track mentality of a sort far beyond Dr Beeching's power to close down. He has written splendid poetry — his play, *The Wallace*, was performed at the Edinburgh International Festival and he has several other plays in his locker — he has given us fine translations of Russian poems including Blók's 'The Twelve' and of French poems; he has written an admirable brief *Introduction to Scottish Literature* and done scholarly work on Gawain Douglas, Robert Fergusson, Robert Burns and others. In addition to all that he is himself a painter and as art-critic of *The Scotsman* in his notices of current exhibitions he has written without pomposity but a great deal of sound sense and with a quick eye to notice and encourage any local sprigs of promise that come into view.

Ladies and gentlemen, I submit that for all these reasons it is good that we should honour our guest — all the more so in that if we fail to do so it is difficult to see anybody else who could.

A Political Speech
transcription from a recording taken at the 1320 Club Symposium, Glasgow University, 6 April 1968

Mr Chairman, Ladies and Gentlemen,

I think I would have had considerable hesitation in rising to move this motion if the wording hadn't fortunately been altered at the last moment. It read originally, 'A debate on the motion that this house is in favour of devolution which would mean creating some form of parliament in Scotland.' Now, I would have hesitated to move that, and the motion now reads, 'This house is in favour of self-government for Scotland.' I couldn't imagine that it would be easy to find any intelligent Scot, man or woman, who would have moved an amendment to the motion as originally framed, but in the upshot, we didn't find anybody, and after discussing the matter, we agreed to dispense with any mover of the amendment and simply throw the matter open for general debate after I've finished speaking. It would have been a novelty in any case to hear any intelligent person, any presumably intelligent person, putting a case against independence. It's contrary to nature. Most of the world's peoples belong to independent nations, and I know of none of them clamouring to give up that independence. Most of them indeed literally fought to retain it, or, where it has been temporarily lost, recover it. So far as I am concerned the spirit that animates me is that expressed in the passage from the Declaration of Arbroath which reads, 'For so long as one hundred men of us remain alive, we shall never under any conditions submit to the domination of the English. It is not for glory or riches or honours that we fight, but only for liberty, which no good man will consent to lose but with his life.' Earlier on today we had some very subtle arguments as to the lets and hindrances if Scotland recovered a measure of self government, from economists. Last night for about eighty minutes on television another team, including Dr McCrone though, debated the same matter. I don't intend to go into these questions at all. The words in the quotation I have just given you from the Declaration of Arbroath, that we fight not for riches, covers all that.

I am not interested in economics. I believe, and my whole nationalist position is grounded in the belief, that where there's a will there's a way, and if we are sufficiently intent on having independence, nothing will stand in our way. We are quite prepared to meet all the sacrifices, if any, that are required. However, it is particularly urgent I think at this juncture — one of the great problems of the modern world is the search for identity — to remember just who we Scots are, and what part we've played in the world. We are too apt to be dismissed by the believers in big units as a small people of no particular consequence in relation to the major problems of modern times; but I think the historian James Anthony Froude, was right when he said that no small people in the history of the world had so profoundly affected the whole of mankind as the Scots people had done. The debate centres largely in the first instance upon whether there is a real, continuing, irrevocable difference between the Scots and the English. I think the quickest way to arrive at the conclusion of that matter, is perhaps to look through the *Dictionary of National Biography*. We find Scot after Scot holding positions in Civil Service and other government appointments in India and Ceylon, who took an active interest in the culture of the peoples amongst whom he was located, who studied their languages, who wrote books about their arts and so on. If you look at the corresponding number of Englishmen who held similar posts in the same countries, you'll find they contributed nothing, they weren't interested in the cultures of these countries and, in fact, after a very long period of the British Raj in India, what have they to their credit? Two things, two great accomplishments, stand to the immortal glory of the British Empire: pig sticking and cocktails. Now that sums it up pretty well. A recent writer has put the matter in a nut shell when he says,

> A great Scottish idea, the one that Scotland gave to the world out of the agonies of the wars of Independence, is freedom, the 'noble thing' of Barbour's famous outburst in *The Bruce*. This is the *sine qua non* of existence, whether of nations or persons, and the tragic irony of Scotland is that she, who gave birth to the idea of national independence and integrity, owing allegiance to no country and no people but itself, should almost alone, of European nations have betrayed and lost this freedom to create new forms of society and art. Truly such a Scotland is not Scotland, it is only a corpse, breeding and spreading corruption.

He goes on to quote from a poem of mine, a few lines which read as follows:

These denationalized Scots have killed the soul
Which is universally human; they are men without souls;
All the more heavily the judgement falls upon them,
Since it is a universal law of life they have sinned against.

There surely is the answer to the particular kind of treachery found in those Anglo-Scots intellectuals who bleat of a false antithesis, internationalism, not nationalism, as if it were possible to have the one without the other. They sin against the universal law of life which invests life in individuals not conglomerations. Yes, even in the ant hill. In the place of living separate identities, having mostly their differences in common, these ghouls would reduce all to a horrible international, characterless, abstract fog, a devitalized nonentity, but their internationalism in fact equals 'English', and behind the pseudo-internationalism of the Anglo-Scots lurks the face of 'The Auld Enemy', English imperialism. The greatest Scots have always deplored the union with England. The common people had no say in the matter, but they protested violently against it. But the greatest Scots, Burns, for example: 'Alas,' he wrote in one of his letters, 'I have often said to myself, what are all the boasted advantages which my country reaps from the union that can counterbalance the annihilation of her independence and even her very name?' The question is put in a way that implies that the answer must be that there are no such advantages. I have put the same question to myself insistently for nearly half a century, and I have been unable to discover any merit in the connection with England whatsoever. Sir Walter Scott summed up the intolerable character of our relationship with England when he said: 'There has been in England a gradual and progressive system of assuming the management of affairs entirely and exclusively proper to Scotland as if we were totally unworthy of having the management of our own affairs.' I could multiply quotations like these from a host of great Scots, but for my present purpose content myself with observing that there has been lately a remarkable convergence of opinion from the most diverse quarters to the same effect; some of them are quite unexpectable. Lord Reith, for example, in his inaugural address as Lord Rector of this university stressed the urgent need to preserve and develop Scotland's distinctive traditions and characteristics for the benefit not only of Scotland, but of the world. A few days later, Dr Harry Whitley of St Giles in Edinburgh, spoke to the same effect, and no less a person than the Earl of Dalkeith warned the Government that Scotland was becoming ripe for UDI. Is it? It would be astonishing if it were, the denationalizing anglicizing process of centuries is not so quickly and easily reversed. I am not greatly impressed, though I welcome it as a step in the right direction, by the upsurge of the Scottish National Party and the fact that that party is now the biggest in Scotland with a hundred thousand paid-up members. The best thing about it is that it has now attracted such a huge proportion of our young people; but what do these young people know of Scotland? They have not been put in possession of their natural national heritage. In their schools and colleges, our native Scottish languages, our Scottish literature, even our history, are inadequately taught if at all, and a virtual monopoly is given over instead to the English counterparts of these subjects.

When I was demobbed in 1920, after being abroad for four or five years, in the interests of the rights of small nations, and poor little Belgium and all that, I found I didn't know anything about Scotland. I applied myself to learn. Travelling since in recent years, in most other European countries, talking to university students, I found that most of them didn't realize that Scotland was a separate country, with history, traditions and achievements of its own quite different from those of its southern neighbour. English propaganda had ensured that, by using the adjective English as if it were synonymous with British. The fact that Scotland has a very different and distinctive identity was lost sight of, but that is being overcome at last. Burns and the Edinburgh *literati* were at odds on the subject. The Edinburgh *literati* told Burns that if he persisted wrongheadedly in writing in Scots, he would limit his public to a small fraction of the Scottish reading public, whereas, if he wrote in English, he would have the whole English reading public at his disposal. It didn't turn out that way; there has never been in the history of literature a poet who has achieved such an enormous international reputation as Burns, and even the international song of human amity is couched in the uncouth Scots language. Not in English. The English can't even pronounce 'Syne' properly, they give it a 'Z'. In the last week or two, I have had sent me periodicals in Danish, German, Magyar and Russian, all with articles on contemporary Scottish literature and translations of poems of mine and other contemporary Scottish poets. So that centuries-long position in relation to Scotland is being altered fundamentally. Scotland is emerging again, culturally at any rate, into the modern world as a separate entity with something of its own to say, some contribution to make to the common pool of culture that no other people can make. Certainly not England. If Scotland recovers its own voice fully, that voice will speak in a way that no

English voice could ever speak. The sudden upsurge of National Party membership may strike people as wonderful, but far more significant is the fact that after centuries of subordination to England, Scottish literature is at last being taught in an increasing number of Scottish schools, and there are now courses in it in most of our universities. Only a few years ago the Scottish Department of Education ruled that pupils deviating into Scots in the classrooms should not be punished but encouraged. That rule could not be implemented, however, simply because most of the teachers themselves were Anglo-Scots, Scots with no knowledge of the Scots tongue, and none of our independent Scottish literary tradition, which, they said, they could not teach because they had never learned how to evaluate it. That change is more significant than the mere party political quibbling about what seem to be important issues. It is the cultural questions, the language and literary questions, that have been the decisive factor in the national regeneration movements of many European countries, and it will not be otherwise with Scotland. No nation was ever restored to its proper dignity owing to a demand for merely practical measures, better wages, better conditions of employment, better transport, and all the rest of it. These are vitally important, but they are subsidiary and first things must be put first. It is because too many people in the National Party have no concern with the things of fundamental importance, with the great spiritual issues underlying the mere statistics of trade and industry, with the ends to which all other things should merely be means, that I don't feel the destiny of Scotland lies with it. At present they are anxious above all not to go too far, they deprecate anglophobia, many do not envisage armed action. Well, no one in his senses wants warfare, but if we are determined to be absolutely independent, it may be, and almost certainly will be forced upon us. I do not believe the English have learned anything from the Irish affair and I believe that they will be more determined to hang on to Scotland than ever, by fair means or preferably foul, since their world rule has diminished so greatly. In any case, even if it doesn't come to that, we'll have violence anyway in Scotland. Scotland never fought while it was independent any aggressive war, but since the Union, it has been dragged at the heels of England into scores of wars, none of which were of any value to Scotland itself. We have a great deal of violence in Scotland today; I could only wish that it were possible that it could be channelled in better directions.

What is the difference between the Scots and the English, how important is it? Robert Louis Stevenson declared that there were no two adjacent peoples in the world so utterly and irrevocably different as the Scots and the English. In this he was re-echoing what was expressed away back in 1549 in *The Complaint of Scotland*, which reads: 'In the days of Moses, the Jews dared not have familiarity with the Samaritans, nor with the Philistines, nor the Romans with the Africans, nor the Greeks with the Persians, by reason that each regarded the other as barbarous.' For every nation regards another nation as barbarous when their two natures and complexions are contrary to theirs, and there are not two nations under the firmament that are more contrary and different from each other than Englishmen and Scotsmen, howbeit they be within one island, and neighbours, and of one language. For Englishmen are subtle and Scotsmen are facile, Englishmen are ambitious in prosperity and Scotsmen are humane in prosperity, Englishmen are humble when they are subdued by force and violence, and Scotsmen are furious when they are violently subdued. Englishmen are cruel when they get victory, and Scotsmen are merciful when they get victory. And to conclude, it is impossible that Scotsmen and Englishmen can remain in concord under one government because their natures and conditions are as different as is the nature of sheep and wolves.

A few words on my own position which puzzles a lot of people in Scotland. This is from an article by Professor David Daiches and he says:

> What have the consequences of the union of 1707 proved to be, what has Scotland become, culturally, nationally, psychologically? Is there a viable Scottish identity available to nourish the artist and to provide a vantage point from which to look out on the world? How is Scotland's past related to her present and to her future and what sort of Scottish future do we want anyway? If Scotsmen of imagination and intelligence have been asking these questions and other questions of the same kind more and more fiercely throughout the last forty years, Hugh MacDiarmid must take a considerable share of the responsibility. His work for a Scottish renaissance was not simply a literary endeavour, it was bound up with questions of Scottish identity which had for the most part been slumbering for nearly two centuries when he came upon the scene, and not only with questions of Scottish identity but the question of the quality of modern industrial democratic society which prevails over the whole western world is also involved. The anglicization of Scotland is part of the general *gleischaltung*[1] of all western

[1] amalgamation (German).

culture and an investigation of its nature and causes is therefore bound up with social and political and economic ideas. Arguments about the use of Lallans or the relative merits of Burns and Dunbar or the place of Gaelic in Scottish culture could not therefore, in the context of any adequately conceived Scottish renaissance movement, be merely arguments about a literary trend or skirmishes preliminary to the emergence of something parallel to the pre-Raphaelite movement or the publishing of the Yellow Book. They were in the last resort not only about the meaning of culture, of nationality, or history, they were, to put it quite simply, about the meaning of life. And that is what Hugh MacDiarmid's poems are about. He could have settled for less. He could have stayed at the head of the Scottish literary revival and become a respected Allan Ramsay type of figure writing introductions to Saltire editions of older Scottish writers and blessing the Lallans-writing young. And indeed, he has played some of the parts played by Ramsay but his driving vision of the fulfilled man in the fulfilled society, a vision which is as much responsible for his choice of language, his kind of imagery and the course of his poetic career from lyricist to discursive epic encyclopaedist as it is for his ever shifting synthesis between nationalism and communism, wouldn't leave him alone. It puzzles, distracts and annoys many of his greatest admirers. When he wrote those early Scots lyrics, he was expected to continue in that vein, he didn't, he turned to English, and to make matters worse turned after a while to a special kind of Whitmanesque, up to a point catalogue poetry, whose essential principle of order escaped most critics. There is, it should at once be added, an essential principle of order in these long encyclopaedic poems that is related to MacDiarmid's vision of reality both human and natural rather than to his kind of Scottish nationalism or his rôle as a Scottish nationalist poet. A major concern of his has long been the search for what Hopkins following Duns Scotus called *haecceitas*. This diverseness and individuating reality of things and a human response to things, nationalism for him is only superficially a political programme, at bottom its object is to provide a means of responding properly to experience.

The three great institutions of Scotland safeguarded under the Treaty of Union — although every safeguarding clause in that treaty, of course, has been violated by the English long ago — the three great institutions which were the bulwarks of the independent Scottish tradition were our educational system, our legal system, and our kirk. Lord Snow, C.P. Snow the novelist, summed up the issue so far as education goes when he wrote,

> For over two hundred years, from the end of the sixteenth century to the beginning of the nineteenth, there were four universities in Scotland and two in England. Further, the content and intention of Scottish University education differed deeply from that of the English. Scottish education was much more European, or the university education of growing up in eighteenth-century New England.

C.P. Snow is referring to a book by Dr George Davie, *The Democratic Intellect*, I think the most important book on any Scottish subject published in my lifetime. And he says,

> This admirable book by Dr Davie is an account of how in the nineteenth century, the Scottish Universities were persuaded, coerced, bullied, and argued into something like English pastiche. Not that this process was straightforward, it is still not quite complete. Scottish education has taken a long time to become undermined and the universities preserved vestiges of an intellectual system and policy radically dissimilar from the English. At its core, the English policy is (*a*) to allow very few students into universities at all; (*b*) to subject those few to courses of intense specialization. The Scottish policy, in this respect, like the American or Russian policy, or in fact the policy of all advanced countries except England [note that phrase] is (*a*) to regard university education as the normal thing for a high proportion of students, and (*b*) to provide courses of considerable generality. Dr Davie thoroughly believes that (*a*) and (*b*) are linked, that is, if you really believe as a matter of social faith, as Scots, Russians and Americans do, that university education should be a democratic affair, then the education itself will inevitably become wider. If you believe as the English do, alone in the world, that university education ought to be restricted, then inevitably, equally inevitably, the disciplines of study will become narrower and more professionalized.

I stress these two phrases, 'all advanced countries except England', and 'The English alone in the world'. Why then should Scotland ever have been linked with a country so utterly at odds with every other so-called civilized country in the world? No one who has really studied the relationship of England and Scotland can be unaware that hatred and contempt of anything Scottish has been and is still being expressed in England to a far greater extent than hatred of England has ever been expressed in Scotland. One has only to go through the parliamentary speeches recorded in *Hansard* to find that hatred and contempt and ignorance of everything Scottish are expressed time and time again, and there's an unceasing attempt to assimilate everything Scottish to English standards. I point out, in addition, to the names I mentioned earlier, Lord Reith, Dr Whitley and others, who have been expressing themselves during this crisis in our affairs, in very similar terms. The two greatest working-class leaders that Scotland has ever thrown up are of the same opinion. Keir Hardie said that if the Scottish Labour MPs in Westminster had only stayed in Scotland, and re-established a parliament in Edinburgh, it would have done more for socialism and more for Scotland, than they could ever achieve at Westminster. The greatest revolutionary working-class leader that Scotland has ever had, John MacLean, went even further. The year before his death in 1923, standing in the Gorbals division of Glasgow, he said, 'I stand as a Scottish Republican.' That's how I stand too, and that's the measure of the devolution that I'm concerned about. I want complete independence, I don't believe in the difficulties that are alleged to exist in the way. I want a Scottish working class republic, based on our ancient traditions, because the difference in democracy in Scotland and England is fundamental and dates back to our Gaelic basis, to the old clan system; we never had the segregations, snobberies, class distinctions that the feudal system gave the English. I'm not an authority on this subject, the subject I'm going to mention (although as you know, I'm an authority on almost everything else), but I'm not an authority on religion. On the dastardly attempt to undermine the Church of Scotland and assimilate it to Anglicanism I would refer to Professor Ian Henderson's book, *Power and Glory*, in which he sees the attempt to fit the kirk out with Bishops to suit the requirements of Lambeth not as a movement of the Holy Spirit, but as a product of historical, geographical, political, sociological and neurotic elements in the relation between England and Scotland. 'Whatever the motives of Anglican imperialism,' he says,

> there is no doubt as to its nature. There are two million communicants in the Church of England, in Scotland there are fifty-six thousand and in the United States of America, two million, one hundred and seventy-four thousand, two hundred and two. On the Continent of Europe, the number of Anglicans is as near nil as makes no odds. In all these countries, the Protestant churches are

> to submit to a complete reconstruction of their power structure, and the extinction of their present ministry, and its replacement by Anglican ordained clergy in order to conform to the preferences of two million Englishmen. This is one of the grossest manifestations of twentieth-century racialism.

But it's in keeping with what we've been accustomed to see England manifesting in all connections during all the time that we've been connected with it. I haven't referred to the great problems of Scotland. The unparalleled drain of emigration from our midst, our unemployment problem always nearly fifty per cent greater than in the worst hit areas of our southern neighbour. Our tremendous housing problem, the fact that we've got the worst slums in Europe; and alongside these great questions, the questions that do arise from our present parliamentary connections, the way in which the parliamentary time-table is overcrowded, and the ridiculously small amount of time allocated to Scottish issues of all kinds, and even then evoking the impatience of the English members. I haven't referred to legislation by appendix, or to the fact that Scotland under the present system is obliged to suffer squeeze and freeze like England although the balance of payments problem is purely an English one. Scotland doesn't suffer from it at all. No, I believe that all these problems and all similar problems can be solved if we get our independence. The Scots people are not inferior in intelligence, in ability, to any people in the world, and if they address themselves to their own affairs, they will speedily find solutions if solutions can be found. The eyes of the fool are on the ends of the earth, and for far too long, the eyes of Scots have been directed away from their own affairs, but they're no use to Scotland, and they certainly can't make any contribution to international culture if they don't first of all put their own house in order, tackle the things that are nearest to hand, and tackle them with all their might. Those of you who saw the TV programme on Scottish affairs last night will agree that the audience there were emphatically of the opinion that I am about to express. I don't think it is necessary now to argue this question of devolution for Scotland. We are going to have it, and we're going to have it very soon, and we can safely reconcile all our religious and other divergences on the basis of one of the profoundest statements in the Bible, one of the profoundest injunctions in the Bible: 'Be ye not unequally yoked together.' We'll choose our own equals, our own peers. At large, we've been internationalists to a far greater extent that the English ever were, we've never had any imperialist longings, our moral position is infinitely stronger than the position of England in any connection has been for centuries past, and it's on that basis that I suggest to you that we don't allow ourselves to be fobbed off with any talk about the problems and difficulties that varying degrees of devolution would present us with. We don't require to bother about that. We're going for devolution right to the end, that's to say for complete independence and we rest our case on the virtue of our own personality and the strength of our own determination.

Thank you.

Appendix

As *Albyn* was about to be published, two further uncollected short monographs were made available to me through a series of serendipitous events. Robert Creeley visited the University of Waikato on 26 July 1995 and I was later in correspondence with him after he had returned to the State University of New York at Buffalo. At around the same time, my wife Rae, the Reference Librarian for the School of Humanities at the University of Waikato, introduced me to an online computer service which gives access to over fifty databases, 'OCLC FirstSearch'. Through one of these databases, 'Worldcat' (which lists about 30 million items held in libraries all over the world), I was able to locate copies of the two essays that follow: both were held in the University Library at Buffalo. (I had previously tried to track them down in Edinburgh to no avail.) I contacted Robert Creeley, who kindly put me in touch with Robert J. Bertholf, the Curator of the Poetry/Rare Books Collection. With great courtesy and generosity, Mr Bertholf promptly forwarded photocopies of the items to me. It was too late to include them in the body of the book, but they are added here as an appendix. The book is richer for their inclusion, and my thanks are due in full measure to Robert Creeley, Robert J. Bertholf and Rae Riach.

Fidelity in Small Things by Hugh MacDiarmid was privately printed in fifty copies for Joseph W. Sault in 1934, in the format of a single folded sheet.

Scotland; and the Question of a Popular Front against Fascism and War by Hugh MacDiarmid was first printed in Dunfermline by J.B. Mackie & Co., Ltd., 98 St Margaret Street, 'for the Publishers, the Hugh MacDiarmid Book Club, Whalsay, via Lerwick, The Shetland Isles'. It dates from 1938, though no date appears on the four-page pamphlet itself.

Fidelity in Small Things

The way to fight an organisation is not to set up a counter organisation. The world is full of organisations. Where are all these movements and counter-movements leading us? Into deeper and deeper difficulties.

The vast proportion of modern social evils would disappear were the Golden Rule of doing unto others as you would they might do unto you, applied.

Collectively we condone and are responsible for iniquities – totally unnecessary and preventible evils – which as individuals we could neither perpetrate nor seek to justify. As individuals most of us are decent, kindly people. In the mass, however, we lose that decency and kindliness, and evince that 'man's inhumanity to man' which makes countless thousands mourn.

In war, in the civil wars of wage slavery and so forth, we are responsible for countless abominations. The only way obviously is to make – not mob acquiescence – but individual conscience the criterion to make it impossible to do collectively what we would not do, or excuse, individually.

In his *Social Substance of Religion*, Gerald Heard stresses the importance of what he calls 'small charitic groups'. This is only what was meant when it was said that 'Where two or three are gathered together'. We must regather together in twos and threes. *There is no other way*. Larger organisations issue in dreadful inhuman automatisms of action which override all genuine human impulses. It is an old truism that the poor help the poor most.

One of the most dreadful disclosures of recent months in Great Britain is that the economic situation in many of the most depressed areas has now rendered that impossible. The old method whereby among some little group of neighbours the one eked the other out during a spell of ill luck, and was in turn eked out when he or she needed it, can no longer operate. It is this mutual help that is the real basis of human relationships. Friendship has no real meaning if it lacks, where necessary, this practical co-efficient.

It is obvious that if we would all get down to this basis, our major social problems would be solved. We would establish a commonwealth of friends, each of whom would at any time help any other in need, and thus make mutual help and true humanity the basis of our social order. No grave hardships could exist where such a principle was the actuating force.

People help one another. It is only a question of 'being faithful in small things' – and that is the only real qualification for being entrusted with greater. As matters stand, the personal responsibility of man to man is ignored or belittled; we are all taken up with large abstractions. We feel that we cannot be held individually responsible for – or have any effective individual influence upon – the huge overriding factors of modern existence. This is a disastrous fallacy. The social aggregates with which we are concerned depend upon the relations of little groups or relatives, neighbours, friends. If these are all right the aggregates built upon them cannot be so hopelessly wrong as they manifestly are today.

Let us be faithful in small things first – helpful to those nearest to us – and on that basis gradually widening out till the principle of humanity and mutual help widens out from our little personal relationships and immediate groups to embrace all mankind.

It is the only way. The opposite method of lip service to large ideals and of beginning with big human conceptions and thinking to bring them down to the small groups and the individuals who compose them has manifestly failed.

We must start again from the bottom up – from the individual true to himself and to those with whom he is intimately related, and on that basis – *and that basis alone* – to all humanity.

World unity is a myth and the federation of all mankind a sheer illusion, unless it rests on these impregnable foundations of personal integrity, friendship and mutual assistance.

Scotland; and the Question of a Popular Front against Fascism and War

Following Scotland's constant great Radical majorities in the nineteenth century – sharply differentiating it from the voting of the English electorate which nevertheless supplies a permanent majority of the members of Parliament and renders the progressive will of the great majority of the Scottish voters ineffective – Scotland, in the twentieth century, has cast a majority of its total votes for Socialism, but its will in this direction has continued to be swamped by the ruinous English connection. Meanwhile – irrespective of what Government has happened to be in power at Westminster – Scottish affairs have been persistently and disastrously neglected, the safeguarding clauses of the Act of Union ignored, Scottish interests of all kinds sacrificed to English interests, and nothing has been left undone to destroy the remnants of Scotland's distinctive national culture and assimilate Scottish education and literary expression to English standards.

Although both the Liberal and the Labour parties have for many decades paid lip-service to the idea of Scottish Home Rule, no progress has been made in this direction; and the question of Scottish Independence has always been the blind spot alike of the Scottish Social Democrats and the Scottish Communists. But the greatest revolutionary working-class leader Scotland has yet produced – the late John Maclean – was significantly different in this respect. The depth of his Marxian analysis forced him to stand for Scottish Autonomy, and a Scottish Workers' Republic. The betrayal of John Maclean's line by the Communist Party of Great Britain has resulted in a loss to Scottish Socialism beyond all reckoning. Even William

Gallacher, MP, who was primarily responsible for it, admits this in his autobiography, *Revolt on the Clyde*. It is obvious that until the Communist Party abandons its present line and reverts to the lead given by John Maclean, it can never carry the masses of the Scottish people. A similar position was to be found in Catalonia – but there the Communist Party altered its line, and, as a direct result, its membership went up by leaps and bounds.

The neglect of Scottish national sentiment by the Scottish Socialists and Communists has played into the hands of the Fascists, who have not been slow to capitalise this neglected force. The result is seen in the proliferation of fascising Boards and in such organisations, backed by leading industrialists and aristocrats and such great war-making corporations as Imperial Chemical Industries (which are simultaneously subscribing for the 'rebuilding' of Scotland and carrying through experiments in the manufacture of still more deadly poison gases) and the Scottish Development Council, which offers a pseudo-satisfaction to Scottish national sentiment in lieu of the autonomy to which Scotland is entitled, and which alone can enable its pressing problems to be dealt with effectively and fully. The record of all the principal supporters of this organisation will not bear examination for a moment from the point of view of the interests of the Scottish workers. But for the English connection, fascism would have little chance of raising its head in overwhelmingly radical Scotland. And Scotland is similarly overwhelmingly opposed to War. Are the young men of Scotland once again to be sacrificed wholesale in another great Imperialist War? There would be no danger of anything of the sort if Scotland were once again an independent nation, as it ought to be. **The last War was Ireland's opportunity; the next must be Scotland's.** There is widespread discussion today of the need for a Popular Front in Britain. What is needed, however, is not a British National People's Front but an International People's Front in the British Isles; a very different matter, and a movement that would signalise a deathblow at the heart of the British Empire. Cut clear of the English connection, Scotland would be as clear from war-making as Norway or Sweden or the other small countries of Europe which recently stood so gallantly by the side of Abyssinia when the English Government, in defiance of all its pledges, and in the teeth of the great Peace Ballot, attempted the crowning infamy of having Abyssinia's credentials rejected at Geneva to please Italy.

Scotland has not participated since Bannockburn in a single war in which Scottish national interests can be truly said to have been in any way involved.

Scotland restored to Independence would not only be another constant factor on the side of European Peace, but would cripple the war-making propensities of reactionary Imperialist England.

In demanding Scottish Independence as an essential factor and condition to be included *and actively pursued* in the programme of a general stand in Great Britain against Fascism and War – in demanding, in other words, not a British National United Front but an International United Front of the workers in the British Isles – the goal envisaged for the United Kingdom is identical with that attained in the USSR, as described by Louis Fischer (writing on 'USSR in 1936' in the American *Nation* for 10th October last) in the following paragraph:

> With the coming of Sovietism the suppressed ethnic units of old Russia emerged as communities with their own individuality, their own cultures, their own governments. They are endlessly grateful for their new existence. Among them the regime finds some of its staunchest supporters. The Bolsheviks leaned over backward to meet the needs of these national minorities. The result is a bulwark against nationalism. Throughout the Soviet Union the observer encounters endless pride in the latest achievements of the country. But it is not a pride in the achievements of 'Russia', for half of the USSR is not Russia. It is made up of scores of national minorities: Stalin, the Georgian; Kaganovich, the Jew; Ordjonekidze, the Georgian; Mikoyan, the Armenian – all of them members of the paramount Politbureau – cannot be proud of 'Russia'. Nor can they suppose that Georgia or Armenia is responsible for the Soviet successes. All the nationalities of the country have contributed to them. The USSR is itself a real international.

So must Great Britain become a real international, and a Popular Front in the United Kingdom against War and Fascism must not be a British Popular Front, but an International Popular Front of the workers of Scotland, England, Wales, and Cornwall. We cannot be proud of Britain; but if our independence is properly conceded we can co-operate with the other nationalities in these islands in pursuance of that opposition to War and Fascism of which the present English Ascendancy Government is, on the contrary, the principal cause and chief fomenter.

All interested in the organisation of such an International United Front in Great Britain instead of a British National United Front are invited to communicate with the Secretary, Hugh MacDiarmid Book Club, Whalsay, via Lerwick, the Shetland Islands. The Hugh MacDiarmid Book Club has been organised to ensure a constant stream of revolutionary Scottish literature directed towards the establishment of an autonomous Scottish Workers' Communist Republic; and (gestetnered) copies of the following essays can now be supplied (2d each, post free), viz. (1) Scottish Culture and Imperialist War; and (2) Brief Survey of Modern Scottish Politics in the Light of Dialectical Materialism.

Commentary

These notes and comments have been kept to a minimum. I am grateful to Angus Calder and Rae Riach for help with a number of these references.

p.1 Albyn: or Scotland and the Future by C.M. Grieve was first published as an attractive little hardback pocket-size book by Kegan Paul in 1927 in the 'To-Day and To-Morrow' series. This was a series advertised as written 'by some of the most distinguished English [*sic*] thinkers, philosophers, doctors, critics, and artists.... Written from various points of view, one book frequently opposing the argument of another, they provide the reader with a survey of numerous aspects of modern thought.' There were over eighty titles in print when MacDiarmid contributed *Albyn*, under headings such as 'Marriage and Morals', 'Science and Medicine', 'Industry and the Machine', 'War', 'Food and Drink', 'Language and Literature', 'Art, Architecture, Music, Drama, Etc.', 'Sport and Exploration' and the heading under which *Albyn* and its companion volume, *Caledonia or the future of the Scots* by G.M. Thomson, appeared, 'Great Britain, the Empire, and America'.

The books were all written in a fluent, accessible style. Notable titles included *Icarus, or the Future of Science* by Bertrand Russell, and its companion volume, *Daedalus, or Science and the Future* by J.B.S. Haldane, *The Future of the Sexes* by Rebecca West, *Pomona, or the Future of the English* by Basil de Selincourt (to which MacDiarmid refers familiarly in *Albyn*), *Mrs Fisher or the Future of Humour* by Robert Graves, and *Hanno, or the Future of Exploration*, which was the first book by James Leslie Mitchell, who was to collaborate with MacDiarmid on *Scottish Scene* and, as Lewis Grassic Gibbon, to produce the modern classic *A Scots Quair* in the early 1930s.

In a letter dated 30 January 1928, written from Montrose, where he was living with his first wife and family and working as a reporter on the local newspaper, MacDiarmid explains the background to *Albyn* to his friend, former schoolmaster and mentor, George Ogilvie:

> *Albyn* (which has been selling well) I am not proud of. A curious story attaches. About a year before it appeared I had written to the publishers suggesting that I should do a vol. entitled

> 'Caledonia: or the Future of Scotland' for their series. They agreed – and then I found I wasn't in the mood. I was too much in amongst the stuff and simply couldn't write a statement in short compass. They wrote me for the MSS several times: but I kept putting them off. Finally a period of months ensued during which I heard nothing from them. Then I happened to hear that they were announcing a book entitled *Caledonia: or the Future of the Scots* by G.M. Thomson. I immediately wrote to them – but they said their acceptance of Thomson's book in no way prevented them accepting mine, written from a different angle – and would I send on my MSS at once? I didn't believe them – so hastily furbished up into a semi-connected form some of the stuff I'd sent out through the afore-mentioned Bureau [MacDiarmid is referring to what he describes as 'a special bureau I formed for the purpose' of 'sending out special articles on Scottish issues and interests of all kinds at the rate of 5 columns per week': this form of syndication was a common journalistic practice, and under the bylines 'A Special Correspondent' and 'Mountboy', MacDiarmid published innumerable articles in local papers all over Scotland in this way. Some of these are collected in *The Raucle Tongue: Hitherto Uncollected Prose*, vol. 1 (Carcanet, 1996).] – just a rough slapping-together of stuff written in a slip-shod and hurried fashion in the first instances. But they took it all right! And to make matters worse didn't send me galley-proofs but only paged proofs – so the corrections I tried to make would have upset the pagination too much. In the finish-up I had to leave it to them to make such corrections as they conveniently could. Needless to say they contrived to make precious few and failed to make some quite indispensible ones. So that's that.

MacDiarmid's modesty was unwarranted. This provocative little book has had a long-term influence and it is noted by Edwin Morgan for its emphasis on extending the 'Scottish Renaissance' from literary into general cultural and political areas of operation (*Hugh MacDiarmid*, Harlow: Longman, 1976, p.30), and by Harvey Oxenhorn as a critical analysis of the educational establishment, which then discouraged spoken Scots and sidelined Scottish literature (*Elemental Things: The Poetry of Hugh MacDiarmid*, Edinburgh University Press, 1984, p.5). Tom Nairn, in *The Break-up of Britain* (2nd edition, London: New Left Books, 1981), quotes extensively from it and engages with MacDiarmid's arguments directly.

George Malcolm Thomson, an author and journalist whose book had prompted MacDiarmid's hasty assembling of *Albyn*, also spurred MacDiarmid into journalistic action. In the same letter to Ogilvie quoted above, MacDiarmid continues: 'Thomson's book gave me a chance for a journalistic grand slam. I had signed articles on it in over 30 different papers (all different articles) including *Irish Statesman, Forward,* the *Outlook,* the *New Age,* etc. etc. Quite a little feat!' The articles mentioned include: 'Scotland and Ireland' in *The Irish Statesman* (22 October 1927), pp.156-8; 'A Silly Book about Scotland' in *Forward* (26 November 1927), p.3 (signed 'L.McN.W.'); 'The Condition of Scotland' in *The Outlook* (12 November 1927), pp.641-2; and 'The Truth about Scotland' in *The New Age* (10 November 1927), pp.16-17. See *The Hugh MacDiarmid-George Ogilvie Letters*, ed. Catherine Kerrigan (Aberdeen University Press, 1988).

p.2 *Scottish Labour members returned to the House of Commons*: In the 1922 General Election, Labour took thirty seats in Scotland, including one Communist elected with Labour support. Previously Labour had held only seven seats in Scotland. Eleven of Glasgow's sixteen seats fell to Labour as well as seven other West of Scotland constituencies. The first Labour government under Ramsay MacDonald was elected in 1923.

p.3 *Scots National League, Scottish Home Rule Association*: In 1928, the year after *Albyn* was first published, these groups united with the Scottish National Movement and Glasgow University Scottish Nationalist Association to form the National Party of Scotland.

the 'Irish Invasion': Irish Catholic immigrants, especially to industrial Glasgow, incited reactionary Scottish Protestants whose nationalist sentiment was basically unionist in politics.

p.4 *many of the emerging artists [must] be Catholics*: Yet the Catholic experience of Scotland remains largely unwritten. Colm Tóibín points out that the almost total absence of Catholic writers in modern Scotland leaves an important gap: the stories of 'the arrival of unskilled and unlettered men and women from Donegal in Ireland into this strange world of factory-work and mines and labour politics; the slow melting into Glasgow of these outsiders; the adherence to Celtic football club; the pub life of the city; the idea for the generation which benefited from free education that they belonged in the city and were outsiders at the same time' – all remain untold. It seemed to Tóibín that the situation in Scotland in this regard in 1993 was analagous to that which pertained in Alabama in 1954. One exception is the work of Thomas Healey, *It Might Have Been Jerusalem* (1991) and *Rolling* (1992) both novels published by Polygon. See 'The Language of the Tribe' in Colm Tóibín, *The Sign of the Cross: Travels in Catholic Europe* (London: Vintage, 1995), pp.162-81.

the Hon. Ruaraidh Erskine of Marr: (1869-1960). A wealthy extremist who advocated ancient cultural roots, he apparently spoke Gaelic and backed up his support of the language with cash and periodicals. MacDiarmid contributed to Marr's *Pictish Review* a series of thoughtful articles under his own name (C.M. Grieve) and as Gillechriosd Mac a'Ghriedhir, as well as poetry. See MacDiarmid, *The Raucle Tongue*.

p.7 *Scottish mediaeval music was ahead of English*: This is remarkably percipient to judge from the recent rediscovery and recordings of Robert Carver. See Carver's motets and settings of the mass on CD GAU 124, GAU 126, GAU 127, John Purser, *Scotland's Music* (Edinburgh: Mainstream, 1992) and D. James Ross, *Musick Fyne: Robert Carver and the Art of Music in Sixteenth Century Scotland* (Edinburgh: The Mercat Press, 1993).

p.13 *Hume Brown*: P. Hume Brown's *History of Scotland* (1911) was shortened and remained in print till the 1960s. It has been described as 'assured, whiggish, patronizing, and principally concerned with high politics, Jacobitism and church history.' See Ian Donnachie and Christopher Whatley, eds., *The Manufacture of Scottish History* (Edinburgh: Polygon, 1992).

p.16 *Tannahill*: Robert Tannahill (1774-1810), poet and songwriter, helped to found a Burns Club in Paisley in 1803; after he committed suicide his fame and popularity spread and his sentimental songs remained in vogue for decades. *Johnny Gibb of Gushetneuk*: (1871) a novel by William Alexander (1826-94). Written largely in Scots it presented scenes of country life and domestic manners, was serialized in the *Aberdeen Free Press* and enjoyed enduring popularity.

p.17 *The Scottish Chapbook*, etc.: Short-lived periodicals of the 1920s advocating independence in literary, intellectual and political spheres. MacDiarmid edited the *Chapbook* (14 issues, monthly, August 1922 – November/December 1923), *The Scottish Nation* (34 issues, weekly, 8 May 1923 – 25 December 1923) and *The Northern Review* (4 issues, monthly, May – September 1924).

p.18 *Dostoevsky's 'Russian Idea'*: 'Dostoevsky's greatest triumph during his lifetime, and at the same time the fullest and most brilliant assertion of his national doctrine, was the Address he delivered in 1880 on the unveiling of the Pushkin memorial in Moscow. Pushkin, said Dostoevsky, was Russia's all-in-all.... This pan-Humanity is the national characteristic of Russia, and Russia's mission is to effect the final synthesis of all mankind.' – D.S. Mirsky, *Modern Russian Literature* (1925), p.48.

Denis Saurat: (1890-1958). MacDiarmid claimed Saurat first coined the phrase 'Scottish Renaissance'. Saurat taught in Glasgow (1918-19), then for several years at the University of Bordeaux, then came to London to direct the Institut Français. Like MacDiarmid, he wrote for *The New Age* in the 1920s. From 1933 he was Professor of French Language and Literature at the University of London.

p.19 *the past two hundred and twenty years*: That is, since the Treaty of Union, 1707: *Albyn* was first published in 1927.

p.20 *Dr J.M. Bulloch*: Popular journalist of the period, worked on the *Aberdeen Free Press*, helped to found *The Tatler* and co-edited *The Scottish Student's Song Book*. Described as a literary critic, he was also a minor versifier and song-writer.

p.21 *discoveries which have recently revolutionized physical science*: Einstein's first theory of relativity was formulated in 1905.

p.22 *the Latest Draft Bill*: A number of draft bills for various forms of devolved political authority had been proposed in the late nineteenth and early twentieth century (in 1894, 1895, 1908, 1911, 1914 and 1920). Even Winston Churchill, in later years strongly opposed to Home Rule for Scotland, spoke in favour of it in Dundee in 1911. But Scottish Nationalism was largely eclipsed by the 1914-18 war. In 1924, George Buchanan presented a Labour Bill for Home Rule, 'the first parliamentary expression of the Scottish Labour demand for Home Rule,' as Andrew Marr puts it. In 1927, when *Albyn* was written, another Labour MP, the Revd James

Barr, introduced a more radical Government of Scotland Bill, which proposed that all Scottish MPs should quit Westminster for a new Edinburgh parliament. Optimism and mass meetings in Scotland were rebuffed at Westminster: debate on the Bill had hardly begun before it was stopped due to lack of parliamentary time. 'It had been squeezed in after a debate on environmental hygiene, and one Labour journalist,' according to Andrew Marr, 'complained that "The claim of Scotland had to come after Bugs, Fleas and Vermin."' See Andrew Marr, *The Battle for Scotland* (London: Penguin Books, 1992), pp.59-62.

MacDiarmid is also referring more generally to post-war political developments. He appears to be linking Scotland's status and potential for autonomous development with the dominions of the Commonwealth such as Canada, Australia or New Zealand. The example of the Irish Free State is also present, but perhaps as a warning as much as a model. The *principle of legislative autonomy* to which he refers on p.24 would apply to the self-governing Dominions.

MacDiarmid is writing at a transitional moment where the Empire is on the point of becoming something else. Yet he is well in advance of the call for freedom which was yet to be heard in Crown Colonies such as Rhodesia and Kenya, where native majorities remained under white minority rule. His notion of a *'British Association of Free Peoples'* may have been proleptic, but there is also a reactionary aspect to its appeal to the coherence of *'Empire'*. Perhaps this might be seen as a strategic argument presenting the case for Scottish Home Rule as a defence of Imperialism; perhaps it is merely an honest attempt to come to terms with the imperial history which generations of Scots spent their lives struggling to build.

p.26 *H.A.L. Fisher*: (1865-1940) Oxford historian, Liberal Statesman, President of the Board of Education under Lloyd George's Premiership (1916-22), introduced important reforming Education Act of 1918.

p.31 *Harry Lauderism*: Sir Harry Lauder (1870-1950), singer and entertainer, knighted in 1919, was enormously popular throughout Britain, the USA and the Commonwealth. His stage costume included kilt, tweed jacket, briar walking stick and beret. MacDiarmid is referring to the international promulgation of tartanry, Scottish kitsch.

p.35 *Scott's Letters of Malachi Malagrowther*: See Paul H. Scott, 'The Malachi Episode' in Sir Walter Scott, *The Letters of Malachi Malagrowther* (Edinburgh: William Blackwood, 1981), pp.ix-xxxiv.

p.38 *the Irish Free State*: MacDiarmid was to visit Dublin the following year, 1928, when he met de Valera, as well as W.B. Yeats, Oliver St John Gogarty and others. See the introduction to the present volume.

'dreamers of dreams': Arthur O'Shaughnessy (1844-81), Irish poet: 'Ode' begins:

We are the music-makers
And we are the dreamers of dreams,
Wandering by lone sea-breakers,
And sitting by desolate streams; –
World-losers and world-forsakers,
On whom the pale moon gleams:
Yet we are the movers and shakers
Of the world for ever, it seems.

p.40 **The Present Position of Scottish Music** by C.M. Grieve was first published as a series of newspaper articles in the *Border Standard* on 20 and 27 November and 4 December 1927, then appears to have been published as a pamphlet by Grieve himself, from Montrose, dated 1927. The present text is from the *Border Standard*. Sections I, II and III appeared on 20 November; Section III was continued on 27 November with Sections IV and V following. Sections VI and VII appeared on 4 December.

p.43 *a Welshman*: Sir Walford Davies. See pp.69-70 of the present volume.

p.47 *Harry Lauderism*: See note to p.31 above.

p.49 Footnote: MacDiarmid is referring to the *Scottish Educational Journal*, where the essay, 'Creative Art and the Scottish Educational System' appeared in two parts, on 5 and 19 November, 1926. It is collected in Hugh MacDiarmid, *Contemporary Scottish Studies* (Carcanet, 1995), pp.401-9. With regard to the Scottish Academy of Music, see MacDiarmid's article of that name, also in *Contemporary Scottish Studies*, pp.409-15.

p.59 **The Present Position of Scottish Arts and Affairs** was published as a pamphlet 'Issued by the Committee of the Scottish Centre of the PEN Club'. The cover of the pamphlet gives the title as *The Present Condition of Scottish Arts and Affairs* but the heading-title in the pamphlet gives the title we have used. MacDiarmid was the founder of the Scottish centre of the PEN Club (Poets, Playwrights, Editors, Essayists and Novelists) in 1927 and at that time, the group he brought together included the President, Lady Margaret Sackville, himself as Honorary Secretary, Alexander McGill as Honorary Treasurer; in Edinburgh, H.J.C. Grierson, Pittendrigh MacGillivray, Lewis Spence and Helen Cruickshank, and in Glasgow, William Power, Edward Scouller, J.M. Reid and Marion C. Lochhead. The pamphlet was 'Printed at the office of the *Stewartry Observer*, Dalbeattie, by I.A. Callan'. It was published anonymously.

p.65 **The Scottish National Association of April Fools** by Gilliechriosd Mac a'Ghreidhir was published as an article in *The Pictish Review*, volume 1, number 6, 28 April 1928 (see note on the Hon. Ruaraidh Erskine of Marr, above), then as a pamphlet by Aberdeen University Press later in the same year.

Cratylus: A younger contemporary of Socrates, he pressed the doctrine of Heraclitus to an extreme point, denying any fixed nature to anything and insisting on the perpetual movement of all things. Plato in his *Cratylus* has the philosopher maintain that all falsehood is impossible: a natural appropriateness will show itself inevitably in the course of things.

p.66 *Roslyn Mitchell*: (1879-1965) Labour MP; *Hugh Robertson*: Roberton (without the 's', 1874-1952) founded the popular saccharine Glasgow Orpheus Choir in 1906; a socialist and pacifist, he accepted a knighthood in 1931. MacDiarmid frequently characterizes him as an Establishment man, as he does the others in this list. Joseph Laing Waugh, for instance, was a 'kailyaird' writer of 'sketches of Scottish life' with titles such as *Cute McCheyne, Cracks wi' Robbie Doo* and *Heroes in Homespun*.

Jacobsen: Shades of anti-Semitism fall here and in a few other places in MacDiarmid's *oeuvre*: it was very much in the air at the time, even in liberal cultured quarters. The remarkable thing is how infrequently MacDiarmid indulges in it.

p.67 *H.L. Mencken*: (1880-1956) American journalist and acerbic wit, he wrote for the New York *Smart Set* and was well known for his iconoclastic attitudes and attacks on censorship, puritanism, moral piety, etc.

the Duce: A pun on the popular name for Mussolini and the dice or card-game colloquialism 'to the deuce with it' (i.e. 'to the devil with it').

p.69 *a pamphlet I had published: The Present Position of Scottish Music* (see above note to p.40).

Will Fyfe: Like Lauder (see note to p.31 above), a music-hall entertainer.

p.70 *a Gowk*: Scots, a cuckoo, but also a fool, a simpleton.

p.71 **Scotland in 1980** by C.M. Grieve was first published in the *Scots Independent* newspaper, volume 3, number 8, in June 1929, then printed as a pamphlet by Grieve himself in Montrose. The text follows the newspaper article, except for the title, which was given in the paper as 'Fifty Years Hence'. The article was the first of a series headed 'Scotland To-morrow'.

The *Scots Independent* was financed by Roland Eugene Muirhead, the prosperous owner of a tannery who subsidized most of the pamphlets and booklets spreading the Nationalist message between the wars. He was known as the 'father of Scottish Nationalism' and the paper was the unofficial organ of the Scots National League, and later 'the Quasi-official voice of Scottish Nationalism'. See Andrew Marr, op. cit., pp.63-7.

Wad that I held...: from *To Circumjack Cencrastus* (1930); see MacDiarmid's *Complete Poems*, vol. 1, (Carcanet, 1993), p.209.

a Scots poet: MacDiarmid himself.

p.72 *Erskine of Marr*: See note to p.4 above.

p.73 *Dr Nigel MacNeill*: (1853-1910), author of *The Literature of the Highlanders: Race, Language, Literature, Poetry and Music* (first published in 1892, a new edition had just appeared from Eneas Mackay, Stirling, in 1929).

pp.73-4 *A Visit to the Four Universities in Scotland*: from *To Circumjack Cencrastus* (1930); see MacDiarmid's *Complete Poems*, vol. 1, pp.203-4.

pp.75-6 *William Livingston*: (1808-70). MacDiarmid included him in *The Golden Treasury of Scottish Poetry* (1940; the most recent edition was published by Canongate, Edinburgh, in 1993).

p.76 *Thomson's work on 'Liberty'*: James Thomson (1700-48) was famous as the poet of *The Seasons* and the author of 'Rule, Britannia!' but he also wrote a long poem entitled 'Liberty' (1735) which proved less popular.

p.77 *Clann Albann*: The 'militaristic neo-Fascist auxiliary' to the Scottish National Party was called into being in MacDiarmid's journalism but few records seem to survive of its membership's activities. See MacDiarmid, *Selected Prose* (Carcanet, 1992), pp.54-60, and pp.170-83. See also Alan Riach, *Hugh MacDiarmid's Epic Poetry* (Edinburgh University Press, 1991), pp.1-14.

p.78 **Aesthetics in Scotland** was never published in MacDiarmid's lifetime. It was first prepared for publication by MacDiarmid's biographer Alan Bold, and published by Mainstream (Edinburgh) in 1984. Alan Bold deduced that it was written in 1950, in a five-apartment outhouse at the home of the Duke of Hamilton, Dungavel House, near Strathaven, Lanarkshire, after MacDiarmid had returned from the Shetlands and ended his spell of work in Glasgow, during the war, in a munitions factory and as a naval officer based at Greenock, servicing British and American men-of-war on the Clyde. The Dungavel location was by constrast a pastoral haven and seems to have encouraged the production of a thoughtful and contemplative essay. Alan Bold has further suggested that the essay was probably sent to T.J. Honeyman, Director of the Glasgow Art Galleries and Museums, and that MacDiarmid intended that it should be published as a pamphlet in 1951. Honeyman and MacDiarmid both applied for the Directorship in 1939, and in a letter of 20 October 1950, MacDiarmid wrote to F.G. Scott, 'My essay on Aesthetics in Scotland – part of which I am to deliver in the Spring as a public (Glasgow Corporation) lecture – will be published in pamphlet form in April or May. I finished it a month or so ago.' Honeyman, Bold concludes, must have found the essay too long to publish as a pamphlet, and kept the TS among his papers until it was passed on to the People's Palace Museum, Glasgow. Internal evidence (references to Eric Newton's *The Meaning of Beauty*, published in 1950, and to the 1950 Edinburgh Festival production of John Home's play *Douglas*) also lends weight to Bold's conclusion that the essay was written in 1950. A manuscript version also exists in Edinburgh University Library. There are two additional passages, one (on p.107) from 1952 (as suggested by the date of the book to which MacDiarmid refers), and the closing paragraph, which dates from 1965, as it refers to the broadsheet *Rocket*, then being edited by Alan Bold, and to which MacDiarmid occasionally contributed.

p.78 *John Tonge*: Author of *The Arts of Scotland* (London: Kegan Paul, Trench, Trubner & Co., 1938), was involved with James H. Whyte in the production of the periodical *The Modern Scot*, a decidedly modernist journal of the 1930s based in St Andrews. Tonge, a homosexual, contributed essays under the name 'A.T. Cunninghame': 'The Scottish 'Nineties' (dealing with Patrick Geddes and the *Evergreen*) and 'The Spenglerian Melodrama' are collected in *Towards a New Scotland: Being a Selection from 'The Modern Scot'* (London: Alexander MacLehose, 1935). MacDiarmid dedicated *In Memoriam James Joyce* (1955) to Tonge and Whyte, as well as to Prince D.S. Mirsky, and 'On a Raised Beach' was dedicated to Whyte. In St Andrews, in the 1930s, they must have provided the poet with much-needed support and intellectual companionship.

p.94 *Thomas Davidson*: See MacDiarmid, 'Thomas Davidson and the Fellowship of the New Life' in *Scottish Eccentrics* (1936; Carcanet, 1993), pp.136-59.

p.109 *in the Domdaniel roots of the sea*: A fabled submarine hall where a sorcerer meets with his disciples. Southey locates it 'under the roots of the ocean' (*Thalaba*, XII, xxiv); Carlyle uses it in the sense of 'infernal cave' or 'den of iniquity' (*Cromwell*, 1871, I, 41).

p.112 *of infinite...softness of sawder*: of great capacity as a flatterer, one who continues to make you feel good at the expense of the truth.

p.125 *here in Glasgow*: See introductory remarks to *Aesthetics in*

Scotland above: this was clearly intended to be delivered as a lecture in Glasgow.

p.129 *the Coronation Stone Episode*: See MacDiarmid, 'The Coronation Stone' in *Selected Prose* (Carcanet, 1992), pp.184-6.

p.130 **Cunninghame Graham: a centenary study** by Hugh MacDiarmid was first published, with the Foreword by R.E. Muirhead (see introductory note on **Scotland in 1980**, above), at the Caledonian Press (Glasgow), in 1952. The flyleaf of the dustwrappers (possibly by MacDiarmid himself) reads as follows:

R.B. Cunninghame Graham was born in May 1852, and in this 40 page pamphlet Hugh MacDiarmid, the greatest poet Scotland has had since the death of Burns, gives a full biographical account of his personality and career, and discusses the thirty-odd books, of which he was the author *seriatim* in the order in which they were published.

Elsewhere Mr MacDiarmid has written: 'I valued Cunninghame Graham beyond rubies. We will never see his like again. He was unique and incomparable – a human equivalent of that pure white stag with great branching horns, the appearance of which, tradition says, will betoken great good luck for Scotland at long last.' Cunninghame Graham certainly heralded and worked manfully for that great Scottish National Awakening which is now in progress.

Sir John Lavery, the great artist, puts the matter in a nutshell in his autobiography, *The Life of a Painter*, when, writing of Cunninghame Graham, with whom he went to Morocco, he says, that Cunninghame Graham's masterpiece was himself. 'Some people complain that he remained an amateur and a playboy. But he was not an amateur in his own art, the art of personality. That art is rare and calls for great devotion and labour. It has few masters. As a portrait painter I have seldom found it.'

In this pamphlet, Hugh MacDiarmid pays a splendid and fully-documented tribute to a great Scotsman whom he knew well and with whom he was for many years closely associated in the Scottish literary and nationalist movements. Cunninghame Graham's character and work are not nearly well enough known to the vast majority of Scots today. It is hoped that the publication of this pamphlet may help to redress that misprizal and neglect, and draw timely attention to the great personal qualities

> and the writings of an outstanding Scotsman whose message to his compatriots was never more needed and calculated to inspire them than it is today.
>
> The pamphlet is introduced by another old friend of Cunninghame Graham's – and fellow-worker with him not only in the Scottish Cause but in all that appertains to social justice and human betterment – Mr R.E. Muirhead.

In *Twentieth Century Scottish Classics* (Glasgow: Book Trust Scotland, 1987), Edwin Morgan points out that the best way to read Cunninghame Graham is to follow his books in the order in which they were published, affirming MacDiarmid's emphasis upon the chronological story. The neglect of his work has been countered in some degree by recent recognition and a valuable critical biography, *Cunninghame Graham* (Cambridge University Press, 1979), by Cedric Watts and Laurence Davis. See also *Joseph Conrad's Letters to Cunninghame Graham* (Cambridge University Press, 1969), edited by C.T. Watts.

p.132 *William Archer*: (1856-1924) Drama critic, playwright, translator of Ibsen, born in Perth, educated at Edinburgh University, he was a vigorous critic of Scottish parochialism. He welcomed the work of Shaw and Wilde and produced twelve volumes of translation of Ibsen. It was Archer who passed on to James Joyce Ibsen's personal thanks and compliments on Joyce's article 'Ibsen's New Drama' in the *Fortnightly Review* of 1 April 1900.

p.133 *Gresham's Law*: That bad money drives out good, or the tendency of cheaper coin to devalue the quality of dearer currency. The law was promulgated by Sir Thomas Gresham to Queen Elizabeth I in 1558 though it had been explained earlier by Copernicus.

p.148 *the Clan Line*: The Clan Line was a cargo-liner shipping company also known as the Scottish Navy, because at one time it had the largest number of ships of any shipping company. As well as the black funnel with two red bands, Clan Line ships had a red house flag with lion rampant. Flourishing from the 1880s to the 1970s, the Clan Line eventually amalgamated with the Union Castle Line and became the British and Commonwealth Shipping Company. Clan Line ships ran mainly out of Glasgow, Liverpool and London, to ports in India, Africa and Australia.

p.151 *he nearly defeated Mr Stanley Baldwin*: see Andrew Marr, op. cit., pp.67-8.

p.162 **Francis George Scott: an essay on the occasion of his seventy-fifth birthday 25th January 1955** by Hugh MacDiarmid was published by M. MacDonald (Edinburgh) in 1955. Scott (1880-1958) was Scotland's foremost modern composer of songs and of European stature in this field, having taken lessons from Roger-Ducasse and comprehended musically the significance of Schoenberg's idiom in some of his settings of MacDiarmid's early lyrics, which date from the 1920s. In his lifetime seven collections of songs were published, and a number of part songs; his orchestral music remains unpublished and although a centenary LP record was produced in 1980, there is no currently available CD recording of his *oeuvre*. Eight of his songs beautifully transcribed for solo piano by Ronald Stevenson are available on *Piano Music from Scotland* (Olympia: OCD 264), played by Murray McLachlan. Maurice Lindsay's *Francis George Scott and the Scottish Renaissance* (Edinburgh: Paul Harris, 1980) remains the only book-length study, and includes valuable correspondence with MacDiarmid.

Other references are worth checking: Ronald Stevenson, 'The Emergence of Scottish Music' in *Memoirs of a Modern Scotland* edited by Karl Miller (London: Faber and Faber, 1970), pp.189-97. And, of course, John Purser, *Scotland's Music* (Edinburgh: Mainstream, 1992), especially 'Chapter XVIII: The Classical Takes Root 1910-1970' (pp.243-58). See also 'Appendix A: Bibliographical Notes' in Lindsay, op.cit., pp.157-64.

p.166 *Contemporary Scottish Studies (1926)*: The most recent edition is published by Carcanet, 1995.

p.167 *Towards a New Scotland*: See note above for p.78, on John Tonge.

p.173 *Mr Ian Whyte*: The hostility towards Scottish composers and arrangers which MacDiarmid displays here is the other side of his vigorous partisanship on behalf of F.G. Scott. There is certainly more to Whyte than this comment suggests. See 'Ian Whyte: A Scottish Composer's Life in Music' by Elizabeth Clark, in *The Music of Scotland* (Hamilton, New Zealand: the University of Waikato Scottish Studies Association Avizandum Editions no. 2, 1994), pp.22-7. And John Purser, op. cit., p.252. See also pp.214-16 of the present volume, where MacDiarmid recycles this material.

p.192 *I have referred elsewhere*: in *Lucky Poet* (Carcanet, 1994), pp.156-7.

p.194 *he coined the descriptive phrase*: See Saurat, 'La Groupe de "La Renaissance Ecossaise"', in *Revue Anglo-Américaine*, April 1924, although MacDiarmid had used the phrase himself in the *Scottish Chapbook* of February 1923, p.182.

p.198 *MacGilleathain's 'An Cuilithionn'*: See 'An Cuilithionn / The Cuillin' in Somhairle MacGill-Eain / Sorley MacLean, *O Choille gu Bearradh / From Wood to Ridge: Collected Poems in Gaelic and English* (Carcanet, 1989), pp.64-131.

p.199 *a federation of independent Celtic workers' republics*: MacDiarmid's republican idealism floats in on the Celtic references from Maurice Walsh (1879-1964), the novelist and friend of Neil Gunn.

p.201 *a good deal more un-English*: MacDiarmid's judgement of Yeats is reaffirmed in his long poem *In Memoriam James Joyce*, also published in the same year as the F.G. Scott essay, 1955. See the *Complete Poems* vol. 2 (Carcanet, 1994), p.757. The passage in question may be sourced in an article entitled 'Yeats' Inner Drama' from the *Times Literary Supplement* (4 February 1939), p.72.

p.205 **Burns Today and Tomorrow** by Hugh MacDiarmid was first published by Castle Wynd Printers (Edinburgh) in 1959. It was the fifth of a uniform series of books by MacDiarmid from the same publishers, having been preceded by the third edition of *A Drunk Man Looks at the Thistle* (1956), *The Battle Continues* (1957), *Three Hymns to Lenin* (1957) and the combined edition of *Stony Limits and Scots Unbound and other poems* (1957).

p.208 *'new Lallans poets'*: Lallans was Burns's term for the language we call Scots and was favoured by a group of poets in the late 1940s and 1950s, pre-eminently Douglas Young but also a number of others, including Maurice Lindsay, whose editing of the journal *Poetry Scotland* (four issues, 1943-9) provided an outlet for their work and whose anthology *Modern Scottish Poetry: An Anthology of the Scottish Renaissance 1920-1945* (London: Faber & Faber, 1946) is a landmark.

p.209 *the School of Scottish Studies*: 'Indifference, and not infrequently antagonism...beset the school in the years following its inception in 1951, after a number of concerned academics from various departments of the university [of Edinburgh] met to discuss the feasibility of a folklore archive similar to those already established on the continent and in Ireland' writes Jim Gilchrist in his essay 'The School of Scottish Studies' (*Cencrastus*, 12, Spring 1983, pp.15-17). The School was incorporated as a Department into the university in 1969 but in 1983 had to raise an appeal for one million pounds to support its activities. See also *The People's Past* (Edinburgh: Polygon, 1980). Hamish Henderson, a long-serving staff member of the School, was very friendly with MacDiarmid in the late 1940s and 1950s; see Henderson, 'Tangling with the Langholm Byspale', *Cencrastus*, 48, Summer 1994, pp.3-13, and 'Flytings Galore: MacDiarmid v. The Folkies', *Cencrastus*, 49, Autumn 1994, pp.15-25; also see *The Armstrong Nose: the Letters of Hamish Henderson*, edited by Alec Finlay (Edinburgh: Polygon, 1996).

p.210 *Yankee-controlled rocket-launching sites*: The development of nuclear weaponry with US bases in the UK was a high priority for defence in 1957 and 1958. On 3 May 1959, Chapelcross (near Annan in Dumfriesshire, MacDiarmid's native area) nuclear power station opened, the first nuclear power station to start operating in Scotland and the second in Britain. Its primary purpose was to produce plutonium for nuclear weapons; as a by-product it was also to produce electricity. A missile range was established on the island of South Uist and was opened on 23 June 1959, when a *Corporal* missile with an inert warhead was fired fifty miles into the Atlantic. See *Keesing's Contemporary Archives: Weekly Diary of World-Events, 1959-1960* vol. XII (Bristol: Keesing's Publications Ltd., n.d.), page and paragraph refs. 16808F and 16871C.

p.214 *I described...as follows*: What follows, down to p.216, seems largely recycled material. See pp.173ff. of the present volume, and the note to p.173 (on Ian Whyte) above.

p.218 *Mr Standfast*: Buchan's novel was published in 1919. The early chapters take the hero, Richard Hannay (of *The Thirty-Nine*

Steps, 1915) to Glasgow, where he encounters working-class socialists and a figure similar to John Maclean is introduced as a thoroughly villainous character.

pp.245-6: The quotation from James Reid should be compared with the same passage as quoted sixteen years earlier, in *Lucky Poet*, pp.417-18, where instead of commenting 'Nonsense!' as he does here, MacDiarmid adds: *'Vive l'anarchie!'* in concurrence with Reid's hyperbolic appraisal.

p.255 *three Scottish writers*: Cf. p.224, where 'the relative continental significance of three Scots' is noted, except that Carlyle is named rather than Scott, along with Byron and Macpherson.

p.256 *the English novelists*: Smollett, of course, was Scottish, but very much involved in the development of an Anglocentric literary tradition.

p.262 *Muir... used his influence to stab the movement in the back*: Edwin Muir and MacDiarmid had been close friends but MacDiarmid took offence at Muir's assertion, in *Scott and Scotland* (London: Routledge, 1936), that Anglocentric literature and the English language were the only possible ways by which Scots could contribute to the greatest literary tradition to which they had the most immediate access. MacDiarmid, to put it bluntly, demanded a plurality of voices, a central loyalty to Scotland, and an opposition to the English ethos, and saw Muir's book as a betrayal. MacDiarmid edited the cheekily entitled *Golden Treasury of Scottish Poetry* (1940; Canongate, 1993), in which his introduction carries forward his argument against Muir, and in 1942 he published an essay which developed the argument further: see 'Scottish Art and Letters: The Present Position and Post-War Prospects', *Selected Prose* (Carcanet, 1992), pp.151-70.

p.270 *a new School of Scottish Studies*: See note to p.209 above.

p.282 *a rocket range*: See note to p.210 above.

p.288 *Edwin Muir*: See note to p.262 above.
the 'Black Belt': The industrial heartland, from Glasgow through Lanarkshire into Edinburgh.

p.297 **David Hume: Scotland's Greatest Son: a transcript of a lecture given at Edinburgh University, April 1961** by Hugh MacDiarmid, was published by The Paperback, Booksellers, Edinburgh, as a pamphlet designed by Peter McGinn and printed by the Caledonian Press (who had also printed the monograph on *Cunninghame Graham*), in 1962. The present text observes a small number of corrections made by MacDiarmid. The philosopher George Davie, who was a good friend of MacDiarmid, who introduced him to Sorley MacLean in 1934, and who visited him in the Shetlands in 1937, has said that MacDiarmid's interest in Hume dates from his reading of the introduction to Professor Norman Kemp Smith's edition of Hume's *Dialogues Concerning Natural Religion* (1935); previously, Davie says, MacDiarmid had spoken of Hume as a pygmy. See *The Letters of Hugh MacDiarmid* edited by Alan Bold (London: Hamish Hamilton, 1984), pp.574-5. See also George Davie, *The Crisis of the Democratic Intellect* (Edinburgh: Polygon, 1986). See also 'You have separated me and my friend', MacDiarmid's poem affirming friendship with Davie and repudiating Kemp Smith, who had warned Davie off having any association with MacDiarmid, in *Complete Poems*, vol. 2 (Carcanet, 1994), p.1468.

Lauder: See note to p.31 above.

p.299 *two cultures*: C.P. Snow's famous Rede lecture of 1959 began by emphasizing this distinction. 'The Two Cultures' began as an article in the *New Statesman*, 6 October 1956.

p.300 *the abandonment of a broad general cultural basis in our education*: A reference to George Davie's seminal work on the changing nature of the Scottish educational system, *The Democratic Intellect: Scotland and her Universities in the 19th Century* (Edinburgh University Press, 1961).

p.301 *Billy Graham*: A celebrity evangelist who achieved international fame in the late 1940s and 1950s at the height of the Cold War and in the context of the threat of nuclear annihilation. He toured England in 1954 in a glare of publicity but according to his biographer, his visit to Scotland in 1955 turned out 'somewhat nipped'. Despite the profusion of cameras, lights, cranes and trolleys in Glasgow's Kelvin Hall, there seemed a 'peculiar indifference to Graham' as if he had 'reconstituted into a polythene blandness all the old fierce theologies' of his Scottish ancestors, and as one visitor to the Kelvin Hall remarked, 'religion has always been more or less the national connoisseurship of the Scots, what opera is to Italy'. Nevertheless, there was widespread popularity for Graham in Scotland. In Protestant Glasgow church attendance increased from an average of 56,503 in 1954 to 67,078 a month after Graham's 'crusade' though it began to ebb again later and there was an actual decrease in church members a month after Graham's visit. See Marshall Frady, *Billy Graham: A Parable of American Righteousness* (Boston/Toronto: Little, Brown and Co., 1979), pp.318-33.

p.309 *Wallace Stevens*: (1879-1955). MacDiarmid reviewed Stevens' first book of poems, *Harmonium*, in *The New Age* in 1924. See *The Raucle Tongue*, vol. 1. The verse comes from a later collection, *Transport to Summer* (1947), from the poem 'Chocorua to Its Neighbour' (stanza xix). See Stevens, *Collected Poems* (London: Faber and Faber, 1984), pp.296-302 (p.300).

p.311 **The Man of (almost) Independent Mind** by Hugh MacDiarmid was published as a pamphlet in Edinburgh by Giles Gordon. Gordon explained how this came about in an introductory note signed G.A.E.G.:

> As co-editor of *New Saltire* I commissioned Dr C.M. Grieve (Hugh MacDiarmid) to write an article for the periodical to commemorate the 250th anniversary of the birth of David Hume. The article was considered not suitable for publication by my co-editor and also by the administrative committee of *New Saltire*. I resigned my position as co-editor as I felt this was a preposterous decision. The article is here printed for the reader to judge its quality for himself.

The cover-title of the pamphlet was *Hugh MacDiarmid on Hume*.

p.313 *Billy Graham*: See note to p.301 above.

p.315 *'in the destructive element to immerse'*: A reference to Joseph Conrad's *Lord Jim*, Chapter 20, where Stein explains the futility of trying to evade 'the destructive element':

> A man that is born falls into a dream like a man who falls into the sea. If he tries to climb out into the air as inexperienced people endeavour to do, he drowns – *nicht war?*... No! I tell you! The

> way is to the destructive element submit yourself, and with the exertions of your hands and feet in the water make the deep, deep sea keep you up.

I am grateful to Professor Marshall Walker for providing this reference.

p.318 **the ugly birds without wings** by Hugh MacDiarmid was published by Allan Donaldson, Edinburgh, 1962. The inside front cover carried this paragraph:

> Hugh MacDiarmid is undoubtedly great. And like all great men before him, he has had the unpleasant experience of meeting the unreasonable and artless criticisms of the nonentities who surround art. But, unlike most others in this respect, MacDiarmid has acquired the reputation of being able to find both the time and humour to offer uninhibited spontaneous replies to them. The instance of this pamphlet portrays that readiness and serves for a final word on a recent bewildering exchange of public addresses which, in truth, do not really affect the answering poet. On the contrary, it is hoped that it is only an opportunity to clarify further his system of immediate reaction to a situation he would regard as extraneous nonsense.

The common perception in the 1990s is probably still that Hugh MacDiarmid and Ian Hamilton Finlay were terrible enemies, opposed to each other personally and aesthetically. This is because of the events subsequent upon the publication (by Chambers in 1959, to mark the bicentenary of the birth of Robert Burns) of an anthology of 'New Scottish Poetry' entitled *Honour'd Shade.*

The book was edited by MacDiarmid's best friend, Norman MacCaig, and the editorial note sounded a warning: 'The absence of any notable name is not necessarily due to editorial negligence.' MacDiarmid was well represented in the anthology, but there was nothing by Ian Hamilton Finlay and nothing by a number of Finlay's contemporaries and acquaintances. This occasioned a series of letters in *The Scotsman* by MacDiarmid in response to the criticism that the anthology was unrepresentative of Scottish poetry. (See *The Letters of Hugh MacDiarmid*, pp.798-806.) MacDiarmid's pamphlet, *the ugly birds without wings*, was his final word on the matter.

The background to the episode should be borne in mind, however. In the 1940s MacDiarmid and Finlay had been friends, and

MacDiarmid was the best man at Finlay's first wedding. As a boy, Finlay had been evacuated to the Orkney Islands during World War II; at the same time MacDiarmid was living in the Shetland Islands. Finlay loved Orkney; he called it 'Arcady'. When they both returned to Glasgow, MacDiarmid worked for an engineering company producing war materials and then as a first engineer in the Merchant Service, servicing British and American men-of-war in the estuaries of the river Clyde, and Finlay was visiting him fairly regularly, for conversation and to borrow books. Finlay was about thirty years younger than MacDiarmid: the older poet was in his fifties, the younger in his late teens or early twenties.

One might understand the parallels in their lives as suggestive of an affinity between them. Neither was really a city man, and perhaps in Glasgow they felt close for that reason too. And that both men should have settled in Lanarkshire, a few miles across some hills from each other (Finlay referred to them, chuckling, in conversation with me in 1995 as 'The MacDiarmid Alps') is a lovely irony. Both are artists of vision and commitment; both have a depth of conviction, an absolute dedication, and a wonderful sense of humour. Even *the ugly birds without wings* was matched by Finlay when he turned MacDiarmid's violent attack to his own advantage, advertising his little magazine *Poor Old Tired Horse* in *The Scotsman* by citing MacDiarmid's judgement upon it: 'utterly vicious and deplorable'. No false piety or stupid modesty blemishes the outspokenness of either man.

p.322 *creative activity in the West Indies in recent years*: Caribbean literary magazines had become increasingly important through the 1950s as West Indian writers began to claim international recognition. It's important to emphasize MacDiarmid's acuity in recognizing the emergent post-colonial literatures. The Nigerian novelist Amos Tutuola is welcomed in *In Memoriam James Joyce* (1955) as the 'the Yoruba writer / Who has begun the structure of new African literature' and he was to introduce an anthology of 'Freedom Poems' from South Africa in 1974. The reference here to West Indian 'creative activity' is possibly to the Guyanese novelist Wilson Harris, whose first novel, *Palace of the Peacock*, was published by Faber and Faber in 1960. It marked a watershed in West Indian literature and the beginning of Harris's career as a major novelist whose later work was to introduce complementary components from Scotland and the Caribbean in a new vision. *Black Marsden* (Faber and Faber, 1972) for example, is 'set' in a Scotland perceived by a West Indian imagination and carries epigraphs from James Hogg and MacDiarmid himself. See Alan Riach, 'The Scottish Element in Wilson Harris', *Scottish Literary Journal*, vol. 18, no. 1 (May 1991), pp.68-81.

p.332 **When the Rat-Race is Over: an essay in honour of the fiftieth birthday of John Gawsworth** by Hugh MacDiarmid was published on 29 June 1962, with the following note: 'Forty numbered copies of this opuscule have been privately printed by the Twyn Barlwm Press, 35 Sutherland Place, London, W.2, each signed by Hugh MacDiarmid and John Gawsworth.'

John Gawsworth was the pseudonym of Terence Ian Fytton Armstrong, a poet, bibliographer and editor of *The Poetry Review*, who was born in Kensington in 1912 and died in 1970. MacDiarmid got to know him in London in the early 1930s and dedicated 'The Little White Rose of Scotland' to him in 1931. By 1933 he was referring to Gawsworth as 'my good friend' (*Letters*, p.503). MacDiarmid stayed in Gawsworth's house in London in 1934 while his second wife Valda Trevlyn and their young son were away in Cornwall. Gawsworth had published poetry, a study of Wyndham Lewis, and an anthology of horror stories (including two by MacDiarmid) by this time. Gawsworth served in Algeria, Tunisia, Sicily, Italy and the Middle East during World War II, later spending time in Cairo and India; he became editor of *Ellery Queen's Mystery Magazine* and edited around sixty collections of verse and prose.

p.335 **Sydney Goodsir Smith** by Hugh MacDiarmid was published by Colin H. Hamilton in Edinburgh in 1963, in an edition limited to 135 copies, 35 signed by the author and issued in a special binding. The text is that of an address at a meeting of the Edinburgh University Scottish Renaissance Society delivered on 14 December 1962, when Smith was presented with the Sir Thomas Urquhart Award for his services to Scots literature. The present text follows that of Kenneth Buthlay, who edited it for publication in his 1968 collection of MacDiarmid's prose, *The Uncanny Scot*.

Sydney Goodsir Smith (1915-75) was born in New Zealand but came to Edinburgh as a young man and was writing poetry in Scots by the 1940s. His poetry developed a conversational mode and while he was a fine lyric poet, he was also unique in producing lengthy sequences of thoughtful, rambly and loquacious poetry in Scots that owed little to ballad metre and song. The sequence of love poems *Under the Eildon Tree* remains his masterwork, but his richly experimental novel *Carotid Cornucopius* is an extreme curiosity: a fully annotated edition would be a thorough introduction to literary Edinburgh of the 1940s and 1950s. He was one of MacDiarmid's close friends and allies, and a boon companion in the 1950s. See Sydney Goodsir Smith, *Collected Poems* (London: John Calder, 1975); *Carotid Cornucopius* (Edinburgh: Macdonald, 1964); and *For Sydney Goodsir Smith* (Loanhead: Macdonald, 1975).

p.339 **A Political Speech: a transcription from a recording taken at the 1320 Club Symposium Glasgow University, 6th April 1968** by Hugh MacDiarmid was published by Reprographia (Edinburgh) in 1972. The 1320 Club was a nationalist organization which also published the magazine *Catalyst*, to which MacDiarmid contributed. The club's title refers to the year of the Declaration of Arbroath, to which MacDiarmid refers in his opening remarks.

Index